E-Commerce Management

Text and Cases

Sandeep Krishnamurthy

University of Washington

THOMSON

SOUTH-WESTERN

Australia · Canada · Mexico · Singapore · Spain · United Kingdom · United States

THOMSON™

★ SOUTH-WESTERN

E-Commerce Management: Text and Cases

Sandeep Krishnamurthy

Editor-in-Chief:
Jack W. Calhoun

Team Leader:
Melissa S. Acuña

Acquisitions Editor:
Steven W. Hazelwood

Developmental Editor:
Taney H. Wilkins

Marketing Manager:
Nicole C. Moore

Production Editor:
Amy A. Brooks

Manufacturing Coordinator:
Diane Lohman

Compositor:
Stratford Publishing Services, Inc.

Printer:
Transcontinental Printing, Inc.
Louiseville, QC

Design Project Manager:
Rik Moore

Internal Designer:
Ted and Trish Knapke,
T&T Knapke Design

Cover Designer:
Brenda Grannan,
Grannan Art & Design

Cover Illustration:
Todd Davidson,
Brand X Pictures

Library of Congress Cataloging-in-
Publication Data
Krishnamurthy, Sandeep.
E-commerce management : text
and cases / Sandeep
Krishnamurthy.
p.   cm.
Includes bibliographical references
and index.
ISBN 0-324-15252-3 (pbk.)
1. Electronic commerce—
Management. 2. Electronic
commerce—Case studies. I. Title.
HF5548.32 .K75 2003
658.8′4—dc21   2002067338

ISBN: 0-324-15252-3

*This book is dedicated to
the grand dames of our family—
Gowramma, Sannamani, Sharada, and Sudhabai—
and to the future—Rishi.*

PREFACE

To the Reader

If you are like me, you cannot perform your job or organize your social life effectively without using e-mail and the Web. Our reliance on these technologies and the extent to which we take them for granted are a testament to the impact that the Internet and the Web have on our lives. These technologies have created a better-informed consumer and a manager who is equipped with up-to-the-second information. New communities have emerged and supply chains have been redesigned. In general, the opportunities created due to the unique properties of these technologies allow us to set higher goals for our businesses and to meet them more effectively.

By embarking on this educational journey, you have put yourself in a position to be a leader in tomorrow's organization. This book was not written for the student who is seeking a career in information systems alone; rather, it was written for the leader who wants to galvanize an organization to embrace and fully apply the capabilities of this new technology.

I want to take this opportunity to welcome you to your education on e-commerce. Writing this book has been a lot of fun for me and I sincerely hope that you get a lot out of it. I have tried to be balanced in presenting both the advantages and disadvantages of some of the new ideas. I encourage you to adopt a similar open and critical stance when reading this book. I expect you will especially enjoy the cases in the book.

You are welcome to e-mail me at sandeep@u.washington.edu with your thoughts and comments while you are reading this book or afterward.

To the Instructor

Let me first thank you for choosing this textbook. I have worked hard to create a product that is inspirational and an excellent educational experience for your students. I hope you find that it meets your needs.

This book was written to help managers harness the transformative power of the Internet to meet business objectives effectively. It is intended as a comprehensive resource for such managers.

This textbook is ideal for an introductory or survey e-commerce class in an MBA program or an undergraduate e-commerce class.

This text has many strengths and unique features, including:

- *Placing E-Commerce in the Right Context.* This text provides the proper perspective on the rise and fall of dot-coms. The causes of the dot-com failures are analyzed, report cards on the different sectors of e-commerce are provided, and the challenges of the future are discussed.

- *Unique Topic Coverage.* This text covers unique topics not found in many other books (e.g., Open Source, Online Research, M-Commerce, Peer-to-Peer Systems); some topics are covered in great depth (e.g., Technical Appendix in the E-Auctions chapter). New ideas are approached in the context of respected theories, and managerial frameworks are discussed.

- *Interdisciplinary Approach.* This text relies on information and theories from many disciplines. These different perspectives have been melded to create an integrative overview of the field.

- *Success-Failure Coverage.* Adopting a balanced style of writing, this book presents both the positives and negatives of new ideas. In-depth case studies analyze well-known companies (e.g., Amazon.com and eBay). Rather than limiting the discussion to successes, the text also includes several cases that cover failures (e.g., Microsoft's Slate.com and Boo.com).

- *Learning Objectives.* Learning Objectives appear at the beginning of each chapter and highlight the major goals to keep in mind while reading through each chapter.

- *Executive Summaries.* An Executive Summary is provided for each chapter, which summarizes the chapter content, ideal for today's busy student.

- *E-Tasks.* End-of-chapter exercises direct students to the Internet, offering numerous opportunities for hands-on learning (e.g., an online scavenger hunt and a viral marketing exercise).

- *Discussion Questions.* Discussion questions are provided for each chapter, which push students to utilize their critical thinking skills and lead to great class discussions.

- *Multi-Course Flexibility.* Written with a managerial focus, this book can be utilized in a variety of courses in information systems, marketing, and management.

- *Dedicated Web Site.* The site, **http://krishnamurthy.swcollege.com**, features additional case studies keeping the content fresh and current. *I have committed to updating the Amazon.com, eBay, and NTT DoCoMo cases at least twice a year.*

You are welcome to e-mail me at sandeep@u.washington.edu with your thoughts and comments while you are reading this book or afterward.

Acknowledgments

I am thankful to many colleagues who responded to my e-mails and gave me feedback. I am especially grateful to Patrick Murphy, University of Notre Dame; Alan Leong, University of Washington; Ron Tilden, University of Washington; Rami Zwick, Hong Kong University of Science and Technology; Patrali Chatterjee, Rutgers University; Rajan Varadarajan, Texas A&M University; P. K. Kannan, University of Maryland; and Lisa Klein, Rice University. I am especially thankful to my good friend, Ian Oxman, for his help with permission marketing.

I would like to thank my MBA students, Eng Lim, Lance Olson, Leyla Beyaz, Garaen Flake, Tushar Mehta, Randy Serroels, and Jennifer Gregor, for their help with the book. Connie Pace, my secretary, helped me extensively with the numerous administrative tasks required during this endeavor. I need to thank Taney Wilkins and Amy Brooks of Southwestern and Linda DeMasi of Publisher's Studio. Thanks also to Fred Hebein of California State University, San Bernardino, who reviewed many chapters. This book could not have become a reality without the support of my wife, Srivani. Thanks also to Jane Bremsky who provided great moral support as always.

ABOUT THE AUTHOR

Sandeep Krishnamurthy is an Associate Professor of E-Commerce and Marketing at the University of Washington. He obtained his Ph.D. from the University of Arizona and has since developed and taught several innovative courses related to E-Commerce for both MBA and undergraduate students. Professor Krishnamurthy has written extensively about E-Commerce in the business and academic press. He is especially known as an international expert on Business Models, E-Marketing, and M-Commerce. Journals in which his scholarly work on E-Commerce have appeared include *Journal of Consumer Affairs, Journal of Computer-Mediated Communication, Quarterly Journal of E-Commerce, Marketing Management, First Monday, Journal of Marketing Research,* and *Journal of Service Marketing.* His writings in the business press have appeared on *Clickz.com, Digitrends.net,* and *Marketingprofs.com.* Press articles in outlets such as *Marketing Computers, Direct Magazine, Wired.com, Medialifemagazine.com, Oracle's Profit Magazine,* and *The Washington Post* have also featured his comments. Professor Krishnamurthy has consulted extensively with companies of all sizes and is in demand as a speaker. You are welcome to e-mail him at sandeep@u.washington.edu or visit his website: http://faculty.washington.edu/sandeep for more information.

BRIEF CONTENTS

PART FOUR: PEERING INTO THE FUTURE

CONTENTS

CHAPTER TWO
Understanding the Internet 24

CHAPTER FIVE
E-Auctions 88

CHAPTER NINE
Permission Marketing 218

CHAPTER TEN

Pricing and Distributing Digital Products 234

PART THREE: INTERNET, GOVERNMENT, AND SOCIETY 311

CHAPTER THIRTEEN
E-Society 312

CHAPTER FOURTEEN
The Internet and Public Policy 328

CHAPTER SIXTEEN
Mobile Commerce 378

CHAPTER SEVENTEEN

Managing E-Commerce in the Future 402

Internet Basics and Business Models

1

Introduction to E-Commerce Management

Learning Objectives

▼ To understand how companies are using the Internet today.

▼ To assess the state of the Internet economy after the recent stock crash.

▼ To understand the importance of the e-commerce triangle—Internet technology, business models, and marketing.

▼ To understand the influences on the manager in the information age—efficiency, value, measurability, dense networking, interactivity, and a global marketplace.

Executive Summary

The Internet has fundamentally altered the way companies do business. Companies using the Internet have reexamined and streamlined their supply chains to reduce inventory-holding costs, reduce the time to market, and improve demand forecasting. Intranets, networks of computers accessible only to employees of a corporation or those granted special access, have helped companies share the knowledge that they create among different business units. In general, companies are using the Internet to add value using the six-C framework—commerce, content, communication, connectivity, community, and computing. Dot-com companies thrived using this framework. However, dot-com companies failed as a result of four major mistakes: they strived to build market share with free or cheap products or services, misunderstood the value of a customer database, underestimated the power of entrenched interests, and/or underestimated the time it takes to change consumer and managerial behavior. Despite these failures, the current state of the Internet is demonstrably healthy: The number of Internet hosts is growing steadily. Most of the top Internet retailers from a few years ago are still in business. A large variety of products are being successfully sold on the Internet. The number of households with access to online services continues to increase.

In a successful e-commerce operation, three elements—internet technology, business model, and marketing—are well integrated. A problem arises when one element is missing or not well executed. Napster, for example, was a case of a technology in search of a business model, as we will discuss later in this chapter. The manager of tomorrow is faced with six new issues—efficiency, value, measurability, dense networking, interactivity, and a global marketplace. Each of these issues has an impact on the others, creating a new conceptual framework for the analysis of managerial problems.

Introduction

The Internet has fundamentally altered the world. This is no longer a futuristic statement made by a technologist; rather, it is a reality that we all take for granted.

Checking e-mail and visiting favorite web sites have become integrated into our lives. Employers commonly expect that a job applicant has visited the company's web site to learn about its market, people, and financials. Children use the Internet for their homework, and educators argue that those who have no access to the Internet are fundamentally disadvantaged. Teenagers chat into the wee hours of the morning and exchange photos with friends in far-off places.

Within an individual business, the Internet has altered every department. Companies using the Internet have reexamined and streamlined their supply chains to reduce inventory-holding costs, reduce the time to market, and improve demand forecasting. Intranets have helped companies share the knowledge that they create among different business units. Salespeople are faced with a better-informed consumer who asks tougher questions. Large internal company meetings at multinationals, such as IBM, have connected employees in different countries. For a comprehensive look at how companies are using the Internet in interesting ways, see the Appendix at the end of the chapter.

The effects of the Internet are, obviously, not limited to corporations. The Internal Revenue Service (IRS) allows individuals to file their returns online. Potential students are able to compare the web sites of leading schools before applying; and many universities permit students to file admission applications online. On November 7, 2000, in a pilot project, voters in Maricopa County, Arizona, were able to cast their votes in a presidential election online for the first time ever.

The purpose of this book is to educate the managers of today and tomorrow about the fundamentals of e-commerce and *help them manage e-commerce within their organizations.* This book is not only for the person who wants to work in the Information Systems department; it is for all managers who are interested in using Internet technology to meet business objectives.

The Rise and Fall of Dot-Coms

In more recent times, the world has seen the rise and fall of the dot-com companies—a loose label for companies mainly serving the Business-to-Consumer (B2C) market. Led by companies such as Amazon.com, dot-coms were sometimes driven to high stock valuations that were not sustainable, and many were forced to close shop or reduce the scope of their operations. Leading dot-com companies that have failed include Pets.com, Alladvantage.com, Bigwords.com, Boo.com, and Mercata.com. Some analysts compared the rash of dot-com failures to the Klondike Gold Rush and the Tulip Craze, because the rise in stock prices was generally due to speculation.

Why did these firms fail? The consensus is that these firms did not follow certain basic business practices. Through observation and analysis, this author has identified four fatal mistakes made by dot-com companies.

The first mistake many dot-com firms made was to build their market share with zero pricing and free services. They aimed to acquire a customer base and *then* worry about what to do with them. As a result, most of their customers visited casually out of curiosity and did not build a sense of loyalty. Dot-com firms that began this way and are still in business are now learning how hard it is to move from free to fee.

The second mistake was to misunderstand the value of a customer database. Managers were under the illusion they had built up an effective customer base when they had simply collected customer information. Registration at a web site or completing a form online does not equate to a strong relationship. A large customer database does not automatically imply a committed and loyal customer base.

The third mistake was to underestimate the ease with which human behavior can change. Many of the dot-com companies proposed new business models, new ways of shopping, and, in general, new ways of doing things. Getting managers and customers to change to the new ways is not a trivial task. Managers have mental models and old habits that they are reluctant to discard, and not all consumers see the value in radically changing their shopping behavior.

The fourth mistake was to underestimate the importance of entrenched interests. Many dot-coms had grandiose visions of building a worldwide marketplace for businesses. But established businesses have relationships and alliances that have been nurtured over several years, and they tend to value stability. They would not want to give those up for the sake of incremental efficiency gains.

The current fashion is to discount completely the B2C companies that failed and question whether a purely online B2C company will ever be profitable. This may also be a mistake. In the future, companies will learn from these mistakes to build better enterprises.

So, what are the dot-com companies doing these days? A recent report followed 125 dot-com companies and how they had adapted to the market downturn. Their main findings indicated that:

- 44% of all Internet companies sampled shifted to "upstream" customers (e.g., moved from selling to consumers to selling to retailers)

- 47% of ninety B2C companies in the sample shifted to a Business-to-Business (B2B) model

- a third of the thirty-five B2Bs migrated upward to larger enterprise customers

- about 16% of the companies adopted "bricks-and-mortar" models

- 14% expanded offerings; an equal number narrowed offerings

- some "serial morphers" have completed as many as three transitions

- some dot-coms have adopted or acquired entirely new businesses

Reality Check

After the crash in the price of dot-com stocks and the subsequent closure of many online firms, many managers have begun to question the utility of these technologies. So, where do we stand now?

First, the Internet is growing at a steady pace. As shown in Table 1.1, the number of Internet hosts (or roughly, the number of domain names in use) has continued to grow at an impressive rate. In January 2002, there were 148 million hosts around the world. This is up from 56 million hosts in July 1999 and about 1 million hosts in January 1993.[1] Moreover, the growth path of the Internet has been spectacular in comparison to other media such as television and radio.

Second, as shown in Table 1.2, a wide variety of domains have experienced great growth. Interestingly, as of July 2001, the ".net" domain has overtaken the ".com" domain name, which continues to be the second most popular domain name. In addition, several other regional names (for example, .jp, .uk, .ca) are growing steadily as well.

Third, computing experts judge the quality of the Internet using three metrics—latency, packet loss, and reachability. *Latency* is the total time taken for a packet (a fundamental piece of information) to travel to a known destination and return back. *Packet loss* is measured by the percent of packets that return intact when a message is transmitted to a known host. *Reachability* refers to the percent of destinations that respond to a packet. A

Table 1.1

Number of Internet Hosts Over Time

January 2002	147,344,723
July 2001	125,888,197
January 2001	109,574,429
July 2000	93,047,785
January 2000	72,398,092
July 1999	56,218,000
January 1999	43,230,000
July 1998	36,739,000
January 1998	29,670,000
July 1997	26,053,000
January 1997	21,819,000
July 1996	16,729,000
January 1996	14,352,000
July 1995	8,200,000
January 1995	5,846,000
July 1994	3,212,000
January 1994	2,217,000
July 1993	1,776,000
January 1993	1,313,000

Source: Internet Software Consortium, "Internet Domain Survey," January 2002, http://www.isc.org/ds/WWW-200101/index.html.

leading Internet expert, Matrix.net, has computed average latency, packet loss, and reachability figures for the Internet since 1993. These graphs are included as Figures 1.1, 1.2, and 1.3. It is clear from these graphs that for the Internet as a whole (line marked 1), there has been a steady decrease in latency and packet loss and a dramatic increase in reachability (from 77.336 in 1994 to 98.02 in 2000). This clearly demonstrates the increasing health of the Internet over time.

Fourth, as shown in Table 1.3, the number of American households with computers and access to online services has steadily grown. Surveys conducted periodically by Harris Interactive indicate that the proportion of users online has increased from 9% of the U.S. population in September/November 1995 to 64% in September/October 2001. However, even at this point, only about 52% of the population had access to online services from home, a percentage that is likely to increase.

The United States dominates the world in terms of Internet usage. As shown in Table 1.4, the United States has 33% of the Internet users worldwide. Two-thirds of all small businesses in the United States have access to the Internet.[2]

Fifth, overall online retail sales have remained steady. Many managers may be under the misconception that because a number of dot-coms have gone under, there was a sharp

Table 1.2
Distribution of Domain Names, July 2001

Number	Domain Name	Number of Hosts	Percent	Name Meaning
1	net	40,542,351	32.2	Networks
2	com	37,502,747	29.8	Commercial
3	edu	7,183,493	5.7	Educational
4	jp	5,887,096	4.7	Japan
5	ca	2,685,100	2.1	Canada
6	de	2,399,004	1.9	Germany
7	uk	2,349,710	1.9	United Kingdom
8	us	2,147,936	1.7	United States
9	it	2,015,621	1.6	Italy
10	mil	1,881,091	1.5	US Military
11	au	1,865,350	1.5	Australia
12	nl	1,763,133	1.4	Netherlands
13	fr	1,404,617	1.1	France
14	org	1,281,090	1.0	Organizations
15	tw	1,280,032	1.0	Taiwan
16	se	1,038,108	0.8	Sweden
17	br	1,025,067	0.8	Brazil
18	es	921,505	0.7	Spain
19	fi	872,618	0.7	Finland
20	gov	786,984	0.6	Government
21	N/A	9,055,544	7.2	All others
		125,888,197	100.0	TOTAL

Source: Internet Software Consortium, "Internet Domain Survey," January 2002, http://www.isc.org/ds/WWW-200101/dist-bynum.html.

drop in the level of online retail sales. This is not true. Figure 1.4 presents a graph of total online retail sales from January 2001 to December 2001. This data is from the Forrester/NRF Online Retail Index. The graph shows the seasonality that is common in all retail operations during the holiday season from October to December. Adjusting for that, this graph shows that total industry-level sales have not dropped and have adopted a steady pattern. The sales in November 2001 are slightly lower than the previous year due to a slowdown in the economy. It is not clear whether this is a long-term trend.

Moreover, as shown in Table 1.5, online retailers are successfully selling a wide variety of product categories, from the top small-ticket item, apparel, to the top big-ticket item, airline tickets.

Figure 1.1
Latency Trend for the Internet as a Whole, 1994–2000

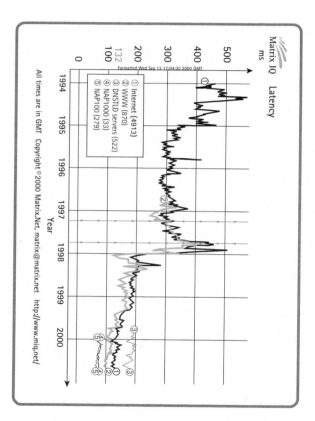

Source: Matrix.Net, "1994 to Present," 2001, http://www.matrix.net/research/history/decade.html.

Figure 1.2
Packet Loss Trend for the Internet as a Whole, 1994–2000

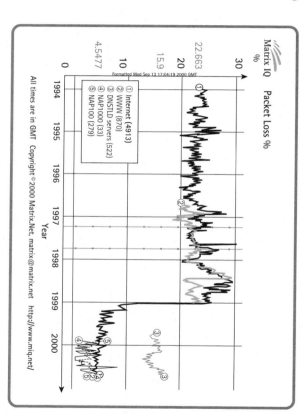

Source: Matrix.Net, "1994 to Present," 2001, http://www.matrix.net/research/history/decade.html.

Figure 1.3
Reachability Trend for the Internet as a Whole, 1994–2000

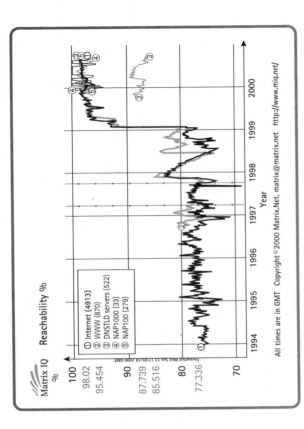

Source: Matrix.Net, "1994 to Present," 2001, http://www.matrix.net/research/history/decade.html.

Table 1.3
Percent of U.S. Households with a PC and Internet

	Use PC	All Online	Online at Home	Online at Work	Online at Other Location
	%	%	%	%	%
September/October 2001	73	64	52	28	19
March/April 2001	72	64	53	27	20
October/November 2000	74	63	49	29	17
April/May 2000	69	57	45	24	15
December 1999	69	56	46	N/A	N/A
January/February 1998	63	35	22	22	N/A
May/June 1997	61	30	16	18	N/A
June/September 1996	54	9	16	16	N/A
September/November 1995	50	9	N/A	N/A	N/A

Source: Humphrey Taylor, "Harris Poll #55: Internet Penetration has Leveled Out Over the Last 12 Months," November 1, 2001, http://www.harrisinteractive.com/harris_poll/index.asp?PID=266.

Table 1.4
Number of Internet Users Worldwide by the End of 2000

Rank	Country	Number of Internet Users	Percent of Internet Users
1	U.S.	134.6	32.54
2	Japan	33.9	8.19
3	Germany	19.9	4.81
4	Canada	15.4	3.72
5	U.K.	16.8	4.06
6	South Korea	19.0	4.59
7	China	22.5	5.44
8	Italy	12.5	3.02
9	France	9.0	2.18
10	Australia	7.6	1.84
11	Taiwan	7.0	1.69
12	Netherlands	5.5	1.33
13	Sweden	4.4	1.06
14	Spain	5.6	1.35
15	Russia	7.5	1.81
	Worldwide	413.7	

Source: Computer Industry Almanac, "Internet Penetration has Leveled Out Over the Last 12 Months," April 24, 2001, http://www.c-i-a.com/pr0401i.htm.

Figure 1.4
Total Online Retail Sales, January 2001– December 2001

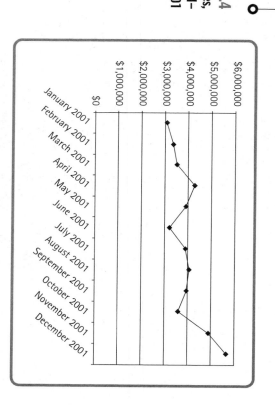

Source: Forrester/NRF Survey, 2001, http://www.forrester.com/.

Table 1.5
Top Products Sold Online in 2001

Small-ticket Items:

Apparel	$ 3,236,731
Toys/video games	1,899,426
Books	2,008,981
Software	1,562,109
Music	1,591,479
Health and beauty	1,429,759
Office supplies	1,254,728
Videos	1,196,141
Jewelry	1,149,369
Sporting goods	903,583
Linens/home décor	956,543
Flowers	668,979
Footwear	830,850
Small appliances	605,332
Tools and hardware	571,057
Garden supplies	312,759
Total small-ticket items	**$ 20,177,826**

Big-ticket Items:

Air tickets	$ 7,592,330
Computer hardware	4,349,737
Hotel reservations	4,218,325
Consumer electronics	2,579,304
Car rental	1,855,950
Food/beverages	1,309,436
Furniture	625,227
Appliances	387,081
Other	4,484,170
Total big-ticket items	**$ 27,401,560**
Total online sales	**$ 47,579,386**

Source: Forrester/ Survey, 2001, http://www.forrester.com/.

As shown in Table 1.6, in September 2000, the National Retail Federation identified the top twenty online retailers. One and a half years later, out of these twenty, seventeen continue to operate. The success stories on this list are not limited to online-only firms (also called pure plays) such as eBay or Amazon; rather, the list also includes firms with experience in the brick-and-mortar world (such firms are called bricks-and-clicks), such as Barnes & Noble.

In addition, a study conducted by McKinsey in mid-2001 indicated that online retailers have higher profit margins than their offline counterparts.[3] On average, the operating profit as a percent of total revenue of the online retailers surveyed was 18%. The corresponding figure for traditional retailers in consumer electronics was 7%, for department stores 10%, and for clothing stores 13%.

Sixth, manufacturers are effectively using the Internet to transact directly with customers. A leading example of this is Cisco Systems. In the fiscal year 2000, 90% of its transactions were conducted online.[4] This is no easy task for a company that reported revenue of $18.93 billion in the same year. This allowed the company to keep its selling costs in check. Other examples of manufacturers selling directly include Dell and airlines.

Seventh, networked organizations have continued to outperform their counterparts. McKinsey defines a networked organization as one "in which companies go far beyond outsourcing and actually collaborate in the delivery of products and services to customers." The leading examples of this type of organization include Charles Schwab, CNET Networks, eBay, E*Trade, Palm, and Qualcomm. Using data from the first quarter of 2001, a study by McKinsey[5] shows that companies such as eBay and Cisco outperform their peers handily. The market value per employee of these two companies were $7.5 million dollars (compared with $0.2 million for retail industry) and $3.4 million ($0.8 for technical industry). Similarly, the revenue per employee of these two companies were $0.1 million (compared with $0.06 for retail industry) and $0.2 million ($0.09 for technical industry).

Eighth, even though several high-profile dot-coms have closed, many continue to operate successfully. CIO.com provides four commandments for online B2C companies who wish to succeed:[6]

1. Be diverse

2. Exploit your channels

3. Be frugal

4. Avoid business models with high customer acquisition costs and low profit margins

Three examples are provided to illustrate these principles:

1. Travelocity diversified and kept revenues streaming in from different avenues. Moreover, it invested more in public relations than advertising and successfully built a strong brand.[7]

2. Eddie Bauer and Sharper Image integrated across three channels—catalog, bricks-and-mortar, and Web. They learned that when customers use more than one channel, their overall loyalty goes way up.

Table 1.6

Top Twenty Internet Retailers as of September 2000

Rank	Company	Type of Company	Primary Web Site(s)	Online Sales to U.S. Consumers	Number of Customers
1	eBay	C2C Pure Play	ebay.com	$3.5–3.7B	10,000,000
2	Amazon.com	B2C Pure Play	amazon.com	1.7–1.9B	12,000,000
3	Dell	Manufacturer	dell.com	1.1–1.3B	600,000
4	buy.com	B2C Pure Play	buy.com	700–800M	3,000,000
5	Egghead.com*	B2C Pure Play	egghead.com, onsale.com (formerly)	500–600M	700,000
6	Gateway	Manufacturer	gateway.com	500–600M	350,000
7	Quixtar	B2C Pure Play	quixtar.com	400–450M	600,000
8	Ubid	B2C Pure Play	ubid.com	275–325M	600,000
9	Barnes & Noble	Bricks-and-Clicks	bn.com	275–325M	3,000,000
10	Cyberian Outpost	B2C Pure Play	outpost.com	200–250M	425,000
11	Value America*	B2C Pure Play	va.com	200–250M	250,000
12	Micro-Warehouse		microware house.com	200–250M	175,000
13	Office Depot	Bricks-and-Clicks	office depot.com, vikingop.com	175–200M	250,000
14	eToys.com*	B2C Pure Play	Etoys.com	150–175M	1,700,000
15	Lands' End	Catalog and Online	Babycenter .com, landsend.com	150–175M	800,000
16	The Spiegel Group	Catalog and Online	spiegel.com, eddiebauer.com, newport-news .com	150–175M	450,000
17	Fingerhut	Retail, Catalog, and Online	fingerhut.com, andysauctions .com, andys garage.com	150–175M	400,000
18	CDW		cdw.com	150–175M	200,000
19	JCPenney	Bricks-and-Clicks	jcpenney.com	150–175M	500,000
20	Gap	Bricks-and-Clicks	gap.com, oldnavy.com, bananarepublic .com	125–150M	800,000

*Ceased operations
Source: http://www.stores.org. © Copyright 2000 NRF Enterprises, Inc. Used with permission.

3. GameColony.com acquired and built its assets on the cheap, frugality that came naturally to the Russian immigrant who founded the company.

Business 2.0 magazine also has presented a list of "habits of persistent dot-coms":[8]

1. Forget the exit strategy–aim to build a real business as opposed to something that will be bought out

2. Niche-ify yourself

3. Aim for high margins

4. Get small fast–large does not necessarily equal larger profits

5. Hunt for bargains at the Web fire sale

Many have pointed out that the financial performance of Internet companies is not a strong enough indicator of the strength of this technology. A better indicator is how much we all depend on these technologies. As noted film critic Roger Ebert has pointed out:

If your interest is in using the Internet, not getting rich from it, the stock price of Cisco is insignificant. In my life, the Web and e-mail play crucial roles every single day. If I had to replace e-mail with the telephone and the fax machine, I would go mad. If I didn't have the research resources of the Web available to me, I would accomplish half as much work. If I couldn't order Saigon Sizzle Sauce at a moment's notice, I might have to move to Saigon.

Overall, the Internet is still growing and is healthier than ever. Although some companies have gone out of business, most large ones are still operating and even thriving. The Internet is here to stay and will be a part of every business in the foreseeable future.

The E-Commerce Triangle

E-commerce management rests on three pillars–Internet and related technologies, business model, and marketing.

Of course, the Internet and related technologies have enabled e-commerce. However, managers who want to understand and manage e-commerce must not simply focus on the nitty-gritty operational details of the technologies. Some aspects are useful and, in fact, necessary (e.g., designing web pages, writing in hypertext). Instead, managers must understand how the Internet and the Web are organized, how sites can be located, and how sites relate to one another. Managers must ask how these technologies affect business variables such as sales, costs, and revenues.

Since even Internet-based corporations exist to make money, the business model is an integral part of e-commerce. A business model is a path to a company's profitability, an integrated application of diverse concepts to ensure that business objectives are met. A business model consists of business objectives, a value delivery system, and a revenue model. The path to shareholder value maximization goes through customer value maximization, so delivering value to the customer is vital. A revenue model is comprised of the set of revenue streams that contribute to the company's profitability. The company must maintain a rich portfolio of revenue streams without losing its focus. In addition, every business that has both a physical and a virtual component, must understand the interrelationship of these two spaces in order to thrive.

Because delivering maximum customer value is important, marketing plays a central role in e-commerce. Once a target audience is chosen, the business must build customer traffic, establish customer loyalty, build strong relationships with its customers, learn how to price and distribute digital products, and identify a distribution and logistics strategy. The goal is to have a satisfied customer.

When a new technology is launched without a solid business model in place, the result is a disaster. Without a clear vision and a revenue model, there is no clear path to profitability.

A glaring example of this is Napster, which was founded by a nineteen-year-old freshman from Northeastern University in Boston. Napster allows users to download music files from one another. Soon, the service attracted a large number of users, but was attacked by the recording industry for encouraging music piracy. Napster also lacked a business model or path to profitability: its service was free. Even though the company now says it will charge its users for downloading music, it is unclear whether consumers who were used to free downloads will be willing to pay for their music. The company is therefore still floundering without a viable business model.

The bottom line is that Internet technology, business models, and marketing are inextricably linked to one another in e-commerce. For success all three must work in sync.

New Conceptual Model

The new conceptual model, shown in Figure 1.5, is based on six elements—efficiency, value, measurability, dense networking, interactivity, and global marketplace.

Although many of these themes are as old as the concept of business, what is new is the *interrelationship* among these elements. Each element influences the next, creating new trade-offs for the manager. He or she therefore needs an integrative understanding of these elements and how they influence one another.

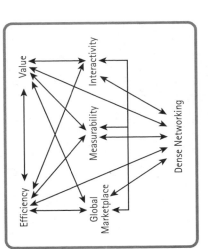

Figure 1.5
Conceptual Model

Efficiency

Most business processes can now be conducted more efficiently (i.e., for less cost in a shorter period of time using fewer resources) using Internet and related technology. Supply chains can be streamlined with greater and better information about demand and inventory resulting in sizeable cost savings. Customers can be contacted in a more efficient manner using technologies such as e-mail. Market research can be conducted more quickly and cheaply.

Value

Using Internet technology, consumers are provided better value through easy ordering, large assortments, profile memory, community, and personalization of products and services. Participants in B2B marketplaces gain access to vendors worldwide. All of us get fresh information on a variety of topics from around the world using the Internet.

Measurability

With Internet technology, what once could not be measured now often can be. For example, advertisers get very little real-time feedback about the performance of their ads on television. Most feedback is based on responses from a sample the day after the ad aired. There could be some correction in the campaign based on this market research, but only a limited amount. With the Internet, advertisers can expect detailed return on investment (ROI) measurements of each campaign for all types of advertisements in real time. As a result, the thinking changes. Managers can launch multiple ads and drop the nonperformers in real time. Similarly, e-tailers can measure the effectiveness of each square inch of their web site and make changes accordingly. Participants in auctions can see an entire bid path and a detailed profile of others that allow them to make better decisions.

Dense Networking

The Internet is the ultimate connector. It helps firms link with other firms (e.g., using strategic alliances, joint ventures, partnerships), firms link with their consumers (e.g., by e-mail and web sites), and consumers link with other consumers in communities (e.g., eBay). A dramatic view of a dense network is shown in Figure 1.6. This is a network of important Internet-related firms and their interrelationships. Interestingly, Microsoft and AOL emerge as the two companies that have the highest number of connections with other firms, making them the most powerful.

Interactivity

A dense network does not automatically imply interactivity; however, it is a great enabler. In a network, interactivity is "many-way" rather than "two-way." Every network member can interact with every other member using the modern tools of communication, such as e-mail, chat, instant messaging, and discussion boards. The implications of this degree of interactivity are tremendous: consumers can quickly respond to poor quality, for example, and partners can ask tough questions of senior managers.

Figure 1.6
Dense Network

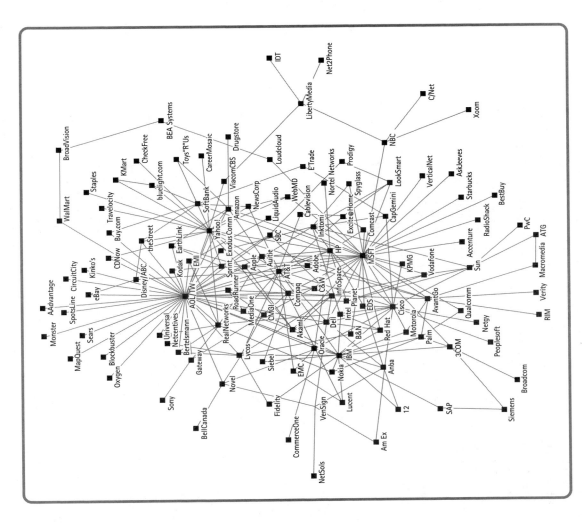

Source: Internet Industry Partnerships, "Network Visualization Using INFLOW 3.0 Software," January 4, 2001, http://www.orgnet.com/netindustry.html.

Global Marketplace

With the Internet, the potential for a global marketplace becomes real. In the words of Intel cofounder Andy Grove,[9]

Internet penetration in the US is substantially ahead of the rest of the world. In the next five years, one thing that is likely to happen is that Internet penetration in the rest of the world is going to replicate what's happened here. And that is going to let a globalization of culture, of

CHAPTER 1 / INTRODUCTION TO E-COMMERCE MANAGEMENT

17

Table 1.7
Worldwide E-Commerce By Region

Region	2000	2001*	2002*	2003*	2004*
North America	206,700	391,200	674,600	1,099,600	1,798,600
Latin America	3,600	9,600	20,700	39,100	66,500
Europe	34,300	68,900	169,800	416,000	979,800
Africa and the Middle East	1,900	3,600	6,500	11,600	19,300
Asia	39,400	76,800	136,800	225,700	338,500
Total	285,900	550,100	1,008,400	1,792,000	3,202,700

*Indicates prediction
Source: Gabriel Spitzer, "Dramatic Slowing for E-Commerce," August 2, 2001, http://www.medialifemagazine.com/news2001/july01/july30/4_thurs/news2thursday.html.

business, of communications achieve a level of pervasiveness that in itself will change the world significantly.

As shown in Table 1.7, e-commerce is expected to grow significantly in all parts of the world. Outside the United States, Europe and Asia are expected to grow especially quickly.

Interrelationship among the Elements

With the Internet, the interrelationship among the elements has never been stronger. Changes made to one are felt by another in Internet time (i.e., much faster than before). These changes are best described by two examples:

In the first example, consumers perceive that the value a company delivers is too low. Increased interactivity among consumers leads to conversations on this topic, some of which are global. The word of mouth is quickly captured in the company's measurement system. The company immediately recognizes that it must rectify the problem by either changing the perception through a direct e-mail campaign or by adding more value.

In the second example, a network of firms work together as partners to meet consumer objectives. Improved information sharing and better measurement systems help them locate an unmet demand in a global market. To solve the problem, they convene an online discussion forum. The group crafts a plan to farm out production to one partner and logistics to another to ready the product for the market.

These examples illustrate the importance of the elements of the new conceptual model and how they affect one another in a networked world.

Conclusion

Let me welcome you on your educational journey. My hope is that this book will expose every manager to the interaction among technology, business models, and marketing so that they might successfully manage e-commerce within their organization.

Notes

(All URLs are current as of March 10, 2002.)

1. The number of hosts is correlated to the number of web pages (since each host may have several thousands of pages). As of March 10, 2002, the search engine Google had indexed 2,073,418,204 web pages.

2. Conversation with Cisco Management, <http://www.cisco.com/warp/public/749/ar2001/online/conversation/index.html>.

3. Tilman Kemmler, Monika Kubicová, Robert Musslewhite, and Rodney Prezeau, "E-Performance II: The Good, The Bad and The Merely Average," The McKinsey Quarterly, 2001 Number 3, Web Exclusive available at <http://www.mckinseyquarterly.com/article_page.asp?ar=1079&tk=292854:1079:24&L2=24&L3=45&pagenum=9> (registration required).

4. John Chambers, "Letter to Shareholders," 2000 Annual Report, available at <http://www.cisco.com/warp/public/749/ar2000/low/letters/index.html#>.

5. Remo Häcki and Julian Lighton, "The Future of the Networked Company," 2001 Number 3, <http://www.mckinseyquarterly.com/article_page.asp?L2=21&L3=37&tk=292854:1091:21&ar=1091&pagenum=1> (registration required).

6. Susannah Patton, "What Works on the Web," September 15, 2001, <http://www.cio.com/archive/091501/works.html>.

7. Sheryl Gatto, "Build a Brand in Internet Time," February 23, 2001, <http://www.digitrends.net/marketing/13638_14609.html>.

8. Ralph King, "Seven Habits of Persistent Dot-Coms," November 2001, <http://www.business2.com/gallery/0,2182,4|30|32,FF.html>, 5 out of the 7 habits selected.

9. John Heilemann, "Andy Grove's Irrational Exuberance," June 2001, <http://www.wired.com/wired/archive/9.06/intel.html?pg=2&topic=&topic_set>.

REVIEW / CHAPTER 1

Discussion Questions

1. Using the data given in Table 1.5, explain why some product categories are more successful in online commerce. Is the Internet better suited for small-ticket or big-ticket items? Why or why not?

2. Using the data given in Table 1.6, consider whether bricks-and-clicks retailers are more likely to succeed online. If so, how do you justify the fact that pure-play retailers are at the top?

3. Does a greater measurability of consumer actions lead to a greater value to the consumer? Why or why not?

4. Can multiple successful business models piggy-back on a single successful technology? Provide examples.

5. Napster is an example of a developed technology that completely ignored the business model. If you were made CEO of Napster on Day 1 of its existence, how would you have managed it differently?

E-Tasks

A scavenger hunt is a great way to get an e-commerce class started, and a great way to learn about the wide variety of information available on the Internet.

Gimmes

1. Look up "advertising" in an online dictionary and print out the result.

2. List the firms ranked 90 to 100 in the *Fortune 500* last year. For each firm, provide revenue in millions of dollars.

3. Identify the web sites of three English-language newspapers based in Pakistan.

Starting to Sweat

1. Who were the top ten Digital Media/Web Properties last month? Rank the properties and also provide the total number of unique visitors for each property.

2. What is Bill Gates' home address?

3. For the 2001 Ford Taurus, obtain the following information:

   a. invoice price for basic car

   b. MSRP for basic car

E−Tasks (continued)

c. destination charge

d. dealer holdback

e. invoice price and MSRP for one optional feature

4. Obtain door-to-door driving directions from the White House to the Capitol.

5. One of Budweiser's more famous ads included the ad that is entitled "Wasaabi." It featured several men saying "Wasaabi" in a funny manner. Find a digital copy of the ad.

Brutal

1. Obtain information about the top ten Network TV programs in terms of viewership for last week. You should be able to find the following for each program:

   a. name

   b. network

   c. rating/share (What is the difference?)

   d. estimated audience size

2. Obtain information about the top ten heaviest spenders on advertising in the year 1997.

3. (Don't spend more than 20 minutes on this one.)

   Consider the following business best-seller—

   Blur: The Speed of Change in the Connected Economy
   Authors: Meyer, Christopher and Davis, Stan
   Publishing date: 04/1999; Publisher: Warner Books, Incorporated
   Binding: Mass Market; Trade Paper; ISBN: 0446675334

   Obtain the top ten cheapest offers on "total price" (i.e., list price plus shipping charge) for this book from Internet-based booksellers. You must include:

   a. total price

   b. name of seller

   c. item price

   d. discount

   e. sales tax

   f. shipping costs

APPENDIX / CHAPTER 1

How Are Companies Using the Internet Today?

Companies' use of Internet technology to meet business objectives can be classified using the six-C framework.

1. Commerce:

- Manufacturers are selling their products directly to consumers (e.g., Dell.com, American Airlines).

- Online retailers are selling products and services to consumers (e.g., Amazon.com, Expedia).

- Large businesses are buying from other businesses in electronic marketplaces (e.g., Covisint).

2. Content:

- Large companies are using the Internet to educate their consumers about their products (e.g., Procter and Gamble has created the Family Care Center at Crest.com to educate consumers about Crest toothpaste).

- News publishers (e.g., CNN, Time, MSNBC, *New York Times*, and *Economist*) have created web sites to publish the latest news.

- E-books are now available on a variety of topics.

- It is common to see web sites with an audio greeting from its CEO.

3. Communication:

- E-mail-based customer service is being used effectively by large companies to answer consumer questions.

- Prospects can sign up for web-based seminars (Webcasts or Webinars) to learn about a company's product.

- Companies are using the Internet to conduct worldwide company meetings.

APPENDIX / CHAPTER 1

4. Connectivity:

- Knowledge management is now a real focus in large corporations, and employees are using large intranets to share their knowledge among corporations.

- With the spread of Internet use, connecting with users or employees in other parts of the world is now a reality.

5. Community:

- Corporations are creating special user communities. For example, the Microsoft Developer Network helps developers learn about the latest Microsoft products from expert developers.

6. Computing:

- Using Internet technology, corporations are able to empower consumers by giving them strong computing tools.

  a. It is now standard among financial service companies to offer portfolio tracking tools.

  b. FedEx and UPS have provided customers with online package tracking software that can be used on any desktop to monitor the status of a package.

  c. Using mapping software, individuals can find directions to any store.

CHAPTER 2

Understanding the Internet

Learning Objectives

To get a brief technical introduction to the Internet and the World Wide Web.

To learn the history of the Internet and the Web.

To understand how the Internet can add value to a business.

To understand the myths about the nature of the Internet.

To study the structure of the Web and how sites relate to one another.

To learn about the laws that govern the Internet (e.g., Metcalfe's Law).

To become familiar with the theories that explain e–commerce—Porter's new theory and Clayton Christiansen's Disruptive Innovation approach.

To understand the e-consumer experience and how shopping and communicating online is different.

Executive Summary

The Internet is a network of networks. The Word Wide Web is a series of documents connected by hypertext links. The Internet was originally built as a decentralized network to withstand a nuclear attack, with the result that the emphasis was on security rather than efficiency. The Internet can add value to a business in many ways: enhancing the value proposition to customers; reducing operational inefficiencies within the organization; streamlining supply chains; increasing connectivity among companies, between a company and its customers, and among consumers; making everything faster; and eliminating distance. The Internet does not, however, change everything—the rules of business still apply. We know that certain types of products cannot be sold well using the Internet (e.g., sensory products, bulky products, those with special delivery considerations). Given the vast number of web sites, it is natural to think of the Web as a fragmented and cluttered medium. It is not. Recent studies have shown that the vast majority of Internet traffic originates from a handful of sites, suggesting a "winner–take–all" market. Moreover, some sites are seen as destinations, others as search originators, and still others as key connectors. Metcalfe's law states that there are increasing returns as the size of the network expands—that is, with the addition of each individual to the network, its value rises by more than the value of that individual. Michael Porter has theorized that the Internet is a competitive neutral weapon. The Internet might provide transitory competitive advantages in terms of efficiency, value, or time to market, but, over time, all firms in an industry will have access. The Internet enables disruptive enterprises that create new markets by serving needs that are ignored by traditional companies who view them as low-profit, small-market opportunities. Shopping online has its advantages and disadvantages: convenient ordering and gathering of product information, but an inanimate shopping experience.

Introduction

To understand e-commerce, one must understand the Internet and the Web. This understanding should be based on perspectives that are managerial, historical, technical, and sociological. The goal of this chapter is to provide the manager with such an understanding.

A Brief Technical Introduction to the Internet and Web

The Internet is a collection of interconnected networks. Every device (e.g., personal computer, cell phone) that is part of the Internet belongs to a network. Many applications are run on the Internet (e.g., e-mail, File Transfer Protocol (FTP), the Web). A machine on the Internet is either a server or a client. The machines that provide services to other machines are servers and those that are used to connect to those services are clients. A server is identified by its application—Web server, e-mail server, and so forth.

The Internet differs from other communication networks (e.g., phones) in that it uses packet switching technology. A packet is a small piece of information that includes a portion of a

A Brief History of the Internet and Web[1]

The Internet was not designed for commercial or widespread use; rather, the primary objective of its designers was to create a decentralized network for the U.S. Department of Defense that could withstand a nuclear attack. The choice of packet-switching technology was, therefore, motivated not by routing efficiency but by security. Interestingly, the Internet was initially envisaged as a *closed network* accessible only to defense employees. The growth of a worldwide decentralized network was unforeseen and unprecedented.

The designers of the Internet created the system using the following principles:

1. No central control.

2. All of the nodes in the network (e.g., PCs and the terminals of mainframe computers) would be equal in status to all other nodes.

3. Each node has the authority to originate, pass, and receive messages.

4. The messages themselves are divided into packets, each with its own address.

message and the destination address. When an e-mail is sent on a packet switching network, the message is chopped up into small packets at the source and is reassembled at the destination. The message travels from source to destination through a network of routers. A *router* is a hardware device that forwards information in a network and usually determines the next step in the path that the packet must take. It does not differentiate between various types of information. The path taken by the packet is not determined ahead of time, but is dynamically constructed as it makes its way to the destination.

The Web is perhaps the most significant application to run on the Internet. The Web is a system that provides access to documents formatted in hypertext that uses languages such as hypertext markup language (HTML) or the extensible markup language (XML). Hypertext is a system of horizontally dispersed information. A web site is a location on the Web that contains documents written in hypertext. Each web site is identified by a unique address called the Uniform Resource Locator (URL), such as http://www.google.com/, or a numeric identifier known as the Internet Protocol (IP) address, which always has four sets of numbers separated by periods (e.g., http://216.239.33.101/). All hypertext documents contain hot spots or links. By clicking on a link, the reader is directed to a new site that may have more links to other sites. A browser is an application that allows users to locate web sites. The two leading browsers are Netscape Navigator and Internet Explorer.

At this time, a variety of applications are being supported on the Internet. Chat refers to the real-time communication between any two or more users on the Internet. Users enter a chat room organized by topic, and what each one types is instantly visible to all others. Instant messaging is a way of creating a private chat room. When an instant message arrives, a pop-up screen appears to alert the user, who can initiate a chat at that point. A discussion board is an online bulletin board, on which a visitor can post a statement that is visible to everyone and anyone can respond to it—it is not real-time.

5. Each packet begins at some specified source node and ends at some specified destination node.

6. Packets are not wedded to any particular route.

These principles are illustrated in Figure 2.1(c), which is derived from the work of one of the founders of the Internet—Paul Baran.[2] As shown in this historic Figure, the goal was not to build a centralized or a decentralized network, but to build a distributed network where each node has the same status.

The early users of the Internet were technically sophisticated. Many users accessed the Internet using the terminals of large mainframe computers. The three key applications on the Internet in the early days were e-mail (sending electronic messages from one user to another), FTP (transferring files from one location to another), and Telnet (remotely accessing the contents of another site). Even though the designers expected transferring files using FTP and Telnet to be the major applications, e-mail was perhaps the most popular.

A key step in the Internet's progression was the development of Gopher by the University of Minnesota (to learn about it, go to gopher://gopher.tc.umn.edu). The name is derived from the university's mascot and Minnesota's nickname. The aim of Gopher was to

Figure 2.1
Centralized, Decentralized, and Distributed Networks

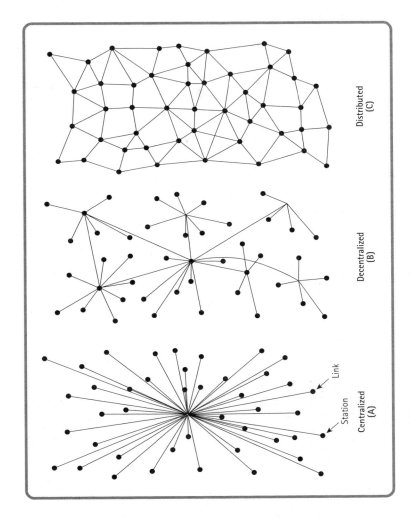

Centralized
(A)

Decentralized
(B)

Distributed
(C)

Station

Link

Source: Paul Baran, "On Distributed Communications," Rand Corporation Memorandum #RM-3420-PR, Santa Monica, CA: RAND 1964. Copyright © RAND 1964. Reprinted by permission.

organize all of the information on the Internet in a hierarchical manner using interconnected menus. Information was placed in directories similar to the directory structure on today's operating system. Using two systems, Veronica and Jughead, users could access information from around the globe on various topics (e.g., the news and weather). The key limitations of Gopher were the use of a text-based interface, not a graphical one, which was only accessible to the more technical user rather than the mainstream consumer, and the use of a hierarchical ordering of information, not a Web-based ordering, which made browsing difficult.

Even though some argue that it is completely different from the Internet, Usenet discussion groups (also called news groups) represent a major step in the evolution of Internet-based technology. These groups are still available at http://groups.google.com. A Usenet group consists of a set of notes posted by individuals from around the world. Groups are organized into subgroups. The primary groups are news, rec (recreation), soc (society), sci (science), and comp (computers). These are free-flowing discussion groups on a variety of topics, including MTV, McDonald's, economics, football, and Unix. They were the first online communities of users. Even though these groups were limited technically, they have contributed considerably to the current way of thinking. For example, the idea of posting a frequently asked questions (FAQ) list originated in Usenet groups.

The most significant development in the Internet was perhaps the World Wide Web, which was developed by Tim Berners-Lee while working at the CERN physics lab in Europe. The key difference between efforts up to this point and the Web was that previous efforts were dominated by hierarchical ways of structuring information (e.g., trees and directories). In contrast, the Web represents a way of thinking of all information as being interconnected. As a result, a tree becomes a special case of a Web.

The difference between the Internet and the Web is best described by Tim Berners-Lee:[3]

The Web is an abstract (imaginary) space of information. On the Net, you find computers—on the Web, you find documents, sounds, videos, . . . information. On the Net, the connections are cables between computers; on the Web, connections are hypertext links. The Web exists because of programs that communicate between computers on the Net. The Web could not be without the Net. The Web made the Net useful because people are really interested in information (not to mention knowledge and wisdom!) and don't really want to have to know about computers and cables.

His vision of the Web:[4]

The dream behind the Web is of a common information space in which we communicate by sharing information. Its universality is essential: the fact that a hypertext link can point to anything, be it personal, local or global, be it draft or highly polished. There was a second part of the dream, too, dependent on the Web being so generally used that it became a realistic mirror (or in fact the primary embodiment) of the ways in which we work and play and socialize. That was that once the state of our interactions was on line, we could then use computers to help us analyze it, make sense of what we are doing, where we individually fit in, and how we can better work together.

Today, the Web is being adapted for the wireless context. This represents unique challenges and the future is obviously still unwritten.

How Can the Internet Add Value to a Business?

The Internet can have a positive impact on any business. More specifically, the Internet can add value in six ways.

1. *Enhancing the value proposition to customers.* The Internet has the potential to enhance the value a firm provides to any given customer. An example of this is Amazon.com, which has provided value to its customers by providing a wide product assortment, a product recommendation engine, e-mail alert technology, and access to product reviews. Similarly, business consumers are able to get more customization, easier transactional capability, and better value-added services as a result of the Internet.

2. *Reducing operational inefficiencies within the organization.* The Internet is being used widely to reduce operational inefficiency within companies. Many organizations have implemented virtual teams for customer service, sales, and product development. Salespeople are using the Internet to give remote presentations to prospects, saving time and money. Consider the recent company-wide meeting at IBM that was held completely online: without flying vast numbers of people to a location, the meeting succeeded in getting 52,600 workers from across the world to participate, leading to over 6,000 proposals and comments.

3. *Streamlining supply chains.* One of the biggest effects of the Internet on business is to streamline the companies' supply chains. Using the Internet, a company can easily share information with suppliers and customers across the globe, allowing it to plan and forecast better. An example is the amazingly large buying alliance Covisint, backed by GM, Ford, and Daimler-Chrysler.

4. *Increasing connectivity.* The Internet is great at linking firms with other firms (e.g., in e-marketplaces), linking firms with their consumers (e.g., by e-mail) and linking consumers with other consumers (e.g., eBay). This creates a dense network, leading to quicker communication among individuals and companies. One consequence of this is that large-scale virtual collaboration is possible among individuals who are spatially distributed. For example, Linux started from an innocuous post from Linus Torvalds on a Usenet group and has emerged as a credible competitor to Microsoft. The interesting thing is that much of this collaboration did not even require the browser—it relied on Usenet and e-mail lists!

5. *Making everything faster.* In the words of Intel's Andy Grove:[5]

It makes everything faster. Genomics discoveries come faster. You can crack data faster. You can build and correct supply lines faster. You can get information faster. . . . The most direct way of increasing productivity is doing the same thing in a lesser period of time—turning things faster. And productivity is the key to everything—greater productivity increases economic growth.

6. *Eliminating distance.* In the words of renowned management author, Peter Drucker:[6]

Today, the Internet eliminates distance for communication. A client of mine, a major financial services company, moved 85 percent of its telephone customer service—calls from customers such as "Where is my dividend check?" –from the Midwest to Bangalore. India has a large population of well-educated, English-speaking women. They go to school to get an American accent. You call from Milwaukee and don't know whom you are talking to. If the question is not routine, she pushes a button and you are speaking to someone over here. As far as the customer is concerned, you have no idea where they are.

What Is the Proper Metaphor for the Internet and Web—Distribution or Communication Channel?

In an attempt to understand the Internet and the Web, some managers have asked whether the Internet is really a distribution or a communication channel. The answer is *both*. These technologies dramatically affect both functions within an organization.

The Internet can lead to a reduction in distribution and selling costs through supplying better information at all steps of the supply chain, low inventory, and a reduction in the sales force. The Web affects both order collection and fulfillment. Consumers have the transactional convenience of shopping from home and, in many cases, tasks are transferred to consumers (e.g., information collection).

At the same time, the Internet leads to several benefits to a firm in the realm of communication. A company can provide detailed information allowing for more rational arguments. For example, a company can clearly describe the advantages of a product over its competing alternatives and provide detailed technical information on its web site. A FAQ section on a web site can educate consumers about products or stores. Complicated arguments can be explained using examples and charts on a web site. In addition, the Internet allows for narrowcasting (rather than broadcasting), in which companies can target specialized market segments and consumers opt into the marketing process. The voice of the consumer becomes important in designing the marketing mix (e.g., consumers set their own prices at Priceline).

The Impact of Internet Technology on Costs and Revenues

Implementing Internet technology does not always lead to lower costs. In some cases, using the Internet could lead to a similar or higher cost structure. In the context of customer service, for example, it has become common to offer e-mail as one channel of communication. E-mail is generally touted as a cheap way of handling this function, and it is, on the basis of handling a single message. Overall costs are equal to the total number of messages from the consumer multiplied by the per-message cost, however, and many businesses learn that the total number of messages goes up with customers who demand quick responses. As a result, more customer service representatives may be required, leading to greater costs. At the same time, customers are better informed when they contact the company, which may require the company to hire better-qualified representatives or retrain existing representatives. In the end, the company's customer service cost may rise, contrary to its expectations.

Similarly, large Customer Relationship Management (CRM) systems, which seek to computerize all interactions between the company, its sales force, its distribution channel, and the customer, have about a 70% failure rate.[7] Many systems never recoup their cost and lead to minimal improvement in revenues. The most important reason for this may be that firms lose sight of why they are implementing CRM, and the project takes on a life of its own. Implementing CRM in smaller departments, rather than the company as a whole, can lead to petty conflict and multiple systems that do not relate to one another. The integration of existing systems with the CRM system becomes an issue. Finally, once a CRM package is customized, it becomes difficult and costly to upgrade. Vendors gain monopoly power and exploit customers. At the end, the results are muddy.

Myths about the Internet[8]

The Internet Changes Everything.[9]

This was a phrase that gained currency in the early days of Internet euphoria. Intel's Andy Grove analyzed it best:

That phrase drove me nuts! The Internet doesn't change everything. It doesn't change supply and demand. It doesn't magically allow you to build businesses by turning investors' money into operating expenses indefinitely. The money always runs out eventually—the Internet doesn't change that, as we have seen.

The current thinking is that the Internet changes a few things—as in how the Internet can add value to a business, discussed earlier.

Anything Can Be Sold Successfully on the Internet

Increasingly, we are learning that this is not true. The products and services that cannot be sold successfully on the Internet fall into four categories:

1. *Experience and sensory products (high-touch products):* We are not comfortable buying certain products—such as clothing, produce, and jewelry—without touching, feeling, or otherwise experiencing them. Of course, there are ways of communicating the qualities of the product. Companies selling clothing online, for example, provide elaborate photographs and allow users to create a virtual model of themselves so that they can virtually "try on" an article of clothing. These efforts may not be sufficient, however, to make the Internet the dominant channel for selling apparel.

2. *Products that are hard to transport.* Products that are bulky (e.g., sofas) have high transportation costs, which may increase the price of the product substantially, and render product returns problematic.

3. *Products with delivery problems.* One of the biggest problems faced by the online grocery business is delivering to a large number of customers who are spread out across urban areas. A driver may be able to make only ten to twenty stops a day, leading to huge delivery costs. As a result, such a business cannot compete effectively with a bricks-and-mortar supermarket, which does not have these costs.

4. *Services where face-to-face interaction matters.* Consider services such as health care and education. In both cases, there is no substitute for consulting a doctor or interacting with a professor and peers in a classroom setting. In both cases, the Internet can help make the face-to-face interaction more productive, but it cannot replace it for a large section of the population. The most effective examples of e-learning have been in the context of teaching the basics or training new employees on company policies and procedures. It is not clear whether more complex forms of learning can be facilitated through the Internet. Similarly, many salespeople now use Internet technology to make sales pitches to prospects, but they still give established clients a visit and a handshake.

No Switching Costs

At one point, it was common to say that on the Internet, your competition is one click away (i.e., there are no switching costs). Although there is some appeal to this statement, in reality we find that the switching costs are not trivial. For example, when a consumer switches from a large e-tailer such as Barnes & Noble (bn.com) to a new one, he or she has to provide detailed personal and payment information. Providing this information to multiple e-tailers is an onerous task. In addition, when one does not know anything about a seller on the Internet, there are "mental transaction costs" relating to trust and privacy.

Disintermediation

At one point, the Internet appeared to remove the need for intermediaries—manufacturers could sell directly to consumers. Although there are stunning examples of this (such as Dell.com), it is not true across the board. In many cases, the Internet has emerged as another sales channel with complementary features. In addition, several infomediaries have emerged to help consumers navigate online choices.

The World Wide Web is Used Across the World

In the early years of the Web, it was predominantly used in America and Europe. Now, markets in Asia are growing at a rapid pace. However, the fact that most of the Web's content is in English limits the appeal of the Web in these markets.

Structure of the Internet

How are all of the sites spread out across the Internet interrelated with one another? This is an important question and three studies provide us with good insight.

Winner–Take–All Markets[10]

The Internet has millions of web sites. Yet, not all of these sites receive the same attention from consumers. Some receive exceptional levels of traffic, while others receive very little. What does the overall traffic pattern on the Internet look like?

To answer this question, researchers from Xerox's Palo Alto research center studied the user logs of 60,000 America Online (AOL) users, covering 120,000 sites in December 1997. Their primary findings indicated that:

- The top 0.1% of the sites accounted for 32.36% of the unique visitors, the top 1% of the sites accounted for 55.63% of the unique visitors, and the top 5% of the sites accounted for 74.81% of the unique visitors. The number one site was Yahoo!.

- In subcategories (e.g., education) the results were similar—the top 10% of the web sites accounted for 60% of the unique visitors.

- Very few sites had a very high number of visitors, and the vast majority of sites ended up with very low user volume.

These results led the researchers to conclude that on the Internet, one finds a winner-take-all market structure. A handful of sites dominate by attracting a large number of visitors. Most languish with a small number of visitors.

Bowtie Structure[11]

Figure 2.2 shows the results from a study of 200 million web pages and 1.5 billion hyper-links conducted by IBM, Compaq, and Alta Vista.

The study found that sites on the Internet are primarily one of three types:

- Originators of searches (IN)—sites that link to others but have very few links to them.
- Destinations of searches (OUT)—sites that are linked to by Core sites. As a result, they can be reached from sites in the Core. However, OUT sites are not linked to other sites.
- Strongly connected sites (Core)—sites that have links to both IN and OUT sites.

In addition, some sites get lost in the mix and are unconnected.

Deep Web

Most search engines capture only the surface of the Web. For example, one study found that search engines cover only about 16% of the overall Web. Large public databases with

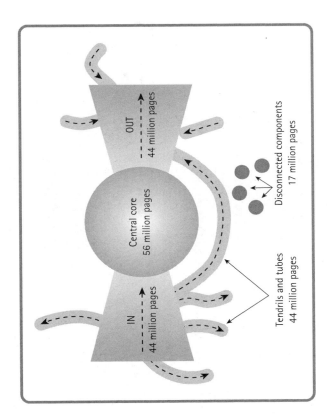

Figure 2.2
Results of the Bowtie Study

Source: Andrei Broder, Ravi Kumar, Farzin Maghoul, Prabhakar Raghavan, Sridher Rajagopalan, Raymic Stata, Andrew Tomkins, and Janet Wiener, May 11, 2000, http://researchweb.watson.ibm.com/resources/news/20000511_bowtie.shtml.

free and valuable information are untapped by most traditional search engines. Examples of such databases include those that are made available by the U.S. Census Bureau, the Securities and Exchange Commission, eBay, Amazon.com, UPS, and the Patent and Trademark Office.

For example, if a user went to Amazon.com and performed a search of its database, he or she would find the necessary information. However, if the same search were done on a standard search engine (e.g., Google), no information available on Amazon.com's pages would appear. Most search engines are unable to tap into such databases because of the way they conduct the search.

The Deep Web, on the other hand, accounts for data from the databases containing information that is accessible only by a direct query. When queried, these Deep Web sites post the results in the form of a dynamically constructed web page with a long URL. By simulating the process a user goes through when searching at the Deep Web site, this information can be made available to the user through one search in one place.

Some preliminary findings about the Deep Web include:[12]

- Public information on the Deep Web is currently 400 to 550 times larger than the commonly defined World Wide Web.

- A full 95% of the Deep Web is publicly accessible information—not subject to fees or subscriptions.

- Deep Web sites tend to be narrower with deeper content than conventional surface sites.

- More than an estimated 100,000 Deep Web sites presently exist.

Conclusion about Web Structure

These three studies give us a good understanding of the structure of the Web. First, the Web has a winner-take-all structure: a small proportion of the sites attract most of the Internet traffic and a large number of sites receive little traffic. What must one do to join this elite club? The research does not help us much with that. Interestingly, the results indicate that the age of the site does not matter much (i.e., there is no first-mover advantage as such).

Second, the connectivity among sites is not uniform. A central core of sites link to others and are also well linked to a variety of sites. Some link to others but are not linked to, and others are linked to, but do not link to many sites. Some sites get lost in the mix and are never found.

This illustrates the artificiality of the browsing or surfing process on the Internet. The final destination of the surfing process is crucially dependent on where one starts to search. Moreover, the mission of every site is different. Some have only a temporary purpose, and thus it makes sense for them to fall in the OUT group. Obviously, the power lies in the Core category, but convincing others to link to your site is perhaps one of the larger challenges on the Web.

Third, getting noticed on the Web is difficult because it is difficult to get listed by a search engine. This is an even larger problem if your site is part of the Deep Web that is not revealed to users who use search engines as their primary means of locating information. Over time, this may change.

Laws That Govern the Internet

Metcalfe's Law

The value of a network increases in proportion to the square of the number of individuals in it. If an individual is worth x and a network has n people, then the value of the network is determined by $x*(n)*(n-1)*0.5 = x*(n^2-n)*0.5$. This implies that networks such as the Internet lead to perpetual increasing returns (i.e., at any point, the value of adding an individual to the network is greater than the value of that particular individual, x).

To illustrate the implications of Metcalfe's law, Figures 2.3a, 2.3b, and 2.3c show the value of the network when each individual is worth \$2 (i.e., $x=2$), given three networks—one with 10 people, one with 100, and one with 1,000.

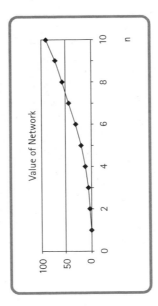

Figure 2.3a
Illustration of Metcalfe's Law
n=10

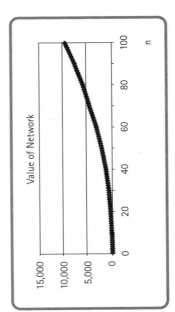

Figure 2.3b
Illustration of Metcalfe's Law
n=100

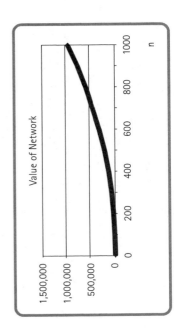

Figure 2.3c
Illustration of Metcalfe's Law
n=1000

Notice that all three curves retain the same basic structure—they rise from left to right in a convex manner with respect to the x-axis. Hence, regardless of the size of the network, its value rises at an increasing rate as it adds more people.

Metcalfe's Law is commonly regarded as an incomplete picture of the Internet for the following reasons:

1. The law assumes that all individuals are equally valuable. This is not true—some are of greater value than others (e.g., opinion leaders, community leaders).

2. The law assumes that all individuals are equal in terms of "communication intensity." This is again not true—some individuals are much more likely to communicate than others.

3. The law does not account properly for free ridership.

An idea related to Metcalfe's Law is that of a *critical mass*. This is a threshold number of people that any network must have to succeed. For example, if there are only ten people on a bulletin board, it may not sustain a sufficiently interesting level of communication. A minimum of 50 people may be needed.

One way to think about this is to imagine Metcalfe's Law in reverse.[13] Large companies, such as AOL and Microsoft, provide large networks of individuals who e-mail and chat with one another. Should these companies be forced to let their users e-mail or chat with the users of their competitor? In other words, should companies erect barriers to create isolated networks or should they encourage users across networks to interact and create one large network? Although the value of the Internet is diminished if companies erect such barriers, many large corporations that are eager to dominate the market hesitate to open their systems to their competitors.

Moore's Law on Internet Traffic

Moore's Law proposes that the capability of microprocessors doubles about every eighteen months. A similar pattern has been seen in Internet traffic both at the aggregate level and at individual institutions. One study revealed that Internet traffic has been doubling about once every year.[14] The researchers pointed out that this rate is much slower than that suggested by earlier claims that traffic doubles once every three to four months. Even with this current rate of traffic growth, the implications for commerce and communication are tremendous.

Cerf's Law

This law is named for Vincent Cerf, one of the pioneers of the Internet. It states that shared databases grow in value according to the number of data item combinations in the database. When the hundreds of thousands of databases on the Internet and other networks are accessible remotely and can be reached in parallel, and when the partial results can be combined and searched anew, the value of these data can grow dramatically.[15]

Theories That Explain the Internet

The Internet as a Neutral Competitive Tool

Michael Porter has provided a controversial new way of thinking about the Internet. He has proclaimed the Internet to be a neutral competitive tool, that is, all competitors in any given industry will use it. According to this way of thinking, Internet use alone is insufficient to gain a competitive edge.

Porter argues that two factors drive profitability—industry structure and the ability to gain a competitive advantage. The Internet affects both. On the one hand, it shifts power to the consumer by better informing him or her of substitutes and prices. At the same time, it lowers the barriers to entry by competitors, eroding competitive advantage.

Porter believes that competitive advantage comes from better knowledge, better people, and great products. He also argues that traditional businesses will effectively merge their conventional strengths with the new capabilities provided by the Internet. In the same vein, Andy Grove of Intel has long proclaimed that every business will become an e-business.

The Internet as a Disruptive Technology

Clayton Christiansen, a Harvard business professor, has proposed the theory of disruptive technology. He argues that traditional companies overlook great opportunities because they initially appear to be low-profit and small-market. Larger companies that are focused on understanding the needs of existing customers and searching for high-end markets may fail to capitalize on such product ideas. However, over time, the products arising from these opportunities could disrupt the marketplace, leading to a new market leader. Christiansen argues that the newer product opportunities create new markets by facilitating consumer behavior in underserved markets.

Christiansen's arguments are consistent with those of a reputed economic thinker, Joseph Schumpeter, who argued that economic growth is driven by entrepreneurial innovation through the introduction of new products, ideas, and methods of manufacture. Schumpter is famous for having identified a process of "creative destruction"—new products destroy markets and the need for existing goods. He also identified creative destruction as the "essential fact of capitalism."

Christiansen does not think that the Internet is always a disruptive technology:[16]

Is the Internet a disruptive technology? You can't say that. If you bring it to Dell, it's a sustaining technology to what Dell's business model was in 1996. It made their processes work better; it helped them meet Dell's customers' needs at lower cost. But when you bring the very same Internet to Compaq, it is very disruptive [to the company's then dealer-only sales model]. So how do we treat that? We praise [CEO Michael] Dell, and we fire Eckhard Pfeiffer [Compaq's former CEO]. In reality, those two managers are probably equally competent.

This seeming contradiction can be resolved if one thinks of the Internet as facilitating disruptive enterprises.[17] Such enterprises share the following characteristics:

1. They were enabled by infrastructural innovations.

2. They reshaped the prevailing business model to earn money in a new way.

3. They served customers as the portals of their day.

4. They enabled customers to do for themselves what only specialists could do before.

5. They migrated up-market as they gradually satisfied the needs once filled by the over-served high end of the market, and branding opportunities shifted from the product to the channel. Instead of adding product features or improving packaging, one could create a retail experience (e.g., Starbucks).

Understanding the E-Consumer Experience

How Shopping Online Is Different from Shopping in a Store

When shopping on the Internet, consumers can shop from the convenience of their homes at any time. Hence, they do not have to worry about traffic, parking, long lines, and poorly trained salespeople. Most transactions do not even require interacting with a salesperson, reducing the psychological costs of negotiation (a boon in certain product categories, such as cars). Transaction costs do not simply vanish, however. For example, consumers still have to provide detailed personal information to shop online.

The availability of information is a great benefit of shopping online. Information is frequently consolidated at one source, making it much easier and cheaper to acquire information than it would be in a brick-and-mortar shopping experience where a consumer may have to travel to multiple stores or place multiple phone calls to get comparative information. Online information is organized and ready to use; placed in different categories, making it easy to learn about the product; and available from retailers and third-party sources (e.g., trade associations, independent third parties), in addition to manufacturers. For example, price comparison engines such as My Simon make it easier to compare prices across retailers.

At the same time, there are also new risks online. There is certainly the prospect of information overload. In addition to good information, there is bad information (e.g., personal web pages, bulletin boards), and consumers may find it hard to distinguish between the two. In some cases, it is easy to ascertain how certain features may work on a product or how operating it feels by simply using or observing the product for a few minutes. Because cyberspace does not allow this, a great deal of information can be required to summarize this experience.

When compared to the traditional store environment, shopping online is an inanimate shopping experience. Consumers do not get pampered and they do not get immediate gratification—frequently, consumers have to wait a long period of time before they receive a product (businesses that tried to accelerate delivery time, such as Kozmo, are now defunct). Consumers accustomed to the sensory nature of shopping at a department store may feel uncomfortable completing all stages of the process online.

Department-store shopping obviously has its drawbacks as well, though: the level of service in brick-and-mortar stores has diminished. Frequently, salespeople are poorly trained, not trained at all, or trained to behave in a predatory manner. Another option, catalog shopping, has many of the same Internet concerns.

Furthermore, real space and cyberspace are not mutually exclusive. Frequently, consumers use both spaces during their purchase process. For example, some consumers may use the Internet to gather information about price and then shop at a bricks-and-mortar store for convenience. On the other hand, other consumers may visit stores to "kick the tires" and then order the product online. Overall, shopping online is a unique experience with its own advantages and disadvantages.

How Communicating Online Is Different

Writing on the Internet using hypertext is completely different from previous forms of writing. Instead of thinking of information as being distributed sequentially (or vertically), one must think of information as being distributed spatially (or as part of a "horizontal" dense network). Managers must learn how to use links in a hypertext document to create a new narrative style as shown in Figure 2.4.

Is learning how to write in hypertext the same as authoring web pages? Not at all. Hypertext is now a reality than transcends the Web. For example, it is now possible to include links in all word-processing and presentation software documents sent as e-mail attachments.

The primary reasons for using hypertext in communication:

- To point out the evidence that substantiates an argument without actually getting into its details.
- To point to a later or earlier section of the document.
- To present the analysis of data without submitting a large dataset or spreadsheet.
- To bring readers who have missed the previous conversation up to speed.

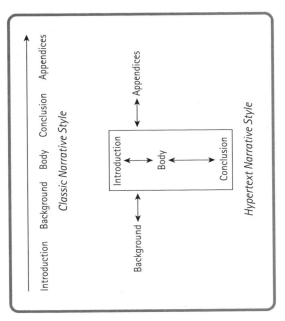

Figure 2.4
Differences in Narrative Style

- To point to alternative points of view.

- To define terms that may be unclear to some (the "Also-see ABC" idea).

A theme that runs through much of the communication on the Internet is interactivity. Rather than having material presented (or broadcasted) without feedback, on the Internet, the communication is "many-way" at the same time. There are many examples of this, such as online newspapers. Rather than presenting news stories as static content, journalists now get immediate and plentiful feedback on the news stories they publish in chat rooms and discussion forums. This changes the mind-set of the journalist from a one-way transmission of information to a many-way transmission. Similarly, the discussion forums at online retailer sites (e.g., Amazon.com) provide the company with immediate feedback about its products. Consumers even learn from one another about how to shop better at the site.

Communicating on the Internet also leads to immediate feedback. A dramatic example is the chat room where users immediately see what others type. As a result, several conversations can occur simultaneously in chat rooms and streams of conversation often intersect with one another. Streams also branch frequently with one group of chatters pursuing a subtopic that is of greater interest to them. Chat room conversations rarely break down into dyadic exchanges, resulting in a dynamic communication environment.[18]

Internet activities have also been characterized by a new word—flow. All of us have felt it at one time. We start browsing and enjoy it so much that we find ourselves immersed in it, losing our sense of time. When one feels the flow, there is a sense of empowerment and enjoyment, leading to greater involvement in the browsing process. As shown in Figure 2.5, to experience flow while engaged in an activity, consumers must perceive a balance between their skills and the challenges of the activity, and both their skills and challenges must be above a critical threshold. Flow has a number of positive consequences from a marketing perspective, including increased consumer learning, exploratory behavior, and a positive subjective experience.[19]

Source: Reprinted by permission, Thomas P. Novak, Donna L. Hoffman, and Y. F. Yung, "Measuring the Customer Experience in Online Environments," *Marketing Science,* 19(1), 22–42. Copyright 2000, the Institute for Operations Research and the Management Sciences (INFORMS), 901 Elkridge Landing Road, Suite 400, Linthicum, Maryland 21090-2909 USA.

figure 2.5
Illustration of Flow

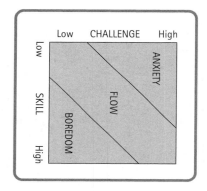

Low   CHALLENGE   High

Low   SKILL   High

ANXIETY

FLOW

BOREDOM

Conclusion

The Internet should be understood at many levels and from the technical, historical, managerial, and customer perspectives. Gaining this rich understanding enables one to tackle the task of designing an Internet business model.

Notes

(All URLs are current as of March 10, 2002.)

1. A detailed history of the Internet is beyond the scope of this book. Interested readers are referred to The Internet Society, *All About the Internet*, available at <http://www.isoc.org/internet/history>.

2. The Rand Corporation, "On Distributed Communications," Memorandum Number RM-3420-PR, 1964, <http://www.rand.org/publications/RM/RM3420/RM3420.chapter1.html>.

3. Richard Griffiths, "History of the Internet, Internet for Historians (and just about everyone else)," October 4, 2001, Available at <http://www.let.leidenuniv.nl/history/ivh/frame_theorie.html>.

4. Tim Berners-Lee, "The World Wide Web: A Very Short Personal History," May 5, 1998, <http://www.w3.org/People/Berners-Lee/ShortHistory.html>.

5. John Heilemann, "Andy Grove's Irrational Exuberance," 9.06, June 2001, <http://www.wired.com/wired/archive/9.06/intel.html?pg=5&topic_set=>.

6. <http://www.business2.com/articles/web/0,1653,17104,00.html>.

7. Jim Ericson, "The Failure of CRM: Looking for Someone to Blame," August 2, 2001, <http://www.line56.com/articles/default.asp?NewsID=2808>.

8. The first three points here are based on the writings of Andrew Odlyzko. Interested readers are referred to <http://www.dtc.umn.edu/~odlyzko/>.

9. John Heilemann, "Andy Grove's Irrational Exuberance."

10. This is based on the research of Adam Huberman. Interested readers are referred to Adam Huberman and L.A. Adamic, "The Nature of Markets in the Word Wide Web," *Quarterly Journal of Electronic Commerce, 1, 203, 2000.*

11. Andrei Broder, Ravi Kumar, Farzin Maghoul, Prabhakar Raghavan, Sridhar Rajagopalan, Raymie Stata, Andrew Tomkins and Janet Wiener, "Graph Structure in the Web," 2000, <http://www.almaden.ibm.com/cs/k53/www9.final>.

12. Michael K. Bergman, "The Deep Web: Surfacing Hidden Value," <http://www.completeplanet.com/Tutorials/DeepWeb/index.asp>.

13. Jakob Nielsen, "Metcalfe's Law in Reverse," July 25, 1999, <http://www.useit.com/alertbox/990725.html>.

14. Andrew Odlyzko, "Internet Growth: Myth and Reality, Use and Abuse," *Journal of Computer Resource Management*, 102, Spring 2001, 23–27.

15. National Academy of Sciences, "A Question of Balance: Private Rights and the Public Interest in Scientific Databases," 1999, <http://www.nap.edu/html/question_balance/ch1.html>.

16. CIO.com, "Disruption is Good: An Interview with Clayton Christiansen," 1997, <http://www.techinformer.com/english/crd_disruptive_49182.html>.

17. Henry C. Co, "Is E-Business A Disruptive Technology," December 19, 2001, <http://www.csupomona.edu/~hco/13eCommerce/ICEB2001DisruptiveTechnology.PDF>.

18. Richard Parrish, "Conversation Analysis of Internet Chat Rooms," <http://www.polisci.wisc.edu/~rdparrish/Chat%20Rooms%20for%20Web%20Site.htm>.

19. Thomas Novak, Donna Hoffman and Y. F. Yung, "Measuring the Flow Construct in Online Environments: A Structural Modeling Approach," eLab working paper, October 1999, <http://www2000.ogsm.vanderbilt.edu/novak/flow.july.1997/flow.htm>.

REVIEW / CHAPTER 2

Discussion Questions

1. What are the advantages and disadvantages of organizing information in the form of a tree (e.g., Gopher) versus a web?

2. According to many experts, the Internet makes everything faster. What is the impact of this increased speed on the costs of the firm? What is its impact on revenues? When does this increased speed lead to greater profits?

3. As discussed in the chapter, the Internet can enhance the value proposition to the consumer. How does it detract from it? From this analysis, would you argue that some consumers are more likely than others to be online shoppers?

4. What is it about Internet technology that facilitates the formation of winner-take-all markets? Why didn't such markets come about before the advent of the Internet?

5. Porter's new theory of the Internet as a neutral competitive tool has been criticized by experts as being too pessimistic about the potential of this new technology. Critically analyze his theory from the perspective of one of these experts.

6. Why don't managers write in hypertext more often?

E-Tasks

1. Visit the following sites: cnn.com, nytimes.com, and msnbc.com. They are the top three news sites online. From the content and layout, can you deduce the target audience for each site? Are the target audiences different for the three sites? If you cannot tell, is that a problem for these sites?

2. Conduct a survey of ten friends. Ask them to keep a diary for five days indicating the names of the sites they visited on any particular day. Prepare a chart with two columns—the name of the web site and the number of times it was mentioned by any one of your friends. Plot these two numbers. Do you observe a winner-take-all structure?

REVIEW / CHAPTER 2

E-Tasks [continued]

3. In this task, the class divides up into groups of different sizes. For example, a class of thirty may be broken up into three groups of three, one group of five, one group of seven, one group of nine. Each group enters a Yahoo! (or other free) chat room. All groups are asked to discuss the same topic. Here are a few suggestions:

- Customer service is an investment, not an expense.

- Let's face it, businesses do not care about customers.

- The Internet changes everything.

- Meeting someone in a chat room is the same thing as meeting them in person.

- E-mail is the killer application, not the Web.

Each group is allowed twenty minutes to chat. Then, each group is responsible for revisiting the transcript of the chat and identifying the total number of comments made by the group. The class then prepares a chart mapping group size with the level of conversation (i.e., total number of comments). If there is a structure similar to Metcalfe's Law here, you must find that the larger groups have more comments per person (not just a greater number of com-ments). Is this true? Why or why not?

CHAPTER 3

Business Model Design

Learning Objectives

▶ To learn about the importance of setting clear objectives before creating an online business or implementing Internet technology.

▶ To learn how to use the Internet toolkit—six-Cs of e-business—to deliver value.

▶ To design the revenue model—understand revenue stream management and profit path analysis.

▶ To learn about how to shift from a free model to a fee-based model.

▶ To learn about the problems that arise when implementing Internet technology.

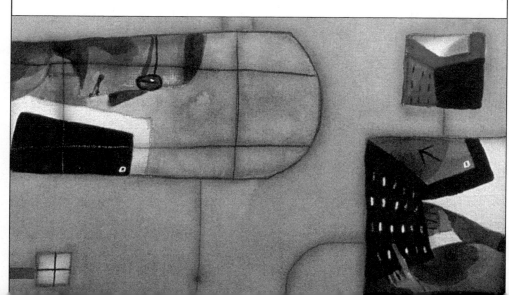

Executive Summary

Anyone planning to create an online business or implement Internet technology in an existing business should first set clear objectives. The company must understand the profit orientation (profit/loss center) of the virtual operation, clearly set short-term and long-term goals, and choose a target audience. Businesses exist to maximize long-term shareholder value, but the path to maximum shareholder value is through the maximization of customer value. The Internet toolkit can help create value for customers in virtual space and the four-Ps of marketing can help deliver value in the physical space. The revenue model consists of the set of the business' revenue streams. Businesses must make careful trade-offs between diversifying revenue streams and losing strategic focus. They must also understand the cost of obtaining revenue in order to understand the profitability of each revenue stream—all of which are interrelated. When moving from a free to a fee-based model, businesses must look at the overall profits and not worry about losing customers. But they should worry about implementation issues, such as aiming for an uninspiring product (yawnware), designing by committee, and assuming a mind-set similar to a traditional business. We will also discuss implementing CRM systems.

Introduction

Every business exists to maximize shareholder value. The path to shareholder value maximization goes through the maximization of value to the customer. Thus, value to the customer must be the driving force in every business. Instead of focusing on designing, producing, and delivering products, the business must articulate what it means by value, deliver it to the consumers, and communicate the value to the consumer. This is the only way a business can ensure maximum earnings and shareholder value in the long run. Using this definition of shareholder value, this chapter discusses how to incorporate the Internet/Web in designing a more effective business.

The process begins by assessing what a business hopes to achieve by incorporating these technologies. First, the business must have a sense of what proportion of its business will be online and how this proportion might change over time. Second, it must clearly understand the purpose of its online operation—is it a profit center (i.e., a source of income) or a loss center (i.e., offered as a service to consumers). Third, it must determine the target audience, in terms of demographics (e.g., age, income), behavior (e.g., surfing pattern), or psychographics (e.g., values, lifestyle).

After gaining a clear understanding of the digitality (i.e., proportion of business online), the purpose, and the target audience, the business must try to clarify the path for delivering maximum customer value. The drivers of value are different in physical and virtual or online spaces. In the physical space, value is driven by the marketing mix or four-Ps of marketing (product, price, place, and promotion). However, in the online space, the Internet toolkit (commerce, cost reduction, communication, connectivity, community, content, and computing), mentioned in Chapter 1, is important.

Delivering customer value is not in itself sufficient for the success of the business; it must be translated into maximizing revenue and profits. The next step is therefore revenue model design. A business can be thought of as a collection of revenue streams, the careful choice of which can determine the long-term health of the business. A business with too few streams is vulnerable to random shocks from the environment, but one with too many suffers from high administrative costs. Fortunately there are simple statistical and managerial tools that can be used to analyze a revenue portfolio.

Finally, implementing the business model is, of course, an entirely separate step from designing it; a perfect model cannot make up for faulty implementation.

Business Assessment

The Digitality of a Business

The *digitality* of a business is the proportion of a business that is online. A business may be completely online and have no physical component; all the employees may telecommute, and the business may sell a digital product, such as software, directly from its web site. Such a business has a digitality of one. On the other hand, a business with no representation in the online space is said to have a digitality of zero. All others fall in between zero and one. At this point, only a few small businesses have zero digitality. Most have a digitality greater than zero but less than one.

The company makes this choice. Taking a portion of a company online requires a careful assessment of the ramifications and does not happen overnight. "Going digital" implies a realignment of the company's power structure and a change in strategic direction. The company must assess these factors carefully before implementing Internet technology.

Every business must also consider how its digitality might change over time. Some businesses that started out as entirely online businesses have added physical components (e.g., Amazon.com has added warehouses close to key markets). And some with a predominantly physical presence (e.g., Wal-Mart) have attempted to build an online presence with varying degrees of success. Each business must carefully consider all implications and prepare a plan to make the transition.

Profit Orientation (Profit or Loss Center)

Every company must determine whether its online operation is a service to consumers or if it will provide income for the organization. Consider, for example, the Crest web site (http://www.crest.com), the leading toothpaste brand owned by Procter & Gamble. The entire site is devoted to educating (predominantly young) users about the benefits of brushing and flossing. The company provides detailed product information, but sells no product from the web site. The web site is strictly a free service to the company's customers and is, therefore, a loss center. On the other hand, if a product or service is sold on the web site (e.g., bn.com), it is a profit center.

A business often goes online quickly with a basic site (sometimes referred to as brochure-ware), which it views as a loss center that is educating a segment of its customers. If the company plans to change the site later into one that sells its products, it must take care to set appropriate customer expectations from the beginning.

Target Audience

Choosing a target audience carefully is one of the most important decisions a business can make. Targeting imposes a sense of focus on the organization, reduces waste of marketing resources, and improves the value delivery to the consumer.

Each web site must be designed to meet the needs of a specific target audience or a set of audiences. If the company targets multiple audiences, it must have a clear sense of priority among them. The web site should be designed so that the members of each audience clearly understand the area that is designated for them. For example, Dell.com targets individuals, businesses, and governments with its web site. The area for each audience is clearly marked on the front page of the site to point traffic from each segment to the appropriate area.

Of course, customers can be divided into a variety of categories, most commonly by demographics (e.g., age, income), behavior (e.g., surfing pattern), or psychographics (e.g., values, lifestyle).

Online customers are typically categorized by their surfing behavior. A study conducted by McKinsey corporation[1] divides consumers into five groups—simplifiers, surfers, bargainers, connectors, routiners, and sportsters. A detailed description of these segments and their implications is presented in Appendix I.

Delivering Value to the Consumer

Although some proportion of almost every business is now virtual (i.e., has a digitality greater than zero), many businesses continue to have a strong physical presence, and very few may ever completely abandon the physical realm. As a result, it is important to distinguish between the value drivers in the physical and the virtual spaces.

The drivers of value in the physical space are the traditional four-Ps of marketing (also called the marketing mix)—product, price, place (i.e., distribution), and promotion. On the other hand, in the virtual space, the Internet toolkit (commerce, communication, connectivity, community, content, and computing) is important in driving value.

Definition of Value

Value to a consumer is his or her perception of the consequence of using a product or service in relation to prior expectations. Consumers perceive additional value if the product exceeds expectations. Consumers commonly make value judgments in relation to price. As shown in Figure 3.1, consumers may compare products based on their price and perceived quality. In general, products that fall below the forty-five-degree line are seen as

Figure 3.1
Price versus Perceived Quality

48

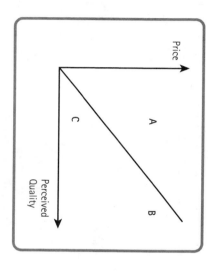

offering greater value than those that fall above the line. In this figure, product B offers greater perceived quality for the same price as product A. On the other hand, product C offers the same perceived quality, but at a much lower price. As a result, consumers perceive products B and C as offering superior value to product A.

However, this is not a complete characterization of customer value. For example, how can a web site that offers educational services to its customer assess the value it delivers? Because it is a free service, price cannot be used to assess value.

Therefore, *value can be more generally defined as the overall evaluation of a product or service based on the perceptions of the net benefits and what must be given up to attain them.* By this definition, the web site just described can focus on factors such as the pleasantness of the browsing experience, the usefulness of the information to answer the important consumer questions, and the reliability of the site (e.g., it does not crash the system).

Managers must follow a five-step process to deliver value to the customer. The first step is to identify how different consumers perceive value. Managers must use research (e.g., focus groups, interviews, surveys), to determine how customers view value—now and in the long run. Particularly useful would be a rank ordering of product attributes based on importance to consumers.

The second step is to choose which value elements will be delivered. Different customer segments desire different values; moreover, the firm's capabilities and core competencies must be matched with what customers want. A firm must choose what it considers to be a value element, and if it's targeting multiple audiences, it must identify the value for each audience.

The next step is to provide the value: build the business in such a way that it manifests the desired elements. In the physical space, this is achieved using the four-Ps; and in the virtual space, it is achieved using the Internet toolkit.

Delivering the desirable value elements is not enough; the company has to tell consumers exactly how value is being delivered. The fourth step is therefore to develop an integrated communications package to help customers learn about the nature of the value.

Finally, one must constantly assess how customers perceive the value being delivered. This is an effort to close the perceptual gap between what the consumers think they are getting and what the company hopes they are getting. Using surveys and other market research techniques, customers should be asked about their perception of value and whether it has led them to be satisfied with the company's offering.

Using the Four Ps to Deliver Value

Because this topic is typically covered in traditional marketing courses in great detail, only a brief discussion is provided here. Methods to use the four-Ps to deliver value might include:

1. Product. The company can begin by providing a product that meets an urgent need of the customer. Other value elements related to product are either functional or hedonic. *Functional value elements* relate to the actual performance of the product. *Hedonic value elements* relate to the utility derived from possessing, using, or displaying the product. With a car, for instance, functional value elements include the horsepower of the engine and the time it takes to reach a speed of sixty miles per hour. Hedonic value elements include brand name, color, and design.

2. Price. When we think of price, we must include mental transaction costs such as waiting in lines, parking time, and so on. Reducing these costs helps the consumer feel that he or she is getting greater value. We've already discussed the issue of value in relation to price and perceived quality.

3. Place (distribution). Distribution ensures that the product is available at the desired location at the desired time. Consumers may take this for granted, but if a product is not delivered to their home on time or if it is not available at their favorite store, they may quickly switch to an alternative.

4. Promotion. Promotion includes communication (e.g., advertising) and providing an economic incentive (e.g., coupons). Promotion alerts consumers to the three other Ps. For example, advertising can help build awareness of a new product, a price cut, or a store opening. In addition, by providing an economic incentive, promotions essentially reduce the price to the consumer, enhancing his or her sense of value.

The Internet Toolkit

Use the six-Cs to deliver value as follows:

1. Commerce. Commerce is perhaps the one C in the Internet toolkit that can have both a strong physical and virtual space component (e.g., Internet retailers such as Amazon.com take orders online, but deliver the products directly to the customer). Wherever relevant, the four-Ps of the physical space must be applied. For example, even if a consumer can place an order in a convenient way, if the product is not delivered on time, there is zero value.

With online commerce, consumers can place orders at any time of the day or night. Moreover, they can shop from the convenience of their homes. Online commerce also provides a large amount of easily available information. The product assortment is larger than that at brick-and-mortar stores. Giving gifts is dramatically simpler—individuals can send gifts to many people from one online store without setting foot in a post office. Some stores provide consumers with "virtual dressing rooms" to try on a dress before ordering it.

2. Communication. The Internet offers a variety of communication technologies, such as e-mail and discussion boards, which provide many benefits, as described in Table 3.1.

These technologies can promote better communication between a firm and its customers and among consumers.

3. Connectivity. Using the Internet, businesses can allow consumers to connect with customers in remote areas all over the world. For example, consumers may be interested to know how their peers would rate a given product. In addition, users can easily connect with other users and with company employees.

4. Community. The value elements in online communities include:[2]

- Socializing: meeting people, playing around, sharing jokes and stories, and just taking an interest in each other.

- Learning from others: individuals benefit from expert users who have extensive product knowledge.

- Working together: distributed work groups within companies and between companies use online communities to build their teams, keep in touch, and even work on projects together. Similarly, community groups (e.g., soccer teams, school groups) have used online forums to work together.

Table 3.1
Value Elements of Different Communication Technologies

Dimension	Description	Example
Co-presence	A and B share the same physical environment.	Avatar-based chat (partial solution)
Visibility	A and B are visible to each other.	Video conferencing
Audibility	A and B can hear each other.	Internet telephony
Co-temporality	B receives the message at the same time A sends it.	Instant message
Simultaneity	A and B can send and receive messages simultaneously.	Chat
Sequentiality	A's and B's turns cannot go out of sequence.	Bulletin board messages
Reviewability	B can review A's message.	E-mail
Revisability	A can revise message for B.	E-mail

Source: Jennifer Preece, Online Communities: Designing Usability and Supporting Sociability (New York: John Wiley & Sons, 2000).

- Having topical conversations: online salons and discussion forums (e.g., the Well at http://www.well.com, Salon's TableTalk at http://www.salon.com, and Cafe Utne at http://www.utne.com) have formed communities of people who enjoy conversations about shared interests.

5. Content. Businesses can use online content to:

- Educate their consumers about how to use the product (e.g., Crest.com's Smiles Central allows families to learn about oral hygiene).
- Provide detailed information about the product to the consumer for a richer shopping experience (e.g., Amazon.com provides buyers with information about the availability of the book, its rank among other books sold there, product reviews, etc.).
- Provide product and price comparison tools (e.g., MySimon.com provides consumers with the tools to compare prices for a variety of products across a number of prominent retail stores).
- Using the commonly used FAQ feature, businesses can lessen the load on service and sales representatives.

6. Computing. Businesses can provide users with complex computing tools, for example:

- Consumers can track packages by visiting FedEx.com.
- Advertising agencies such as Doubleclick provide complex real-time reports to advertisers.
- Using Ditech's portfolio tracker, individuals can track changes in the stocks of their choice in real time.
- Using ESPN Gamecast, individuals can track every pitch thrown in a baseball game in progress.

A detailed six-Cs checklist is provided in Appendix II at the end of the chapter.

The Revenue Model

Revenue Stream Management

Every new business aims to maximize its profits. Businesses make money online in five ways:[3]

1. *Commerce*–selling products or services to consumers or businesses.
2. *Advertising*–selling advertising space to interested advertisers.
3. *Fees*–charging fees to consumers (individuals or businesses) for subscribing to content or service or for auction participation, charging brokering fees for consummating a transaction or finder's fee, and charging fees for the use of technology.
4. *Sale of consumer information*–aggregating consumer behavior information and selling it to interested companies.

5. *Credit*—receiving money from the consumer on Day 1 and paying vendors after a long period of time. This is also called creating a "float."

The primary issue for a new e-business is choosing its revenue streams. In fact, a new e-business is really a collection of revenue streams. Revenue streams are the most effective metrics by which to judge a business.

Each revenue stream differs based on these four dimensions:

- Strength—a strong revenue stream is one that adds the most to the profitability of the organization.

- Stability—a stable revenue stream is not easily altered by changes in the business environment.

- Cyclicality—a cyclical revenue stream does not provide consistent returns to the company. As a result, it is dangerous for a company to count on a single revenue stream that is vulnerable to a cyclical market.

- Resource needs—the amount of money, time, technology, people and other resources a revenue stream requires.

Revenue Stream Management versus Product Portfolio Analysis

Revenue stream management (RSM) differs significantly from product portfolio techniques such as the Boston Consulting Group (BCG) Matrix. Of course, products lead to revenue, but focusing on products exclusively limits the scope of a firm's operations to just the first of the five methods of earning money (i.e., commerce). RSM provides a general form of analysis that can include any revenue stream.

Why Focus on RSM for an E-Business?

There are two important reasons why RSM is important to an e-business:

1. E-businesses typically have intangible and informational assets. These assets can be leveraged many times to obtain multiple streams of income. For example, some firms use customer information to target advertising as well as to create market research reports.

2. One of the primary benefits of the Internet is the ease of linkage between firms. E-businesses typically have horizontal and vertical linkages with other firms, and each linkage has the potential to be a revenue stream. Therefore, learning about RSM is vital for an e-business.

Revenue Information

Consider two businesses—Business I and Business II. Business I has five revenue streams and Business II has three revenue streams. The data are shown in Tables 3.2a and 3.2b.

Cost of Obtaining Revenue (COOR)

One must also incorporate the COOR. For example, it may be possible to get high revenue figures if millions of consumers visit your web site, but if the cost of bringing in consumers is very high, it is not profitable.

Table 3.2a
Revenue Streams of Business I

	Revenue, $
Revenue Stream 1	100,000
Revenue Stream 2	20,000
Revenue Stream 3	50,000
Revenue Stream 4	10,000
Revenue Stream 5	500

Table 3.2b
Revenue Streams of Business II

	Revenue, $
Revenue Stream 1	80,000
Revenue Stream 2	100,000
Revenue Stream 3	150,000

Table 3.3a
Profit Picture of Business I

	Revenue, $	COOR, $	Profit, $
Revenue Stream 1	100,000	50,000	50,000
Revenue Stream 2	20,000	15,000	5,000
Revenue Stream 3	50,000	12,500	37,500
Revenue Stream 4	10,000	2,500	7,500
Revenue Stream 5	500	0	500
			100,500

Table 3.3b
Profit Picture of Business II

	Revenue, $	COOR, $	Profit, $
Revenue Stream 1	80,000	60,000	20,000
Revenue Stream 2	100,000	90,000	10,000
Revenue Stream 3	150,000	112,500	37,500
			67,500

Costs are of two types—fixed and variable. Fixed costs are incurred irrespective of the level of revenue, whereas variable costs escalate in direct proportion to the revenue. For example, a company that decides to make money through advertising will have to invest in a certain number of servers and in software before it earns its first dollar. Over time, it will also incur the cost of salaries to operate the advertising engine. This is shown in Tables 3.3a and 3.3b.

In this case, we find that both businesses are profitable—a good sign. Business I is more profitable than Business II.

Portfolio Analysis

The key question in portfolio analysis is whether to develop a large portfolio of revenue streams to reduce the risk of failure or focus on a few streams in order to concentrate on the company's core competence. A business that relies on one revenue stream is putting itself in a vulnerable position, since if that revenue stream is threatened by a weak economy, a worker strike, or some other factor beyond the company's control, the company will go out of business.

On the other hand, if a company includes multiple streams, it may lose focus and gain too many administrative problems for it to be viable. One way of dealing with this is to quantify administrative difficulties as a cost and apportion that cost to different revenue streams, so that it is reflected in the COOR figures.

How does a company decide if it has too many revenue streams or too few? A simple statistical analysis (Table 3.4) provides more insight.

Although the first three rows are easy to understand, the coefficient of variation (CV) may be new. The CV is the ratio of the mean over standard deviation. The CV value helps us make sense of the standard deviation figure by telling us if it is too high or too low: a high CV value indicates a low level of standard deviation and vice versa. The CV value therefore gives us a simple measure of the extent of diversification in the portfolio.

Business I has five revenue streams with a mean of $20,100 and a CV of 0.91. This indicates to us that it is well diversified.

Look at Table 3.3a again. Should Business I drop revenue stream 5? A casual look at the profit numbers reveals that revenue stream 5 is contributing the least–$500. If the company drops this, the CV number goes up to 1.12 and the mean goes up to $25,000. This suggests that the company can focus better if it drops revenue stream 5. However, one could also argue that this stream does not ask anything of the company because the COOR value is 0. In many businesses, small revenue streams can bog the company down by creating administrative problems.

Other factors might include:

1. If the company is convinced that stream 5 has the highest growth potential, it could retain it.

2. If stream 5 meets a specific nonrevenue-related company objective (e.g., service to a customer, serving a market), it may be wise to retain it.

Table 3.4
Revenue Stream Analysis

	Business I	Business II
Number of revenue streams	5	3
Mean value of profit from revenue stream	$20,100	$22,500
Standard Deviation	$22,179.38	$13,919.41
Coefficient of Variation (Mean/Std. Dev.)	0.91	1.62

Business II has only three revenue streams with a mean of $22,500 and a CV of 1.62. Because the company has only three streams, dropping one in order to focus the company is not an issue. The real contributor to the high CV is the high COOR for revenue stream 2. The company should focus on reducing that stream.

Interrelationship Among Revenue Streams

Revenue streams are interrelated. The two revenue streams advertising and subscription, for example, are negatively correlated; that is, if one is high, the other is most likely low. Think about it. If you set a high subscription fee, you will not get many consumers. As a result, your advertising rates will be low. If you set a low subscription fee, you will get a lot of consumers. Now, you can set a very high advertising rate. In fact, this can be expressed through a simple graph as shown in Figure 3.2.

Two revenue streams might instead be positively correlated. For example, as a web site attracts more consumers, it is able to set a higher advertising rate and at the same time make more money from market research by packaging consumer information to interested firms. In this case, the relationship between the two is shown in Figure 3.3.

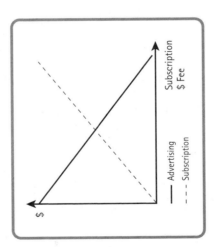

Figure 3.2
Negative Correlation Between Advertising and Subscription

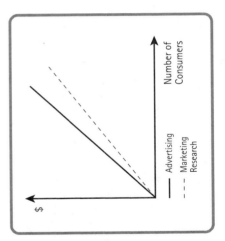

Figure 3.3
Positive Correlation Between Advertising and Marketing Research

Figure 3.4
Low Correlation Between
Advertising and Marketing
Research

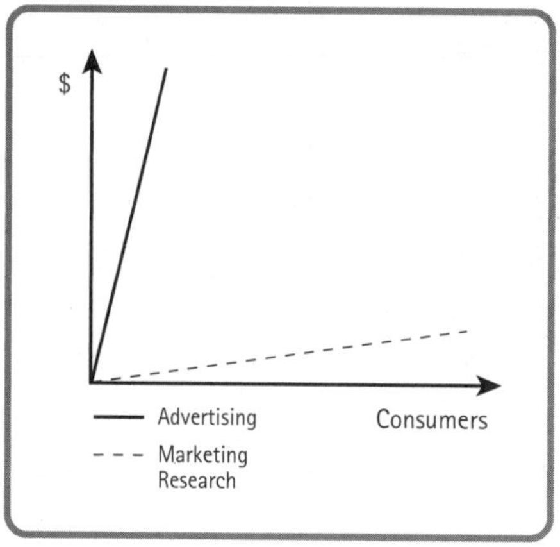

Of course, the degree of correlation can vary. Compare Figure 3.3 to Figure 3.4. Both have the same streams, but they turn out to be less correlated in the case shown in Figure 3.4.

How should a business determine the extent of correlation between or among two or more revenue streams? The first instinct of managers may be to conduct a correlation analysis over time, but they shouldn't. The proper approach is to conduct a survey or an experiment.

Use as an example a business that is trying to decide the appropriate subscription price. After conducting survey research, it has come up with Table 3.5 (details of this are presented in the section on free versus paid).

A simple correlation between the advertising and subscription revenue columns yields a value of −0.46684. As expected, the correlation is negative and is at a moderate level.

Revenue Stream Decisions

At different points in time, managers have to make the following decisions:

- Add a new revenue stream

Table 3.5
Free to Fee

Subscription Price	Number of Customers	Incremental Attrition	Advertising Revenue	Subscription Revenue	Total Revenue
$ 0	100,000	N/A	$200,000	0	$200,000
5	75,000	25,000	150,000	$375,000	525,000
10	40,000	35,000	80,000	400,000	480,000
15	35,000	5,000	70,000	525,000	595,000
20	10,000	25,000	20,000	200,000	220,000

- Remove an existing revenue stream

- Restructure an existing revenue stream

When does an e-business add a new revenue stream? The following factors must be considered:

1. The incremental profit (i.e., compare the incremental revenue with the incremental cost of obtaining that revenue).

2. The impact on existing revenue streams—will the new stream be correlated with an existing stream? If so, it could affect overall revenue and profitability and must be considered carefully.

3. The administrative difficulties of multiple revenue streams. In general, administrative problems rise in proportion to the square of the number of revenue streams. Consequently, if you have fifty-three streams and are thinking about adding another, there is probably something wrong.

Profit Path Analysis

One of the tools available to businesses interested in improving their revenue is to look at the determinants of their revenue streams. For an example see Table 3.6. Look at Business I and name the revenue streams.

The next step is to set up a specific profit path as shown in Figure 3.5.

There are two sources of profit in this business. The first one is clearly driven by the quantity of customer traffic. The second one is driven by four factors—price, service, reputation, and assortment. Note that even though the quality of content leads directly to a profit of only $500, it influences the quantity of traffic and thus may have a larger influence. The profit path analysis is a simple diagnostic tool that is very useful when a firm has a large number of revenue streams.

Table 3.6
Revenue Stream Determinants

	Determinants	Revenue, $	COOR, $	Profit, $
Commerce (B2C)	Price, Service, Reputation, Assortment	100,000	50,000	50,000
Advertising	Quantity of Traffic	20,000	15,000	5,000
Commissions	Quantity of Traffic	50,000	12,500	37,500
Fees from merchants in eMall	Quantity of Traffic	10,000	2,500	7,500
Subscriptions to premium content	Quality of Content	500	0	500
			Total	100,500

Figure 3.5
Profit Path Analysis

58

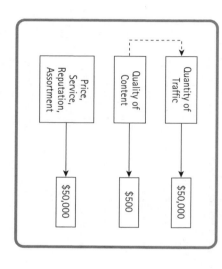

Forecasting Revenue Streams

When venture capitalists look at a business plan, they focus on the sales forecasts. If you are starting a new business, adopt a conservative approach. The following is one example—subscription fee.

Subscription Fee Revenue Expected in Year 1 $200,000

(20,000 subscribers at the rate of $10 per year)

The strategy is to hold the subscription fee constant for two years and then increase it to $15 per person per year.

Number of Subscribers		Revenue
Year 1	20,000	$200,000
Year 2	24,000 (20% growth)	240,000
Year 3	20,000 (Attrition rate = 4,000)	300,000
Year 4	22,000	330,000
Year 5	23,000	345,000

Forecasting Techniques

1. Use expert forecasts. Companies such as Jupiter Communications and Forrester Research are famous for arriving at estimates of future sales levels for various industries.

2. Consider similar industries. If you are interested in forecasting sales for DVDs, you can consider the growth rates of CDs. Obviously, this is an imperfect technique but it is helpful.

3. Understand the cyclical nature of some revenue streams. Advertising is a cyclical business: when the economy is strong, ad rates are high; when the economy is in a recession, ad rates are low.

4. Extrapolate from the big picture. If you are interested in understanding the number of people who might come to your site, start with forecasts of your sector. For example, if the B2C sector is expected to grow at a rate of 23% over the next year, you could argue that your growth rate is in the region of 10–15%.

Pitfalls in Setting Forecasts

1. Too aggressive—steady growth rates of 25% or more may lead to overcommitment of resources and excessive investment.

2. No fundamental logic for the growth—why do you expect such a high growth rate? What is the underlying logic?

3. Inadequate vision of the meaning of the growth—do you realize the number of employees that will be necessary to manage that growth rate?

4. Not planning for all situations—are you prepared for very high or very low levels of any given revenue stream?

Free versus Paid

Is it possible to convert consumers who have signed on to a free service to paying consumers? This is a big question facing Internet businesses. Many businesses built their customer base by giving their basic service for free. The companies were flush with venture capital and had the resources to do this. Moreover their investors advised the companies to act this way, in order to build market share and drive out smaller competitors.

But after they amassed market share and drove out smaller competitors, a lot of businesses realized that they did not have adequate revenue. So they started harassing their customers (e.g., free Internet service providers now restrict the number of hours free users get) and trying to convert them into paying customers (e.g., Netzero has created the Platinum service, in which users get faster connections with no banner ads if they pay a flat monthly fee). At this point, consumers do not have much choice because most free operators have disappeared. Hence, it is possible that consumers will start paying. On the other hand, if the advertising market picks up, consumers may not have to pay.

One lesson that many businesses have learned is that making an abrupt change from an all-free web site to an all-paid web site leads to disaster (see the Slatanic case). The more appropriate strategy may be to create separate versions of the product and offer a paid product with more features for a price. Even then, not all consumers will switch; managers must prepare for attrition.

Specifically, companies must consider the level of attrition at different pricing levels. The pricing plan that leads to the lowest level of attrition will often not be the most profitable. When one moves from a free business model to a paid business model, one must shift focus from expanding customer traffic to maximizing profits from a smaller set of customers.

To understand these dynamics, consider a business that provided free content and made its money through advertising. Assume that each customer visits the site about 100 times a month and the company is able to charge advertisers $20 per 1,000 exposures. Now, the company is deciding to move to a system where it can charge for its content.

This point is made in Table 3.5. In this case, the greatest profits are found when the price is $15. Some managers may continue to apply free business model thinking by trying to go with $5 pricing, leading to 75,000 customers. But in fact, greater revenue can be made with greater customer attrition. Of course, the cost of running the business at the new prices is not factored into Table 3.5. Including that could complicate the matter further.

Revenue Stream Decisions Affect User Experience

Let us compare three sites. All three connect users with experts in a number of areas, but they differ in terms of their business model and their RSM strategies.

Site 1 believes that it must locate experts in different areas. Consequently, it carefully chooses experts and pays them to be part of the site. Users pay nothing to consult with the experts. The company makes money by selling advertising space on a targeted basis and from "paid links" to other companies.

Site 2 believes it must create a community of experts. Consequently, it does not choose experts—users proclaim themselves to be experts and they are in business. Other users then pay to talk to the experts by phone or e-mail. The company makes money in two ways—it receives the money from the users on Day 1 and holds onto it until Day 30 when it pays the experts, and it takes 5% of the money.

Site 3 also believes it must connect users with experts. This site designates individuals as experts in specific areas after an application and interview process. All experts go through a training process. They then maintain a set of links on their topic. Users can contact the experts and do not have to pay. The experts are paid a share of the advertising revenue on their page. The greater the number of visitors to a site, the more money they make. The experts themselves are therefore expected to become recruiters for the site.

How might the user experience be different for these three sites? First, we would expect to find more "experts" in any given category on Site 2 because the requirements for becoming an expert are low. The lowest number of experts will be on Site 1 because the company will want to minimize the number of people it has to pay. Second, how about the number of users? We will probably see more users on Sites 1 and 3, where they do not have to pay anything to get advice. On the other hand, those users who care about the quality of the advice will go to Site 2. Third, Site 2 has no advertising—it makes its money from commissions. Therefore, users see no banners—a great user experience.

Implementation Issues

Even though an e-business may be designed effectively, if it is not well implemented, the results could be poor. The fact that many of these implementations take place within a short time frame (i.e., "Internet time") increases the possibility that they will be implemented poorly.

Implementation Challenges for Online Firms

Online firms face unique implementation challenges:[4]

• Internet time. Frequently, the implementation of the business model in an online space has to be done very quickly. This creates a sense of urgency and some element of the business model may be forgotten or not implemented to the satisfaction of the designers.

• Higher visibility of errors. A web site is a public space. Anybody can read the entire code used to prepare it. If access to the web site is denied to some users, the word can spread like wildfire, leading to bad publicity. A spelling mistake or grammatical error in the content can lead to a loss in business.

• Lower switching costs. On the Internet, competition is, as they say, just a click away. If users visit a site and are dissatisfied with what they see, they can easily move to a competitor's site. Although they may return in the future, their loyalty may be weakened.

• More complex linkages. Online firms typically have linkages to several partners. In some cases, the site development may be farmed out to different vendors, coordination among which may be tricky.

Implementation of E–Commerce by Physical Companies

Many companies with a strong physical presence resist implementing Internet technology. Consider the results from this survey of fifty-four CIOs conducted by *CIO Magazine* in January 1998. Seventy-six percent of the participants indicated that they faced resistance from employees and colleagues when implementing an Internet/intranet/extranet. Moreover, 57% of the participants indicated that there were dramatic differences of opinion within the company as to what the Internet venture would provide. The primary cause of this resistance was fear of the technology and failure to understand the potential value of its implementation.[5]

Consider the case of CRM systems. Recent studies have shown that the systems have about a 70% failure rate.[6] This incredibly high number is largely attributed to faulty implementation. Following are the most common reasons why CRM systems fail:[7]

1. *Losing sight of why the CRM system is being implemented.* In many cases, the implementation of large systems such as CRM takes on a life of its own. Frequently, companies get carried away with the details of the system and forget why they wanted to implement it in the first place—to improve customer loyalty and sales per customer. A CRM package by itself will not make this happen. Firms must be willing to evaluate the current customer experience and implement standard business methods before implementing new technology. A CRM system cannot hide a basic failure to understand the company from the customer's point of view.

2. *Not having a clear executive sponsor who owns the CRM vision.* CRM is expensive and extensive. An enterprise-wide CRM implementation is bound to challenge the firm to the core. Without an executive sponsor, such a project is bound to flounder and lose direction, and the system vendor may end up dictating the terms.

3. *Implementing CRM in silos.* Many companies implement CRM to replace several disparate systems and create a unified view of the customer. If one group creates the "order" processes and another group creates the "care" processes, the customers may feel like they are dealing with two different departments. If there is no coordination between these departments, the problem is accentuated further.

4. *Underestimating the difficulties of integration.* A CRM strategy cannot succeed without integration. Integrating CRM systems with other internal systems such as enterprise resource planning (ERP) and other enterprise applications is difficult, but it is necessary to give the customer a superior experience. CRM packages do not offer adequate tools for ERP integration, resulting in systems that cannot share data between acquisition points, making it impossible to create customer profiles that include such information as shipping preferences and spending habits.[8] Integration failures result in manual steps across multiple departments or applications, often resulting in duplicate data entry, wasted effort, and data errors.

5. *Package upgrades.* Once a CRM package is customized, it is difficult and costly to upgrade. The best way to lower this risk is to evaluate all customizations carefully and leverage the support of the CRM vendor. Firms should demand that vendors review the customizations they require and point out the areas that might be difficult to upgrade.

Finally, a recent study identified the best practices when implementing Internet technology into traditional organizations based on research of 800 businesses.[9] The best practices:

1. Have an overarching plan that drives its Internet implementation. One central office must have the overall authority for this process.

2. Avoid design by committee, which leads to a product that everybody can live with as opposed to one that inspires.

3. Don't take the path of least resistance and create a simple "yawner app." Instead, aim for an inspirational product.

4. To build the web site, choose vendors who understand your business. Try to work with one vendor so that there is accountability.

5. Do not duplicate your traditional business assumptions online. The Internet is a fundamentally different medium.

6. Allocate adequate resources to make the Internet venture successful.

7. Provide incentives for business units to collaborate in cyberspace.

8. Consider the activities of both online and offline competitors.

9. Build an Internet culture. Train employees to use the Internet effectively.

10. Allow customer input to drive design.

Conclusion

The business model is a plan for profitability and maximum shareholder value—which necessarily implies maximum value to the customer. RSM provides the manager with a valuable statistical and managerial tool to design and manage a revenue model. Implementing the business model design can result in problems and must be actively managed for success.

Notes

(All URLs are current as of March 10, 2002.)

1. John E. Forsyth, Johanne Lavoie, and Tim McGuire, "Segmenting the E-Market," Number 4, 2000, <http://www.mckinseyquarterly.com/article_page.asp?tk=292854:939:24&tar=939&L2=24&L3=44> (registration required).

2. This has been taken directly from Sue Boetcher, Heather Duggan and Nancy White, "What is a Virtual Community and Why Would You Ever Need One?," January 2002, <http://www.fullcirc.com/community/communitywhatwhy.htm>.

3. The focus is on company operation and not on capital investment. Therefore, receiving money from a venture capitalist in exchange for equity does not constitute a revenue stream.

4. This is adapted from Jeffrey Rayport and Bernard Jaworski, *E-Commerce* (Boston: McGraw Hill-Irwin-MarketspaceU, 2001).

5. Kathleen Kotwica, "Survey: Internet Implementation and Management," January 1998, <http://www.cio.com/behavior/edit/survey1.html>.

6. Jim Ericson, "The Failure of CRM: Looking for Someone to Blame," August 2, 2001, <http://www.line56.com/articles/default.asp?NewsID=2808>.

7. My thanks to my MBA students, Jennifer Gregor and Randy Serroels, for this information.

8. Lee Pender, "CRM from Scratch," *CIO Magazine*, August 15, 2000.

9. Rosabeth Moss Kanter, "The Ten Deadly Mistakes of Wanna-Dots," *Harvard Business Review*, January 2001.

REVIEW / CHAPTER 3

Discussion Questions

1. How is the digitality (i.e., the extent to which a firm is online) of a firm related to its competitive advantage? Can a company be competitive with a physical presence only? With an online presence only?

2. What are the challenges of designing a web site for many target audiences as opposed to one? Should a company create several new sites, each with its own distinct domain name, instead of creating one home page that directs audiences to their appropriate space?

3. There are five ways that companies make money online—commerce, advertising, fees, sale of consumer information, and credit. Can you order these revenue streams as to their money-making power for any given company?

4. How does the managerial challenge change with the degree of correlation among a company's revenue streams?

5. Is it always better to begin as a paid service instead of trying to move from a free service to a paid service?

6. We discussed three "expert" businesses and how the consumer experience would be different. Which would you go to for advice? Which will be most profitable? Are the topics covered on these sites likely to be different?

E-Tasks

1. The year is late 1994. E-commerce is just starting. We are barely beginning to understand what the Internet is all about.

You are part of a select group that has been invited to a retreat in the mountains. Your job is to talk about the "business models of the future—what will work and what will not." The audience is tough-minded and forward-thinking. They want to know the future as much as you do. It includes visionaries, industry leaders, and brilliant professors.

Your job is to convince the audience of the importance of the business model that you have been assigned. Assume that none of these businesses exists yet. Describe your vision of this business and why it has a role in the future. Feel free to use your vision of the Internet eight years from today to justify the business.

Choose from this list of companies:

- Yahoo!
- C/Net

REVIEW / CHAPTER 3

E-Tasks [continued]

- eTrade
- Charles Schwab
- eSteel

Be prepared to make a ten-minute presentation.

2. Nielsen's Net Ratings provides information about the top monthly properties on their web site: http://www.nielsen-netratings.com. Choose three properties from this list. Visit their web sites and identify how they provide value to their customers. Use the Internet toolkit as a framework. Prepare a one-page report describing the strengths and weaknesses of each site.

3. Visit http://www.bricksorclicks.com. This is an interactive simulation built by Knowledge Dynamics. In the words of the company:

   BricksorClicks.com puts you in the role of CEO at a traditional toy manufacturer. The company, called ToyBlocks Inc., must confront the challenges of launching an online sales channel while managing and maintaining their current traditional sales channels.

   You will make decisions over eight periods. In each period, you will make decisions about allocating a fixed marketing budget across three existing channels. In addition, you will have to decide when to launch the online store—if at all. Participate in this interactive simulation and see if you show up on the high score list. What are the assumptions made when preparing the simulation? Do you find that some of them are unrealistic? Why?

APPENDIX I / CHAPTER 3

Segmenting the E-Market

Trying to span all segments with a single offer won't work. E-marketers should cultivate core-segment customers who buy items of greater than average value.

With the novelty and excitement of Internet companies giving way to sober demands for bottom-line results, marketers must get serious about matching their site strategies to the needs of their target customer segments. The first step should be to identify those segments that do (or could) make up the audience of a site and to tailor its value proposition or consumer experience accordingly.

Our research suggests that current active online consumers fall into six segments: Simplifiers, Surfers, Bargainers, Connectors, Routiners, and Sportsters. Each segment is defined by the online behavior of its members—traits such as the amount of time they actively spend online, the number of pages and sites they access, the time they spend actively viewing each page, and the kinds of sites they visit (exhibit, on the next page). The challenge is that each of these segments has different needs, so marketers must distinguish among the segments their sites attract and match their site strategies to the needs of the target. Otherwise, those marketers risk attracting unprofitable visitors and alienating the most profitable ones.[1]

For marketers whose profitability depends on the number of transactions at their sites, Simplifiers are the most attractive consumers, since they account for more than 50 percent of all online transactions. But Simplifiers are challenging to serve and easy to lose, for they want ease of access and end-to-end convenience. Simplifiers like readily available product information, reliable customer service, and easy returns, and they respond positively to any evidence—conveyed through advertising or on-site messages—that it is easier or faster to do business on- than offline. They dislike unsolicited e-mail, uninviting chat rooms, pop-up windows intended to encourage impulse buys, and other features that complicate their on- and offline experience. Few sites give Simplifiers everything they want: other research we have conducted shows that even heavy online shoppers think that offline customer service is better than its online counterpart. Amazon.com's one-click ordering process is a good example of a feature designed for Simplifiers.

Surfers account for only 8 percent of the user population but for 32 percent of all time spent online—far more than any other segment—and they access upward of four times as many pages as do average users. Surfers use the Internet for many reasons (for example, to explore, shop, find information, and be entertained) but move quickly among sites, continually seeking new online experiences. To attract and, more important, retain Surfers, a site must offer a strong online brand, cutting-edge design and features, constant updates, and a rich variety of products and services.

Exhibit
The Online Consumer:
Six Degrees of Separation

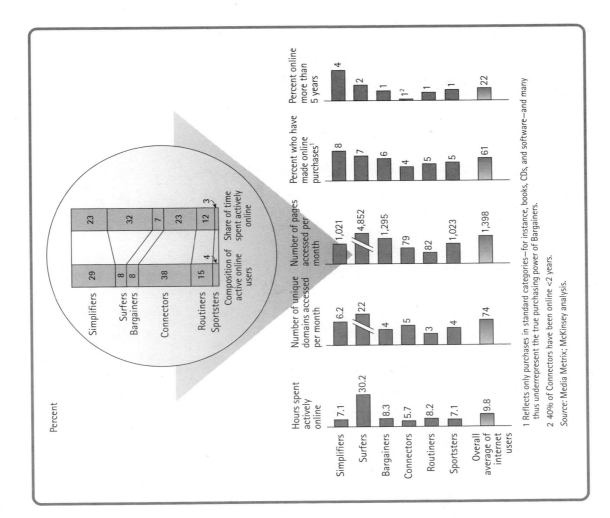

Percent

Composition of active online users

Simplifiers	29
Surfers	8
Bargainers	8
Connectors	38
Routiners	15
Sportsters	4

Share of time spent actively online

Simplifiers	23
Surfers	32
Bargainers	7
Connectors	23
Routiners	12
Sportsters	3

	Hours spent actively online	Number of unique domains accessed per month	Number of pages accessed per month	Percent who have made online purchases[1]	Percent online more than 5 years
Simplifiers	7.1	6.2	1,021	8	4
Surfers	30.2	22	4,852	7	2
Bargainers	8.3	4	1,295	6	1
Connectors	5.7	5	79	4	1[2]
Routiners	8.2	3	82	5	1
Sportsters	7.1	4	1,023	5	1
Overall average of internet users	9.8	74	1,398	61	22

1 Reflects only purchases in standard categories—for instance, books, CDs, and software—and many thus underrepresent the true purchasing power of Bargainers.

2 40% of Connectors have been online <2 years.

Source: Media Metrix; McKinsey analysis.

APPENDIX I / CHAPTER 3

Bargainers care mainly about getting a good deal. Although they make up just 8 percent of the active online population and spend less time online than average users do, they generate 52 percent of all visits to eBay, the busiest auction site. Other favorite sites include uBid and Priceline.com (two other auction sites) as well as the financial-information site Quote.com. Bargainers enjoy the search for a good price, control over transactions, and the sense of community that sites such as eBay offer.

Sixty-four percent of all Bargainers have made online purchases from standard categories such as books, compact discs, and software.[2] To get Bargainers to repeat their visits, a site must appeal to them on both the rational and the emotional levels; eBay, for example, devotes an entire section to a newsletter, chat groups, a library, and opportunities to make donations to charities.

Connectors, as their name suggests, use the Internet mainly to relate to other people through chat services such as ICQ and through sites such as Blue Mountain Arts, which permits them to send electronic greeting cards free of charge. Connectors tend to be novices: 40 percent of them have been online for less than two years, and only 42 percent of them have made purchases online (against 61 percent overall). Connectors are trying to figure out what is available to them and what has value.

Marketers must focus on ways to shape the habits of Connectors so that they graduate to a more attractive segment, such as the Simplifiers. One approach is to help Connectors find their way around the Internet, earning their trust as they go. Readersdigest.com is particularly good at this approach, giving special help to subscribers over the age of 50. The site includes features explaining how users can protect themselves online and how e-mail works as well as simple explanations of technology, "netiquette" lessons, and features such as "Create a family newsletter on your PC!" Wal-Mart stores, Staples, and other bricks-and-mortar-based brands that make their Internet addresses highly visible on packaging, advertising, and mailings have an advantage with Connectors, whose inexperience makes them willing to accept advice from trusted guides about online content.

Routiners use the Internet for content—usually news and financial information—and spend more than 80 percent of their online time surfing through their ten favorite sites. The Wall Street Journal's interactive edition and MSNBC's online site are among the most popular sites for the members of this group. The superior and exclusive content of those sites makes Routiners feel like insiders.

Sportsters behave like Routiners but gravitate to sports and entertainment sites. They view content as entertainment, so sites must be fresh, colorful, and interactive to attract them. The popular home page of the sports site ESPN.com, for instance, features sports results, polls, chat rooms, fantasy games, news updates, and radio broadcasts.

Generating revenue from the efforts of the Sportsters and the Routiners to find information is a real challenge. An obvious way of meeting it—though probably the most diffi-

APPENDIX I / CHAPTER 3

cult—is to transform visitors from consumers of free content into paying subscribers. Quote.com, for instance, provides some information free of charge but offers considerably more to the site's paying subscribers. ESPN.com generates significant revenue from subscription fees for its fantasy sports leagues. Other options include the creation of links to transaction-based sites and the use of targeted advertising and promotions to influence the offline purchasing behavior of visitors.

Whatever approach marketers take, they should avoid trying to span all segments with a single offer and thus diluting the Internet experience so that it appeals to no one, least of all their core segment. They are better off cultivating core-segment customers who repeatedly purchase items of greater than average value. In time, new technologies will permit marketers to display the content and products that most appeal to particular user segments. Ultimately, segments based on demographics will give way to offerings informed by the tastes and needs of individuals.

—John E. Forsyth, Johanne Lavoie, and Tim McGuire

Notes

1. McKinsey and Media Metrix, which measures Internet and digital-media audiences, analyzed on-line behavior using a sample of the most active online consumers in the Media Metrix U.S. panel of 50,000 users (those who have been online in each of three straight months).
2. This figure does not include nonstandard purchases such as collectibles.

John Forsyth is a principal in the Stamford office, Johanne Lavoie is an associate principal in the Montréal office, and Tim McGuire is a principal in the Toronto office. Copyright © 2000 McKinsey & Company. All rights reserved.

APPENDIX II / CHAPTER 3

The Six–Cs Checklist

Commerce

1. Who are your target customers?

2. What type of commerce are you going to feature (e.g., sale at fixed-price, auctions)?

3. Which commerce-related activities (e.g., payment system, shopping cart technology) are you willing to farm out?

4. What are you going to sell?

5. Do you have a competitive advantage with this product or service?

6. Is this product or service well suited for sale on the Internet?

7. Will you have a substantial margin?

8. What does the competitive picture look like online and offline?

Communication

1. What are your communication objectives?

2. What is your target audience and what are its information needs?

3. Does your organization have a larger communication plan? Has it been revised lately?

4. What technologies will you use to communicate with your stakeholders?

5. Will you set rules for how users can communicate with one another on your site?

6. Will you offer free e-mail accounts to your consumers?

7. Will you monitor what is said in chat areas? How will you fund this activity?

Connectivity

1. How are your users connecting to your web site?

2. Can you target users who are using higher speeds of connectivity?

3. How will you deal with the users who do not have connectivity?

APPENDIX II / CHAPTER 3

Community

1. What steps are you going to take to build a community of users?

2. Are you interested in hosting a community or would you prefer that users build a community of their own elsewhere?

3. How can you engage users in activities beyond commerce?

4. What strategies are competitors using to build community?

5. Will the community be open to the public or only to a select group?

6. How will you manage community rules and administer access rights?

7. How will you protect privacy rights?

8. How will you establish trust in your community?

Content

1. What types of content are you going to provide on your site?

2. Who will influence the nature of the content (e.g., advertisers, users)?

3. How will the content on your site work in relation with your brand image?

4. What proportion of content will be created by users?

5. What proportion of content will be purchased from an external content provider?

6. How frequently will you update the content?

7. How does your content rate in relation to the competition?

Computing

1. What hardware configuration will you use?

2. What software architecture will you use?

3. What constraints do these place on your growth?

4. What computing tools can you provide the consumer?

5. What is the range of customer traffic that you are able to accommodate on your site? Have you built enough redundancy in your system?

CHAPTER 4

Types of Business Models

Learning Objectives

▼ To understand the different types of Internet business models—B2B, B2C, Consumer-to-Consumer (C2C), and Consumer-to-Business (C2B).

▼ To study the functioning of pure–play B2C business models—how they make money, the different types, and what separates the best from the rest.

▼ To understand the functioning of pure–play B2B business models—how they make money, what they offer to large businesses, the different types, and what separates the best from the rest.

▼ To understand C2B firms (discussion on C2C is deferred).

▼ To learn about the bricks-and-clicks approach to building a business model.

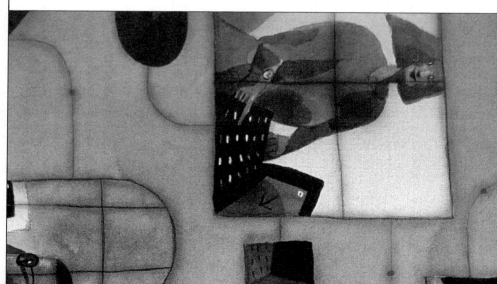

Executive Summary

Internet business models are classified in two ways—businesses that operate online only are pure-play businesses; those that operate both online and in a physical space are bricks-and-clicks businesses. In addition, business models are classified based on the nature of the buyer and seller. This leads to the familiar groupings—B2B, B2C, C2C, and C2B. All pure-play B2C businesses can be classified as direct sellers, intermediaries, advertising-based models, community-based models, or fee-based models. We will briefly discuss electronic data interchange (EDI) and extranets. B2B marketplaces can be either horizontal or vertical and could be biased in the favor of the buyer, the seller, or neither. Factors that separate the top marketplaces from the rest include their high number of buyers and sellers, their higher number of transactions, their higher transaction fee, and the right service bundle. Industry analysts view bricks-and-clicks businesses as superior because they combine the complementary capabilities of both the physical and virtual spaces. Creating the proper organizational structure for a bricks-and-clicks company can be a challenge, as can achieving synergies between the physical and virtual operations.

Introduction

All Internet businesses can be placed into two categories—pure plays and bricks-and-clicks (also known as surf-and-turf and clicks-and-mortar). *Pure-play* businesses, such as Amazon.com, eBay (commerce), and Slate.com (content), have an online presence only. On the other hand, *bricks-and-clicks* businesses combine a physical presence with an online presence, as do, for example, Barnes & Noble and bn.com, Nordstrom department stores and Nordstrom.com (commerce), the *New York Times* and nytimes.com (content). Pure-play businesses use the capabilities of the Internet to create a new business. Bricks-and-clicks businesses use the Internet to supplement their existing businesses. Businesses also can be classified on the basis of the type of buyer (business or consumer) or seller (business or consumer).[1]

Buyer

		Business	Consumer
Seller	Business	B2B (e.g., I2.com)	B2C (e.g., Amazon.com)
	Consumer	C2B (e.g., Ideas.com)	C2C (e.g., eBay.com)

Based on these two classification schemes, this chapter discusses

- pure-play B2C business models
- pure-play B2B business models
- a brief overview of pure-play C2C and C2B business models
- bricks-and-clicks business models

B2C Pure-Play Business Models

Pure-play business models in the B2C sector can be broadly classified as:

- direct sellers
- intermediaries
- advertising-based models
- community-based models
- fee-based models

Direct Sellers

Direct sellers make money by selling products or services to consumers. Their primary source of income is the margin on each transaction. There are two types of direct sellers—e-tailers and manufacturers. E-tailers, such as Amazon.com, collect orders from consumers and either directly ship the products or pass the order on to wholesalers or manufacturers for delivery.

Manufacturers that sell directly are using the power of the Internet to reach customers directly. A prime example of this is Dell.com. Rather than selling through intermediaries such as CompUSA, Dell gains market power by establishing direct customer relationships. The airlines too are directly selling to consumers from their web sites, circumventing traditional intermediaries (e.g., the travel agents). This process of eliminating intermediaries is known as *disintermediation*.

Disintermediation is not new. As shown in Figure 4.1, there are a wide variety of channel structures. The left-most channel with three intermediaries is common in food and meat markets. The channel with a wholesaler supplying to retailers that then supply to consumers is standard in the beer market, for example. For many supermarket and drugstore products, the manufacturers deal directly with retailers. Moreover, catalog companies have sold directly to consumers for a while. In fact, before there was Dell.com, Dell quite successfully sold computers by catalog.

What is new is that with the Internet it has become possible to have direct contact with the customer easily and cheaply. As a result, intermediaries have been under tremendous pressure to prove that they add value. Because the value added could potentially be low or nonexistent, disintermediation spreads. For instance, before the Internet, in the travel industry, travel agents were very powerful. Now, airlines successfully sell directly to consumers, and because they avoid paying commissions to agents, they can offer consumers cheaper tickets and special deals.

Of course, the actual contortions in the distribution process are more complicated than simply bypassing inefficient intermediaries. In many distribution channels, traditional retailers have taken on the role of the manufacturer-assembler; CompUSA, for example, has launched an online business allowing consumers to assemble their own PC. This pits them directly in competition with giants such as Dell and Compaq. Similarly, wholesalers with strong relationships with manufacturers are trying to sell directly to consumers.

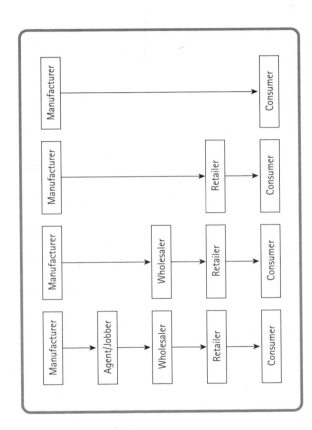

Figure 4.1
The Process of Disintermediation

Intermediaries

Online intermediaries (not to be confused with the physical intermediaries discussed previously) are the largest number of B2C companies today. These companies facilitate transactions between buyers and sellers and receive a percentage of the value of each transaction.

B2C intermediaries are of two types—brokers and infomediaries. *Brokers* facilitate transactions between buyers and sellers. *Infomediaries* act as a filter between companies and consumers. Individuals provide the infomediary with personal information and, in turn, receive targeted ads and offers. Companies can buy aggregated market research reports and target individuals based on data held private by the infomediary. Brokers make money by charging a fee on each transaction, while infomediaries make money by selling market research reports and helping advertisers target their ads.

The types of brokers include:

- buy/sell fulfillment—a corporation that helps consumers place buy and sell orders (e.g., the online stock broker eTrade).

- virtual mall—a company that helps consumers buy from a variety of stores. The company makes money on each transaction (e.g., Yahoo! Stores).

- metamediary—an intermediary that offers consumers access to a variety of stores and provides transaction services such as financial services (e.g., Amazon's zShops).

- bounty broker—an intermediary that offers a fee to locate a person, place, or idea (e.g., Bounty Quest).

- search agent—a company, such as MySimon, that helps consumers compare different stores. It makes money from the merchants.

Advertising-Based Businesses

These businesses have ad inventory on their site and sell it to interested parties. There are two guiding philosophies in such businesses—high-traffic or niche.

The high-traffic philosophy is that advertisers care about reaching a large audience and will, therefore, pay a high rate for a site that can deliver large numbers. This is true in other media as well—the most expensive ad spot on television is the Super Bowl, which is watched by about 40% of American households. Examples of online businesses built on the high-traffic philosophy are the portals Yahoo! and AOL. Since these sites attract a large percentage of online users, they are able to charge high ad rates.

The niche philosophy states that advertisers care about reaching a small target group that is well defined, clearly identified, and desirable in terms of influence or buying power. The idea here is to trump not the quantity, but the quality of the audience in terms of its desirability to the advertisers. A good example of a niche audience may be wsj.com, which attracts business professionals from around the world and has a high-quality position.

Community-Based Model

Community-based models allow users worldwide to interact with one another on the basis of interest areas. Examples include:

- Yahoo! clubs provide users with a free space that includes a discussion board, e-mail, chat, and file uploads. Clubs may be moderated or not.

- Talkcity allows users interested in any topic to chat with one another.

These businesses make money by accumulating loyal users and then targeting them with advertising. In a way, they are a subset of the advertising-based business. AOL is perhaps an anomaly because it charges its users a flat fee per month and provides them access to community services such as chat and e-mail.

Fee-Based Model

This type of business charges viewers a subscription fee to view its content. There are many variations:

- All content is fee-based (e.g., wsj.com).

- Some content is fee-based (e.g., Salon Premium offers special content at a price).

- Niche content is fee-based (e.g., mlb.com charges a fee for sport events).

Challenges Faced by B2C Pure-Play Businesses

Keen observation of this industry so far indicates that an online business cannot survive on advertising dollars alone. There are many reasons for this.

First, unfortunately for the Internet advertising industry, the banner was linked to the click-through—an intermediate behavioral measure with no intrinsic meaning. On no other medium is advertising linked to direct action. As a result, when advertisers did not see immediate action, they lost faith in the medium. Now, industry experts say that the long-term effect (i.e., those that viewed the ad, did not click, but returned to the site later) is stronger than the click-through effect. However, selling the idea of the long-term effect to advertisers at this late stage has proven challenging.

Online advertising companies have alienated many customers by using annoying techniques such as push banners, rich media, forced exposure, pop-ups, pop-unders, ultra-large creatives, and so on. Such advertising is motivated by the short-term desire to maximize click-throughs rather than value.

Finally, advertising is a cyclical business in all media, and firms adjust their advertising budgets based on the business outlook. It is also an intensely competitive business. Many dot-commers did not fully appreciate this, or believed that online advertising would be different.

Building traffic continues to be the biggest challenge faced by online businesses, followed by sustaining customer loyalty. Due to the winner-take-all market structure described in Chapter 2, very few sites dominate in any given category. As a result, it is very hard for small sites to break through the clutter. As for the loyalty question, online consumers are very price sensitive and can easily be lured away—and if a consumer has been attracted by a price promotion, retaining him or her is difficult. Overall, the challenges are to break through the clutter to build traffic and to offer true value to sustain loyalty.

What Separates the Top B2C Companies from the Rest?

A study by McKinsey found five characteristics that distinguish the top B2C companies:[2]

- The top performer had 3.2 times more unique visitors per month than the median. Interestingly, the top performer had over 2,500 times the number of visitors than the worst performer.

- The top performer's conversion rate of new visitors (18%) was about twice the median.

- The top performer's revenue per transaction was about 2.5 times the median.

- The top performer's average gross margin was about three times the median.

- There were no significant differences in the number of transactions per customer and the visitor acquisition cost.

The number of visitors, the conversion rate, the revenue per transaction, and the gross margin are the key differentiators between top performers and the average company.

But how does a company become a leader in the B2C area? Communication effectiveness and value to the customer. If you are an online business, you must find a way to communicate your existence to prospective consumers. Your goal is to increase the awareness of your brand name and to build positive brand associations. Then, when a consumer visits your web site, you must offer sufficient value to convert this visiter into a loyal customer. Offering value but being buried in the clutter does you no good, nor does getting people to your site but not providing them tangible value. The bottom line is that success in the B2C sector requires both effective communication and value to the customer.

The Bricks-and-Clicks Business Model

In many spheres, it makes sense to combine online capabilities with the advantages of traditional bricks-and-mortar firms. This might be through either a partnership (e.g., AOL and Wal-Mart, Drugstore.com and Rite Aid) or by ownership (e.g., Barnes & Noble and bn.com). Such bricks-and-clicks companies treat the Internet as one channel to reach consumers and then integrate it with existing channels.

In the retail industry, bricks-and-clicks have several advantages:

1. For some product categories, such as produce, furniture, and apparel, individuals have to touch, feel, sit on, or try on a product before buying. With these products, selling exclusively online is an expensive proposition. With a bricks-and-clicks partnership, users can visit a bricks-and-mortar store to experience the product and order it there. They could use the Internet to locate the store, track their order status, and get an e-mail when something similar becomes available again.

2. Delivering products is a hassle for dot-com stores. Frequently, the consumer is not home to receive a delivery and later has to stand in line at the post office or shipment center to receive the product. If the product is simply left outside the home, it may be damaged by weather or miscreants. Delivery partnerships can help avoid these problems by allowing users, for example, to place orders online and pick up the items at a local store.

3. Similarly, returning products can be tricky. A bulky product such as a couch can be difficult and expensive to return if the consumer does not like it. Here again, partnering with bricks-and-mortar stores is an ideal solution: these stores can sell the returned item to another consumer in the store, or, if it must be shipped back to the manufacturer, they could add it to other items to create a complete shipping load, reducing the cost of shipping per item.

4. Salespeople help customers in bricks-and-mortar environments by answering product-related questions, providing feedback about the suitability of a product, and suggesting other products that work as well. Combining the power of face-to-face selling with the informational display at online retailers can lead to great results.

Which Is More Successful—Bricks-and-Clicks or Pure Plays?

A survey conducted by McKinsey found that bricks-and-clicks outperformed pure plays on many dimensions.[3] On average, bricks-and-clicks companies had a customer acquisition cost of $62 compared to $146 for pure plays. Moreover, the conversion rate in bricks-and-clicks companies is higher—the customer to visitor ratio is 7.1 and only 4.8 for pure plays. Although the number of transactions per customer is similar (1.34 transactions per customer per month for bricks-and-clicks in comparison to 1.28 for pure plays), the customer maintenance costs are much greater for pure plays ($245 for pure plays in comparison to $103 for bricks-and-clicks).

Because bricks-and-clicks benefit from the established brand name, marketing arrangements with suppliers, and existing information systems, they tend to do better than pure plays. One wonders, though, if the picture might change over time.

Organizing for Bricks-and-Clicks[4]

The key managerial issue with bricks-and-clicks is determining the extent to which the online operation will be integrated with the existing physical operation. Different organizational models exist.

The first approach is to spin off the online venture. For example, Barnes & Noble spun off bn.com as a separate entity that would compete with Amazon.com. Such a spin-off creates a focused enterprise that can pursue venture capital funding without the constraints of "the mother ship." The disadvantage is that the new venture cannot leverage the assets of the parent company, making it harder to compete. Moreover, it is hard to create a new identity for the online version.

Another approach is to create a strategic partnership. For example, Rite Aid has a broad partnership with Drugstore.com. Rather than invest in expensive online storefront technology, Rite Aid lets consumers place orders at Drugstore.com, at which time, the existing relationship with the consumer and the neighborhood drugstore kicks in. Consumers can pick up their prescriptions at their local Rite Aid.

A third approach is to create a joint venture between a bricks-and-mortar store and an online company. For example, KB Toys partnered with an online company—Brainplay .com—rather than create its own online store. The result was KBKids.com.

A final approach is to integrate the online operation with the existing physical operation by creating a division within the company. Office Depot took this route. This made sense for them because they already had a large catalog operation in place, complete with a call center and over 2,000 delivery trucks. Moreover, they had earlier created a sophisticated information system that they were able to leverage.

Synergies between Physical and Online Stores

If a company owns a physical and an online store, how can it organize these stores in a way that maximizes the synergies between the two stores? This is an area where stores have struggled.

Consider the large discount stores Wal-Mart and Kmart. At their physical stores, the number of items on sale for less than $5 is tremendous, but the same is not true for the online store. When shipping costs are added to the price of inexpensive items, consumers are no longer interested and the discount stores cannot make a profit. So discount stores simply have to choose products they can sell well online. Laptops, for example, are available online at discount store web sites, but not at the store because the manufacturer can ship them directly to the consumer and the retailer can collect a commission for the order.[5]

Others have tried to use kiosk technology to entice those customers already in a physical store to order a product from a web site. For example, Compaq has partnered with retail stores such as RadioShack to allow consumers to customize a computer for their needs, and Borders Books and Music stores provide kiosks that allow consumers to place orders with Borders.com. The retail stores gain by this arrangement because it taps a sale that would otherwise have left the store: they make some money from it as a commission rather than none. The online store also gains because the partnership allows them access to a previously untapped pool of consumers.[6]

Bricks-and-Clicks in Other Areas

The discussion so far has focused on the retail industry; however, marrying online competencies with physical ones is by no means limited to retail.

Consider higher education. There are now attempts at collaborations between online universities, such as University of Phoenix, and community colleges and universities. Students benefit from online instruction coupled with physical contact with the instructor and peers. The online vendors view this as a way to rebut critics of online instruction. In another model, vendors have emerged who can supply courses to a school, which might choose to farm out some courses to reduce the cost of instruction.

In the area of news and publishing, television networks (e.g., abcnews.com), cable news channels (e.g., cnn.com), news magazines (e.g., time.com), and newspapers (e.g., nytimes. com) have launched their own web sites. The relationship between the online presence and the other mode of news delivery is very important. For example, all of the content at nytimes.com is available for free if an individual registers, but a single copy of the paper costs at least seventy-five cents. The news agency has to decide whether it will continue to offer free content in one area and paid content in another.

B2B Pure-Play Business Models

Business markets are unique in many ways. For example, they may exhibit any of the following characteristics:

- High value of purchases (e.g., airplanes)
- Large order size (e.g., 900 computers)
- Items purchased (e.g., lathe machines, paints)
- Purchase specificity (e.g., technical specifications)
- Team buying (buying center)
- Vendor/value analysis (e.g., vendor qualification)
- Team selling—especially for high value products
- Leasing
- Competitive bidding (e.g., sealed bids)
- Derived demand (e.g., reduced demand for airline flights reduces the demand for airplanes from Boeing)

- Cyclical demand
- Number and location of buyers
- Use of buying specialists
- Special services required

Businesses buy from, sell to, and partner with other businesses. The interactions among businesses and the scope for B2B e-commerce is shown in Figure 4.2. The activities can be classified as supply chain management, demand management, and support activities.

Exchanges between firms in the B2B setting take place in two areas—EDI/Extranets and B2B marketplaces.

EDI/Extranets

Every firm is affiliated with a network, which includes the firm's supply chain as well as strategic partners. Each company aims to share information and transact with these partners. The first approach to do this was EDI, a practice that predates the Internet; however, EDI systems were based on proprietary technology that essentially created a closed network. Systems did not speak to one another and firms had to go to great lengths to create the semblance of a network.

With the emergence of Internet technology, all firms have a single standard by which to communicate, which makes it easier to build systems that talk to one another. Most companies first create internal networks called intranets that are accessible only by the employees of the company. The external world is kept out by a software program called the firewall. The next step is to create an extranet—an intranet that is adapted so that external parties are provided varying degrees of access to information. A supplier, for example,

	Supply Chain Management Activities	Demand Management Activities	Support Activities
Transactional-oriented Activities	• Purchasing • Paying	• Selling • Collecting	• Financing • Cash Management
Collaboration-oriented Activities	• Sourcing • Forecasting • Scheduling • Inventory Management • Production Planning and Control • Transportation Planning and Control	• Customer Service • Product/Service Information and Support • Product Configuration • Product Design • Sales Forecasting • Sales Analysis	• Planning • Training • Human Resources Management • Skills Management

Figure 4.2
The Business-to-Business Electronic Commerce Scope

Source: Alan Lindsay, Marcos Peralta, Matt Thiel, and Colleen Tierney, "How to Engage Trading Parties in Extranet Initiatives," Fall 1998, http://www.ecommerce.vanderbilt.edu/research/papers/html/

may have access to demand information to assist with forecasting his manufacturing activities. One example of an extranet is the FedEx web site where paying customers can track orders. Harley-Davidson has launched an extranet (www.h-dnet.com) through which dealers can file warranty claims, check recall status, submit financial statements, and order parts and accessories.

Other uses of extranets include:[7]

- Private newsgroups that cooperating companies use to share valuable experiences and ideas.

- Groupware that allows several companies to collaborate when developing new products or services.

- Training programs or other educational material that companies develop and share.

- Shared product catalogs accessible only to wholesalers or those in the trade.

- Project management and control for companies that are part of a common work project.

With both the EDI and the extranet, participation is by invitation only. The most common form of an extranet is called a *hub and spoke system*, which is popular with large companies that have great market power. These companies can dictate the nature of the firms that deal with them, with the result that the entire extranet revolves around them. Firms who want to deal with the company have varying levels of access; the most trusted firms have the highest levels.

Some experts have criticized this as an arrogant system and have called for the creation of a network of firms who have equal access to everybody's information. Most large companies have resisted this idea, arguing that it is tantamount to surrendering their market power.

B2B Marketplaces[8]

The term "net markets" broadly describes all online marketplaces where buyers and sellers congregate to exchange goods and services for money. Such markets are also called "Butterfly markets" or "Butterfly hubs." If one wing of the butterfly is made up of buyers and one wing is made up of sellers; where they meet—the body of the butterfly—is the hub.

Net markets can be organized either horizontally or vertically. *Horizontal markets* cut across many industries, typically providing a common service, such as financial services; benefits management; and maintenance, repair, and operating (MRO) equipment. Popular horizontal markets include Ariba Network and Commerce One's MarketSite.net.

Vertical markets concentrate on one specific industry, such as agriculture or chemicals, and seek to provide all of the services it needs. Popular examples are VerticalNet, Chemconnect, and Covisint.

There are three common types of net markets:

1. *Buy-centric markets* are organized by large, influential buyers as a place where small and fragmented sellers can sell their goods. This is great for buyers because it permits quick and easy price-comparison shopping. Popular examples are Kmart's Retail Link, FreeMarkets.com, and Covisint.

2. *Sell-centric markets* are markets where one or more big sellers build a marketplace for small, fragmented buyers. Typically, revenues are derived from ads, commissions on sales, or fees for delivering qualified leads to suppliers. Buyers must beware of rising prices because the sellers hold all the power here. Popular examples are Grainger.com, GE Global Exchange, DoveBid, GoFish.com, GlobalFoodExchange.com, E2open.com, and TradeOut.com.

3. *Neutral exchanges* appear when both the sellers and the buyers are fragmented. In this environment, a third party creates a neutral exchange and performs the transactions through a bid/ask system. Some of these exchanges are struggling financially. Popular examples are Altra, Paper Exchange, and Arbinet.

Why Would an Established Business Use These Marketplaces?

In general, an established business will use these marketplaces for the following reasons:

- Selection of buyers or sellers (global markets) is greater
- Dynamic markets may be a great place to move inventory quickly
- Efficient exchange process minimizes employee time
- Prices are low due to expanded access to sellers
- Some one-time deals are available only to online audiences

A Fortune 1000 company with established buying channels and procedures, for example, would benefit from participating in a buy-centric exchange rather than an unestablished neutral exchange. Along these lines, Covisint is a large purchasing alliance in the auto industry backed by the giants—General Motors, Ford Motor Company, and Daimler-Chrysler; and Boeing, Raytheon, BAE Systems, and Lockheed Martin have announced the formation of an aerospace parts exchange with more than 37,000 participants.[9] Similar exchanges have been announced by retailers, metal companies, thermoplastics companies, and many others.

Challenges Faced by E-Marketplaces

Building traffic is a big challenge for e-hubs. For neutral exchanges success requires critical mass on both sides of the exchange; high-caliber sellers simply will not participate unless there is a critical mass of buyers, and *vice versa.*

One way of dealing with traffic uncertainty may be to abandon neutrality. Because buy-centric and sell-centric sites do not have to worry about traffic generation on one side (i.e., on the buyer side for buy-centric sites and on the seller side for sell-centric sites), they can focus on adding value.

An issue related to critical mass is competing e-marketplaces. Buyers (especially large companies) will not participate in multiple markets, with the result that a few hubs may dominate the market. But in this case the power dynamic may be such that large firms already dominate the marketplace.

A third issue is to integrate other sales channels with e-marketplaces. Large companies already have a sales force and a purchasing and selling channel, all of which must be integrated with e-marketplaces.

What Separates the Top B2B Companies from the Rest?

McKinsey conducted a survey of sixty independent B2B companies in the United States and Europe.[10] They compiled a performance scorecard and identified what separated the top quartile companies from the rest.

The study's primary findings:

- The top marketplaces have a high number of buyers and sellers.

- The top marketplaces have a higher number of transactions even though the total value of the transactions is smaller.

- The top companies are able to charge a higher transaction fee and earn more nontransaction revenue.

- The top corporations offer financial services, not content or advertising.

How does a business become a leader in the B2B sector? Unlike in the B2C sector, in the B2B sector a leader must gain the support of the larger companies in the industry. A marketplace that tries to create power for itself may be viewed with suspicion, whereas if the same marketplace offers to work with a coalition of the larger companies, it may succeed. Having gained the support of the companies, the marketplace must then offer the proper value-added services and customized transactions.

Pure–Play C2C Business Models

C2C businesses involve exchanges between or among two or more individuals. The chapters on auctions and peer-to-peer applications and the eBay case discuss C2C businesses extensively.

Pure–Play C2B Business Models

C2B models involve interactions originating from the consumer. This represents a new form of conducting business with the voice of the consumer shaping the interaction. The consumer is not, strictly speaking, the seller *per se* in all C2B businesses, but in all cases the consumer originates the transaction.

Such businesses fall into the following categories:

- *Idea collectors.* Individuals have wonderful ideas about how to improve existing products, features that can be added to new products, and other spheres related to their lives. A company that can motivate consumers to submit their ideas, may be able to buy new ideas at a reasonable price. This is the premise of the C2B company Ideas.com.

- *Reverse auctions.* Companies such as Priceline.com and Pricemate.com allow consumers to submit binding bids (i.e., covered by credit card) for the purchase of products such as airline tickets. The e-auctions chapter presents a detailed analysis of reverse auctions.

- *Complaint centers.* EComplaints.com allows individuals to post complaints about a business, view others' complaints about any given business, and interact directly with the business in question. The company presents a business' response time and effectiveness for public display, and makes its money by selling aggregated complaint research data.

- *Paid advertising models.* Companies such as Cybergold and Alladvantage.com sought to pay consumers to view targeted ads. The advertisers would get better targeting and consumers would get to see ads for products they cared about. Due to a variety of issues (e.g., consumers not viewing ads, non-updated profiles), however, this idea has yet to succeed.

All of these business models attempt to empower the consumer in their interaction with corporations.

Conclusion

The Internet affects almost all businesses; however, each business is different and recognizing the nature of the business can help managers better manage the Internet's impact. This chapter has presented a wide variety of business contexts and the different types of business models that operate within each context.

Notes

(All URLs are current as of March 10, 2002.)

1. One other term is in use—B2B2C. This refers to transactions in which a business sells a service or product to a consumer using another business as an intermediary. One could think of this as B2B businesses managing derived demand.
2. Tilman Kemmler, Monika Kubicová, Robert Musslewhite, and Rodney Prezeau, "E-Performance II: The Good, The Bad and The Merely Average," *McKinsey Quarterly*, No. 3, 2001, Web exclusive, available at <http://www.mckinseyquarterly.com/article_page.asp?ar=1079&ttk=292854: 1079:24&L2=24&L3=45&pagenum=9> (registration required).
3. Ibid.
4. This is drawn from Ranjay Gulati and Jason Garino, "Get The Right Mix of Bricks and Clicks," *Harvard Business Review*, May–June, 2000, 107–114.
5. This was informed by Tedeschi, "Discount Giants Learn Online Lessons: Film, Yes; Shampoo, No," nytimes.com, September 26, 2001.
6. Maileen Hamto, "Seven Rules for Thriving in the New Economy," *Rice News*, 10(20), February 8, 2001, <http://www.rice.edu/projects/reno/rn/20010208/Templates/neweconomy.html>.
7. Mark Merkow, "Extraordinary Extranets," WebReference.Com, <http://www.webreference.com/content/extranet/index.html>.
8. This section is based almost entirely on Community B2B, "B2B Fundamentals," <http://www.communityb2b.com/library/fundamentals.cfm>.
9. Janette Adams, "Airbus Boosts B2B Exchange," June 19, 2000, <http://www.redherring.com/industries/2000/0619/ind-staralliance061900.html>.
10. Bertil Chappuis, Ron Lemmens, Haim Mendelson, and Denise Villars, "A Performance Index for B2B Marketplaces," *McKinsey Quarterly*, No. 2, 2001, <http://www.mckinseyquarterly.com/article_page.asp?ar=1077&ttk=292854:1077:24&L2=1077:24&L3=45&pagenum=11>.

REVIEW / CHAPTER 4

Discussion Questions

1. Why haven't intermediaries disappeared in traditional physical channels? Will intermediaries become less important in certain channels?

2. As discussed in the chapter, advertising-based models either try to attract high traffic or target a niche. Can a business do both? Use Yahoo! as an example in your answer.

3. Annoying ad techniques (e.g., pop-ups) lead to greater click-throughs, but are they good for the advertiser? Would you advertise using a pop-up?

4. When is the experience inside a store important to consumers? Can some products be sold without this experience? Alternatively, are bricks-and-clicks the only viable strategy for online retail?

5. What are the challenges in making B2B marketplaces a success?

E-Tasks

1. Compare the web sites of Amazon.com, a B2C pure play, and bn.com, a bricks-and-clicks. Has bn.com leveraged its bricks-and-clicks capability well on its web site? What features could it add to its web site that would make it a more successful bricks-and-clicks company?

2. Visit the web site of MySimon (www.mysimon.com). This site allows you to compare prices from different online retailers. Conduct a search for a book that you like. You must be able to see information about the book, the rating of the retailer, if it is in stock, and the price information. Using this information, answer the following questions:

   a. Would you perform such a price comparison before each purchase? Have you done so in the past? Will you do so in the future?

   b. Will you buy from an unknown retailer if it is selling at a low price?

   c. How do these sites complicate the life of online retailers?

   d. Should online retailers block entry to these sites?

   e. How does MySimon make money and what implications does that have for the consumer?

REVIEW / CHAPTER 4

E-Tasks [continued]

3. Bizrate and Gomez are the two leading infomediaries on the Web. Visit their web sites and compare their ratings of the top online retailers in a category of your choice. Which site adds more value for the consumer? How does each site make money and what implications does this have for consumers?

4. Consider these B2B exchanges in the chemicals industry—CheMatch.com, ChemConnect, Chemdex, Envera, e-Chemicals.com, ElastomerSolutions.com, SciQuest.com, ChemicalBid.com, chemicalmarket.com, and Elemica. Visit three of these marketplaces and describe how they have differentiated themselves from their competition. If you managed a chemicals company, which one would you join and why?

CHAPTER 5

E-Auctions

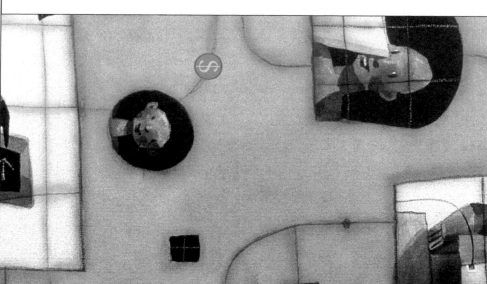

Learning Objectives

▼ To understand what an auction is and what it is not.

▼ To understand the auction's potential benefits to a buyer and a seller.

▼ To learn about the different types of auctions and how they can affect final outcomes.

▼ To study the different business models of firms that organize online auctions.

▼ To learn about the different types of consumer behavior that manifest themselves in auctions.

▼ To understand the potential for fraud in auctions and to explore ways of limiting it.

▼ To be exposed to an advanced economic theory of auctions.

Executive Summary

Auctions are dynamic pricing markets where the final price is not known ahead of time. The price is determined by a system of bidding. The Internet has enabled auctions on a large scale with buyers and sellers from all corners of the globe. Auctions do not always lead to lower prices. They are great mechanisms for disposing of items on short notice and they are perhaps the cheapest way of selling. Most auctions work in a bid-up fashion with the highest bidder winning; however, there are a variety of other auction types. Auction participants must carefully study the rules because small changes in auction rules can lead to major differences in the outcome. There are two auction-related business models—listing (e.g., eBay) and merchants (e.g., uBid). The former do not take title to the goods being sold and the latter do. Strategic behavior in auctions includes shilling, sniping, and siphoning. Fraud is rampant in auctions, but micropayment systems, rating systems, escrow, and mediation may alleviate it.

Introduction

An auction is a market of buyers and sellers. Typically, multiple buyers compete to obtain one or more items from one seller. The bidding process determines the sale price, which cannot be predicted with certainty by either the buyer or the seller. The best known example of an online auction is eBay (see Case 3), but there are also uBid, Onsale, Yahoo! Auctions, and Amazon.com Auctions, among others.

Online auctions have several advantages over traditional auctions. First, in online auctions, the audience does not have to be physically present to participate, which means that individuals can place their bids at any time, and a large audience can be put together on relatively short notice. Second, because of search engines and hierarchy-based classification schemes, consumers can easily locate the auctions with the products they want.

Third, online auctions create global markets for a local product. Consider Figure 5.1. Think of a product that has a small local market—Pez dispensers (a collector item made of plastic with a cartoon character that dispenses candy). Assume that in each of six markets, the proportion of potential traders is about 10% of the market. To make matters

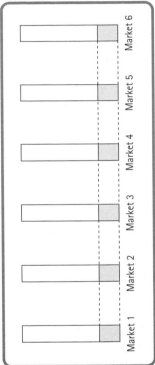

Market 1   Market 2   Market 3   Market 4   Market 5   Market 6

Figure 5.1
Connectivity Between
Markets Enhances
Bidder Pool

simple, assume that each market is made up of 1,000 people. That means, in each market about 100 people are potential buyers or sellers of Pez dispensers. In the old way of thinking, there might be an auction once a year in each of these six markets so that individuals could buy or sell Pez dispensers. But, when markets are interrelated through technologies such as the Internet, we now have a market of 600 people. We frequently find that obscure products that have limited appeal are suddenly being sold to interested buyers who live in faraway places.

But online auctions also have their share of disadvantages.[1] First, buyers cannot see, touch, or feel the product that they are buying before placing their bid. Of course, this is a standard problem with buying anything through the Web, however, the implications with auctions can be more profound, especially when consumers buy from other consumers. Second, there is the potential for fraud by both the buyer and the seller–the buyer may not pay and the seller may not deliver the goods.

Online auctions appeal to sellers as a cheap means of selling their product, since they involve a low level of overhead.[2] Because the auctioneer rather than the seller bears the onus of generating traffic, marketing costs are dramatically reduced. Online auctions appeal to buyers for the following reasons:[3]

First, online auctions are an *entertaining way* of buying a product. With the advent of modern retailing institutions (e.g., supermarket, department store), consumers have become accustomed to buying from stores that quote a fixed price. The suspense of the dynamic price and the competition make auctions entertaining; the constant bidding action keeps people hooked.[4] Some have suggested that auctions have made shopping interesting again for the male shopper.

Second, auctions have led to the *formation of trading communities.* eBay is a great example of a trading community. In many cases, the same individuals are buyers as well as sellers. In addition, a common interest in an obscure collectible or antique creates strong relationships among individuals.

When a Seller Must Choose Auctions

Many times, sellers face a choice. They can either sell their goods at a fixed price or auction them off. Auctions benefit the seller only under some circumstances; they are not a "silver bullet."

First, *auctions work well for products that are idiosyncratically valued.* Consider products such as Pez dispensers, Beanie Babies, and Brady Bunch lunch boxes. Consumers differ in how they value these products. Some place a sentimental value on products such as the Brady Bunch lunch box, whereas others may think it useless. Auctions makes sense for such items, which typically include art and antiques.

Second, *auctions work well when one can put together a large group of bidders.* The price one gets at an auction depends heavily on the size of the bidder pool. If the number of bidders is small, each individual knows that a small bid can win, and the price never goes high. On the other hand, if the number of bidders is large, the ensuing competition leads to higher prices. Traditionally, sellers advertise upcoming auctions through ads or mailers.

Since online auctions can run for an extended period, they can be continually advertised while they are taking place. With online auctions, keeping the auction open for a long period of time allows more bidders to participate.

Unlike consumer auctions, B2B auctions tend to be for higher value technical products where buyers and sellers are both organizations. As a result, what matters more is not the sheer number of participants, but rather that the key players are present. For example, it is important that Boeing attend auctions in the aerospace industry. In many cases, participation in a B2B auction is by invitation only, so the seller knows ahead of time how many people will be participating.

In the B2B setting, auctions are used frequently to clear inventory. In many cases, companies are saddled with inventories (and, hence, holding costs) that would take too long to dispense with through the regular retail process. They therefore conduct auctions to move the products quickly. Auctions typically work well for products with a limited shelf life (e.g., flowers, airline tickets) and overstocked products—especially from previous product versions and discontinued items.[5] In fact, the Dutch auction (discussed later) was used extensively in the Dutch flower markets to quickly move flowers from the wholesale warehouses to individual retailers.

Understanding Different Auction Types

Understanding the rules of each type of auction is extremely important for a buyer or a seller. Minute changes in the rules can lead to dramatically different results.

The first decision to be made is the type of auction mechanism to be used. Table 5.1 shows several varieties of auctions.

The most common variety used today is the English auction (also called the straight or Yankee auction). The bidding starts from a minimum price and the highest bidder wins and pays what he or she bid. Another kind of auction, the second-price auction, is a favorite of economists because its bidders voluntarily reveal their true willingness to pay (this is analyzed in greater detail in the Appendix).[6]

The key feature of the Dutch auction is the short time to sale. It works most effectively in the B2B setting when firms are trying to get rid of perishable items such as flowers and fish. But the Dutch auction, especially of multiple-item products, typically results in low prices; therefore, it is not a good way to sell high-priced items such as homes or computers.

The reverse auction is an interesting model of commerce. The process starts with "asks" from buyers. Sellers compete to serve the buyer. The top bid is accepted and the buyer and seller are matched. The main difference between the bidding here and other auctions is that it is backed by a credit card (i.e., the buyer makes a promise that he or she will buy if the bid price is reached. Also, there is no interaction among bidders. Priceline.com is the best known online example of this auction type. However, Priceline.com consumers may not necessarily be "winning" with this arrangement because there are several extra costs to the consumers:[7]

1. No guarantee of acceptance. Your bid may or may not be accepted. If it is rejected, you have to place a new bid.

Table 5.1
Comparison of Auction Formats

Auction Name	Online Example	Buyers/ Sellers	Bidding Procedure	Who Wins	Winner Pays
1 English	uBid, Yahoo!, OnSale	1 Seller/ Multiple Buyers	Bid up from minimum price	Highest bidder	Highest bid
2 Second-Price	eBay	1 Seller/ Multiple Buyers	Bid up from minimum price	Highest bidder	Second-highest bid
3 Dutch	Ticktock, Outletzoo	1 Seller/ Multiple Buyers	Bid down from maximum price	First bidder	First bid
4 Dutch Auction-Multiple Items	eBay	1 Seller/ Multiple Buyers	Starts at minimum asking price; buyers specify quantity and price	Highest bidders	Lowest bid
5 Sealed English Auction		1 Seller/ Multiple Buyers	Sealed bids	Highest bidders	Highest bid
6 Reverse Auction	Priceline	1 Buyer/ Multiple Sellers	Buyer submits binding bid	Buyer matched with seller who accepts bid	Binding bid
7 Double Auction	Fastparts	Multiple Buyers/ Multiple Sellers	Buyers and sellers constantly update bids	Highest bidder	Highest bid
8 Anglo-Dutch Auction		1 Seller/ Multiple Buyers	Ascending auction till two buyers remain—then sealed bids	Highest bidder	Highest bid

Source: Paul Klemperer, "What Really Matters in Auction Design," February 2001, <http://www.nuff.ox.ac.uk/users/klemperer/design3aweb.pdf>.

2. Pay before price is known. You have to give your credit card information and agree to be charged before you know whether you've even got a deal.

3. No choice. You don't get to choose the airline that you will use. You cannot specify the time of day you will leave or whether you will make an intermediate stop.

At the same time, there are extra benefits to sellers. Because each customer reveals the maximum amount he or she is willing to pay, the company can maximize its profits. Second, because there is no advertised sale price, price expectations in the future are not revised. Third, this is a great tool to manage capacity. For example, in the last minutes and hours before a plane leaves, an airline would rather get $50 than lose money on an empty seat.

After choosing the auction type, sellers must make the following decisions:

1. *Setting the reserve.* In some cases, a minimum price is established by the seller before the auction begins. If the top bid does not meet the reserve price, the seller may withdraw the item and no sale occurs. The reserve price may be publicly announced before the auction begins (open) or hidden from all bidders (sealed). Setting the reserve price is a tricky decision. If it is set too low, it is viewed as a minimum price and the final sale price may be only marginally higher than the reserve. On the other hand, setting it too high may price out a substantial portion of the market, leading to a low bidder pool. In fact, economic theory suggests that if the reserve is set optimally (i.e., just right), then all auctions will yield similar revenue.[8] Similarly, revealing the reserve price is a strategic decision that may help the seller only if it is set adequately high.

2. *Choosing a buyout price (optional).* Some auction houses (e.g., Yahoo!) offer a buyout price. This is a price at which the auction stops. That is, the seller agrees ahead of time to reveal the maximum price he or she is seeking from the auction. In some sense, setting a buyout price makes an auction similar to selling by a retail (fixed price) process. The seller is likely to choose an artificially high buyout price to encourage aggressive bidding.

3. *Private versus public.* One of the decisions auctioneers have to make is whether the auction is private or public. If it is public, the onus of generating traffic is on the auction facilitator; if it is private, the onus shifts to the seller. Private auctions may work when sellers use relationships that existed prior to the Internet to organize the auction.

Auction Categories

Based on the nature of the buyer and seller, auctions can be categorized into three categories—C2C, B2C, and B2B. Table 5.2 describes the top sites in each category.

If you work for a company that is interested in selling or buying goods using auctions regularly or semi-regularly, you must decide whether to develop your own auction site or participate at an auction facilitator site. Developing your own auction site allows you to control the rules and the number and type of bidders and keep the auction completely private—but it is costly. An alternative might be to collaborate with one's "competitors" (e.g., in the auto industry, the Big-3 automakers have announced a buying alliance). The biggest challenge when building your own auction site is attracting a sufficient bidder base.

Developing your own auction site is a true option only for B2Bs. Most B2C companies participate in auctions conducted by facilitators. There are two business models that auction facilitators use—the listing model (used by eBay) and the merchant model (used by OnSale).

In the *listing model*, the auction facilitator is strictly an intermediary. In other words, the listing agent's only role is to bring buyers and sellers together; it does not take possession of the goods, inspect the goods, or vouch for the quality of the goods.

Table 5.2
Top Auction Sites by Category in Alphabetical Order

	C2C	B2C	B2B
1	Amazon.com Auctions	Amazon.com zShops	DoveBid
2	Collecting Exchange	FirstAuction	eBay Business eXchange
3	eBay	Onsale Auctions	Liquidation.com
4	Excite Auctions	Teletrade	Microsoft bCentral
5	Haggle Online	uBid	Online Asset Exchange
6	Half.com		Onvia.com
7	Lycos Auctions		
8	MSN Auctions		
9	Onlineauction.com		
10	Yahoo! Auctions		

Source: http://www.auctionwatch.com.

In the *merchant model*, the auction facilitator buys goods from many places and puts them up for sale at auction. In this model, the buyer has the assurance that the seller has inspected the goods and vouches for the quality—a particular benefit for high-ticket items.

On the Internet, most auction sites adopt the listing model—70% according to one survey. Another survey found that of 142 auction sites, 96 were listing sites and 25 were merchant sites.[9] A small number of sites adopt a combination approach.

How do online auction sites earn money? Most auction sites charge several types of fees, the most common of which are insertion and final value fees. Sellers pay *insertion fees* to list their item, regardless of a sale; *final value fees* are paid only if the item sells and are a percentage of the final sale price. Auction sites also charge to set a reserve price and to relist (i.e., if the item does not sell the first time). Tables 5.3 and 5.4 show a comparison of these rates.

Interestingly, eBay manages to dominate the auction market despite having competitors who charge neither an insertion nor a final value fee! Sites that do not charge an insertion fee, such as Lycos, expected to make money using an advertising-based model. Moreover, because eBay had a head start on many other auction sites, these other sites felt the need to make their services free in order to make any headway into the auction business. eBay has, nevertheless, clearly cemented its dominant position in the business with its large number of committed buyers and sellers. Establishing such a large base is hard for a new-comer because it is difficult to get a trader to switch from eBay. Zero fees are not attrac-tive if the number of potential buyers is small.

Table 5.3
Comparison of Insertion Fees for Leading C2C Auction Sites

Auction Site	$0.01 to $9.99	$10 to $24.99	$25 to $49.99	$50 and Up	Reserve Listing	Relist Fee
Amazon.com Auctions	$0.10	$0.10	$0.10	$0.10	No Fee	1x w/o fee
eBay	$0.30	$0.55	$1.10	$2.20–$3.30	$.50–$1	1x w/o fee
Excite Auctions	Free	Free	Free	Free	Free	Free
Haggle Online	Free	Free	Free	Free	No Fee	No limit
Half.com	Free	Free	Free	Free	n/a	Free
Lycos Auctions	Free	Free	Free	Free	No Fee	No limit
MSN Auctions	Free	Free	Free	Free	No Fee	No limit
Onlineauction.com	Free	Free	Free	Free	No Fee	No limit
Yahoo! Auctions	$0.20	$0.35	$0.75	$1.50	$0.40–$0.75	No

Source: http://www.auctionwatch.com, updated January 25, 2001.

Table 5.4
Comparison of Final Value Fees for Leading C2C Sites

Auction Site	$25 and less	$25.01 to $1,000	$1,000 and Up	$1,500 Sale
Amazon.com Auctions	5% ($1.25)	$1.25 + 2.5%	$25.63 + 1.25%	$31.88
eBay	5% ($1.25)	$1.25 + 2.5%	$25.63 + 1.25	$31.88
Excite Auctions	5% ($1.25)	2.5% ($24.38)	1.25%	$31.88
Haggle Online	Free	Free	Free	Free
Half.com	15%	15%	15%	$225
Lycos Auctions	Free	Free	Free	Free
MSN Auctions	5% ($1.25)	2.5% ($24.38)	1.25%	$31.88
Onlineauction.com	5%	5%	5%	$75.00
ReverseAuction	3%	3%	3%	$45
Yahoo! Auctions	Free	Free	Free	Free

Source: http://www.auctionwatch.com, updated January 25, 2001.

Bidder Behavior

The English auction is famous for being susceptible to the *winner's curse* (the Appendix offers a longer and more technical explanation). Buyers differ in their enthusiasm for a product. The most enthusiastic will bid up the price, and the "winner" pays a price far above his or her valuation of the product. In this way, by "winning" the auction, the person loses by paying a very high price. One way to avoid the winner's curse is to research previous auctions of similar items.[10]

Traditionally, a "going, going, gone" procedure is used to end a single bidding process; however, on the Internet, because there is no live auctioneer, a closing time is specified: an auction might, for example, be open for seven days. Many bidders adopt a strategy called *sniping* to win in such auctions. They wait until the last few minutes to place a bid, and because other bidders do not have enough time to respond, they better their chances of winning the auction. Online auction sites have devised two techniques to prevent sniping.[11] The first technique, used by OnSale and Yahoo!, among others, is to offer an *automatic extension period*, in which, for instance, if there is bidding activity during the last five minutes of an auction, it is automatically extended by another five minutes. This provides other bidders some more time to modify their bids and in that sense, it makes the auction "fair."

The second technique is *proxy bidding*, which is being used by eBay and other sites. Here, an individual can set up a proxy by specifying the highest price he or she is willing to bid. The proxy then bids on behalf of the individual in prespecified increments until the maximum price is reached. If a bid is received during the last few minutes and the value of the bid is less than the maximum price specified to the proxy, a bid is automatically registered, rendering sniping ineffective.

Shilling is the classic way by which a seller increases the price of the sale. Typically, the seller disguises his or her identity and submits an artificially high bid, raising the bar for interested buyers, and leading to a higher sale price. Shilling is illegal, but the law against it is hard to enforce.

Bid shielding is the reverse of shilling in that it is an attempt by a buyer to ward off other bidders to keep the final price low. In this case, an accomplice places a very high bid that is unlikely to be exceeded. Then, at the very last moment, the accomplice withdraws the bid, leaving a clear path for the second highest bidder who set up the scheme in the first place.

Bid siphoning is when a competing seller contacts bidders at an auction and offers to sell them the item. This leads to a reduction in the number of bidders and, potentially, a lower sale price. The competing seller also does not have to pay any fees to the auction facilitator and therefore has an unfair advantage.

A leading auctions expert makes the following observations about expected strategic behavior in different auctions:

1. In auctions where buyers bid up from a minimum price (called "ascending auctions"), in the early stages of the auction, buyers try to signal to others that they must bid low.

2. Ascending auctions are more susceptible to illegal cartel formation than sealed-bid auctions.

3. If the reserve price is set too low, collusion between bidders may lead to a low sale price.

4. In ascending auctions, the "winner's curse" leads to higher bids.

5. Ascending auctions encourage predatory behavior–stronger bidder threatening weaker bidders.

Fraud

Fraud is a big problem with auctions. Even though eBay claims that fraud occurs only in one of every 25,000 transactions,[12] the prospect of deadbeat buyers who do not pay is a genuine problem with online auctions. A survey conducted by eMarketer indicated that the leading category of online crime is auction fraud, with the average amount involved being $600.[13] Similarly, the Internet Fraud Watch reported that the number one type of fraud on the Internet was related to online auctions.[14]

Four deterrents to fraud have emerged:

1. Micropayment systems. These are designed for the efficient transfer of small amounts of money from buyers to sellers. In this way, sellers are assured payment before they ship the product. The leading micropayment systems are Paypal, eBay's Billpoint, Yahoo!'s paydirect, and Amazon.com's Amazon Payments.

2. Rating systems. eBay has pioneered a system of feedback between buyers. Specifically, buyers rate sellers based on previous transactions. eBay provides an index that involves the difference between the number of positive and negative comments. Unfortunately, the feedback system can also be manipulated–e.g., a seller can ask an accomplice to post positive comments–but in most cases, such an index is a reasonable data point.

A leading auction user group suggests the following points when evaluating ratings:[15]

- Numbers alone are deceiving–individuals must study detailed comments.

- Feedback comments reflect both parties.

- A big number doesn't always mean a quality transaction.

- A zero doesn't mean a bad seller–it just means that the seller is new.

3. Escrow systems. Leading examples are SafeBuyer.com, i-Escrow Inc, and Escrow.com. These intermediaries obtain possession of the item being sold and the money to ensure a safe exchange. But they require fees from the seller and buyer.

4. Mediation services. These services have emerged to settle disputes arising from auctions. An example is squaretrade.com, which specializes in mediating disputes and conflict resolution.

In addition, the FTC has prepared detailed documentation to help consumers participate in auctions. See http://www.ftc.gov/bcp/conline/pubs/alerts/gonealrt.htm, for example.

Conclusion

Online auctions are here to stay. Managers who are considering using auctions to buy or sell must understand the different auction mechanisms and bidder behaviors in order to succeed.

Notes

(All URLs are current as of March 10, 2002.)

1. David Lucking-Reiley, "Auctions on the Internet: What's Being Auctioned and How?," working paper, Department of Economics, Vanderbilt University, 1999.

2. Bruce Gottlieb, "Ebay or the Highway: Its Size Is Its Selling Point and Curse," July 7, 2000, <http://slate.msn.com/default.aspx?id=85756>.

3. Miriam Herschlag and Rami Zwick, "Internet Auctions: A Popular and Professional Literature Review," *Quarterly Journal of Electronic Commerce*, 1(2), (2000): 161–186.

4. Steven Landsburg, "My Way to the eBay," April 9, 1999, <http://slate.msn.com/default. aspx?id=22998>.

5. Stefan Klein, "Introduction to Electronic Auctions," *Electronic Markets* (1997): 3–6.

6. Steven Landsburg, Sidebar to "My Way to the eBay," April 9, 1999, <http://slate.msn.com/ default.aspx?id=22998&sidebar=23035> provides a detailed explanation of why this is the case.

7. Ira Carnahan, "The Economics of Priceline," May 19, 2000, <http://slate.msn.com/default. aspx?id=82827>.

8. Paul Klemperer, ed., *The Economic Theory of Auctions* (MA: Edward Elgar Publishing, 2000).

9. Lucking-Reiley, "Auctions on the Internet."

10. Peter Coy, "Online Auctions: Going, Going, Gone . . . Sucker!," March 20, 2000, <http://www. businessweek.com/2000/00_12/b3673131.htm>.

11. Lucking-Reiley, "Auctions on the Internet."

12. Coy, "Online Auctions."

13. Clare Haney, "Most of US Net Crime At Auctions," January 11, 2001, <http://www.cnn.com/ 2001/TECH/computing/01/11/auction.crime.idg/index.html>.

14. Internet Fraud Watch, "Home Page," <http://www.fraud.org/internet/intset.htm>.

15. Scott Samuel, "Understanding What Feedback Means," <http://www.auctionusers.org/education/ p1s003.shtml>.

16. This is primarily based on Paul Klemperer, *Auction Theory: A Guide to the Literature*, March 1999, which is available at <http://econwpa.wustl.edu:8089/eps/mic/papers/9903/9903002.pdf>.

17. Steven Landsburg, "My Way to the eBay."

18. Bruce Gottlieb, "The Agony of Victory," March 19, 1999, <http://slate.msn.com/?id=21810>.

19. Ibid.

20. Paul Klemperer, "What Really Matters in Auction Design," February 2001, <http://www.nuff. ox.ac.uk/users/klemperer/design3aweb.pdf>.

REVIEW / CHAPTER 5

Discussion Questions

1. What is the incremental value added by the Internet to an auction?

2. What types of products or services cannot be sold using auctions? Why?

3. How might your thinking change if you were a buyer in an English auction as opposed to a second-price auction?

4. Why did Yahoo! fail to pull customers from eBay though its auctions were completely free?

5. Is the seller better off revealing the reserve price? Why or why not?

6. If you anticipate sniping, are you better off having a very short auction? Why or why not?

7. In your opinion, which of the four techniques to prevent fraud has the highest chance of succeeding?

E-Tasks

1. Visit eBay's Australia and Singapore stores. What differences do you find with the auctions there in comparison to the U.S. store?

2. Compare the design of the Yahoo!, eBay, and Amazon auction sites. What are the differences? Which differences matter most to consumers?

APPENDIX / CHAPTER 5

A Brief Description of Economic Theory of Auctions[16] (Advanced)

The central aspect of auctions is the asymmetric information among participants. Each participant knows how much he or she values the item, but this information is not openly available to others. Every participant is not equally astute when valuing the item—some may have better research than others, or others may be needlessly optimistic.

Potential buyers gain considerable advantage from acting as if they do not value the item very highly. The seller has no way of finding out each person's valuation of the good being sold. As a result, the seller stands a real chance of receiving a low price from a group of buyers who may pretend not to care about the item's value. To avoid this, economists have developed the second-price auction. In this auction type, the bids proceed in an ascending manner, and the person who has the highest bid wins and pays the second-highest bid. The following example illustrates how this makes revealing the true valuation of the item a strategy for all players:[17]

Suppose an antique water pitcher is worth $300 to me, and I'm deciding whether to bid $300 or to bid less, say, $250. Consider various scenarios and see what happens under each.

Scenario A: The highest bid other than my own is $200. Under either strategy (i.e., whether I bid $250 or $300), I get the pitcher for $200. In this scenario, both strategies are equally good.

Scenario B: The highest bid other than my own is $275. If I bid $250, I lose. But if I bid $300, I get the pitcher for $275, which is a bargain. In this scenario, it is better to bid $300.

Scenario C: The highest bid other than my own is $350. Under either strategy, I lose. In this scenario, as in Scenario A, both strategies are equally good.

The bottom line: Bidding $300 is sometimes better, and never worse, than bidding $250. So, I should bid $300, and I can be confident that no matter what scenario develops, I will not regret my bid.

Auctions are broadly classified into two types—private-value and pure common-value. In *private-value auctions*, each participant knows for certain what his or her valuation of the good is, but this valuation is not known to others. In the *pure common-value auction*, there is one true value for the good being auctioned (e.g., a piece of land that may have crude oil). However, this true value is hard to assess—even for experts. In pure common-value auctions, participants are very sensitive to others' bids because they may assume that others are bidding in a certain way because they have access to additional research. This sort of thinking, however, may lead to erroneous bidding and result in people's over-paying. This is the winner's curse.

APPENDIX / CHAPTER 5

The winner's curse is also illustrated in this classic example:[18]

Suppose several petroleum firms are bidding on the drilling rights to a piece of tundra. No firm is certain how much oil is underneath the property, so they hire a team of engineers to poke at the surface rocks and make a guess. The guesses will likely range from too low to too high. Some firm's engineer will probably guess correctly, but that firm will not win the auction. The winner will be the firm with the engineer who was most optimistic. The winning firm ultimately will not get as much oil as their engineer promised, meaning the firm paid too much. In short, the auction "winner" is ultimately a loser.

Even though there is an economic theorem proving that a truly rational participant can avoid the winner's curse, most evidence points to the contrary. For instance, an empirical examination of bidding on oil fields showed that even seasoned firms made excessively high bids.[19]

Auction design is very important. Small changes in the auction's rules can lead to major differences in the final outcome. Paul Klemperer, a professor at Nuffield College in Oxford, UK, and a leading auction expert, discusses this in detail in the context of the auction of a wireless spectrum in various European countries.[20] He points out how even with the same auction design (Anglo-Dutch), subtle differences in the number of participants, the reserve price, and other rules led to major swings in the revenues earned.

Nevertheless, a powerful concept in economics called the *revenue equivalence theorem* states that for a given set of assumptions a wide variety of auctions will yield similar results. For example, in auctions where individuals know how much they value the object being auctioned, but not how much others value the item, the person who values the item most gets the item. A detailed discussion is beyond the scope of this Appendix. Interested readers may read the paper at http://econwpa.wustl.edu:8089/eps/mic/papers/9903/9903002.pdf.

amazon.com

Amazon.com—
A Business History: Case 1

Introduction

Amazon.com is perhaps the company most closely associated with the e-commerce phenomenon. The Seattle, Washington–based company has grown from a book seller to a virtual Wal-Mart of the Web, selling products as diverse as music CDs, cookware, toys and games, and tools and hardware. The company has also grown at a tremendous rate with revenue rising from about $150 million in 1997 to $3.1 billion in 2001. However, the rise in revenue has led to a commensurate increase in operating losses, leaving the company with a large deficit. The company did make its first quarterly profit of $5 million in the fourth quarter of 2001, but this was dwarfed by large cumulative losses. Its share price, as shown in Figure C1.1, is perhaps the biggest symbol of the rise and fall of the dot-coms.

The purpose of this case is to present a balanced and up-to-date business history of the company.

Background

The story of the formation of Amazon.com has been repeated to the point of legend. The company was founded by Jeff Bezos, a computer science and electrical engineering graduate from Princeton University. Bezos had moved to Seattle after resigning as the senior vice president at D.E. Shaw, a Wall Street investment bank. He did not know much about the Internet, but, he came across a statistic that the Internet was growing at a rate of 2,300%, which convinced him that it was a large growth opportunity. Not knowing much more, he plunged into the world of e-commerce with no prior retailing experience.[1]

He located the company in Seattle because the city had a large pool of technical talent and was close to one of the largest book wholesalers, in Roseburg, Oregon, because the company began as a bookseller. Moreover, the sales tax laws for online retailers state that a company has to collect sales tax in the state in which it is incorporated. This means that the price of all orders originating in the state is increased by the sales tax, leading to a competitive disadvantage in that state. Therefore, it was logical to locate in a small state and be uncompetitive on a smaller number of transactions rather than potentially lose customers in a big state such as California or New York.

The company went online in July 1995 and went public in May 1997. As a symbol of the company's frugality, Bezos and the first team built desks out of doors and four-by-fours. The company was started in a garage, and, ironically, initial business meetings took place at a local Barnes & Noble store.

Bezos' first choice for the company name was Cadabra. He quickly dropped this name when a lawyer he contacted mistook it for cadaver. He picked Amazon because it started with the letter A, signified something big, and was easy to spell.

For his contribution, Jeff Bezos was picked as the 1999 *Time* person of the year at the age of thirty-five, making him the fourth-youngest person selected. Describing why it chose Bezos, *Time* magazine said, "Bezos' vision of the online retailing universe was so complete, his Amazon.com site so elegant and appealing that it

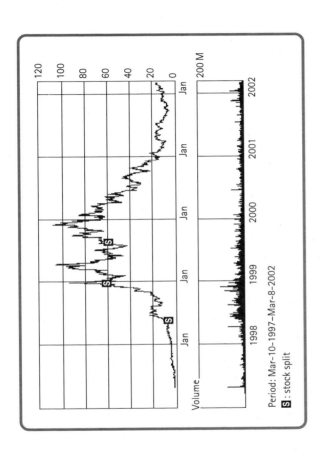

Figure C1.1
Amazon.com's Stock Price Path

Period: Mar-10-1997–Mar-8-2002

S : stock split

Volume

200 M

Source: Quicken.com, accessed on March 6, 2002.

became from Day One the point of reference for anyone who had anything to sell online."[2]

Vision and Value

Jeff Bezos was one of the few people to understand the special nature of Internet retailing and e-commerce. This is how he compares e-tailing to traditional retailing:[3]

Look at e-retailing. The key trade that we make is that we trade real estate for technology. Real estate is the key cost of physical retailers. That's why there's the old saw: location, location, location. Real estate gets more expensive every year, and technology gets cheaper every year. And it gets cheaper fast.

There were really two elements to his vision:

1. He wanted to build the world's most customer-centric company.

2. He wanted to establish a place where customers could buy anything.

This is how he characterizes his vision of customer-centrism:[4]

Our goal is to be Earth's most customer-centric company. I will leave it to others to say if we've achieved that. But why? The answer is three things: The first is that customer-centric means figuring out what your customers want by asking them, then figuring out how to give it to them, and then giving it to them. That's the traditional meaning of customer-centric, and we're focused on it. The second is innovating on behalf of customers, figuring out what they don't know they want and giving it to them. The third meaning, unique to the Internet, is the idea of personalization: Redecorating the store for each and every individual customer. If we have 10.7 million customers, as we did at the end of the last quarter, then we should have 10.7 million stores.

Amazon.com recently launched a "Your Store" service, thus translating Bezos' vision into a reality.

He strived to understand what was unique about the Internet to developing a customer-centric company:[5]

In the online world, businesses have the opportunity to develop very deep relationships with customers, both through accepting preferences of customers and then observing their purchase behavior over time, so that you can get that individualized knowledge of the customer and use that individualized knowledge of the customer to accelerate their discovery process. If we can do that, then the customers are going to feel a deep loyalty to us, because we know them so well.

The value elements Amazon.com sought to deliver are illustrated in this Bezos quote:[6]

Bill Gates laid it out in a magazine interview. He said, "I buy all my books at Amazon.com because I'm busy and it's convenient. They have a big selection, and they've been reliable." Those are three of our four core value propositions: convenience, selection, service. The only one he left out is price: we are the broadest discounters in the world in any product category. But maybe price isn't so important to Bill Gates.

Some of Bezos' critics have said that the extent of customer-centricism of the company is about the same as any other company. Bezos has been seen as generating hype and nothing more.

In any case, Bezos' vision has been translated into a large customer base and loyalty rate.

Amazon.com's customer base has grown rapidly over the past several years. Customer accounts grew from 1.5 million in December 1997 to 24.7 million in December 2001.[7] The percentage of repeat customers increased from 64% in 1998 to 78% in 2000. In the fourth quarter of 2001, Amazon spent $7 to acquire a new customer, and the average customer spending was $123.

In addition to customer-centricism, Bezos wanted Amazon.com to be the place where you could buy anything and everything online. Although the company started out as the world's biggest bookstore, it aimed eventually to become the world's biggest store. The company has made some progress along these lines by expanding into new product categories, such as cookware and tools, and also providing new services such as auctions. However, Bezos has conceded that becoming the place to buy any product is a "multi-decade proposition."

Financial Analysis of Amazon.com

The financial statements of Amazon are shown in Tables C1.1, C1.2, and C1.3. Table C1.1 presents the historical income statements of the

Table C1.1
Amazon.com's Historical Income Statements
(2001 YTD figures are up to September 30)

		Year ended December 31			
	2001	2000	1999	1998	1997
Net sales	$ 3,122,433	$ 2,761,983	$ 1,639,839	$ 609,819	$ 147,787
Cost of sales	2,323,875	2,106,206	1,349,194	476,155	118,969
Gross profit	798,558	655,777	290,645	133,664	28,818
	25.6%	23.7%	17.7%	21.9%	19.5%
Operating expenses:					
Fulfillment	374,250	414,509	237,312	65,227	15,944
Marketing	138,283	179,980	175,838	67,427	24,133
Technology and content	241,165	269,326	159,722	46,424	13,384
General and administrative	89,862	108,962	70,144	15,618	6,741
Stock-based compensation (1)	4,637	24,797	30,618	1,889	1,211

Year ended December 31

	2001	2000	1999	1998	1997
Amortization of goodwill and other intangibles (1)	181,033	321,772	214,694	42,599	—
Impairment-related and other (1)	181,585	200,311	8,072	3,535	—
Total operating expenses	1,210,815	1,519,657	896,400	242,719	61,413
Loss from operations	(412,257)	(863,880)	(605,755)	(109,055)	(32,595)
Interest income	29,103	40,821	45,451	14,053	1,901
Interest expense	(139,232)	(130,921)	(84,566)	(26,639)	(326)
Other income (expense)	(1,900)	(10,058)	1,671	—	—
Non-cash investment gains and losses (1)	(2,141)	(142,639)	—	—	—
Net interest income (expense) and other	(114,170)	(242,797)	(37,444)	(12,586)	1,575
Loss before equity in losses of equity-method investees	(526,427)	(1,106,677)	(643,199)	(121,641)	(31,020)
Equity in losses of equity-method investees, net (1)	(30,327)	(304,596)	(76,769)	(2,905)	—
Cumulative effect of change in accounting principle (1)	(10,523)	—	—	—	—
Net loss–GAAP	$ (567,277)	$ (1,411,273)	$ (719,968)	$ (124,546)	$ (31,020)
Basic and diluted loss per share	$ (1.56)	$ (4.02)	$ (2.20)	$ (0.42)	$ (0.12)
Basic and diluted loss per share—pro forma	$ (1.56)	$ (1.19)	$ (1.19)	$ (0.25)	$ (0.11)
Shares used in computation of basic and diluted loss per share	364,211	350,873	326,753	296,344	260,682

(1) Amounts excluded from pro forma calculations
Source: Courtesy Amazon.com Inc., http://www.iredge.com/IREdge/IREdge.asp?c=002239&f=2019, accessed March 6, 2002.

Table C1.2
Amazon.com's Historical Balance Sheet Statements

	2001	2000	1999	1998	1997
ASSETS					
Current assets:					
Cash and cash equivalents	$540,282	$ 822,435	$ 133,309	$ 71,583	$110,119
Marketable securities	456,303	278,087	572,879	301,862	15,256
Inventories	143,722	174,563	220,646	29,501	8,971
Prepaid expenses and other current assets	67,613	86,044	79,643	21,308	3,363
Total current assets	1,207,920	1,361,129	1,006,477	424,254	137,709
Fixed assets, net	271,751	366,416	317,613	29,791	9,726
Goodwill, net	45,367	158,990	534,699	174,052	0
Other intangibles, net	34,382	96,335	195,445	4,586	0
Investments in equity-method investees	10,387	52,073	226,727	7,740	0
Other equity investments	17,972	40,177	144,735	0	0
Other assets	49,768	60,049	40,154	8,037	2,409
Total assets	$1,637,547	2,135,169	2,465,850	648,460	149,844
LIABILITIES AND STOCKHOLDERS' EQUITY (DEFICIT)					
Current liabilities:					
Accounts payable	$444,748	$ 485,383	$ 463,026	$113,273	$ 33,027
Accrued expenses and other current liabilities	305,064	272,683	176,208	47,484	8,871
Unearned revenue	87,978	131,117	54,790	0	816
Interest payable	68,632	69,196	24,888	10	177
Current portion of long-term debt and other	14,992	16,577	14,322	808	1,660
Total current liabilities	921,414	974,956	733,234	161,575	44,551

	2001	2000	1999	1998	1997
Long-term debt and other	2,156,133	2,127,464	1,466,338	348,140	76,702
Commitments and contingencies					
Stockholders' equity (deficit):					
Preferred stock, $0.01 par value:					
Authorized shares—500,000					
Issued and outstanding shares—none	—	0	0	0	0
Common stock, $0.01 par value:					
Authorized shares— 5,000,000					
Issued and outstanding shares	3,732	3,571	3,452	3,186	2,898
Additional paid-in capital	1,462,769	1,338,303	1,194,369	297,438	65,137
Deferred stock-based compensation	(9,853)	(13,448)	(47,806)	(1,625)	(1,930)
Accumulated other comprehensive income (loss)	(36,070)	(2,376)	(1,709)	1,806	0
Accumulated deficit	(2,860,578)	(2,293,301)	(882,028)	(162,060)	(37,514)
Total stockholders' equity (deficit)	(1,440,000)	(967,251)	266,278	138,745	28,591
Total liabilities and stockholders' equity (deficit)	1,637,547	2,135,169	2,465,850	648,460	149,844

Source: Courtesy Amazon.com Inc., http://www.iredge.com/IREdge/IREdge.asp?c=0022239&f=2019, accessed March 6, 2002.

company, Table C1.2 provides the historical balance sheets, and Table C1.3 provides segment-level analysis.

Following are a few highlights from the financial statements:

- Sales have grown from $147 million in 1997 to about $3.1 billion in 2001. The average growth rate during this period was 141%.
- The gross margin during this period has averaged 21.68%.

Table C1.3
Segment-Level Sales and Profitability Information

		2001	2000	1999
Net Sales				
U.S. Books, Music, and DVD/Video		$ 1,688,752	$ 1,698,266	$ 1,308,294
U.S. Electronics, Tools, and Kitchen		547,190	484,151	150,654
	Total U.S. Retail	2,235,942	2,182,417	1,458,948
U.S. Services		225,117	198,491	13,148
	Total U.S.	2,461,059	2,380,908	1,472,096
International		661,374	381,075	167,743
	Consolidated Totals	3,122,433	2,761,983	1,639,839
Gross Profit				
U.S. Books, Music, and DVD/Video		453,129	417,452	262,871
U.S. Electronics, Tools, and Kitchen		78,384	44,655	(20,086)
	Total U.S. Retail	531,513	462,107	242,785
U.S. Services		126,439	116,234	12,285
	Total U.S.	657,952	578,341	255,070
International		140,606	77,436	35,575
	Consolidated Totals	798,558	655,777	290,645
Pro forma income (loss) from operations				
U.S. Books, Music, and DVD/Video		156,753	71,441	(31,000)
U.S. Electronics, Tools, and Kitchen		(140,685)	(269,890)	(163,827)
	Total U.S. Retail	16,068	(198,449)	(194,827)
U.S. Services		42,042	26,519	(78,320)
	Total U.S.	58,110	(171,930)	(273,147)
International		(103,112)	(145,070)	(79,223)
	Consolidated Totals	(45,002)	(317,000)	(352,370)

Source: Courtesy Amazon.com Inc., http://www.iredge.com/IREdge/IREdge.asp?c=002239&f=2019, accessed March 6, 2002.

- The ratio of marketing expenses to sales revenue has decreased from 16.33% in 1997 to 4.43% in 2001.

- The interest expenses have risen from $326,000 in 1997 to $139 million in 2001.

- The loss from operations has increased from $32,595 in 1997 to $412,257 in 2001.

- The sales from book, music, and video have leveled off, but this is a very profitable segment. On the other hand, the electronics, tools, and kitchen segment is growing rapidly, but is not very profitable.

Given its diverse set of products and services, it is hard to identify appropriate competitors. Bn.com is frequently thought of as a strong competitor in the books, music, and video categories. Its operating statement for 1998, 1999, and 2000 is shown in Table C1.4. Note that the level of sales is much lower than Amazon. Moreover, it spent a much greater percent of its sales on marketing and fulfillment—nearly 42% in the year 2000.

Amazon.com has also been praised for its innovative financing strategy—using a convertible bond issue. Professor Ufuk Ince from the University of Washington, Bothell, provides a detailed explanation that is attached as an appendix at the end of the chapter.

Books—The Entry Point

Amazon.com started out as an online bookseller. Indeed, to some, Amazon.com will always be a bookseller. Selling books on the Internet made sense at many levels.

To Jeff Bezos, the primary advantage was selection.[8]

Books are incredibly unusual in one respect, and that is that there are more items in the book category than there are items in any other category by far. There are more than 3 million different titles available and active in print worldwide. When you have this huge number of titles, a couple of things start to happen.

First of all, you can use computers to sort, search, and organize. Second, you can create a super-valuable customer proposition that can only be done online, and that is selection. There are lots of categories where selection is proven to be important: books, in particular, with the book superstores, but also in home construction materials, with Home Depot, and toys with Toys "R" Us. Online, you can have this vast catalog of millions of titles, whereas in the physical world, the largest physical superstores are only about 175,000 titles, and there are only three that big.

In addition, as a product, books were:

- Easy to ship because they are not bulky

- A low-value item and hence, low-risk

- Informational products, making them amenable to selling them via online storefronts using features such as sample chapters, table of contents, editorial reviews, and customer reviews.

Moreover, Amazon.com felt that it could add maximal value given the archaic and inefficient structure of the $23 billion American publishing industry. An overview of the structure of the industry is provided in Exhibits C1.I and C1.II.

The primary features of this publishing industry are:[9]

- Concentration at all levels of the supply chain—publishers, printers, wholesalers. The top ten publishers accounted for 20% of the new titles, the top five printers represent 40% of the market, the largest wholesaler accounts for 33% of all books shipped.

- No dominant player on the retail side—even No. 1 Barnes & Noble has only about 11% of the U.S. market.

- Publishers guarantee the sale of all books. Retailers can simply return a book if it does not sell within a predefined time frame. As a result, in 1998, the return rate of hardcover books was around 32% and those for softcover books was about 27%.

Table C1.4
Consolidated Statement of Operations of bn.com (All figures in thousands unless otherwise stated, bn.com was a subsidiary of Barnes & Noble up to October 31, 1998)

	2001	Year Ended 12/31/2000	Year Ended 12/31/1999	Year Ended 12/31/1998
Net sales	$289,562	320,115	193,730	61,834
Cost of sales	222,766	261,801	159,937	47,569
Gross profit	66,796	58,314	33,793	14,265
Operating expenses:				
Marketing, sales and fulfillment	31,820	132,483	101,077	70,423
Technology and web site development	47,560	40,391	21,006	8,532
General and administrative	34,859	31,293	18,842	12,026
Depreciation and amortization	23,626	36,088	15,510	7,140
Impairment and other special charges	—	75,051	—	—
Stock based compensation	—	11,740	—	—
Equity in net loss of equity investments including amortization of intangibles	20,593	30,728	—	—
Total operating expense	189,592	357,774	156,435	98,121
Operating loss	(122,796)	(299,460)	(122,642)	(83,856)
Interest income, net	6,265	23,737	20,238	708
Loss before minority interest	(116,531)	(275,723)	(102,404)	(83,148)
Minority interest	84,396	210,320	54,253	—
Net loss—historical	($32,135)	(65,403)	(48,151)	(83,148)
Basic net loss per common share	($0.24)	($2.02)	($0.72)	($0.48)
Basic weighted average common shares outstanding	43,787	32,386	28,778	28,797
Diluted net loss per share	($0.24)	($2.02)	($0.72)	($0.48)

Source: 10Q, November 2001.

- It is a hit-and-miss business with major fluctuations in sales. Even though publishers incur the fixed costs of book production and editing for all books, only a few are very successful.

- Retailers bear the fixed costs of displaying the product in a bricks-and-mortar location.[10]

Bezos also commented on the traditional nature of the publishing industry in an amusing anecdote:

The wholesalers had 10-book minimum orders. I tried to negotiate with them and said, "Let us just pay a small fee, and you waive the 10-book order," and so on. But they wouldn't go for it. So we fig-

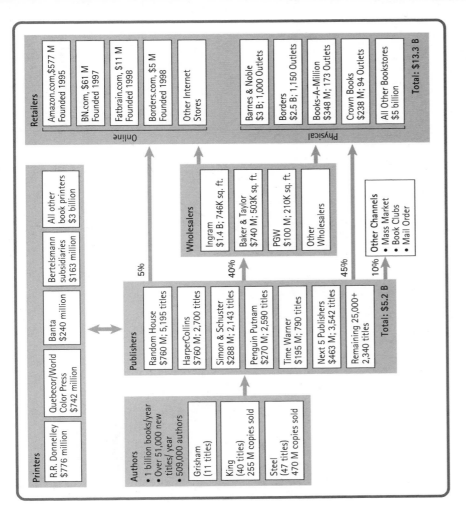

Source: Simba Information Inc. Trade Book Publishing 1999. Standard and Poor's Publishing Industry Surveys, company annual reports, and BAH analysis.

ured out a loophole. It turned out that you just had to place an order for 10 books; you didn't actually have to get 10 books. We found an obscure book on lichens that none of our wholesalers actually carried.

So whenever we wanted to order one book, we ordered the book we wanted, and then nine copies of this lichen book. They would deliver the one that we wanted, along with a very sincere apology about not having been able to fulfill the nine copies of the lichen book order. That worked very well for exercising our systems. I've since talked and joked at length with the people at these companies about this. They actually think it's very funny.

Amazon changed the traditional book publishing industry in the following ways:

- It reduced book return rates from about 30% to 3%. Industry experts estimate that about $100 million is spent on returns. Moreover, "a truly efficient supply network, which processed only saleable books, could save over $2 billion—quite an opportunity given that industry profits from the one billion trade books total about $4 billion today."[11] Reducing this by a factor of ten can lead to an immensely profitable business.

- It relied on the existing distribution structure, building warehouses only for the top

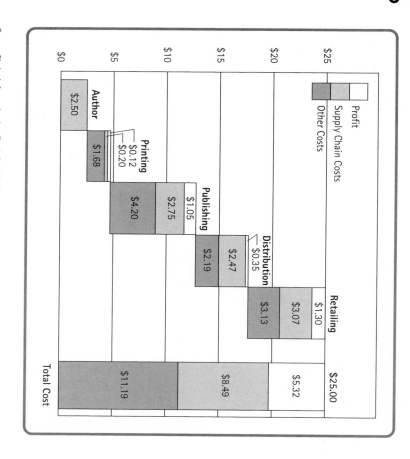

Source: Simba Information Inc. Trade Book Publishing 1999, Standard and Poor's Publishing Industry Surveys, Brill's Content Magazine, October 1998, and BAH analysis.

sellers and quick moving items. As a result, its inventory turnaround is much quicker than bricks-and-mortar stores.

- "Physical bookstores must stock up to 160 days' worth of inventory to provide the kind of in-store selection people want. Yet, they must pay distributors and publishers forty-five to ninety days after they buy the books—so on average, they carry the costs of those books for up to four months. Amazon, by contrast, carries only fifteen days' worth of inventory and is paid immediately by credit card. So, it gets about a month's use of interest-free money."[12]

- Amazon.com passes on the cost savings in the form of price reductions to consumers.

Currently Amazon offers 30% off all the *New York Times* best-sellers, for example.

- Amazon "has broken the principle of critical mass for the book market. For the first time, small and independent publishers, as well as authors, could place their products directly in a (online) store with global reach and without investments (except paying for transporting books to Amazon.com's distribution center)."[13]

Amazon's primary competition in this market was from bricks-and-clicks stores such as Bn.com (and Barnes & Noble). Bn.com, for instance, has noted the following sources of competitive advantage:[14]

- Superior brand recognition of the Barnes & Noble brand name and the security from knowing that it is associated with the 1,000 retail bookstores nationwide.

- The use of Barnes & Noble's distribution center enables bn.com to offer more than 880,000 in-stock book titles for fast delivery, representing the largest standing inventory of any online bookseller.

- The ability to conduct cross-marketing, co-promotion, and customer acquisition programs with Bertelsmann's U.S. book clubs and Bertelsmann's Books Online in various countries including the United Kingdom, Germany, France, the Netherlands, Italy, Spain, Norway, Sweden, Japan, and China, which provide bn.com with: (i) access to millions of established book buyers; (ii) the opportunity to directly promote its online store to this large audience of proven buyers; and (iii) a potential new stream of customers that it will be able to acquire at a significantly lower acquisition cost as compared with customers acquired through other marketing channels.

- Participation in Barnes & Noble's membership loyalty program, Readers' Advantage, which offers discounts and other benefits to members. For a $25 annual membership fee, participating customers receive 10% additional discounts at Barnes & Noble stores and 5% additional discounts at bn.com. Customer sign-up benefits include a one-year subscription to *Book* magazine and a free canvas tote bag. The program benefits also include invitations to members-only events.

Amazon.com also continued the onslaught on independent booksellers.

Small independent bookstores have been pounded by two waves of change over the past decade, reducing their numbers from 6,500 in 1991 to 3,500 in 1998. First, the major chains introduced the category-killer superstores with up to 60,000 square feet of retail space and 175,000 titles in stock. With the addition of coffee shops, they changed book buying from a traditional retail activity to something akin to an intellectual social outing. In July 1995, Amazon launched the second wave by allowing consumers to browse 4.5 million titles from the comfort of their own computers.[15]

Independent booksellers responded in two ways:[16]

- In 1999, the American Booksellers Association announced BookSense.com, a web site allowing customers to order books over the Internet with their local independent bookstore getting a commission on each sale.

- BookSite.com allows small bricks-and-mortar bookstores to add an online storefront and with e-commerce tools and Internet ordering to supplement their inventory.

However, it is not clear whether either approach has led to a credible threat to Amazon.

The dominance of Amazon in the book market was made abundantly clear by the capitulation of a major competitor, Borders.

In April 2001, Amazon made an astonishing alliance—with rival Borders. For years now the Borders Group has sought in vain to offer a web site that would compete effectively with Amazon. Borders became a force in book retailing thanks to its superior computerized inventory management system dating back to the 1970s. It never figured out how to translate its computer expertise into an effective web site. In April, Borders eliminated all staff positions in Borders.com, and announced that Amazon will front-end its online bookselling.[17]

Should Amazon.com Have Remained a Bookstore?

Amazon.com rapidly expanded into a number of products. Following is a timeline for the first few product introductions:[18]

- June 1998: music
- November 1998: DVD/video
- July 1999: toys and electronics
- November 1999: home improvement, software, and video games

Its foray into music was dramatic. "In Amazon's first full quarter selling music CDs, ending last September, it drew $14.4 million in sales, quickly edging out two-year-old cyber-leader CDnow Inc."[19] However, it is not clear if it could translate such success into products as disparate as cookware and hardware.

The following arguments have been made in *favor of rapid diversification.*

Cross-Selling

Amazon wanted to get a greater share of each customer's overall shopping basket. They felt that they had already established a relationship with the customer with books. All that remained was to leverage this trust by persuading consumers to buy everything else from them.

Economies of Scale

From a technology standpoint, the company had already incurred the fixed costs of developing software for the online storefronts. Expanding into other product categories allowed the company to spread these fixed costs across a larger pool of transactions leading to greater profits. As Bezos put it:[20]

On the Internet, companies are scale businesses, characterized by high fixed costs and relatively low variable costs. You can be two sizes: You can be big, or you can be small. It's very hard to be medium. A lot of medium-sized companies had the financing rug pulled out from under them before they could get big. . . .

When we open a new category, it's basically the same software. We get to leverage the same customer base, our brand name, and the infrastructure. It's very low-cost for us to open a new category, whereas to have a pure-play single-line store is very expensive. They'll end up spending much more on technology and other fixed costs than we will just because our earlier stores are already covering those costs.

Brand

Amazon established a relationship with its first customers on the basis of being a bookseller. Redefining this relationship in terms of other product categories is not a trivial task. A typical customer reaction might be, "Many of us old customers have a hard time thinking of Amazon as a place to buy a set of Polk home theater speakers or a set of Calphalon cookware. For me, the Earth's Biggest Bookstore moniker has occupied a spot in my mind since it began appearing in those tiny bottom-of-page-one advertisements in the *New York Times*."[21]

Forever Small

Selling books alone would not catapult Amazon as the leading e-tailer and a cutting-edge firm. They would forever be constrained by the small market they operated in. Moving into other product categories allowed them to become a dominant retailer. The operating statement of bn.com in Table C1.4 can be cited as evidence of this. Bn.com chose to focus its energy on the book, music, and video markets, with the result that its revenue is and may always be much smaller than Amazon's. The data from Table C1.5 corroborates this, showing that visitors to Amazon.com increased from 14 million in March 2000 to 18 million in March 2001, whereas visitors to bn.com decreased from 5.4 million to 4.9 million.

Blessing of Wall Street

Perhaps the most important reason for Amazon to diversify was that at the time it was a darling of Wall Street. Skeptics were overruled by high-flying optimists who viewed Amazon as the symbol of the new economy and a new way of doing business. As a result, Amazon made the best use of the opportunity.

On the other hand, many arguments have been made *against* expanding into new product categories.

Table C1.5

Top Internet Retailing Sites in Terms of Unique Visitors, March 2000 vs. March 2001

Rank	March 2000		March 2001	
1	Amazon.com	14,349,000	Amazon.com	18,229,000
2	bn.com	5,404,000	X10.com	8,406,000
3	CDNow	4,737,000	bn.com	4,877,000
4	Ticketmaster	3,617,000	CDNow	4,694,000
5	McAfee	3,549,000	Apple.com	4,029,000
6	hp.com	3,441,000	hp.com	4,018,000
7	Apple.com	3,185,000	Magazineoutlet.com	3,906,000
8	Enews.com	2,901,000	Sears.com	3,842,000
9	Iprint.com	2,871,000	Ticketmaster.com	3,813,000
10	Buy.com	2,624,000	Dell.com	3,800,000

Source: Media Metrix.

New Products Lead to New Challenges

As mentioned earlier, books provided certain unique advantages to Amazon. Moving into new product areas provided new challenges:

- Bulky products—consider cookware items such as pans, blenders, and grills. These items are hard to stock and expensive to ship and return.

- Noninformational products—books are informational products that lend themselves to features such as reviews and sample chapters. Except for music and video, all of the other products that Amazon sells are noninformational products that lack these advantages. As a result, the advantage of selling them online may be limited.

In the consumer electronics business, for example, Amazon.com has not been able to buy directly from leading manufacturers such as Sony, Panasonic, and Pioneer. As a result, Amazon is forced to buy products from distributors, giving it a hefty competitive disadvantage that may be hard to overcome. In addition, selling at prices lower than the manufacturer wanted strained relationships with such giants as JVC.[22]

There are many reasons for this estranged relationship with electronics manufacturers.[23] In the electronics business, manufacturers have a stringent set of requirements governing how a retailer will display and sell their products. Only retailers who pass this "test" are pronounced authorized dealers. Authorized dealers get lower prices, money for cooperative advertising, and the right to sell warranties. Large manufacturers did not want to jeopardize existing relationships with retailers by selling through Amazon—which they feared would sell at lower prices. At the same time, some manufacturers wanted to set up their own online stores. For example, Sony sells electronics through sonystyle.com and deals with the online counterparts of established players such as Best Buy and Circuit City.

Moreover, some manufacturers felt that Amazon did not have a sufficient history in the business and were turned off by its string of losses. Amazon may have appeared too unconventional for them—Amazon's reliance on e-mail as the primary customer service tool, for example, did not please some manufacturers.

Electronics represent the fastest growing part of Amazon's business, while the book, music, and video portions have leveled off. As one analyst from Prudential said, "It has been our contention that if the most profitable part of Amazon's business is not growing, and the most unprofitable part of its business is growing rapidly, the company will begin to experience economic deterioration."

In the final analysis, the company has showed an inability to grasp the intricacies of some of the businesses it entered. Bn.com has not diversified beyond books, music, and videos.

Competition

Amazon.com was the first-mover in the book market, but this was not the case in most other product categories. For example, e-tailers such as CDNow were already in place before Amazon.com appeared in the music category. As a result, Amazon exposed itself to new levels of competition, creating new vulnerabilities. In many cases, established players in the bricks-and-mortar space had also established a presence in the online arena. Moreover, as bricks-and-mortar stores, such as JC Penney and Circuit City, expanded to the online arena, Amazon was faced with escalating levels of competition.

Cost of Complexity

Amazon.com's costs are not driven by technology alone, but depend significantly on the handling of physical goods and inventory. As the magnitude and variety of the goods increase, the cost of real estate, labor, and inventory also increase.[24] This increased cost dragged the company down to some degree.

The Associates Program

Amazon pioneered the concept of the associates program—what is now also referred to as affiliate programs. The basic idea:

- Small sites would act as traffic generators for the company.

- These sites would post content on their site with a link to Amazon.

- Each site would receive a commission of 15% for any referred purchase and 5% for any other purchase made by that consumer.

- The company would benefit not only by traffic generation, but also by branding. Because the small sites would carry an Amazon logo, it would enhance the online presence of the company.

- The company paid for the customer traffic after the fact as opposed to traditional advertising where companies pay ahead of time without knowing the level of traffic it will generate.

The company also obtained a patent for its affiliate program,[25] which was somewhat controversial. The program itself has been quite successful—the company reports signing up at least 200,000 associates. At this point, the vast majority of e-tailers have an associate program. But because Amazon was the first, it was able to sign up many small sites.

Moving beyond Retailing: Partnering, Auctions, and the Zshops Initiative

In addition to expanding into new product categories, Amazon.com proceeded in two new directions. The first initiative was to partner with e-tailers that sold products Amazon did not carry and did not plan to carry. The second one was to host several small businesses as part of the Zshops initiative. As Jeff Bezos explained, "It's not a shift in the model. It's something we had always thought about. For at least a year, we've been talking about ourselves as a 'platform.' It's a foundation or a workbench from which you can do a lot of things. In our case, it consists of customers, technology, e-commerce expertise, distribution centers, and brand."[26]

With each of these initiatives, the company leveraged its reputation and minimized its risk, but it also relinquished control over the consumer experience. In addition, it created layers of complexity and cost due to issues of due diligence and cost and monitoring partners and participants in auctions and Zshops.

Partnerships

The partnering approach was designed to let another firm bear the risk of selling products with unique problems but still share in the potential upside from such a venture. Specifically, Amazon acquired ownership stakes in many companies including Drugstore.com, HomeGrocer.com, Pets.com, Ashford.com, Gear.com, Audible.com, Greenlight.com, Living.com, and Della.com. According to various estimates, Amazon spent at least $160 million on those investments.[27] In some cases, the investment was sizeable—Amazon acquired a 46% stake in Drugstore.com and 50% in Pets.com.[28]

Bezos' comments on the deal with Drugstore.com reveal the intention behind partnerships:[29]

Take Drugstore.com as an example. That is a very complicated business, because you have to be regulated in all 50 states in a very careful way. You have two payers because you pay the $5 copay, and the insurance company takes care of the rest. That leads to a different set of technology systems to make that work. So, it becomes clear very quickly that because they're up and running and they have that customer experience nailed, it would be much better for our customers to offer them that experience than to put our energy and time into trying to replicate it.[30]

However, these investments have proved to be disastrous. In most cases, the fees paid to Amazon by these partners were in their stock, which lost most of its value.[30]

Zshops

Amazon.com got into the store hosting business with its Zshops initiative. This pitted it against portals such as Yahoo! and MSN.

The idea can be summarized as follows:

- Amazon.com provides a place for all kinds of small- and medium-sized businesses to sell products.
- The company provides a guarantee that essentially insures the buyer in the event of nondelivery or the supply of a defective product.
- Sellers are provided a cheap way to sell their products to an already established customer base that trusts the company.
- Amazon gets a sales presence in products it does not carry.

The company earns money from the sellers in Zshops primarily in the following ways:[31]

1. Listing fees (required)—every seller pays $39.99 per month to maintain as many as 40,000 items. If the number of listings exceeds 40,000 at any given time, sellers are charged a $0.10 listing fee for each additional individual listing.

2. Merchandising fees (optional)—sellers can draw attention to their listings with Amazon.com merchandising features.

3. Zshops closing fees (required)—a closing fee is assessed when the item sells at the following rates:
   - If the item sells for $0.01–$25.00, Amazon collects a 5% closing fee.
   - If the item sells for $25.01–$1,000.00, Amazon collects $1.25 plus 2.5% of any amount greater than $25.
   - If the item sells for $1,000.01 or more, Amazon collects $25.63 plus 1.25% of any amount greater than $1,000.

This initiative had the following advantages:[32]

1. It increased Amazon's inventory possibilities a thousand times over without adding inventory cost.

2. It created new, eventually high-margin, revenue streams in the form of a monthly fee

paid to Amazon for listing items on its site, and in the form of a transaction fee paid to Amazon whenever a listed item was sold.

3. If successful, Zshops could increase the number of customer visits to Amazon several fold.

4. Zshops will provide another means for Amazon to cross-promote items over numerous product lines, creating tangential sales.

5. Zshops should only strengthen the Amazon community because members are able to rate all outside sellers and their products.

Zshops also presents new challenges to the company:

- If the company does not attract high-quality brands, the presence of these sellers can attenuate the strength of the brand and lead to brand confusion. It could further muddle the answer to the question "What is Amazon and what does it stand for?"

- It takes away from its core competence of retailing and presents it with new levels of cost and competition.

- The company takes on the risk of a fraudulent seller with this approach.

- It may create additional competition for the firm. In the words of Jeff Bezos:

The Zshops compete against us. I am constantly finding toys on our site that a Zshop is also selling, sometimes at a lower price. If you are used to having very strong control, that is a terrifying notion. But I really believe you can build a more robust company if you give up a bit of that control in this organic marketplace.[33]

Auctions

On March 30, 1999, Amazon.com announced that it was introducing Amazon.com Auctions.[34] This was a bold move on the part of Amazon to overthrow the large Internet auction house eBay. The rationale for Amazon's entry into auctions:

1. Cross-selling—Amazon wanted to leverage its large customer base and encourage them to become buyers or sellers on its auction service.

2. eBay's focus was almost exclusively on small businesses (e.g., antique dealers) and collectors. The thinking at that time was that Amazon may introduce new kinds of buyers and sellers, leading to a different market dynamic.

3. Competition—at this point, variable price mechanisms such as auctions were being projected as the dominant form of e-commerce in the future. As a result, a number of companies introduced auctions. Consider the moves made by Amazon's competitors in March 1999.[35]

- PriceLine.com, the reverse auctioneer, went public on March 30, rocketing to 57 and closing at 70.

- eBay forged a $75 million deal with AOL on March 25 to promote its eBay auctions.

- Catalogue retailer Sharper Image began offering online auctions of new and excess merchandise on March 1.

- Computer e-tailer Cyberian Outpost launched a site on March 16.

How did Amazon's approach differ from previous efforts?

- Amazon provided a money-back guarantee for purchases below $250.[36] Because seller-side fraud is a big issue with auctions, this was a radical move.

- In addition, Amazon invited a group of merchants to set up shop on its auction site.

The fee structure on the auction side is very similar to the Zshops fee structure described previously. The biggest challenge in this arena was to find a way to topple the giant, eBay. Table C1.6 shows that Amazon's auction venture was not very successful. eBay continues to dominate auctions.

International Growth

Even without opening web sites and distribution centers abroad, Amazon.com has consistently served a global audience. In July 1995, the company's customers came from forty-five different countries.[37] Currently, the company sells to over 150 countries.[38] As shown in Table C1.3, in the year 2000, about 13.8% of all revenues came from the international market. The company realized that closely targeting some markets could increase revenue even more.

Jeff Bezos said this about being a global seller:[39]

We got an order from somebody in Bulgaria, and this person sent us cash through the mail to pay for their order. And they sent us two crisp $100 bills. And they put these two $100 bills inside a floppy disk. And then they put a note on the cover of the floppy disk, and they mailed this whole thing to us. And the note on the cover of the floppy disk said, 'The money is inside the floppy disk. The customs inspectors steal the money, but they don't read English.' That shows you the effort to which people will go to be able to buy things.

As a result of global interest, in 1998, the company launched a site in Germany—Amazon.de—and a site in the UK—Amazon.co.uk, both of

which focused on books, music, and videos. The company adopted an acquisition strategy to achieve this goal. It acquired two European e-commerce sites in early 1998 (Telebuch in Germany and Bookpages in the United Kingdom) and then relaunched them as Amazon.com-branded sites. The sites had loyal followings, allowing the company to gain a customer base in these markets. To serve the markets, the company opened customer service centers in Slough, England; Resenburg, Germany; and in The Hague, and hired multilingual service representatives.[40]

Later, the company expanded into France[41] (April 2000) and Japan (November 2000). With the French, Japanese, and German stores, the company was forced to deal with creating content in local languages. In addition, with international expansion, the company had to become sensitive to local cultures.

Amazon.com Technology

In the ultimate analysis, the true core competence of Amazon may be its technology and the web site that manifests it. First, Amazon took a fundamentally different approach to developing an online store. As described by Salon.com's Scott Rosenberg

Five years ago, entrepreneurs thought the way to duplicate the retail experience online was to build

Table C1.6
Top Auction Sites Ranked by Revenue Share, May 2001 (U.S.)

	Auction Site*	Revenue Share	Satisfaction Rate	Conversion Rate
1.	eBay.com**	64.30%	8.42	22.50%
2.	uBid.com	14.70%	7.87	11.00%
3.	Egghead.com (Onsale.com)	4.00%	7.75	8.00%
4.	Yahoo! Auctions	2.40%	7.84	4.40%
5.	Amazon Auctions	2.00%	7.64	6.50%

*Auction sites do not include travel related sites.
**Figures for eBay.com do not include figures for Half.com.
***All revenue figures are for May 2001.
Source: Reproduced with permission. © NetRatings, Inc. 2001. All rights reserved.

AMAZON.COM—A BUSINESS HISTORY: CASE 1

virtual replicas of physical stores: The theory was that you had to orient users spatially; the Holy Grail was the 3-D walk-through. Amazon never went down that path. Its founder, Jeff Bezos, and his talented crew of site builders seemed to understand from Day 1 that information organized thoughtfully can create its own experience—one entirely different from the familiar store geography of aisles and shelves. They started with a vast but bare database of books in print and kept adding new layers of valuable information to it.[42]

Second, Amazon pioneered new ways to enhance the shopping experience. Here is a partial list of their innovations:

- One-click shopping. Amazon.com recognized that one of the most important ways in which it could increase value was to reduce the transactional burden on customers. If the company could remember all of the relevant information about the customer, the individual could breeze through the ordering process. This also established switching costs, making it irksome to switch to other online stores that may or may not have any given customer's information. In a controversial move, the company also obtained a patent on its one-click shopping system and successfully stalled its usage by its rival—bn.com.[43]

- Product review information. All products on Amazon can be reviewed. Publishers provide editorial reviews for books, but for all products, customer reviews are available. Moreover, customers can rate each other's reviews: a rating figure is placed against each review to help customers decide whether to read it.

- Purchase circles. Suppose you are interested in learning about the books being read by your rival firm or scientists at MIT—Amazon provides you a means to do this. In the company's words:[44]

We group the items we send to particular zip and postal codes, and the items ordered from each domain name. We then aggregate this anonymous data and apply an algorithm that constructs bestseller lists of items that are more popular with each specific group than with the general population. No personally identifiable information is used to create purchase circle lists. The regularity with which a purchase circle is updated depends on its size and the activity of a purchase circle group. Large purchase circles are updated weekly; smaller ones are updated monthly.

- E-mail alerts. Amazon allows consumers to keep tabs on their favorite author or musician. Individuals can enter the name of their favorite author, for example, and when that person's next book comes along, Amazon e-mails the customer with an alert—in some cases, before the book is available to the public.

- Recommendations. The company uses collaborative filtering and other personalization techniques to recommend books and music to users. The company remembers the name of each customer and the web site greets each individual as he or she logs in. Then, when the user picks a book, the system recommends a few other books that may be of interest, encouraging users to browse and buy more than they had originally intended.

- Wish list. Each individual can create a wish list of items he or she would like to acquire. This list is public so that a friend or acquaintance could order and send you the items you want.

- The page you made. The web site creates a special page of recently viewed portions of the site. Consumers who have forgotten something that they looked at a few minutes ago can go to this page to locate it.

These innovations resulted in Amazon's leadership role. Table C1.7 shows that Amazon dominates others in multiple product categories based on how well it serves its customers.

Amazon.com is the Leader: Top E–Tailers in Books, Toys, Videos, and Music (Max. score possible is 10)

	Books (Spring 2000)		Toys (Fall 2000)		Videos (Summer 2000)		Music (Summer 2000)	
1	Amazon.com	8.66	Amazon.com	8.02	Amazon.com	8.40	Amazon.com	8.16
2	barnesandnoble.com	7.63	SmarterKids.com	7.99	BUY.COM	8.25	CheckOut	7.67
3	BUY.COM	7.50	ZanyBrainy.com	7.33	CDNOW	7.73	BUY.COM	7.51
4	Borders.com	7.38	KBkids.com	7.06	Express.com	7.58	Barnes	7.47
5	Booksamillion	7.35	Wal-Mart	6.33	800.com	7.29	CDNOW	7.24
6	fatbrain.com	6.71	NuttyPutty.com	6.30	CheckOut Enter.	7.25	SamGoody	6.89
7	Wal-Mart	6.60	JC Penney	5.73	Blockbuster	7.03	Tower	6.86
8	gohastings.com	5.92	Target	5.61	Bigstar.com	6.90	Express.com	6.85
9	varsitybooks.com	5.83	FAO Schwarz	5.56	Borders.com	6.86	ARTISTdirect.com	6.45
10	BookBuyer Outlet	5.43			SamGoody.com	6.83	MuZic	6.31

Source: Gomez.com, accessed July 27th 2001.

The 2001 Holiday Shopping Season and Amazon's First Profit

Amazon.com reasserted its dominance in the e-tailing sector during the 2001 holiday season. According to Nielsen's Net Ratings, it was the number one site in terms of the total number of unique visitors during the month of November 2001—about 31 million. It was followed by Yahoo! Shopping with 27 million and eBay with about 26 million.

Moreover, as shown in Table C1.8, Amazon.com ranked among the top ten fastest growing e-tailers, which was significant because this list usually has e-tailers who do not make the top ten list in terms of total traffic.

Buoyed by this dominant performance, Amazon.com posted its first quarterly profit of $5.8 million in the fourth quarter of 2001. According to Bezos, the most important factor in achieving this milestone may have been the reduction in prices.[45]

Without a question, it was the very significant reduction in prices that we put in place in the fourth quarter [that contributed most to profits]. We had always had low prices, but in the fourth quarter we really lowered prices—for example, 30% off on books over $20. That had a substantial effect on volume. You can't do that until you have the operating efficiency to afford to do it. We just saw it a little bit faster than we expected.

Other factors helped, such as a favorable exchange rate with the Euro, lower fulfillment costs (down 17% from previous year), and better inventory management.[46] The company has made great improvements in operations and shipped 35% more items with the same number of employees. This feat was achieved by farming out the fulfillment operations of certain products.

Table C1.8

Top Ten Fastest Growing E-tailers in the 2001 Holiday Shopping Season, U.S., Combined Home and Work

		Shopping Trips, Nov.–Dec. 2000, in thousands	Shopping Trips, Nov.–Dec. 2001, in thousands	% change
1	Columbia House	7,958	25,386	219.0
2	Fingerhut.com	3,300	8,051	144.0
3	Overstock.com	6,215	12,894	107.5
4	Officedepot.com	5,222	10,003	91.6
5	Apple.com	10,322	17,642	70.9
6	Bestbuy.com	13,735	22,389	63.0
7	hp.com	17,043	26,067	53.0
8	Staples.com	5,609	8,509	51.7
9	Amazon.com	133,197	198,822	49.3
10	Circuitcity.com	6,346	8,950	41.0

After posting this profit, the company quickly announced that it may not make quarterly profits again for a while. Retailers pay out suppliers in the first quarter of the year and demand slackens, making it tough to turn a profit in this quarter. Amazon also carries about $2.2 billion in long-term debt that is expected to place a heavy burden. The company may have overinvested in distribution and some experts note that only 40% of warehouse capacity is being used. Some, citing the reduced expenditure on marketing as evidence, worry that the company has sacrificed too much growth in sales by starting to focus on profits.[47]

Amazon announced a free shipping deal in the same press release that touted its first quarterly profit. The company said that it would offer free shipping on any sale (on items other than toys, video games, baby products, and third-party goods) worth more than $99. Bezos has argued that, based on what the company knows about price elasticity, this offer may increase sales volume and the order size. However, critics quickly pointed out the greater price pressure this would place on a company that had barely come out of the red. Bezos is confident that costs can be cut further, leading to profits in the future; others are not as certain. Experts have pointed out that due to fine-print restrictions, a small proportion of consumers may benefit from this offer. From a competitive standpoint, bn.com already had such an offer and Buy.com quickly followed with a similar deal, so it is not clear whether Amazon will pick up market share from these retailers.

A Discussion of Amazon.com's Cumulative Losses

When the discussion has turned to Amazon's first quarterly profit, it is appropriate to revisit the reasons for the company's large cumulative losses: a deficit of over $1.4 billion dollars. The main arguments for the poor cumulative performance of the company:

1. *The company overspent on marketing and advertising.* Table C1.1 shows marketing expenses, which were as high as 16.33% of net sales in the year 1997 and had reduced to 10.72% in the year 1999. The company drasti-

cally reduced marketing expenses to about 6.52% of net sales in the year 2000 and to 4.43% of net sales in the year 2001.

Some critics argue that Amazon.com built a strong brand early on. As a result, the incremental sales as a result of the holiday advertising campaign were small and the company would have been closer to profitability if it had reduced marketing expenses sooner.

2. *Poor investments.* As indicated earlier, Amazon.com invested in a number of online retailing companies such as Drugstore.com, HomeGrocer.com, and Pets.com. Most of these investments did not pay off (Pets.com and Homegrocer.com/ Webvan are out of business) and the company wrote off about $135 million in the year 2000 alone.

3. *It grew too soon.* Amazon.com rapidly diversified into a number of product categories and added new services such as Zshops and auctions. The company may not have fully understood the impact on the cost structure as it added these products and services. Some observers have pointed out that with only the book, music, and video segments being profitable, the company may be forced to reevaluate other products.

4. *Technology features versus cost.* As described in the technology section, Amazon.com has introduced an amazing array of technologies on its web site. It has been an industry leader in this regard. Although developing these technologies in-house gives the company total control, it is expensive. Some observers have asked if Amazon would have been better off adding fewer features and controlling costs.

Conclusion

Amazon.com is a leader. As Table C1.7 shows, it stands head and shoulders above its competition in many categories.

However, the company stands at a critical juncture today. Profits have proven elusive. Jeff

Bezos has long argued that focusing on profits means giving up on growth opportunities and is not in the interest of the company. But recently he said, "This is the right time to focus on the fundamental economics of our business, even if it means sacrificing growth." He has promised to focus more on growth next year.[48]

Amazon has written off the vast majority of the money it invested in online firms. The company does not have adequate cash to operate for a long period of time, and it has accumulated a vast deficit. But Amazon is still making new acquisitions and forming new partnerships; it announced a key partnership with Target in September 2001. Target agreed to use Amazon.com technology for order fulfillment and customer care services on its Target.com, Marshall Fields.com, Mervyns.com, and GiftCatalog.com web sites.[49] It acquired the operations of the defunct Egghead.com on December 19, 2001, providing Amazon.com another channel to reach customers.[50] The company also announced a partnership with Circuit City on December 11, 2001,[51] through which customers can now place an order for an electronics item at Amazon.com and pick it up at their local Circuit City.

The company continues to add innovative features on its web site. It added the "millions of tabs" feature in September, giving customers their own tab completely customized to their needs. Amazon.com also added computers and e-books to its site.

One problem that analysts have identified is that the growth in the number of customers has slowed down. As one analyst has said, "Everyone who wanted to buy a book online has already heard of Amazon."[52] An expert within Amazon has come up with this solution: "Amazon should increase its holdings of best sellers and stop holding slow-selling titles."[53] He views this as the way to reduce costs and move toward profitability.

The company has attracted a $100-million investment from AOL, fueling speculation that this may be the first step toward a merger.[54] Moreover, there is some sentiment that the long-term future of the company may be as a technology provider. This speculation is based on the alliance with Toys "R" Us—Amazon runs the online storefront and Toys "R" Us controls inventory and logistics.

The future of the company is unwritten and will prove to be as interesting as its past.

Discussion Questions

1. What is the lasting legacy of Amazon.com?

2. What did Amazon.com get right and what did it get wrong?

3. Should Amazon have remained an online bookstore? Critically evaluate the arguments for and against quick diversification.

4. Can Amazon.com successfully compete with bricks-and-clicks stores such as Barnes & Noble?

5. Note from the financial statements that services (e.g., auctions, Zshops) represent a smaller proportion of the company's revenues in comparison to product sales and technology partnerships. What is the role for services in the long term for the company?

6. a. Using data from Table C1.1, plot net sales and loss from operations from 1997–2001 on one chart. What trends to you see?

   b. On one chart, using information from Table C1.1 plot:

      I. Marketing costs / revenue from 1997–2001.

      II. Fulfillment costs / revenue from 1997–2001.

      III. Technology and content costs / revenue from 1997–2001.

   How has the company changed its spending strategy over time?

7. You should be able to obtain the answers to these questions from the financial statement:

   - Debt is more risky to issue.

   - Equity is, in general, more costly to issue for the company than debt.

   a. Compute the ratio of operating income to sales, and gross profit to sales. See how these ratios have changed over time. Compare with bn.com and eBay.com. What do you learn from this?

   b. Compute the current ratio (current assets/current liabilities) and the quick ratio (current assets – inventories) / (current liabilities). See how these ratios have changed over time. Compare with bn.com and eBay.com. What do you learn from this?

   c. Study the accumulated deficit and how it has changed over time. How did Amazon.com fall into this perilous position?

   d. Monitor interest payments over time. How have they changed and what do we learn from that?

8. Several arguments have been provided for Amazon's lack of profitability. Using the financial statements, identify the ones that are most applicable.

9. Can small booksellers compete with a large site such as Amazon.com? What would you do if you were a small bookseller online?

10. Based on what we know, paint a picture of how Amazon.com will look in one year and in five years.

APPENDIX

Professor Ufuk Ince's Explanation of Amazon's Convertible Bond Issue

The choice between equity and debt is a fundamental question in practical, as well as theoretical, finance. We still do not know everything about this subject and it still maintains its place as a major research area. Some of the things we do know:

Several additional characteristics of these two financing choices make them attractive or unattractive compared to each other:

- Interest payments are tax deductible for the corporation and dividend payments are not. This makes debt more attractive than equity. This is true even for a nondividend paying company such as AMZN for reasons I skip here for brevity.

- An argument that is also empirically observed in favor of some debt: managers seem to work harder and waste less capital if they have a debt obligation that they have to meet at periodic intervals; it seems to discipline them.

- Even though some debt is good, when it gets too much, the risk of bankruptcy tends to outweigh the benefits of debt—even if the company never actually goes bankrupt. Customers do not like to deal with a company that may go bankrupt soon, and many employees do not like to work for one. Many such indirect costs make a heavy debt load dangerous.

The empirical observation is that debt level is highly industry-specific. Heavy manufacturing industries can usually live with much higher debt loads than service or high-tech industries that tend to have more intangible assets.

To understand the choice of AMZN in January 1999, let us look at the $1.25 billion issue in detail: This was not really a straight (plain-vanilla) debt issue. It was a hybrid (between debt and equity) security issue that is known as a convertible bond (CB). *In fact, it is the largest CB issue ever in the history of finance.* It was originally set to be a $500 million issue, but was later bumped up to $1.25 billion due to intense investor interest.

A CB pays interest every six months just like a regular bond issue, but it gives the investor who purchases it the option to convert it into (a certain number of) shares of stock of the same

company. That is, the bonds that require regular interest payments may turn into AMZN shares at some point in the future, at the investors' choosing.

The CB of AMZN was issued when its stock was trading at about the mid-$120s. It is a ten-year bond and is convertible to about six AMZN shares at any time from the date of issue until maturity. Of course, the investors will decide to convert only if the shares become more valuable than the bond itself. The stock price that makes the conversion profitable is $156 per share. This was about a 25% premium over where the stock was trading at the time of the issue. That is, the stock had to appreciate to $156 or above for the debt issue to become a stock issue. Another important feature of the AMZN CB was the rate of interest—4.75% annually.

Why would a company issue a CB instead of straight debt or equity? To understand this, one must realize that at the time of the issue, the company and the investors do not know what will happen with the stock price. The company may want to issue stock, but at the then current price of $120, it may have felt that the stock was undervalued. That is, if it were to issue stock at that time, it would have undersold the stake in the company, hurting or diluting existing stockholders' stake. By issuing a CB that would become stock at $156 dollar level, in effect, AMZN issues (pseudo) stock at the time it needs the cash (January 1999) and not at the low price of $120. When and if the market price appreciates in the future to and beyond $156 the bonds will turn into stock and the company will have issued stock at that higher price, but got the cash much earlier—when it needed it to finance its immense investment throughout 1999.

Why do investors buy into this scheme? Because they are betting that the stock will appreciate beyond $156, which would entitle them to get a piece of the action at $156 per share instead of whatever high-market price everyone else might be paying. Of course, we all know *now* that AMZN stock has never reached $156, and in fact plunged down to $17 in two-and-a-half years. That means the investors never got to convert their bonds into stock, and AMZN was not able to have stock issued at a higher price.

Does this mean AMZN and the investors made a huge mistake together? No, and that's the beauty of a CB issue—it is a contingent security. That is, because no one knows what will happen in the future, the contingent security takes care of possible future scenarios. What did the investors gain by buying a CB instead of stock? They did not get the upside potential because of

the stock price crash, but they did not completely lose either: they still have a piece of paper that keeps paying them real cash every six months. If they had AMZN shares, they would have twelve cents to the dollar of their original investment and no dividends whatsoever.

What did AMZN gain by issuing a CB instead of straight bonds? The interest rate is 4.75%, which is at least two percentage points lower than what a comparable ten-year Treasury Note was paying at the time. Thus, a company as risky and speculative as AMZN was able to borrow at two points less than the safest borrower; it got extremely cheap financing.

Notes

(All URLs are current as of March 10, 2002.)

1. Jeff Bezos, "A Bookstore By Any Other Name," July 27, 1998, <http://www.commonwealthclub.org/98-07bezos-speech.html>.

2. Joshua Cooper Ramo, "Amazing Person.com," 1999, <http://www.time.com/time/poy/intro.html>.

3. Robert Hof, "Q&A with Amazon's Jeff Bezos," March 26, 2001, <http://www.businessweek.com/magazine/content/01_13/b3725027.htm>.

4. Nina Gregory, "Of Amazonian Proportions," December 1999, <http://www.earthlink.net/partner/usaa/blink/dec99/celebrity.html>.

5. Jeff Bezos, "A Bookstore By Any Other Name," July 27, 1998.

6. William Taylor, "Who's Writing the Book on Web Business?," October 1996, <http://pf.fastcompany.com/online/05/starwave2.html>.

7. Amazon.com, 1999 Annual Report 10K, <http://www.edgar-online.com/bin/edgardoc/finSys_main.asp?dcn=0000891020-00-000622>, "About Amazon.com," Amazon.com web site, <http://www.amazon.com/exec/obidos/subst/misc/company-info.html/ref=gw_m_b_aa/105-5691616-3591150>.

8. Jeff Bezos, "A Bookstore By Any Other Name," July 27, 1998.

9. Tomothy M. Laseter, Patrick W. Houston, Joshua L. Wright, and Juliana Y. Park, "Amazon Your Industry: Extracting Value from the Value Chain," First Quarter 2000, <http://www.strategy-business.com/strategy/00109/page1.html>.

10. Robert Hof, "Amazon.com: The Wild World of Web Commerce," 1998, <http://www.businessweek.com/1998/50/b3608001.htm>.

11. Tomothy M. Laseter, Patrick W. Houston, Joshua L. Wright, and Juliana Y. Park, "Amazon Your Industry: Extracting Value from the Value Chain."

12. Robert Hof, "Amazon.com: The Wild World of Web Commerce."

13. "Amazon.com: Case Study," 1999, http://www.umich.edu/~cisdept/bba/320/1999/fall/amazon.html.

14. Adapted from BN.com 100 statement, April 2001.

15. Tomothy M. Laseter, Patrick W. Houston, Joshua L. Wright, and Juliana Y. Park, "Amazon Your Industry: Extracting Value from the Value Chain."

16. Richard Wiggins, "Of Jeff Bezos and Leo Durocher," 6(5), May 2001, <http://www.firstmonday.org/issues/issue6_5/wiggins/index.html>.

17. Ibid.

18. Amazon.com, 1999 Annual Report 10-K/A, page 5.

19. Robert Hof, "Amazon.com: The Wild World of Web Commerce."

20. The first quote is from Robert Hof, "Q&A with Amazon's Jeff Bezos," March 26, 2001, <http://www.businessweek.com/magazine/content/01_13/b3725027.htm>.

21. Richard Wiggins, "Of Jeff Bezos and Leo Durocher."

22. Tim Arango, "Amazon's Foe in Race to Profitability: The Middleman," June 4, 2001, <http://www.thestreet.com/_cnet/stocks/timarango/1449487.html>.

23. This entire discussion is based on Tim Arango, "Amazon's Foe in Race to Profitability: The Middleman," June 4, 2001, <http://www.thestreet.com/_cnet/stocks/timarango/1449487.html>.

24. Thanks to my student, Eng Lim, for pointing this out.

25. Staff reporter, "Amazon gets patent for affiliate program," Feb 27, 2000, <http://www.zdnet.com/zdnn/stories/news/0,4586,2449914,00.html?chkpt=zdnntop>.

26. Robert Hof, "Jeff Bezos: There's No Shift in the Model."

27. Compiled from various Amazon.com Press Releases.

28. Ibid.

29. Robert Hof, "Jeff Bezos: There's No Shift in the Model."

30. http://www.thestandard.com/article/0,1902,23702,00.html?body_page=1.

31. Amazon's Zshops Page, <http://www.amazon.com/exec/obidos/tg/browse/-/537918/102-0043307-5091367>.

32. Jeff Fisher and David Gardner, "Surprise! Meet the New Amazon," September 29, 1999, <http://www.fool.com/portfolios/rulebreaker/1999/rulebreaker990929.htm>.

33. Wired Editors, "Amazon.com and Beyond," July, 2000, <http://www.wired.com/wired/archive/8.07/bezos_pr.html>.

34. Robert Hof, "Online Auctions: Going, Going, Gone," 1999, <http://www.businessweek.com/1999/99_15/b3624066.htm>.

35. Ibid.

36. Amazon.com Press Release, "Amazon.com Launches Online Auction Site," March 30, 1999, <http://www.corporate-ir.net/ireye/ir_site.zhtml?ticker=AMZN&script=410&layout=8&item_id=232870>.

37. Diego Piacentini, "Case Study: Amazon.com," May 18, 2000, <http://usinfo.state.gov/topical/global/ecom/00051809.htm>.

38. Robert Hof, "The Crucial Mission: Provide Customers with What They Want," March 16, 1999, <http://www.businessweek.com/ebiz/9903/316bezos.htm>.

39. Ibid.

40. Diego Piacentini, "Case Study: Amazon.com."

41. Lori Enos, "Amazon Storms Into France," August 29, 2000, <http://www.ecommercetimes.com/perl/story/4142.html>.

42. Scott Rosenberg, "Miles of Aisles," May 21, 2001, <http://www.salon.com/tech/col/rose/2001/05/23/amazon/index.html>.

43. Scott Rosenberg, "Amazon to World: We Control How Many Times You Must Click!," December 21, 1999, <http://www.salon.com/tech/log/1999/12/21/bezos/index.html>.

44. Amazon.com Services Page, <http://www.amazon.com/exec/obidos/tg/stores/browse/-/help/468604/103-2854054-5173445>.

45. Douglas Harbrecht, "Jeff Bezos: Amazon is Something Genuinely New," Jan 28, 2002, <http://www.businessweek.com/bwdaily/dnflash/jan2002/nf20020128_0062.htm>.

46. Robert Hof, "How Amazon Cleared the Profitability Hurdle," February 4, 2002, <http://www.businessweek.com/magazine/content/02_05/b3768079.htm>.

47. Heather Green, "How Hard Should Amazon Swing?," Jan 14, 2002, <http://www.businessweek.com/magazine/content/02_02/b3765097.htm>.

48. Saul Hansell, "A Front-Row Seat As Amazon Gets Serious," nytimes.com, May 20, 2001.

49. Amazon.com Press Release, "Target and Amazon.com Team to Advance E-commerce Initiatives," September 11, 2001, <http://www.corporate-ir.net/ireye/ir_site.zhtml?ticker=AMZN&script= 410&layout=8&item_id=229577>.

50. Beth Cox, "Amazon Relaunches Egghead.com," December 19, 2001, <http://www.internetnews.com/ ec-news/article/0,,4_942931,00.html>.

51. Amazon.com Press Release, "Amazon.com to Further Expand Electronics Selection and Provide In-store Pickup at Circuit City Stores; to Launch in Time for Holiday Shopping," 2001, <http://www. corporate-ir.net/ireye/ir_site.zhtml?ticker=AMZN&script=410&layout=8&item_id=201929>.

52. Saul Hansell, "AOL Invests $100 million in Amazon.com," July 24, 2001, <http://www.nytimes.com/ 2001/07/24/technology/ebusiness/24AMAZ.html>.

53. Saul Hansell, "A Front-Row Seat As Amazon Gets Serious."

54. Saul Hansell, "AOL Invests $100 million in Amazon.com."

boo.com

The Failure of Boo.com: Case 2

Introduction

Boo.com was one of the most anticipated e-tailing sites around the world. The company was attempting to become a fashion merchandise seller in several different markets, with the dream of creating a global brand.

Surprisingly, after a glitzy launch during the end of 1999, Boo.com announced in mid-May 2000 that it had put the company's assets up for liquidation. During a period of one year, the company had spent $135 million with spectacularly poor results.[1] By April 1999, gross sales were only $500,000 a month, and Boo.com was spending $1 million more than it was earning every week. Only $500,000 of the initial investment remained.[2]

The demise of Boo.com stands as a spectacular landmark in the history of e-commerce. AOL vice president of e-commerce, Patrick Gates, said,[3] "Boo.com was one of the big reality checks for everyone. I don't think any of us were surprised specifically. I sensed that there would be some issues there based on the product mix and sort of high-flying technology. But that one made a lot of people look back and go, 'Wow.'"

The event contributed in large measure to dire predictions about B2C commerce and to widespread pessimism about the dot-com revolution. Soon after the closure of Boo.com, The Gartner Group, for example, announced that up to 95% of e-tailers could go out of business by mid-2001.[4] Similarly, Price Waterhouse Coopers announced that one in four British online firms would run out of cash by 2000.[5] Boo.com's failure also led to a widespread sentiment that selling apparel on the Web would not succeed, which forced even online retailers that had made steady progress, such as Dressmart.com, to fold.[6]

In addition to its historic significance, an analysis of Boo.com offers rich insights into everything that should be avoided when launching an e-tailing business. Analyzing the company reveals serious flaws on many fronts—from its web site design to its promotion to its grandiose strategic ambition.

Background

Boo.com was founded by two Swedish entrepreneurs: Kajsa Leander, a fashion model, and Ernst Malmsten. Before Boo.com, they had created the Swedish Internet bookstore bokus.com in 1997 and sold it the following year. Boo.com was backed by Paris-based Europ@web, the private investment company of LVMH Chairman Bernard Arnault; 21 Investimenti of Italy, the private investment company of the Benetton family; Bain Capital Inc. of Boston; and the New York investment firm Goldman Sachs & Co.[7]

Boo.com first announced that it would launch by the end of May 1999; however, due to software problems, the web site actually launched in November 1999. The company failed to meet its sales targets by January 2000. It fired 100 staff members and reduced its product prices by up to 40%. In May 2000, Rob Shepherd quit as chief technology officer, the third high-level personnel loss in a month. Finally, on May 17, 2000, after failed attempts at selling the site to other retailers and trying to get more funding from the shareholders, Boo.com announced that it was shutting down.

The rights to the name Boo.com were acquired by Fashionmall.com for 250,000 British pounds.[8] In February 2001, Boo.com recast itself as a fashion and style portal that provided fashion advice and reviews. It also provided links to small boutiques where customers could go to buy the products.[9] The new site was also less data-intensive making downloading easier.[10]

An Analysis of Firm Strategy

Ernst Malmsten, a cofounder, said, "We have been too visionary."[11] As implausible as it may sound, this statement may provide us a glimpse at the flaw in the firm's strategy.

Boo.com believed in the big-splash theory of firm strategy. The firm wanted to be a global fashion super retailer. The company hoped to have a major presence in multiple prominent fashion markets—at one point, it had offices in London, New York, Munich, Stockholm, Paris, and Amsterdam.[12] It aimed to leverage the power of the Internet by serving brands that were local powerhouses or global superstars to the consumers in these markets. And it intended to provide access to consumers in different multiple languages and transact business in multiple currencies.

The vision for the firm can be summarized in one word: grandiose. Although this strategy can be faulted on many counts, envisioning a global reach is not in itself a mistake. It is, however, problematic to hope to achieve that all at once. Because the company's web site was launched simultaneously in several countries, the firm had to ensure that it had an effective presence in all of those countries. As a result, its resources were spread thin. The company may have been better served by starting small and spreading out over time.

The company also failed to consider those companies with strong brand names (e.g., Land's End, Nordstrom) that had already established strong presences in the markets that they wished to attack. Many of these companies had a long history in these markets due to catalog or bricks-and-mortar operations. Consequently, they had an advantage in resources, as well as in brand name.

Boo.com furthermore chose a product category, fashion goods, that is hard to sell on the Internet. Individuals like to touch and feel the fabric, try on a dress, and experience the product firsthand before buying it. In spite of these challenges, companies such as Land's End are successfully selling apparel online today by using systems such as virtual dressing rooms. Although Boo.com had a lot of functionality on its web site, it did not adequately focus on the functionality that could best help its consumers.

The global vision for the company led to several execution problems. An ex-employee described a few.[13]

Multiple Currencies

If you want to trade globally, you can't only offer US dollars. As a result, you need to figure out a way to handle multiple currencies ranging from dollars to pounds to francs, to deutschmarks, to kroners, etc. . . . If you are planning on doing this well, you have to peg your prices to a particular value. However, you have to realize that prices are not the same in every country and what may seem expensive in the US can be seen as cheap in other countries. This is where you have to make a decision as to whether you want to set a fixed price in the local currency or set a more dynamic price that is affected by currency exchanges and other fluctuations. It's a fascinating problem in and of itself but it's one that we discovered to be a big pain to deal with. In the end, Boo built a system that allowed us to set a different price for each country or set a single price for all countries and have that price be translated in the proper currency based on a set exchange rate. It was a bit of a kludge but it worked and, to this day, I haven't seen an Ecommerce shop with a similar system.

A global e-tailer must worry about optimally setting prices in multiple markets. One price is not valid across all markets; the price must be have underestimated the cost of achieving this on the Web.

On-the-Fly Tax Calculation

This one almost killed me. In the US, it's relatively easy to deal with taxation. For the most part, the only taxes you have to pay are for states in which you have a physical presence. Where it gets tricky is when your servers are located in one area and your offices are in another. Technically, that is two locations. In the case of Boo, it got worse. For example, a sale to France was taxed three ways. Why? Quite simply because the company had offices in Paris, its servers were located in London, UK and its distribution center was in Cologne, Germany. However, the interesting part of the problem was that we were making a sale but not delivering a good in the UK, delivering a good but not making a sale in Germany, and making a sale and delivering a good in France. This was just one example. Multiply that by the number of countries the company was doing business in and it soon got VERY complicated. Add to that the fact that certain goods were coming from China or Taiwan and the picture got so clouded that we had to bring in tax attorneys to help us on the details.

The Web has certainly complicated the matters of international taxation. To this day, there is no consistent set of global rules on taxation and the laws in this area are still emerging. Clearly, international coordination is necessary to solve some of these problems. Boo.com's vision was perhaps premature.

Integration with Multiple Fulfillment Partners

The main issue here was dealing with different file formats for DeutschePost (the European fulfillment company) and UPS (the company that did fulfillment for the US). What we ended up doing was create an EDI link to those guys (Deutsche-Post was not web-enabled yet) and create a set of filters for each of them. A simple answer to a simple problem but this little answer cost about

set for each market in terms of the buying power of the market, its market size, and so forth. In addition, e-tailers must worry about the signals that the prices send. Price signals quality in the fashion business, and maintaining a consistent position across nations is certainly an important objective. All in all, developing a system that allowed them to set prices in multiple ways across countries was certainly one achievement of Boo.com.

Multiple Languages

First of all, forget translation software packages. They are still relatively immature and there is (at this point anyway) little hope that they will mature much beyond their current point in the near future. If you've taken any linguistics course, you know that grammatical rules can hardly be standardized for several languages. For example, something as simple as a verb can become a whole new set of problems. In English, there is a relatively small set of basic rules. The verb "to want" breaks down into "I want, you want, he wants, we want, you want, they want." Notice that there are only two basic variations here. In French, the same verb "vouloir" breaks down as follows: "Je veux, tu veux, il veut, nous voulons, vous voulez, ils veulent." In this case, there are 5 different variations. In Spanish, it's six … and so on. Take that problem and try to automate it and you are building a system that is bound to fail. The way we worked around it at Boo was to create a system where the copy was translated by hand by people who were fluent in the language. Unfortunately, another problem cropped up: British English and American English are EXTREMELY different. Considering that the assumption was that one version of each language was sufficient, problems cropped up and some of the perfectly normal British English stuff ended up being very offensive in the US. THAT was a major problem.

On the one hand, to be accepted by markets in different countries, the content has to be in different languages. Moreover, the language and product selection must be sensitive to the local cultures in order to truly appeal. Boo.com may

131

150 man hours of work as the content had to be migrated from the old (untagged) setup to the new one. Because the original database was originally set up wrong, we had to totally reorganize the schema and refit the content into it.

Working with multiple fulfillment partners can lead to new levels of complexity because the company has to work with different systems and cultures.

Problems with the Web Site

Boo.com had spectacular problems with its web site when it first launched. The site was designed with excessive graphics, movies, audio, and video. Examples of such features included short movies that featured the brands for sale and a personal shopping assistant called Miss Boo who made remarks to assist shoppers. They tended to see Miss Boo as an annoyance because of the irrelevance of her comments. For example, when a user clicked on the Acupuncture Deep Greco Fashion Velcro shoe, Miss Boo popped up exclaiming: "Tie me up, tie me down in a shoe that looks like it's been attacked by Gulliver's Lilliputians."[15]

Every product on the Boo.com web site had a 3-D image. Photographing the products to create these images cost up to half a million dollars a month.[16]

A company spokesperson explained, saying, "We realize we're selling clothing. But we're selling a lifestyle item, not a commodity, so we wanted to build a different type of experience. Some of it is around rich graphics, some of it is around rich elements of design. In some cases, this was

not ideal for the customer experience. So we're taking this information and trying to make it better."[17] However, an analyst for Forrester Research rightly points out[18] that this was the wrong strategy for web site design at the time because "99% of European and 98% of US homes lacked the high-bandwidth access needed to fully benefit from the site." The company rolled out a site for low-bandwidth users in February 2000, but the target market had already been alienated. Moreover, Boo.com was built using Macromedia's Flash program, which at the point of the launch, was loaded on the computers of only a small proportion of the population.

The initial response to the web site was awful. An article in the *Wall Street Journal* reported:[19]

Perhaps the most telling sign of what went wrong can be found in a statement made by cofounder, Ms. Leander,[14] "We kind of forgot about the consumer." In other words, the company's grandiose vision was not put in place with the explicit intention of serving consumers and providing them value—that was a secondary purpose! Businesses often fail when they forget the consumer.

On Day 1, according to Boo, only 50% of consumers who typed in the address www.boo.com actually made it onto the site. There were a variety of reasons: The site didn't run on some combinations of browser software and hardware, particularly Macintoshes. The abundance of graphics and animation made it extremely slow, even for customers with high-speed connections. Many of those with low-bandwidth connections found it impossible to access the site, or simply gave up, Boo says. And, worst of all, those who did manage to make it onto the site were unable to purchase anything because of a glitch in the checkout process that unexpectedly returned customers to the opening screen just before the transaction was completed.

A web-site reviewer for the *Wall Street Journal* coined a new term, "Boo rage." She reported that she had spent three hours attempting to order a skirt.[20] Also, "the first 17 times I tried to submit my order, my browser crashed. I also endured pages that took forever to download, was randomly tossed off of the site, and was besieged by a ridiculous number of questions when registering."

The Web usability guru Jakob Nielsen wrote this scathing review in December 1999.[21]

In general, Boo.com became a victim of Internet time. Businesses move faster in Internet time; e-tailing systems take much longer to develop. In this case, the web site was not fully designed when it was launched, which meant changes had to be made in public, reducing consumer confidence.

The Badly Designed Advertising Campaign

Another problem faced by Boo.com was that it overspent on advertising early on. It created a great deal of consumer interest, but then the web site launch was delayed by about five months, during which time, consumers finally got fed up.

Anticipating a May 1999 launch, Boo.com announced a two-year $65 million advertising budget after hiring the London ad agency BMP DDB. The agency created a campaign showing geeky kids playing sports in cool clothes that would be available from Boo.com.[22]

According to Marina Galanti, the second marketing director, when the launch got delayed, the ad campaign was modified to make it "more about mood and attitude and less about sports." The launch was rescheduled for July and teaser ads began running in magazines. However, teaser ad campaigns work only when the firm knows exactly when the final product is going to be available. In this case, the tease campaign backfired because the site did not launch until November 1999. It also placed the spotlight on the company while it was still tinkering with the web site.

The company believed in going on an all-out blitz rather than building the business gradually. As described in a *Wall Street Journal* article,[23] "the company launched press, television, cinema and outdoor campaigns in six countries and expanded to nine others, spending about $25 million—much of it still owed to the agencies that created and executed the ads."

Boo.com takes itself too seriously. Instead of making it easy to shop, the site insists on getting in your face with a clumsy interface. It's as if the site is more intent on making you notice the design than on selling products. Boo should be congratulated, though, on running a site that supports 18 countries equally well in terms of both language and shipping.

Screen Pollution

Boo insists on launching several of its own windows. My own browser window is left with the message "Nothing happens on this page, except that you may want to bookmark it." Fat chance, especially since the windows forced upon me are frozen and can't be adapted to my window or font preferences.

This site is simply slow and unpleasant. All product information is squeezed into a tiny window, with only about one square inch allocated to the product description. Since most products require more text than will fit in this hole, Boo requires the user to use a set of non-standard scroll widgets to expose the rest of the text, 20 words at a time. Getting to a product requires precise manipulation of hierarchical menus followed by pointing to minuscule icons and horizontal scrolling. Not nice.

Miss Boo, the Shopping Assistant

She is prettier than Microsoft's Bob but just as annoying. Web sites do need personality, but in the form of real humans with real opinions and real advice. I prefer the interactive content experiments in the site's magazine section, such as a feature on the similarities between stone-age living and some current fashion products.

What's a Boobag?

It's a shopping cart, actually, and unlike other carts it contains miniature photos of your products. It is also possible to drape the items on a mannequin to see how they look as an outfit, though too much dragging and low-level interface manipulation is required.

After setting grandiose expectations, Boo.com seemed to have faltered in its marketing strategy. Panicked by low sales, the company abandoned its image as a high-end retailer and started offering huge discounts—but without modifying its advertising.[24]

It seemed to some that the company had simply not catered to its target market and had failed to make a connection. Simon Mathews, managing director of Optimedia International, a media planning firm, said, "Boo.com's advertising strategy was emblematic of what was wrong with its business." The focus was on showboating instead of selling a product with clear substance. They never gave people a real reason to buy their clothes."[25]

Poor Management Quality

Boo.com has also been criticized for poor management quality. The firm had few management controls and many of the personnel were consultants with little relevant business experience.[26] The company is also said to have been too enamored with the fashion industry: senior managers were rewarded with five-star hotels and first-class airline tickets to attend fashion shows in cities such as Paris and Milan. Early employees were also rewarded with Palm Pilots and other perks.[27]

But the poor management went further than simple extravagance, as an ex-employee recounts.[28]

When I joined the company in August, the launch was behind schedule by three months and we had ten weeks to the Xmas season. The first thing I asked to see was the project plan. It didn't exist. People were working on bits and pieces of the project without communicating with other people they were affecting. Within a week, we put together a MS-project chart and things started to move properly.

Lack of communications to and from the top was definitely a problem as well as a lack of understanding of Internet time. . . .

Boo.com set out to do too many things and ended up doing none of them. The site was designed to create an immersive online retailing experience, but most users did not have broadband connectivity to benefit from it. The ad campaign built traffic to the site when it was not up. The management quality was poor and in the end, Boo's failure did not particularly surprise anyone who had worked for or with the company. Future attempts at building a global online apparel retailer will surely learn from the experiences of Boo.

The Future

Boo.com failed to create an immersive retailing experience online. The question for the future is will it ever be possible? Some studies now show that online users respond more to text than to pictures, which seems to support the approach taken by Amazon.com. But the jury is still out on this question.

Discussion Questions

1. Was Boo.com doomed more by its faulty strategy or by its poor implementation?

2. Can apparel ever be sold successfully on the Web? How about other fashion products such as jewelry and perfume?

3. What can the Web add to apparel sales that a catalog cannot?

4. What is the appropriate way to use graphics when designing a web site?

5. Was Boo.com just ahead of its time? Will there ever be a global online retailer?

6. Will the impending broadband revolution help sites that want to create an immersive retail experience online?

Notes

(All URLs are current as of March 15, 2002.)

1. Keith Regan and Macaluso, "Boo.com Saga Ends with Asset Sale," *E-commerce Times*, May 30, 2000.

2. Bryan Glick, "Boo.com's Fall Makes Realism the Fashion," May 24, 2000, <http://www.vnunet.com/Analysis/1102339>.

3. John Weisman, "The Making of E-Commerce: 10 Key Moments, Part II," August 23, 2000, <http://www.ecommercetimes.com/news/articles2000/000823-1.shtml>.

4. Tiffany Kary, "Dot-com Bankruptcies: Who Will Survive?," September 29, 2000, <http://www.zdnet.com/ecommerce/stories/main/0,10475,2635323,00.html>.

5. Bryan Glick, "Boo.com's Fall Makes Realism the Fashion."

6. Mick Brady, "The Web's Touchy-Feely Fashion Challenge," August 28, 2000, <http://www.ecommercetimes.com/perl/story/4131.html>.

7. Cate T. Corcoran, "E-Commerce (A Special Report). Industry by Industry—More Than Style: Fashion sites need to be exciting and stylish; And, as this tale of two ventures shows, they also need to be practical," *Wall Street Journal*, April 17, 2000, R 68.

8. Karen Holloway, "Boo.com Reborn as Lifestyle Portal," October 30, 2000, <http://www.karenholloway.com/boo.htm>.

9. John Parker, "Boo.com Reborn," *Traffic World*, 265(9) (2001):23.

10. Scott Tillett, "It's Back from the Dead: Boo.com," *Internet Week*, 834 (2000):11.

11. John Weisman, "The Making of E-Commerce: 10 Key Moments, Part II," August 23, 2000, <http://www.ecommercetimes.com/news/articles2000/000823-1.shtml>.

12. Erik Portanger and Stephanie Gruner, "Boo.com to Move Into Receivership As Funds Dry Up," *Wall Street Journal*, (2000): B16.

13. Tristan Louis, "What I Learned at Boo.com," May 19, 2000, <http://www.tnl.net/newsletter/2000/boobust.asp>.

14. Corcoran, "E-Commerce (A Special Report)."

15. Corcoran, "E-Commerce (A Special Report)."

16. Bryan Glick, "Boo.com's Fall Makes Realism the Fashion."

17. Corcoran, "E-Commerce (A Special Report)."

18. John Cassy and Mary O'Hara, "It All Ends in Tears at Boo.com," May 19, 2000, <http://www.shopping unlimited.co.uk/newsandviews/story/0,5804,222624,00.html>.

19. Corcoran, "E-Commerce (A Special Report)."

20. Andrea Petersen, "Watching the Web: Buzzkill," *Wall Street Journal*, November 11, 1999, B, 19:5.

21. Jakob Nielsen, "Boo's Demise," May 2000, <http://www.useit.com/alertbox/20000528_boo.html>.

22. Sarah Ellison, "Boo.com: Buried by Badly Managed Buzz," *Wall Street Journal*, May 23, 2000, B10.

23. Ibid.

24. Ibid.

25. Ibid.

26. John Cassy and Mary O'Hara, "It All Ends in Tears at Boo.com."

27. Erik Portanger and Stephanie Gruner, "Boo.com to Move Into Receivership As Funds Dry Up."

28. Tristan Louis, "What I Learned at Boo.com."

eBay–A Business History: Case 3

Introduction

eBay is a vibrant gathering place where consumers can sell anything to interested buyers. Items sold include Harley Davidsons, cars, antique vases, stamps, coins, dolls, Beanie Babies, jewelry, computers, software, concert tickets, and cameras. The list is endless.

Meg Whitman, the current CEO, described the nature of the company in this way:[1]

We think of eBay as a global, online trading company. That might sound foreign, but that's because we really did create something entirely new that took unique advantage of the Internet. It connects many-to-many every single day. You can come to eBay to buy or sell practically anything in both the auction format and most recently, with the acquisition of Half.com, in the fixed-price format. Every day thousands and thousands of people come to buy and sell, everything from Beanie Babies to cars to skis.

eBay views itself as an intermediary that helps buyers meet sellers. Making that match makes money for eBay. And because sellers ship the items directly to the buyers, eBay does not have any distribution or fulfillment costs, which gives it a tremendous advantage.

One way to think of eBay is as a giant "classified advertisement" page. Individuals can advertise an item that they want to sell for a price and buyers can contact the sellers directly, eBay is also considered an auction house, because buyers bid on items and the highest bidder wins.

Some have also described the company as a large swap meet or yard sale where people buy directly the sellers.

eBay is one of the best recognized online brands today. Table C3.1 shows that by August 1999, the company rated third behind Amazon.com and Priceline.com in a survey of online brands. Even at that early date, more than 46% of the American population had become aware of the brand. It is no wonder that eBay is now a household name in the United States and in many corners of the globe.

Background

Kevin Pursglove, the senior director of communications, describes the fascinating story of eBay's formation:[2]

There's a great Silicon Valley story here about a gentleman named Pierre Omidyar. He was working as a software developer here in Silicon Valley, and he had always been fascinated by how you can establish marketplaces to buy and sell goods and services. He had also been fascinated by how you can bring together fragmented audiences.

Because of his interest in the Internet, and his background in software, he developed a software program that allowed people, in one spot, to list items of various interest and various degrees. It allowed people to be able to come to that very same site and look at what's for sale and bid on and buy those items. He used the auction process as the method for establishing how merchandise is valued and eventually how it is exchanged between buyer and seller.

A key component that prompted him to do this was at the time his fiancée—now wife—was inter-

Table C3.1
Top Ten Online Brands

		August 1999		Spring 1999	
---	Brand	Percent Awareness	Million adults	Percent Awareness	Million adults
1	Amazon.com	60.10	117.8	51.70	101.3
2	Priceline.com	55.40	108.6	46.50	91.1
3	eBay	46.40	90.9	32.20	63.1
4	E*Trade	43.80	85.8	29.90	58.6
5	eToys	26.20	51.3	21.60	42.3
6	HotJobs	26.00	50.9	17.60	34.5
7	Monster.com	24.10	47.2	17.40	34.1
8	AutobyTel	22.60	44.3	17.90	35.0
9	CDNow	20.20	39.6	17.20	33.7
10	Reel.com	19.40	38.0	14.90	29.2

Source: Michael Pastore, "Top Online Brands Becoming Household Names," 1999, http://cyberatlas.internet.com/markets/retailing/article/0,,6061_189911,00.html. Copyright 2002 INT Media Group, Incorporated. All rights reserved.

ested in her Pez (dispenser) collection. She was experiencing a frustration that many collectors have experienced, and that is often times when you're collecting a particular item or you have a passion for a particular hobby, your ability to buy and trade or sell with other people of similar interests is limited by geographical considerations. Or if you trade through a trade publication, often volunteers produce those publications, and the interval between publications can often run several weeks if not months.

All of that was shortened down when Pierre, at the prompting of his wife and her interest in Pez dispenser collections, used his interest in fragmented markets and efficient marketplaces as a laboratory for what eventually became eBay.

Services Offered by eBay

The company started with the basic auction service. It now offers a variety of services:

- *Billpoint.* One of the big challenges in an online auction environment is to ensure that the sellers are paid for the item that has been auctioned. eBay has created an online bill payment service in collaboration with Wells Fargo Bank that facilitates credit card payments between buyers and sellers. Buyers also are free to use other services such as Paypal.

- *Half.com.* One of the biggest uses of eBay is to sell previously owned merchandise; however, such merchandise does not have to be sold in an auction format. Half.com fills this gap by providing previously owned items in a fixed-price format.

- *eBay International.* eBay has consciously tried to create a global marketplace. Even though users from other countries may bid on U.S. auctions, the legal and financial barriers prevent easy trading. To overcome this, eBay now has country-specific sites in Austria, Australia, Canada, France, Germany, Ireland, Italy, Japan, Korea, New Zealand, Switzerland, and the United Kingdom.

- *eBay Motors.* In addition to used cars, this site features motorcycles and auto parts. The company has created a unique trading environment with such services as financing, inspections, escrow, auto insurance, vehicle shipping, title and registration, and a "lemon" check (e.g., a check for defective products).

- *eBay Stores.* eBay Stores expands the marketplace for sellers by allowing them to create customized shopping destinations to merchandise their items on eBay. For buyers, eBay Stores represents a convenient way to access sellers' goods and services. Buyers who shop at eBay Stores are able to make immediate, multiple-item purchases using either a fixed-price or auction-style format.

- *eBay Professional Services.* Professional Services on eBay serves the fast-growing but fragmented small business marketplace by providing a destination on eBay to find professionals and freelancers for all kinds of business needs such as web design, accounting, writing, and technical support.

- *eBay Local Trading.* eBay has local sites in sixty markets in the United States. These sites feature items that are located nearby. As a result, buyers pay low shipping rates—especially for difficult-to-ship items such as automobiles, furniture, or appliances.

- *eBay Premier.* This is a specialty site on eBay that showcases fine art, antiques, fine wines, and rare collectibles from leading auction houses and dealers around the world. Through its "Premier Guarantee" program, all sellers on eBay Premier stand behind and guarantee the authenticity of their items.

- *eBay Live Auctions.* This feature allows consumers to participate in auctions being conducted by the world's leading auction houses.

In addition, the company has sponsored special auctions. For example, after the tragedy of September 11, 2001, eBay sponsored the "Auction for America." Rather than paying the seller, the proceeds from the purchase of any listed item went automatically to a charity of the buyer's choice. The company challenged its users to raise $100 million in 100 days and started the campaign by making a donation of $1 million.

Why Is eBay Unique?

Even early on, eBay had a completely different view of the world and the Internet and how it applied to retailing. While most companies were interested in opening online stores where they could sell products to consumers, Pierre Omidyar was interested in creating a trading community. As Omidyar said:[3]

The first commercial efforts were from larger companies that were saying, "Gee, we can use the Internet to sell stuff to people." Clearly, if you're coming from a democratic, libertarian point of view, having corporations just cram more products down people's throats doesn't seem like a lot of fun. I really wanted to give the individual the power to be a producer as well.

Meg Whitman, the CEO of eBay, has identified three reasons why eBay was successful.[4] First, she said that in her mind,[5] successful consumer business models either create an entirely new business that could not have existed without the Web or offer a service that becomes much more efficient with the Web. Of eBay, she said:

We created a business that took unique advantage of the properties of the Net—the Net's ability to connect many to many—allowing a business to be created where there was no land-based analog. If you can't buy your book at Amazon, you can still go down to Barnes & Noble. eBay has no land-based analog—not in one place. It was a business model that was created out of the technology called the Internet. Some of the most successful companies are those that had an entirely new model that could not have existed without the Net. eBay might be one of the only businesses that was created on the Internet.

Whitman identified the business model as another reason for the company's success. The idea was not just to create a new concept; rather, it was to create a concept that could be profitable.

The third reason was, in her words,[6] "old-fashioned execution—building a company to last, building cost behind revenues, not ahead of revenues, having a returns-based investment philosophy." She described how the company exerted strong financial discipline by measuring the return of every dollar spent on marketing and technology. Moreover, eBay never planned to grow for growth's sake; its goal was always to be profitable.

Understanding the Dominance of eBay

In May 2001, eBay earned 64.3% of all spending on online auctions, up from 57.8% the previous year. It has clearly established itself as the leader over rivals such as Amazon.com and Yahoo![7]

One study put its market share as high as 85%, and there have been allegations that eBay violates antitrust laws because of its dominance.[8]

Figures C3.1 through C3.4 clearly illustrate the extent of its dominance. These figures were compiled by the Nielsen's NetRatings service in collaboration with Auction Watch over a period ranging from November 1999 to November 2000. As these figures show, during this time span, eBay simply dominated its rivals on a variety of measures: there was absolutely no competition in the areas of total number of unique customers and the total number of pages viewed. Yahoo! briefly overtook eBay in terms of number of pages viewed per person, but only briefly. eBay does show some weakness, however, in the number of visits per month.

eBay's competitive advantage may come from the sheer number of registered users. As shown in Table C3.2, at the end of 2001, eBay had over 42.2 million registered users, up from 41,000 in 1996! This is a huge advantage over its rivals because in the auction market, the greater the

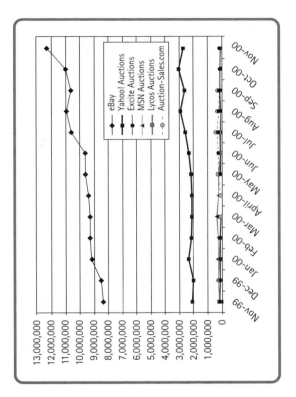

Figure C3.1
Unique Visitors

Source: Auctionwatch.com, "AW Metrics Monitor," 2000, <http://www.auctionwatch.com/awdaily/reviews/metrics/index.html>.

Figure C3.2
Total Number of Pages Viewed

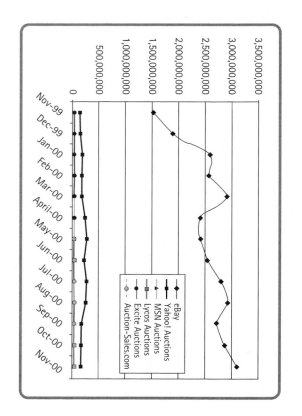

Source: Auctionwatch.com, "AW Metrics Monitor," 2000, <http://www.auctionwatch.com/awdaily/reviews/metrics/index.html>.

Figure C3.3
Pages Viewed Per Person

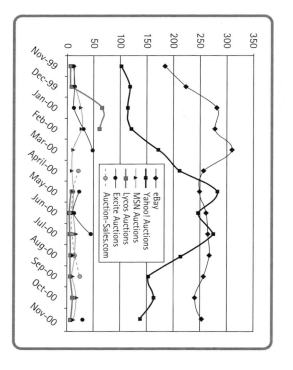

Source: Auctionwatch.com, "AW Metrics Monitor," 2000, <http://www.auctionwatch.com/awdaily/reviews/metrics/index.html>.

Figure C3.4
Number of Visits Per Person in a Month

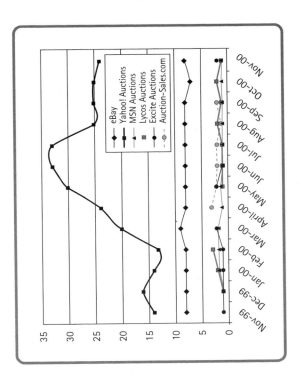

Source: Auctionwatch.com, "AW Metrics Monitor," 2000, <http://www.auctionwatch.com/awdaily/reviews/metrics/index.html>.

Table C3.2
Operational Information

	1996	1997	1998	1999	2000	2001
Number of registered users at end of year, in thousands	41	341	2,181	10,006	22,472	42,400
Gross merchandise sales, in millions	$7	$95	$745	$2,805	$5,422	$9,320
Number of items listed, in thousands	289	4,394	33,668	129,560	264,653	423,000

Source: eBay company 10-K form, March 8, 2001 and quarterly earnings releases for 2001.

number of buyers, the greater the advantage for sellers and *vice versa.*

As Meg Whitman described it:[9]

We had three years to build a very vibrant marketplace and because buyers want to be where the sellers are, and sellers want to be where the buyers are, it is an incredibly compelling environment, and it's difficult to start another market. The analogy I often use is the New York Stock Exchange and NASDAQ—it's very hard to create another stock exchange today because the action is on those two exchanges.

A third-party firm, Auction Watch, rates top auction sites on five dimensions: inventory, bidding, services/fees, support, functionality, and community (see Table C3.3). eBay gets high marks on all dimensions, and is the only company to score four on the community dimension.

Table C3.3
Ratings of Top Auction Sites

Auction Site	Inventory	Bidding	Services/Fees	Support	Functionality	Community
Amazon.com Auctions	4	2	4	3	4	2
AuctionAddict.com	2	1	3	3	2	2
Bid.com	1	1	3	3	2	N/A
CNET Auctions	3	2	2	2	3	1
Collecting Nation	2	2	3	3	2	3
Dell Auction	2	2	3	3	3	1
eBay	4	3	3	2	3	4
eBay Premier	2	1	2	3	4	N/A
edeal Marketplace	3	1	4	2	2	3
eHammer	3	4	3	3	2	1
eOrbis.com	2	1	3	4	3	1
eWanted.com	2	2	3	3	3	2
Excite Auctions	2	2	4	3	2	1
First Auction	2	3	2	3	3	N/A
Haggle Online	2	2	3	2	2	2
Lycos Auctions	2	2	3	4	3	2
MSN Auctions	3	2	3	2	3	2
NBCi Auctions	3	2	3	3	3	2
Onsale	3	3	2	4	2	2
Pottery Auction	2	2	3	4	3	2
Sothebys.com	4	3	3	3	3	N/A
SportsAuction	3	N/A	2	3	3	N/A
uBid	3	3	3	4	3	N/A
Yahoo! Auctions	4	3	3	1	4	2
Yahoo! Store	3	N/A	3	2	4	N/A
ZDNet Auctions	3	3	3	2	2	2

1 = below average, 2 = average, 3 = good, 4 = excellent
Source: Auction Watch Ratings, accessed in January 2002, http://www.auctionwatch.com/awdaily/reviews/ratings.html.

At the same time, the company has said that it currently accounts for less than 0.5% of all goods sold in each of its product categories. The company's goal is to triple this to 1.5% of all purchases by 2005—that means selling goods valued at $30 billion by 2005, an ambitious target. eBay's real challenge is attracting those users who buy in fixed-price environments (both on and offline) to the online auction environment.

As Meg Whitman puts it:[10]

But you know who our real competitor is? It's not the other online auction companies. It's the challenge of getting people to do on eBay what they do in the offline world. So all of our collectors, sporting cards, toys, antiques—all those kinds of things most people still buy in antique shops or at collectible trade shows. So our challenge is actually to get the offline transactions transferred online because it's more efficient, more fun, and there's a bigger selection. Our real competitor is, in many ways, the old way of doing things.

In one way, eBay really does not have much competition online. Some have argued that eBay's real impact is being felt by the flea market, antique and collectible shows, and newspaper classified ads:

Hardest hit so far are antiques and collectibles shows, which aggregate items like eBay does, but less efficiently. Joe Spotts, president of L&S Management, owns two shows—one in Denver, the other in Kansas City, Mo.—and he says the number of vendors at both has slid 30% in the past 18 months. And eBay is the reason. "It has the potential of absolutely destroying the business," says Spotts. "I've seen several shows around the country that are near shutting down." Flea markets could be the next to suffer. When the National Flea Market Association held its annual meeting in Orlando, Fla., in October, 100 members jammed into a session on the Internet future to hear dire predictions of what the Net would do to their land-based businesses.

Although these businesses may be hurt, many small businesses have used eBay as a channel to sell their products and have increased the size of their operation. This is a typical story:[11]

David James, for example, opened his shop in Alexandria, Va., eight years ago. He deals mostly in what the trade calls smalls: candlesticks, glassware, and other such collectibles. He's still got the store, but today his business—and his life—revolve around a warehouse a few miles away, where he stores the treasures he has gleaned from scouting

estate sales and flea markets. From a cramped, windowless cubicle, he monitors the hundreds of auctions he has posted—moving anywhere from $40,000 to $75,000 a month. He has hired a full-time employee to oversee his eBay business and plans to move to a new space complete with a miniprocessing center.

eBay's Stellar Financial Performance

eBay is one of the most successful companies on the Internet in recent times, as evidenced by the consolidated statement of income on Table C3.4 and the balance sheet on Table C3.5.

Table C3.4 shows that the company has had positive gross profit and net income since at least 1997. Its income position has only strengthened over time. This is an important point in the e-commerce space because many large and successful companies (notably Amazon.com, see Case 1) have never made a profit. The company has realized perhaps more than others that[12] "there's only one economy, and it judges you on standards like profitability, strong investment strategy, and your balance sheet."

The largest revenue source for the company is "fees and services." eBay earns money on every transaction on its site by charging the seller of an item two fees—the Insertion fee and the Final Value fee. The Insertion fee is paid by the seller for having her product featured on the site and ranges from $0.25 to $2.00 depending on the value of the opening bid. The Final Value fee is charged only if the transaction is successfully completed and ranges from 1.25% to 5% of the final sales price. In addition to these fees, the company earns money if individuals want their items to be highlighted in some way in order to stand out. For example, for a fee of $99.95, sellers can have their item featured on eBay's home page.

The company also adopted a prudent marketing approach. It relied on some print and radio advertising,[13] however, it attracted most of its consumers through word of mouth generated by consumer experiences. As a result, marketing

Table C3.4

Consolidated Statement of Income [All figures in thousands of dollars except per-share data.]

	1996	1997	1998	1999	2000	2001
Net revenues	$32,051	$ 41,370	$ 86,129	$224,724	$431,424	$748,821
Cost of net revenues	6,803	8,404	16,094	57,588	95,453	134,816
Gross profit	25,248	32,966	70,035	167,136	335,971	614,005
Operating expenses:						
Sales and marketing	13,139	15,618	35,976	96,239	166,767	253,474
Product development	28	831	4,640	24,847	55,863	75,288
General and administrative	5,661	6,534	15,849	43,919	73,027	105,784
Payroll expense on employee stock options	—	—	—	—	2,337	2,442
Amortization of acquired intangibles	—	—	805	1,145	1,433	36,591
Merger related costs	—	—	—	4,359	1,550	—
Total operating expenses	18,828	22,983	57,270	170,509	300,977	473,579
Income (loss) from operations	6,420	9,983	12,765	(3,373)	34,994	140,426
Interest and other income (expense), net	(2,607)	(1,951)	(703)	21,412	46,025	46,276
Income before income taxes	3,813	8,032	12,062	18,039	81,019	170,457
Provision for income taxes	(475)	(971)	(4,789)	(8,472)	(32,725)	(80,009)
Net income	3,338	7,061	7,273	9,567	48,294	90,448
Net income per share:						
Basic	$0.20	$0.14	$0.07	$0.04	$0.19	$0.34
Diluted	$0.04	$0.04	$0.03	$0.04	$0.17	$0.32
Weighted average shares:						
Basic	16,979	48,854	104,128	217,674	251,776	268,971
Diluted	90,119	169,550	233,519	273,033	280,346	280,595

Source: eBay company 10-K forms.

Table C3.5

Balance Sheet Information
(All figures in thousands of dollars except when noted.)

	1998	1999	2000	2001
Current assets:				
Cash and cash equivalents	$31,790	$221,801	$201,873	$523,969
Short-term investments	40,401	181,086	354,166	199,450
Accounts receivable, net	6,369	36,538	67,163	101,703
Other current assets	4,825	25,882	52,262	58,683
Total current assets	83,385	465,307	675,464	883,805
Long-term investments	7,831	373,988	218,197	286,998
Property and equipment, net	1,267	112,202	125,161	142,349
Intangible and other assets, net	$31,790	12,689	23,299	198,639
Restricted cash and investments	—	—	126,390	129,614
Deferred tax assets		5,639	13,892	21,540
Other assets		—	10,236	15,584
Total Assets	$92,483	$969,825	$1,182,403	1,678,529
Liabilities and Stockholders' Equity				
Current liabilities:				
Accounts payable	$1,385	$32,133	$31,725	$33,235
Accrued expenses and other current liabilities	4,971	32,675	66,697	94,593
Deferred revenue and customer advances	—	5,997	12,656	15,583
Short-term debt	—	15,781	15,272	16,111
Income taxes payable	—	6,455	11,092	20,617
Total current liabilities	8,038	93,041	137,442	180,139
Long-term debt	—	15,018	11,404	12,008
Other liabilities	—	5,905	6,549	19,493
Minority interests	—	1,732	13,248	37,751
Total Liabilities	115,696		168,643	249,391

(continued)

Table C3.5 (continued)

	1998	1999	2000	2001
Commitments and contingencies				
Stockholders' equity:				
Preferred Stock, $0.001 par value; 10,000 shares authorized, no shares issued or outstanding	—	—	—	
Common Stock, $0.001 par value; 900,000 shares authorized; 262,087 and 269,250 shares issued and outstanding	121	262	269	277
Additional paid-in capital	86,265	831,121	941,285	1,275,240
Notes receivable from stockholders	(1,130)	(11)	—	
Unearned stock-based compensation	(4,139)	(8,704)	(1,423)	(2,367)
Retained earnings	3,328	26,367	74,504	164,633
Accumulated other comprehensive income (loss)	—	5,094	(875)	(8,645)
Total stockholders' equity	84,445	854,129	1,013,760	1,429,138
	$92,483	$969,825	$1,182,403	$1,678,529

Source: eBay company 10-K forms.

expenses hovered around 40% of total net revenues from 1996 through 2000. Moreover, as shown in Table C3.6, eBay has advertised prudently: due to the strong word-of-mouth and community aspects, its advertising "bought" it much greater awareness compared to that of other leading online companies.

Further information about the operation of the company is shown in Table C3.2. On all dimensions, we see tremendous growth from 1996 through 2000. In 1999, the company had over 10 million registered users, had been responsible for sales of almost $3 billion, and had listed almost 130 million items.

The auction format also helped eBay create a sense of excitement in the shopping process. As a result, the company always appears on the lists of top sites in terms of stickiness (i.e., average time spent on the site). The data shown for the month of October 2001 in Table C3.7 is typical: eBay's users spent an average of 96.3 minutes per month in comparison to Amazon users' 16.8 minutes.

Cultural Impact

Eighteen-year-old Sterling Jones of Ontario, Canada, put his soul on auction on eBay. The offer stayed up for two days, and then Jones was sent an e-mail that read: "Although you may not have been aware, eBay does not allow the auctioning of human souls." The story goes on to say that[14] "according to an eBay spokes-

Table C3.6
ROI on Advertising Spending

Brand	1999 Ad Spending (millions) (1)	Top of Mind Brand Awareness (2)	Branding Bang for Ad Buck (2)/(1)
eBay	$ 5.50	22%	4.000
Excite	3.20	8	2.500
CDNow	10.50	22	2.100
Yahoo!	29.20	38	1.301
Amazon	35.20	45	1.278
Buy.com	17.00	6	0.353
IWON.com	18.40	6	0.326
AOL	83.20	22	0.264
Priceline	49.60	5	0.101
Monster	29.00	2	0.069
E*Trade	124.20	5	0.040
Ameritrade	103.70	1	0.010

man, Kevin Pursglove, there's no proof Jones can make good to the winning bidder. At one time, the gentleman would have to make a pretty strong case to us that he could deliver his soul,' Pursglove told *Salon.* 'Now, assuming that he has a soul, we also have language in our user agreement that prohibits the sale of body parts. That's against U.S. law. If the soul exists, one would assume it is some way a part of the human body.'"

Stories about items for sale on eBay have had a huge cultural impact. At one time, the raft on which Elian Gonzalez made it to Miami without his mother, was put up for auction.[15] One individual put his vote up for sale.[16] The auction of Beanie Babies on eBay took on a life of its own, with reporters discussing the price at which a certain doll was sold. At one time, a group of software engineers placed themselves on the auction block for employers. eBay has been investigated for auctioning items made from the body parts of animals on the endangered species list.[17] A convicted murderer offered tick-

ets to his execution on eBay and received no bids.[18] In almost all of these cases, eBay has stepped in and stopped the auction; however, the publicity from these cases has led people to offer all sorts of creative products for sale.

The talk show host Rosie O'Donnell partnered with eBay to sell items that were autographed by the guests on her show. The proceeds from the auction went to charity. Several consumers got into the business of buying items and selling them on eBay for a profit. Consider this story:[19]

Sally Rosenthal, who is based in Palo Alto, Calif., said that while at a Target store in Silicon Valley watching collectors line up to buy Star Wars trinkets, she started talking to a couple in their early 40s, with infant in tow, who had been returning to the shelves every 20 minutes. The couple systematically bought up $4,000 worth of stuff, each buying the maximum items that Target allowed each customer, then going back for more.

Table C3.7
Top 20 Digital Properties, October 2001

Rank	Top Web and Digital Media Properties	Unique Visitors (000)	Total Usage Minutes (000,000)	Average Minutes Per Month
1	AOL Time Warner Network	83,871	44,894	535.3
2	MSN-Microsoft Sites	70,720	10,994	155.5
3	Yahoo!	68,364	10,494	153.5
4	Terra Lycos	39,514	701	17.7
5	X10.COM	39,334	64	1.6
6	Vivendi-Universal Sites	36,458	535	14.7
7	About/Primedia	33,220	491	14.8
8	eBay	25,945	2,498	96.3
9	Walt Disney Internet Group	25,386	931	36.7
10	eUniverse Network	25,156	298	11.8
11	Amazon	24,298	408	16.8
12	Excite Network	21,723	1,127	51.9
13	Infospace Network	21,381	182	8.5
14	CNET Networks	21,368	402	18.8
15	Google Sites	21,146	500	23.6
16	American Greetings	20,814	225	10.8
17	Viacom Online	17,008	396	23.3
18	Ask Jeeves	16,741	250	14.9
19	Columbia House Sites	15,560	81	5.2
20	AT&T Web Sites	15,248	452	29.6

Source: Ryan Oettinger, "Jupiter Media Metrix Announces US Top 50 Web and Digital Media Properties for October 2001," November 13, 2001, <http://www.jmm.com/xp/jmm/press/2001/pr_111301.xml>.

"They said they'd decided that the lowest risk with the fastest, highest return," Ms. Rosenthal said, "was to buy Star Wars merchandise, then post it on eBay for a seven-day auction, with a reserve"—the lowest price they would take—"of double their money." Thus, at the end of seven days, they would double their investment, maybe doing even better, "or they would return the merchandise, making it zero risk; their only investment was their time and running around to buy the stuff."

Consumers have reported rounding up merchandise from yard sales and selling it on eBay.

Problems with eBay

If eBay has led to major consumer participation, it has also led to some bad consumer experiences. In fact, there is a club on Yahoo! devoted to eBay consumer horror stories at http://clubs.yahoo.com/clubs/ebayhorrorstories.

The National Consumer League's Internet Fraud Watch identifies auctions as the number one source of fraud-related complaints. Auctions were the basis of 87% of all complaints they received in 1999 and 68% of all complaints filed in 1998.[20]

In several cases, sellers have exaggerated the value of the item or presented an item as being something that it is not.[21] In other cases, "buyer rings" help increase the final price: an associate of the seller places a fake bid to encourage others to increase their bid amount, leading to a higher price. In a publicized case, "a Sacramento, Calif., attorney named Kenneth Walton had entered his own bid of $4,500 for a painting that eventually fetched a winning bid of $135,805."[22]

eBay is taking several steps to overcome this. The most important step is the seller rating system, in which buyers rate their experience with the seller. Jakob Nielsen is an industry expert in the area of usability; that is, ensuring that the user experience is maximized. (If you wish to learn more about him, visit http://www.useit.com). He analyzed the reputation ratings in this way:[23]

eBay (auction site) keeps reputation ratings for all the people who offer things for sale on the site. After buying a collectible in an auction, you can go back to the site and rate the seller for prompt shipping and whether the physical item actually matched the description in the auction. This is the most literal of the current reputation managers: eBay literally keeps track of the reputation of each seller. Prospective buyers can feel safe bidding on items from people they have never heard of: if the reputation ratings show that many previous buyers were treated well and thought that the textual descriptions matched the actual collectible, then the seller is almost certainly honest and worth dealing with. Also, sellers are highly motivated to offer great service to every single buyer: a single customer with a bad experience will ruin a seller's perfect reputation rating and multiple bad experiences (quickly followed by negative ratings) will put a seller out of business for good.

However, even these ratings can be manipulated, since a seller can ask friends to fill out

positive evaluations. For this reason, perhaps, recent studies show that consumers pay more attention to negative than to positive reviews when making their decisions.

For high-value items, a paid escrow service (i.e., a service where a third party holds on to the item of the seller and the cash from the buyer and makes the exchange for a commission) and insurance are available. Because most of the items sold on eBay are of a lower value (in the $50 range), these services may not apply to a broad range of products.

The Future of eBay

The company is totally committed to the Internet. As CEO Meg Whitman put it,[24] "The Internet is not dead. When I talk about the future of the Internet many people say, 'What future?' But I believe the Internet's best days are still ahead."

eBay realizes that it has a powerful place in the market with a loyal customer base. On January 17, 2002, the company announced that, for the first time since 1996, it was increasing the Final Value fee, which is the fee paid to the company when an item is sold.[25] Such fee increases can be expected in the future, leading to strong profits.

A clear direction of growth for eBay is in foreign markets. eBay currently operates in eight of the top ten countries by online market size outside of the United States. It has a presence in major Asian markets, Japan, South Korea, and Singapore, and plans to expand to Taiwan and China soon. It is gaining users 50% faster in Europe than in the United States, and gross merchandise sales are growing 135% faster.[26]

eBay has also identified m-commerce as a potential growth area. Specifically, eBay is working with Microsoft's .Net initiative to provide access to its auction services to cell phone users.[27] With this technology, consumers will be able to bid on auctions using their cell phones, which will make it even easier for users to participate in auctions, and should increase usage.

eBay appears to feel that sticking exclusively to the auction format limits its growth prospects. As a result, it has said that it will pursue fixed-price retailing, which it started by buying Half.com.

Discussion Questions

1. What factors contributed to the success of eBay?

2. a. Plot net sales and profits from 1996–2001.

   b. Using data in Table C3.2, plot the total number of registered users versus gross merchandise sales over time. What trends do you see?

   c. On one chart, plot this information from 1996–2001:

      I. Ratio of sales and marketing costs/revenue.

      II. Ratio of product development costs/revenue.

   d. Plot net income with total number of registered users and number of items listed.

   e. Compute the ratio of gross merchandise sales in Table C3.2 with net revenue in Table C3.4 from 1996–2001. What does this tell you?

3. You should be able to obtain the answers to these questions from the financial statement in Table C3.5:

   a. Compute the ratio of operating income to sales and gross profit to sales. See how these ratios have changed over time. Compare with Amazon.com and bn.com (data available in Case 1). What do you learn from this?

   b. Compute the current ratio (current assets/current liabilities) and the quick ratio (current assets – inventories) / (current liabilities). See how these ratios have changed over time. Compare with Amazon.com and bn.com (data available in Case 1). What do you learn from this?

4. Will auctions continue to be the dominant format at eBay? Will fixed-price retailing through Half.com always be a secondary business?

5. Is eBay a retailer? Discuss.

6. Would the merger of eBay and Amazon.com be a good idea? For whom?

7. How can eBay leverage its community more to improve its market position?

Notes

(All URLs are current as of March 15, 2002.)

1. Charlie Rose, "Q&A with Meg Whitman," July/August 2001, <http://business.cisco.com/app/tree.taf?asset_id=58046>.

2. Matthew Beale, "E-Commerce Success Story: eBay," <http://www.ecommercetimes.com/success_stories/success-ebay.shtml>.

3. Adam Cohen, "Coffee with Pierre," December 1999, <http://www.time.com/time/poy/pierre.html>.

4. Robert D. Hof, "Q&A with eBay's Meg Whitman," March 26, 2001, <http://www.businessweek.com/magazine/content/01_13/b3725036.htm>.

5. <http://www.worth.com/content_articles/0501_ceo_qa_whitman.html>, accessed December 2001.

6. Robert D. Hof, "Q&A with eBay's Meg Whitman."

7. Troy Wolverton, "eBay Riding Net Auction Industry's Wave," June 28, 2001, <http://news.cnet.com/news/0-1007-200-6407299.html>.

8. Oscar Cisneros, "eBay Accused of Monopolization," July 31, 2000, <http://www.wired.com/news/business/0,1367,37871,00.html>.

9. Charlie Rose, "Q&A with Meg Whitman."

10. Ibid.
11. Andrew Ferguson, "Auction Nation," December 1999, <http://www.time.com/time/poy/auction.html>.
12. Elizabeth Hurt, "Whitman: We Will Survive," March 14, 2001, <http://www.business2.com/articles/web/0,1653,15559,00.html>.
13. Matthew Beale, "E-Commerce Success Story: eBay."
14. Stephen Lemons, "eFaust Foiled," February 25, 2000, <http://www.salon.com/people/log/2000/02/25/soul/index.html>.
15. Darryl Lindsey, "Bidding for the Boat," May 3, 2000, <http://www.salon.com/news/feature/2000/05/03/soundbite/index.html>.
16. Katharine Mieszkowski, "Democracy for Sale," August 17, 2000, <http://www.salon.com/tech/log/2000/08/17/vote_sale/index.html>.
17. Lucy Chubb, "eBay Under Scrutiny for Endangered Species Auction Items," January 21, 2000, <http://www.enn.com/enn-news-archive/2000/01/01212000/ebay_9252.asp>.
18. Richard Zitrin, "Killer Put Tickets to His Execution on Ebay," May 25, 2000, <http://www.apbnews.com/newscenter/internetcrime/2000/05/25/executeauction0525_01.html>.
19. Dennis Caruso, "Success Stories from eBay," May 24, 1999, <http://www10.nytimes.com/library/tech/99/05/biztech/articles/24digi.html>.
20. Internet Fraud Watch, "Home Page," <www.fraud.org/internet/intset.htm>.
21. Bensinger, "Collecting: The Perils of Online Auctions," *Wall Street Journal*, Mar 5, 1999.
22. wsj.com, accessed May 24, 2000.
23. Jakob Nielsen, "Reputation Managers Are Happening," September 5, 1999, <http://www.useit.com/alertbox/990905.html>.
24. Patricia Jacobus, "eBay's Whitman: Net Has Lots of Fight Left," March 14, 2001, <http://news.cnet.com/news/0-1007-200-5137192.html>.
25. Beth Cox, "eBay Hikes User Fees," January 17, 2002, <http://www.internetnews.com/ec-news/article/0,,4_957321,00.html>.
26. Magnus Bjornsson, "eBay's Position in the Industry," Spring 2001, <http://www.cs.brandeis.edu/~magnus/ief248a/eBay/fiveforces.html>.
27. Kristen Kenedy, "The Future's In Portability, Say Sun, EBay Execs," March 15, 2001, <http://www.internetweek.com/story/INW20010315S0001>.

PART TWO

E-Marketing

CHAPTER 6

Building Customer Traffic

Learning Objectives

▼ To gain a solid understanding of the customer acquisition process on the Internet.

▼ To learn the benefits and challenges of using viral marketing to build site traffic.

▼ To understand the field of search engine optimization.

▼ To gain a comprehensive understanding of Internet advertising techniques.

▼ To understand how to use promotions effectively on the Internet.

▼ To understand affiliate and associate programs.

▼ To learn how to build an effective web site.

▼ To learn the appropriate mix of offline and online techniques to build site traffic.

Executive Summary

The most difficult task for any company is to acquire and retain a large customer base. This chapter uses an integrated marketing communication perspective to introduce online techniques that can help marketers acquire and retain customers. It will follow the AIDA model (attention, interest, desire, action) as a guide when discussing the techniques.

Companies can now do a profitability analysis on each customer by comparing revenues from him or her with the acquisition and retention cost. Viral marketing proposes leveraging relationships among consumers to spread a message. Even though word of mouth is a time-honored marketing technique, viral marketing has become more important due to the enhanced connectivity among individuals. Search engines can help consumers locate your site online; however, each engine uses different rules to locate and classify information. Search engine optimization is a technique that tries to place a web site in the top five to ten results located by most search engines. Building an effective web site must be a part of an integrated marketing campaign; the web site is often the last step (i.e., action) in the AIDA framework. The quality of a web site depends on the quality of information, the quality of the information's structure, and the information's usability. Although Internet advertising has grown at a tremendous clip, banner ads suffer from measurement problems and an overemphasis on the click–through. Providing free products and other promotions has become exceedingly common; some sites have even offered permanent free shipping to their customers. When designing a campaign, a company must set objectives ahead of time and be clear on how it defines success. It must also choose a mix of media based on the relative strengths of each medium.

Introduction

Companies communicate with consumers in so many ways—television ads, radio ads, direct mail, product packaging, in-store displays, outdoor advertising (e.g., blimp, billboard), newspaper articles, infomercials, press releases, coupons, web sites, and banner advertisements. This chapter uses an integrated marketing communication (IMC) perspective. The Internet is a medium of communication that must work with all other media to communicate a coherent and consistent message to the consumer.[1] IMC posits that a variety of communication disciplines (e.g., advertising, computer-mediated communication, direct marketing, sales promotion, public relations) must work together to ensure maximum clarity, consistency, and communication impact. The integration of the communication message allows the development of a unique and strong brand image. IMC begins with understanding the consumer by collecting data about each consumer and using it effectively to target him or her.

This chapter will refer to the AIDA model. AIDA stands for the four steps in persuasion—attention, interest, desire, and action. Unless the consumer is aware of the existence of a brand, he or she cannot take an interest in it. Interest can arise from a deeper understanding of the attributes and functions of the product. Interest alone, however, does not lead to action. Consumers must think well of the product and value it higher than competitive alternatives. Only after a strong desire is developed will the consumer take action and buy the product.

The first step in the AIDA framework, to capture the attention of potential users, is hard to achieve on the Web, for three reasons. First, the Web is a fragmented medium with billions of web pages competing for consumer attention. Second, the Web is constantly changing (e.g., your site's appearance at the "top of the pile" in most search engines today is no guarantee you will retain that spot tomorrow). Third, users have a limited attention span and have established loyalty to a few sites that they trust. As discussed in Chapter 2, the Internet exhibits a winner-take-all market structure.

Of course, getting people's attention and enticing them to visit your web site is not everything. The AIDA framework makes it clear that the ultimate goal is the action—be it buying a product, registering at the site, downloading software, or signing up for a Web event. Getting to the action is the difficult part.

Whether a person visiting your site for the first time becomes interested in what you have to say depends on how you have organized your site and the quality of information you present. A consumer can easily judge the personality of the company from a web site or other communication. If the company appears to be unprofessional or uses obnoxious or obtrusive techniques, the consumer will click away. You need a way to get consumers to like your company and have a strong desire to buy from it. The problem is that you have to do it in a digital environment with no face-to-face or direct contact. Using the AIDA framework, we will look at a variety of (mainly) online techniques that can be used to capture the consumer.

Understanding the Customer Acquisition Process

Cost–Benefit Analysis

The customer acquisition process requires a comparison of the incremental benefit of attracting a customer with the incremental cost of doing so. The benefit is measured in terms of the *lifetime value of the customer*, defined as the discounted cash flows (i.e., potential revenues less costs of attracting and retaining) that are expected to arise from this customer over his or her lifetime. Customer equity is the sum of the lifetime value across all customers in the company's database.

The two cost components to developing a relationship with a customer are the *customer acquisition cost* and the *customer retention cost*. The customer acquisition cost is the up-front marketing and advertising expenses of enticing a customer to begin a relationship with your company. The retention cost consists of the marketing expenses incurred over the lifetime of the individual in trying to convince him or her to continue to do business with your company.

A survey conducted by the Boston Consulting Group found that the customer acquisition cost for online retailers was about $40 during the second quarter of 2000.[2] In general, the cost of retaining a customer is much smaller than that of acquiring a new one. Loyal customers buy more and purchase more often at full price, and they do not have to be educated or "sold to." As a result, the marketing expense on loyal customers is minimal. On the other hand, the costs associated with new customers include new account setup, credit searches, and advertising expenses, and the total can be very high.

Consumer Profitability Analysis

By creating an appropriate consumer database, every company can measure the profits that arise from each individual. Profits are simply the revenue from the individual less the sum of acquisition and retention costs to date.

Consumers who contribute the most to the company's bottom line should be rewarded. Companies now routinely identify consumers who are the most desirable (in terms of profitability). When a phone call arrives at a call center, a computer can quickly check to determine whether the customer is on "the A list." If so, the person moves up in the queue and gets to speak to a representative quickly. On the other hand, consumers who are "high-maintenance," leading to low profits or even losses, must be "fired." A company can effectively "fire" a customer by telling him or her that it has done everything it can to satisfy the person and perhaps it is time for that person to try an alternative.

Building a Customer Database

There are three approaches to cultivating a database:

- *Defense.* This program is designed to retain the company's loyal customers. These individuals are rewarded and provided special access not offered to others.

- *Tough offense.* This program is designed to entice the loyal customers of the competition to switch. This could prove expensive (especially if there is retaliation by the competitor) and must be managed carefully.

- *Easy offense.* This is designed to capture the "low-hanging fruit." Consumers who are known to be price-switchers are persuaded to purchase by using price promotions such as coupons or sales.

Once a database is in place, the company can try to encourage customers to buy more or in other categories. Consider the approach of Amazon.com. It entered the marketplace selling books, but once it had created a database of individuals, the company tried to do two things—up-sell and cross-sell. *Up-sell* means trying to sell more to existing customers, which Amazon.com tried to do by introducing new features. When consumers searched for a particular book, they were provided with a list of other books of potential interest. Consumers received e-mail updates when their favorite author's latest book hit the market. The other approach was to *cross-sell.* The idea here was to sell other products to existing customers. Amazon.com's expansion plan was based on trying to sell its book customers music CDs, videos, kitchen gadgets, and so on.

Setting a Budget for Customer Acquisition

There are two factors to keep in mind when setting the budget:

1. Diminishing returns. The budget is appropriate if it is at the point where increasing it by a dollar leads to less than a dollar in profits. After a point, increasing the budget does lead to more customers—but the cost of getting them outweighs their value.

2. Competition. One has to monitor and keep pace with what the competition is doing to acquire customers, but setting the budget at the same level as a competitor may be unwise because it can lead to escalating acquisition costs.

Attracting Customers within a Company

The target audience is sometimes located within the company for which a web site is created. The challenge then is not to get noticed in a public space, but to stand out among the hundreds of sites on the company's intranet. This is especially an issue for Fortune 500 companies where each division may be creating multiple web sites.

Companies are very concerned that all information reaches the intended audience. If a site with valuable information does not reach the appropriate audience, company knowledge is being underused. A division may order a market research study when the answer to the question may be available in another division's documents. Simply incorporating a search engine may not suffice because different divisions may use different terms.

Companies are trying new tricks to overcome this problem. For example, many company web sites have a "what's new" section describing new sites, and most companies also have e-mail newsletters, which can advertise internal sites.

Viral Marketing

Viral marketing proposes that messages can be rapidly disseminated from consumer to consumer, leading to large-scale market acceptance. With the advent of the Internet, marketers must think of markets as networks of consumers rather than an amorphous mass and use this knowledge to enhance the spread of their message.

Why Viral Marketing Now?

Marketers have long recognized the importance of word-of-mouth advertising, but its relative importance in the marketing campaign has now changed, for three reasons.

First, many social networks are now online. How many of your friends do not have an e-mail address? Did you answer zero? A large portion of the American population would.

Second, contacting individuals using the Web is much faster than contacting people using postal mail or the telephone. All of us can contact our entire social network in a relatively short time by using communication technologies such as e-mail, chat, and instant messaging. It does not cost us more to add 100 more e-mail addresses to our list.

Finally, the critical-mass effect plays an important role. As more customers sign up, each one can contact many more. Soon, the total number contacted rises exponentially. This is the result of Metcalfe's Law (the value of a network rises at an increasing rate with the addition of each individual), discussed in Chapter 2.

Three Types of Viral Marketing

There are three "flavors" of viral marketing: incidental contagion, contagion due to transaction consummation, and consumers as professional recruiters.

Incidental Contagion

In this case, the consumer is not made aware of his or her role in the message dissemination process. Consumers sign on to a service and while using the service, unwittingly increase the awareness of a product. Consumers do not perform any special promotional tasks and do not receive any reward.

Hotmail is an example of incidental contagion; it grew by leaps and bounds by doing something simple. At the bottom of each e-mail message, a small line promoted Hotmail: "Get Your Private, Free Email at http://www.hotmail.com." Recipients of these messages were thus quickly alerted to the Hotmail web site. This led to phenomenal growth, with more than 12 million people signing up for a Hotmail account during the site's first 18 months. Hotmail spent only $500,000 on marketing and promotion during this period, an acquisition cost of about four cents per customer.

Contagion Due to Transaction Consummation

Typically, in this case, a firm makes an attractive product available for free provided that all interested parties register for the service. In other words, a service is available to a particular individual only if others sign up, giving the user an incentive to persuade others to sign up as well, leading to rapid growth. Two classic examples of this are ICQ and PayPal.

The real-time chat service ICQ (short for "I seek you") signed up 12 million users using this approach. In order to chat with your friends, they had to have the service too. Those friends signed up their friends and ICQ eventually sold out to AOL for about $300 million.

More recently, PayPal, which allows users to make small payments to one another online, paid its early users $10 to sign up and a few more dollars for each new member they referred. People liked the service, and it pulled in more than three million users during its first nine months. Once it reached a critical mass, PayPal reduced its payments to $5.

Consumers as Professional Recruiters

In this case, consumers are encouraged to contact others and inform them about the product. There are two different versions of this. In the first approach, no incentives are provided to the consumer; the "tell your friend" icon might apear right next to a product display or a news story. The second approach is perhaps the most aggressive—an explicit incentive structure is set up to reward consumers who bring in the most traffic. As salespeople, consumers use the AIDA framework to persuade their friends to buy a product or read a message.

When to Use Viral Marketing

Viral marketing is not for everyone and every situation. From a *strategic standpoint*, it is called for when you care only about the quantity, rather than the quality, of traffic. Viral marketing works best when you are interested in getting a lot of people to do something and you are not choosy about who the people are. Viral campaigns also work well for markets that are homogenous, not heterogeneous. Consider a market where every single consumer is expected to spend $50 at your store over the next two years. Now, consider a second market where 10% of your market is expected to spend more than $10,000 in the next two years, 50% of your market is expected to spend between $5,000 and $10,000, and the remaining 40% is expected to spend less than $5,000. Viral marketing is better for market 1. In market 2, you are better off having a targeted campaign to ensure that you get the top 10% followed by the 50%.

Products for Which Viral Marketing Works Best

It works best for products or services that have one or more of the following characteristics:

Uniqueness

Viral marketing works very well for products that are market creators, products or services that are nothing like what is available in the market and that represent a new way of thinking. Think of Hotmail. At the point of its launch, most e-mail providers charged a flat service fee. Providing free e-mail represented a new way of thinking about customer acquisition.

Exciting Product Concept

Remember that in viral marketing success depends on individuals passing the message on to others. This is the "action" in the AIDA framework. They will do so only if they are excited about the product and the value proposition. Therefore, viral marketing is great for products that are entertaining, colorful, and exhilarating to use.

Simple Product Concept

If a consumer has to explain what a product is to his or her friend, neighbor, or acquaintance, the product should be as simple as possible. The Hotmail concept was simple and could be described in two words—"Free e-mail." Naturally, it was easy to disseminate.

Low Trial Cost

When a consumer attempts to try a product, the total cost of adopting the product must be low. The total cost of adoption can be broken down into several components—switching cost, price of the product, and transaction cost.

The *switching cost* refers to the cost of moving from an old product that is currently satisfying a need to your new product. A person who has to go through a huge hassle is unlikely to move to the new product. Consider, for example, a consumer who has customized a portal, such as Yahoo! or Lycos, with his or her bookmarks, stock portfolio, weather settings, and local movies. If he or she had to do this all over again at a new portal, it would not be worth the time.

The second cost component is the *price of the product*. Viral marketing works best for products or services that are free or inexpensive, such as digital products, free communication technologies, and so forth.

Finally, there is the *transaction cost* of actually making the move. Consider this case. I have received an e-mail from a friend informing me of a new service. When I try to sign on, I am told that I have to fill out a ten-page survey, providing all sorts of details about my life. It is highly unlikely that I will sign on. In order for a viral campaign to succeed, the actual sign-up or registration process must be seamless.

Negative Aspects of Uiral Marketing

Viral marketing does have some disadvantages.

Brand Control

Viral marketing reduces your control over your branding. Since you don't know ahead of time whom an individual is going to contact, many of your messages may end up with people outside the target audience. Moreover, in some cases, individuals may modify or add to the message or add something to it, which leads unfortunately to variability in how your brand is perceived.

Uncharted Growth

Viral marketing can lead to unanticipated growth paths. Hotmail, for example, is now one of the leading e-mail providers in India. It is not clear whether it expected or even wanted that. But many individuals started e-mailing friends in India, who e-mailed many more. Such growth paths may lead to abrupt changes in strategic direction, which can be problematic.

Lack of Measurement

You can't always track who received the e-mails and what they did with them. It is only possible to measure the number of people who opened an e-mail if it is sent out using HTML. But if the message is opened using the preview options in programs such as Outlook, it counts as an opened message even if it is immediately deleted unread. In many cases, it may not be possible to tell if people who adopted your service did so because of your viral marketing technique. So, the results of viral marketing are difficult to track and measure.

Spam Threats

Finally, if done poorly, viral marketing can lead to large-scale spam (unsolicited commercial e-mail, see the Appendix in Chapter 14 for a detailed discussion) issues. Consider a company that pays individuals to e-mail their friends to convince them to buy one of its products. If the individual who receives the e-mail had only given the friend permission

Figure 6.1
Social Network Analysis

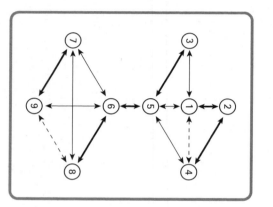

to send e-mail of a personal nature, receiving an unsolicited commercial e-mail can weaken relationships among consumers. In some cases, individuals who want to earn more money simply go out and spam people, which can damage your company image.

What Can Be Done to Manage the Viral Marketing Process?

Although viral marketing offers an organic, customer-led path for growth, it requires continuous managerial oversight. How can you do that?

First, *pick the initial recipients of the message carefully*. The whole viral marketing process starts off with the first few message recipients. They have to pass the message on to others who then pass it on to others. These viral pioneers must be popular (have access to a large social network), influential (have persuasive power over others), and represen-tative of your target market.

Figure 6.1 is a description of a social network. The numbers refer to people. The interactions among individuals are coded. A bold line indicates a strong relationship, a thin line indi-cates a relationship of moderate strength, and a dashed line indicates a weak relationship.

Whom would you pick to start the viral campaign? Person 1 should certainly play a vital role because he or she knows four people in the network. However, the key to spreading the message is to ensure that either person 5 or 6 gets the message and passes it on. These two people play a *bridging role* in bringing together two social networks (the top and the bottom). Identifying individuals who occupy such positions is key to the campaign's suc-cess. In general, *influential members of social networks have ties with many others and frequently play a bridging role with two or more subnetworks*.

One of the mistakes that firms make when putting together viral campaigns is choosing the first set of individuals out of convenience (e.g., the friends of employees) rather than by any strategic consideration. This could work if the target audience looks like the indi-viduals chosen, however, it is generally not a good rule to follow.

Second, *pick the message carefully.* Design a message that communicates the value proposition clearly and simply, so that it is easy for consumers to pass the message on. Strive for methods that ensure consistency of the brand image. If you are going to provide consumers incentives for passing on the message, think about how it will affect the final results. For example, incentives can reduce the credibility of the sender in some cases.

Third, *put control mechanisms in place.* Think about how you will measure the impact of your viral marketing campaign. One simple way of doing this is asking new customers where they heard about your service. You must constantly monitor how consumers are spreading the message.

As with any other form of promotion, viral marketing works for *products that offer genuine value to consumers.* If the product is bad, viral marketing can sink it fast.

Search Engine Optimization

Understanding Search Engines

Search engines (e.g., www.google.com) and directories (e.g., www.yahoo.com) are designed to help consumers navigate the millions of pages on the World Wide Web. Users can, of course, simply type the address of a site they are interested in or go to a site using their bookmarks, but frequently they need to search for information—for example, if they are purchasing a product about which they know little.

Search engines use software programs called spiders or crawlers to search the Web and create a large database (known as the index) of what is available online. The spider visits a web page, reads it, and then follows links on the page to other sites. The spider returns to the site on a regular basis, such as every month or two, to look for changes. Search engine software helps make sense of the index by using rules that correlate pages to specific search queries.

A directory, on the other hand, uses human beings to classify pages into different categories. Owners of pages fill out a form and are placed into different categories based on a decision by the person who manages that category.

Search engines are of different types:

- Paid listing search engines—only includes listings from companies who have paid to be included (e.g., GoTo.com, bay9.com).
- Reward-based search engines—rewards consumers for using the engine by entering them into a contest (e.g., iWon.com, eFind.com).
- Community-based directories—links are contributed by members (e.g., Zeal.com, Dmoz.com).
- Meta search engine—searches across multiple search engines (e.g., Metacrawler, Vivisimo.com, IxQuick.com).

- Global search engines—focus is on a global market (e.g., Diabolos.com, Euroseek.com, Goo, Khoj.com).

- Natural language query—allows users to ask questions using full-form English instead of keywords (e.g., Ask Jeeves).

Identifying the largest search engines and directories is tricky. Google.com is the search engine with the largest index—it has over 3 billion pages. This includes discussions in newsgroups and files. However, if one considers the number of people who actually use a search engine or directory, the picture is somewhat different as shown in Table 6.1. Yahoo!, MSN, and AOL dominate with over 50% of online users estimated to have used each one of them. Google is sixth on this list.

People often use search engines to locate information on the Internet. According to surveys:

- More than 75% of surfers use search engines to traverse the Web according to a Real-Names survey dated April 2000.

- An IMT Strategies research study conducted in April 2000 indicated that 45.8% of Web users cited search engines as their top choice for finding web sites.

Table 6.1
Top Search Engines

	Reach (percent)
Yahoo.com	58.80
MSN.com	52.30
AOL.com	50.40
Go.com	22.10
Netscape.com	20.00
Google.com	18.40
Excite.com	11.90
Lycos.com	11.80
iWon.com	7.70
AltaVista.com	6.90
Overture.com	6.80
Looksmart.com	6.00
AskJeeves.com	4.90
Hotbot.com	2.20
NBCi.com	0.30

- Iconocast reported in August 2000 that 81% of United Kingdom users find web sites through search engines.

About 130 million searches are conducted each day at Google.com.[3] Interestingly, on September 11, 2001, soon after the terrorist attacks, the top search items on Google included CNN and MSNBC. Instead of directly going to cnn.com or msnbc.com, users used Google to locate the sites. This may have been because both sites were temporarily down, but it illustrates how users rely on search engines to locate information on the Internet.[4]

Optimization Process

When individuals search for information using these sites, they are presented with hundreds of selections. Consumers will not read through all selections. Though all of the results of a search are vying for the attention of the consumer, only the top few are likely to catch his or her eye. Of course, as the AIDA framework tells us, it is not enough to capture the attention of the consumer: the attention must be converted into action (i.e., a visit to a web site and, eventually, a purchase).

Certainly, though, if you design your site so that you show up in the top five, you will get more traffic. As shown in Table 6.2, the higher the rank in the search engine, the greater the proportion of consumer traffic that visit your site.

Hence, search-engine optimization (SEO) has become an important marketing concern. SEO is the practice of fine-tuning the design and content of the site with the hope that it will lead to a higher ranking for some searches done by the leading search engines.

Search engines rank pages using:

- Keywords in the title
- Keywords near the top

Table 6.2
Ranking Drives Traffic

Rank	Percent of traffic
1	10.0
2	5.0
3	2.5
4	1.5
5	1.0
6	1.0
7	1.0
8	0.5
9	0.5
10	0.5

Source: Courtesy of 7search.com and its family of Internet services.

- Frequency of keywords
- Link popularity (number of links pointed at a site)
- Penalty for search engine keyword spamming (i.e., if you try to include every popular keyword with the hope that you will show up near the top in many searches, there is a penalty–you may show up at the end of the list)

However, each search engine uses this information to come up with the rankings differently. Because search engines use different algorithms and take different approaches to rank pages, being high in one may mean being low in another. Also, one needs to constantly update the site's tags to show up in the top few.

What are some of the specific things companies do to boost their ratings? A survey conducted by Iconocast in November 2000 yielded the following information about strategy. The number one strategy (61% of respondents) was to change the meta tags on the page. All web pages are written using HTML, which has a set of commands known as tags that determine how the page looks. A meta tag does not affect how the page looks; rather, it is a secret instruction to visiting search engines on where to put the page in the index. Choosing these tags wisely is very important.

The second most popular strategy (44% of respondents) was to change the page title. The third most common strategy (32%) was to link reciprocally. In other words, site A and site B agree that they will place a link to the other's site on their page. In this way, a wider audience is exposed to both pages. The fourth most popular strategy (28%) is to purchase multiple domain names, and the fifth (21%) is to have multiple home pages.

SEO is expensive. The alternative is to use the pay-for-position approach. Rather than trying to guess where your site might end up in a search process, you can simply pay a search engine to place you in the top five. Many search engines now provide this service. For example, Google provides paid links at the top or on the side of a page in a separate box. Search engines such as Google take pains to mark clearly which links are paid. They do this to assure consumers that the integrity of the search process has not been compromised. GoTo.com does something interesting: all of its links are paid. It believes this leads to the most relevance. It tells the users what a source has paid for every link.

How do managers study the effectiveness of search engines? An Iconocast survey revealed the following: 53% of managers measure traffic from specific search engines, 49% conduct a logfile analysis of search terms (a log file is a list of searches conducted by one person; see Chapter 12 for a longer discussion), 42% compare competitive rankings, and 29% examine competitive meta tags.

One expert provided these suggestions on how to design web pages so that they appear at the top in search engine rankings:[5]

- Give the engines plenty of keyword-rich text to work with. Since search engines process textual information, it is important to design the text properly. Text must be placed at the top of the page and keywords must be integrated into the content of the page and must be placed at the beginning of paragraphs and headings.

- Ensure that the search engines have plenty of basic links to follow. When a search engine's spider visits a page, it first collects information about the page and then tries to follow any links to other pages. Many search engines cannot follow links that are generated using programs—especially if they have the "question mark" in the address. Ensuring that the links are current and appropriate is important.

- Provide a site map. Site maps help search engine spiders to find all of the pages on a particular site.
- Provide meta tags. As discussed earlier, providing meta tags that describe the site helps immensely in raising search engine rankings.

Search Engine Limitations

Search engines alone will not help consumers find every site relevant to their needs. Increasingly, search engines tap into smaller and smaller fractions of the overall Web with no engine capturing more than 16% of Web content. In addition, web debris (e.g., pages that are no longer updated, expired pages) reduces the effectiveness of search engines.

Internet Advertising

Internet advertising presents an interesting puzzle to marketing managers. On the one hand, total spending on Internet advertising has exploded. Figure 6.2 shows that such spending has risen from $30 million in the first quarter of 1996 to $2.2 billion in the fourth quarter of 2000. Even though current spending has dipped below the $2 billion mark, the Internet has clearly arrived as a legitimate new medium.

Many traditional advertisers have also unveiled major Internet advertising campaigns. Examples include Sprint, Procter & Gamble, Eddie Bauer, Visa, Toyota, Adidas, and British Airways. As shown in Table 6.3, the top ten advertisers spent about $161 million in the first half of 2001—about 8.5% of overall advertising. There is greater domination on the revenue side, where the top ten sites accounted for 38% of the overall market.

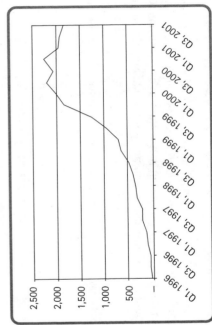

Figure 6.2
Total Spending on Internet Advertising ($ millions)

Source: Compiled from press releases at http://www.iab.net.

Table 6.3
Top Sites by Advertising Revenue and Top Advertisers (Information for first half of 2001)

Top Ad Revenue by Site

1	Yahoo!	$197,282,923
2	AOL.com	174,263,850
3	Excite	90,453,160
4	Lycos	61,892,893
5	AltaVista	50,577,473
6	Netscape	48,007,442
7	Webcrawler	38,903,498
8	ESPN.com	23,677,857
9	Go.com	23,625,735
10	Weather.com	20,084,731
	Total	$728,769,562

Top Online Advertisers

1	General Motors	$ 25,415,811
2	eBay	24,356,260
3	Amazon.com Inc.	16,200,820
4	Classmates Online	15,108,190
5	J.P. Morgan Chase	14,914,052
6	Barnes & Noble	14,368,801
7	Verisign Inc.	13,711,014
8	AOL Time Warner	13,333,416
9	Providian Corp.	12,769,892
10	Bank One Corp.	11,187,960
	Total	$161,366,216

Top Online Advertising by Industry

1	Retail	$ 299,404,537
2	Media and Advertising	261,440,537
3	Financial	177,879,435
4	Computers and Software	149,753,786
5	Local Services and Amusements	143,964,572
6	Public Transportation, Hotels and Resorts	68,016,488
7	Automotive, Auto Accessories and Equipment	66,261,445
8	Telecommunications	42,318,614
9	Government and Organizations	39,589,868
10	Insurance and Real Estate	38,961,553
	Total	$1,287,590,835

In 1998, the Internet overtook outdoor advertising (e.g., billboards) in total expenditure. However, as shown in Table 6.4, at the end of 2000, the Internet had less than a 2% media share.[6] The traditional giant media still dominate, but in the next few years the Internet is expected to break into the top five media.

The news on Internet advertising isn't all good. The most widely used metric for testing the effectiveness of banner advertising is the click-through rate, the proportion of viewers who clicked on a banner ad to visit the advertiser's web site. These rates have steadily

Table 6.4
Media Share

Medium	Advertising expenditures			Medium as % of total	
	2000	1999	% change	2000	1999
Magazine	$ 16,697	$ 14,672	13.8	6.9	6.6
Sunday magazine	1,110	1,006	10.3	0.5	0.5
Newspaper	18,817	17,797	5.7	7.7	8.0
National newspaper	3,785	3,320	14.0	1.6	1.5
Outdoor	2,391	1,989	20.2	1.0	0.9
Network TV	18,417	16,354	12.6	7.6	7.4
Spot TV	17,107	15,115	13.2	7.0	6.8
Syndicated TV	2,804	2,650	5.8	1.2	1.2
Cable TV networks	9,506	8,181	16.2	3.9	3.7
Network radio	871	417	108.7	0.4	0.2
National spot radio	2,672	2,349	13.8	1.1	1.1
Internet	4,333	2,832	53.0	1.8	1.3
Yellow Pages	13,228	12,652	4.6	5.4	5.7
Measured media	111,739	99,335	12.5	45.9	44.7
Unmeasured spending estimates	131,941	122,973	7.3	54.1	55.3
Total U.S. advertising	$243,680	$222,308	9.8	100.0	100.0

Notes: Dollars are in millions. *Measured media for 100 Leaders and all advertisers from Taylor Nelson Sofres' CMR, except Yellow Pages for the 100 Leaders, from Yellow Pages Publishers Association. **Figures extrapolated from Robert J. Coen's media analysis at Universal McCann (AA, June 11, 2001) are shown in italic for comparison. In the Coen figures shown, spot radio, spot TV and cable TV include national and local spot buys; magazine includes business publications.

Source: Advertising Age, http://AdAge.com.

diminished, with the latest data suggesting an average click-through rate of about 0.5%. In addition, a recent study of the eye movements of consumers as they browsed the Web showed that consumers pay scant attention to banners and may actively avoid them.[7] Furthermore, getting a reliable estimate of the number of consumers who actually viewed an ad is problematic.

For many managers, this is the puzzle. On the one hand, the total Internet advertising expenditure has exploded and many leading firms have unveiled advertising campaigns on the Internet. On the other, the Internet is still an unproven medium with shaky measurement systems and seemingly poor results. How does a manager making advertising decisions balance these seemingly contradictory pieces of information when designing an effective campaign?

Banner Ads and Sponsorships

Banners are small rectangles that appear on the top, bottom, and sides of the content in a web site. When a consumer visits a web site, the banners appear; if he or she clicks on a banner, the user is automatically taken to the advertised web site. Banners come in many sizes, ranging from small buttons to skyscrapers, which occupy a large portion of the screen.

The three important banner ad variations are interstitials, pop-ups, and pop-unders. An *interstitial* banner ad appears when the user transitions from one web site to another. It occupies the entire computer screen, and can either be automatically timed out or the user may be asked to initiate closure. *Pop-up ads* appear abruptly when a consumer first visits a site or at any other point during the browsing experience. The difference between pop-ups and *pop-unders* is that the latter open up in a new window that is visible only when the user closes the current window. The advantage of interstitials, pop-ups, and pop-unders is that they catch users by surprise. The disadvantage is that they are likely to annoy customers.

With site sponsorships, advertisers sign long-term agreements to have their logo displayed at all times on a given web site. As with banners, consumers can click on the logo to visit the sponsor's site.

How should managers think of banner ads? No consumer visits the Web to view a banner ad. The focus of the consumer is on activities, such as reading the news or buying a book. The banner ads are, therefore, incidental to the browsing experience. They are most closely comparable to billboards—viewing the message is incidental to the consumer's experience. This means that since consumers rarely pay close attention to the ads' messages, creative strategies using imagery, animation, and succinct slogans work best.

The banner ad is best thought of as a brand-building device that improves brand awareness and attitude. A banner rarely generates immediate consumer action, and then only if it is accompanied by a sizeable promotion. Banners can be targeted to the individual user by an advertising network, such as Doubleclick, using cookie technology. In most cases, banners must appear on multiple web sites to reach a sufficient number of target consumers.

Understanding the Click-Through

The click-through rate has become a dominant measure of banner ad effectiveness. Articles in the press lament the decline of click-through rates and question the long-term viability of the medium. Managers of successful web sites trumpet their amazing click-through rates, and articles proliferate about how to design ads to maximize click-throughs. I think that this current phase is misguided, and both advertisers and agencies must think hard about exactly what click-throughs mean. As the AIDA framework teaches us, it is important to move beyond getting the consumer's attention to making them take the desired action.

Think about it in two ways. If consumers do not click on an ad, does that make it ineffective? If consumers do click on an ad, does that make it effective? I would argue that the answer to both questions is a resounding "No"!

Start with the first question: Should we conclude that ads that are not clicked on are ineffective? The Internet is the only medium that has a two-stage consumer response process: consumers are first supposed to see the ad and then to click on it. In all other advertising media, consumers are expected simply to view an ad and go on with their lives—yet many of these ads on other media improve brand attitudes and sales.

We know from other media, in fact, that consumers rarely take an action immediately after viewing an ad. Ads work incrementally to improve awareness and brand attitudes. Anticipating an immediate response after an ad is viewed may be an unrealistic expectation.

Even if a consumer is interested in a product, he or she may or may not be ready to buy. Consider an ad for a mortgage service. I may actually be interested in it when I see the banner ad in the morning as I read the news on cnn.com, and in the evening, I may remember the name and visit the site. Thus, the ad has had a tremendous impact on me. But, I did not click through!

Now, consider the flip side: If a consumer clicks on an ad, does that automatically make it effective? Of course not. Frequently, we see that there is no clear post-click call for action. A consumer may click on a banner and be taken to a site with 10,000 sub-pages. The consumer may be befuddled by this, back off, and never return. But the advertiser counts this as a click-through and is delighted at the result.

This is a particular problem with ads designed to resemble a site's content (e.g., with buttons that say "OK!" or "Click here!"). Consumers may be misled and click through, but then they realize their folly and beat a hasty retreat. Hence, they are counted as click-throughs even though the ad was not effective for these consumers.

Click-throughs are not meaningless, but don't pull the plug on your banner advertising simply on account of a low click-through rate. Instead, look at the big picture in terms of affecting awareness rates and attitudes. If you do have a high click-through rate, consider whether it reflects true consumer response or is an artifact of your ad design.

In the long run, serious advertisers and ad agencies will go beyond click-throughs. They will do what advertisers in most other media do–track the effectiveness of ads by conducting market research, which should basically track what some industry people currently dismiss as the "warm fuzzies." Consumer attitudes toward the ad and the brand and consumer awareness and knowledge are some of the key variables that should be tracked. As the medium grows, market research companies will be better able to do this for the large majority of ads, leading to a more sophisticated approach to banner advertising.

Targeting with Banner Ads

The advantage of advertising on the Internet is that one can narrowly define the target market. There are four types of targeting offered: content targeting, behavioral targeting, user targeting, and tech targeting.

Content targeting involves delivering ads based on the content of a web site or interest category chosen by a consumer. For example, an advertisement for an HP printer might be displayed on the search results page when a user types "printer" into a search engine.

Behavioral targeting involves delivering ads based on how and when a visitor uses the Web. First is psychographic targeting (i.e., ads are shown to consumers matching a certain psychographic profile). Second, frequency control is provided (i.e., an ad is delivered such that every consumer sees it three to four times—no more, no less). Third, time control can be achieved (i.e., an ad for a product is shown at a time when it is most likely to have the highest impact). For example, a McDonald's banner can be shown around 11 A.M. when people are starting to think about lunch.

User targeting involves delivering ads based on the specific traits of a visitor. An advertisement might appear only to people within a certain geographic location, within a certain industry, or who use a certain domain name (e.g., ads shown to North American users visiting your site from .org domain names).

Tech targeting involves delivering ads based on the visitor's browser type, operating system, or ISP (e.g., Apple might target ads for a new product only to consumers using Macintosh computers).

Challenges of Banner Ads

The greatest challenge of banner advertising is measurement. First, no standard term defines the number of consumers who have viewed a banner ad. Three terms related to viewing are hits, impressions, and page views. Each time a Web server sends a file to a browser, it is recorded in the server's log file as a "hit." *Hits* are generated for every element of a requested page, including graphics, text, and interactive items. If a user views a page containing two graphics, three hits are recorded—one for the page itself and one for each graphic. "Valid hits" are a refinement of hits that exclude error messages and other useless information. *Page views* refers to the number of times a user requests a page that may contain a particular ad but these results must be adjusted for the fact that they may overstate ad impressions if users choose to turn the graphics off. *Impressions* refers to the number of times an ad banner is downloaded and presumably seen by visitors. If an ad appears on multiple pages simultaneously, this statistic may understate the number of ad impressions due to browser caching—a practice where recently used pages are stored on a local server to increase access speeds to the Web. There is no way of knowing whether an ad was actually loaded, and most servers record an ad as served even if it was not. Most advertising is bought on a cost per thousand impressions basis. Because impressions are not reliable measures of the number of ads downloaded to users, many advertisers are leery of the Internet.

Second, many sites use IP addresses as a means of identifying "hits." Because IP addresses are not uniquely assigned to individuals, this identification process may lead to 39% underestimation of visits, a 64% overestimation of page views, and a 79% overestimation of the time spent on each visit. Naturally, this also waters down the ads' targeting.

Third, there is no standard way to identify the largest, and hence most desirable, sites on the Web. Jupiter Media Metrix and Nielsen's Net Ratings are the two firms that measure the traffic ratings of web sites. Both companies recruit participants who install software on their PC to monitor their browsing patterns. The way this data is collected significantly undercounts two populations: users who browse the Internet from work (only 7,000 of Media Metrix's 40,000 sample users have a PC at work) and global users. There are also significant differences in the methodology used by these two firms. Net Ratings enumerates the universe of Internet users on a monthly basis and uses single panel recruitment and data collection methods. On the other hand, Media Metrix sporadically updates its universe estimate and uses multiple recruitment and collection methods. These differences make it difficult to achieve a consensus about the largest sites.

How are sponsorships different from banner ads? Unlike banner ads, which are placed on a variety of sites based on user characteristics, sponsorship is a long-term promotional agreement with a few sites. In other words, the trade-off is between breadth (banner) and depth (sponsorships).

The primary purpose of the sponsorship is to leverage the traffic and brand strength of a web site to obtain traffic for one's own site and buttress one's own brand. Hence, portal sites such as AOL and Yahoo! are the leading candidates for sponsorship deals. Smaller sites may, however, offer access to a more targeted set of consumers.

How does one choose between banner ads and sponsorships? Because banner ads are the dominant form of advertising on the Internet, consumers have become familiar with them. Banner ads are also directly comparable to billboards and print ads, so they act as ready frames of reference. Moreover, because they are not very intrusive, they do not provoke a negative reaction, as do some other techniques, such as spam. Banner ads are excellent brand-building devices because they can reinforce messages well.

For a banner ad to succeed, two components are necessary: pre-click excitement and a post-click call for action. Pre-click excitement is essential for all ads, but it may or may not lead to a click-through. If consumers do not click through the ad is not necessarily a failure. Such ads may have improved brand attitude and consumer awareness of the web site, which lead to positive results in the long run.

If a consumer does click on the ads, he or she should encounter a clear post-click call for action. Confronted by a large web site with thousands of sub-pages, a consumer may not know what to do. The ads that work best take consumers to a page where the expected action is clear.

Sponsorship arrangements provide several advantages over banner ads. Typically, they are long-term deals, which means consumers consistently view brand information when they visit a particular web site. Also, because consumers associate the contents of the web site with the sponsor, sponsorship helps build positive associations. Therefore, sponsorships are a good tool for brand building and traffic generation.

The disadvantage of sponsorships is that, unlike with banners, there is little scope to present brand content beyond the logo. The advertiser has to work within the framework of the content site, and cannot try different creative styles. Sponsorships should not therefore be the sole advertising option for a company.

E-mail advertising is discussed in detail in Chapter 12.

The Web Site as a Marketing Tool

A company's web site is central to its marketing strategy. Frequently, the goal of advertising and promotion is to direct consumers to the company's web site. (This is expected to be the case even with mobile commerce; e.g., transactions enabled by handheld devices such as cell phones and personal digital assistants.) The site is where consumer actions take place. Users can read news stories, forward them to others, download recipes, buy products, download software, or talk to others, among other things. Thus, going back to the AIDA framework, the web site represents the last step (action) and in that way is the culmination of the marketing process.

Three Design Elements

Firms must keep in mind three elements when designing a web site: purpose, target audience(s), and expected behavior.

The first element is *purpose*. Why does the site exist? What does it hope to accomplish? What is the essence of the site? These questions must be answered and there must be a consensus among the firm's key decision makers about the answers.

At this stage, it is important to define the stance of the site, its overall position. For instance, is the site formal or informal? Is its purpose serious or fun? Answering these questions drives the design process.

The second element is the *target audience*. Web designers must understand clearly who will benefit from the site. It is useful to prepare a short description of the audience and display it prominently. Defining the target audience is always tricky: the definition must not be too broad or too narrow, and the audience must be both substantial and reachable.

Once you have defined the target audience, you should ask, What do they want? How do they think? How much time will they have when they come to your site? What are their objectives when they arrive at your site? How will they connect to the site (e.g., modem, DSL, cable modem, T1 line)?

The last thing to consider is the *expected behavior* at the site. Do you expect the reader to go over the information and then go home? Will the reader visit the site once or many times? If repeat behavior is important, how will the site bring the reader back? Will the reader want to print some of the information?

Is your web site going to be static (one-way) or interactive (two-way)? If you expect interactivity, then your site must accommodate that. For instance, the reader must be able to send e-mail with questions, compliments, or suggestions. Many sites provide forms where users can fill out their information for future contact.

Quality of a Web Site

There are three aspects of web site quality: information quality, information structure quality, and usability. The quality of a web site is strongly related to the quality of information it provides. Users judge site quality to be poor if the information provided is factually incorrect. Incorrect information inconveniences users because they must visit many sources to recheck it. Second, information that is obviously propaganda or unconditional praise leads to increased cynicism among users. Third, incorrect spelling and poor grammar obviously affect user opinion. Finally, link quality matters. Broken links (i.e., links that do not work and lead to a "page not found" message) and wrong links (i.e., links that take you to a place that you did not expect) detract from the quality of information.

Not only must the information be of a high quality, it must be organized effectively. A good information structure helps individuals understand the scope of the information provided and helps them quickly locate the information they care about. Four things detract from information structure quality: too many categories, too few categories, not enough information in a category, and no logical category arrangement.

Finally, the term *usability* captures the quality of the user experience. High usability indicates great navigation and easy access, leading to a satisfying user experience. The top web design problems related to usability are:[8]

Long Download Times

Studies now show that users are very impatient about long download times. Many users switch away to another page if the page does not load in a few seconds.

Outdated Information

Users must understand the overall structure of the page at all times and where they are in relation to the home page. Providing a site map or a consistent menu visible on all pages alleviates this problem. Also, many users now make assumptions about the layout. For example, they assume that they can click on the site logo in the left-hand corner and go to the home page. If this does not happen, they may become confused.

Nonstandard Link Colors

Colors have meaning online. Typically, dark blue is reserved for unread links and a light brown is reserved for links that have been clicked on before. Unfortunately, this is not standardized, leading to user confusion.

Scrolling Text and Animations

A document with a lot of text accessible only if users scroll to the bottom is badly designed. Each page should have a small chunk of information that can be easily understood. And keep it visually simple: many users are irritated by flashing, blinking, or noisy things that may detract from their main objective.

Free Products and Promotions

A great way to entice consumers to visit your web site is to provide a promotion, such as free shipping. Amazon.com announced in January 2002 that, for all orders over $99, shipping is free. Consumers can participate in sweepstakes and contests online (see Appendix I for a list of companies that provide this) and download free products such as

Figure 6.3a
On-Site Promotions

Figure 6.3b
Intermediary–Based Promotions

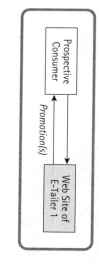

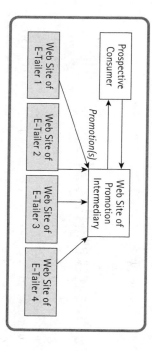

screensavers and games (see Appendix II for a list of companies that provide this). Offering consumers electronic coupons that can be redeemed on or offline has also become very common (see Appendix III for a list of companies that provide this).

Let us look at online coupons more closely to determine why they may be better than traditional paper coupons. The most common way to distribute coupons is through the Sunday newspaper. If you want coupons, you must go through hundreds of coupons before you find the few that are suited to your tastes. The result of this targeting approach is that the redemption rate is around 1–2%.

There is a better chance online of targeting consumers with what they want. The individual can simply run a search on the product that is of greatest interest. Some e-tailers are able to identify a visitor as a frequent shopper as soon as they arrive at their site, allowing them to target these consumers more effectively. Also, on the Internet, a user can print out coupons just before shopping. With the advent of mobile commerce, it is going to be even more common to receive targeted coupons online.

How are promotions different from advertising? First, unlike most advertising, they lead to an immediate increase in sales and have a direct impact on consumer behavior. Second, they provide consumers with a lower price. Third, they are time-bound (i.e., they are available for a short period of time), and last, they may require participation by the consumers (e.g., filling out forms).

Two Promotion Models

As shown in Figures 6.3a and 6.3b, on the Web, there are two promotion models: direct and intermediary-based.

In the *direct model*, a seller provides its current or prospective customers with the promotion directly. For example, bn.com frequently e-mails coupons to its existing customers.

Other stores provide coupons to consumers who visit their site. The advantages of this method are that there is a direct channel of communication with the consumers, and the company can control the message. It is a great way to get returning customers to buy again and to buy more, but it may not work well for first-time consumers.

The second way of distributing coupons is through an *intermediary* (e.g., freeoffers.com). The intermediary either provides coupons to local bricks-and-mortar stores (e.g., valpak. com) or to online retailers. The first advantage of using this model is that the cost of building traffic is spread across several companies and is, therefore, lower than what an individual e-tailer might have spent. The second advantage is that the synergies across e-tailers can be exploited (e.g., a clothing e-tailer and a shoe e-tailer can have a joint promotion).

The disadvantages to the intermediary approach are that consumers can easily compare what competitors are offering and switch to them; it may be hard to attract the attention of the consumer when the list of e-tailers is large; brand confusion may result; and if the target consumers of each e-tailer is different, the scope for synergy may be limited. The value of the intermediary to an individual e-tailer member reduces with the number of members.

Affiliate or Associate Programs

This concept was pioneered by Amazon.com's Jeff Bezos, who described it as a micro-franchising strategy. For example, a small site that specializes in Egyptian art signs up for the Amazon.com associates program. As part of the agreement, the site posts a small Amazon.com banner and encourages its visitors to purchase books on Egyptian art from Amazon.com. Whenever a consumer who is referred from the small site buys something at Amazon.com, the site receives a commission of 15% of the sale.

Amazon.com signed up associates at a frenetic pace. By February 1998, Amazon.com had attracted more than 30,000 webmasters. By June 1998, it had 60,000; by July 1999, more than 300,000; by June 2000, it was over the 450,000 mark.[9] At one point, about 30% of its revenue came from such sites.

Benefits of Associate Programs

Associate programs benefit both the advertiser (e.g., Amazon.com) and the associate. The advertiser gets the traffic from the site and the associate gets a commission every time a customer they refer buys something. But the advertiser pays for the extra traffic only when there is action—a purchase in the case of Amazon.com. Amazon.com does not pay for all of the consumers who may browse and exit. Moreover, advertisers typically do not pay out commissions until they hit a minimum target amount, and even then, they pay out the amount at intervals.

Associate programs are also a great branding tool; in addition to providing incremental traffic, these programs provide greater publicity: small banners are displayed at thousands of sites for basically no charge!

Moreover, associate programs are a decentralized traffic generation tool. Instead of going to one large portal site such as Yahoo! to generate traffic, this method uses thousands of small sites. This spreads out the cost of traffic generation and reduces the risk to the advertiser.

Variations of the Basic Idea

Some associate programs are *two-tiered*. These programs reward publishers for signing up other publishers. Thus, if company X signs up companies Y and Z, it will earn a commission on the combined sales of X, Y, and Z.

Some online firms have used associate programs to create online malls. A site joins the associate program of several online retailers and displays the links to these e-tailers on its site. The site makes money every time somebody clicks on any of the links. This may reduce the prominence of any given retailer and to avoid this many online retailers now ask for an *exclusivity agreement.*

One other variation is for a site to share a portion of the commission with either the end-user or with a nonprofit organization. Consider iGive.com. This company allows consumers to shop from a variety of e-tailers with the promise that it will provide half the commission it gets to a nonprofit organization.

Designing an Integrated Marketing Communication Campaign

Designing a promotional mix implies aligning managerial objectives with the right promotional vehicle.

Objectives

The first step in planning a campaign is to define what the firm wants to achieve. Objectives can be divided into three categories: cognitive, affective, and conative.

Cognitive objectives relate to changes in an individual's thought process, including attracting attention and increasing consumer knowledge. *Affective* objectives relate to consumer emotions—primarily, getting consumers to like your ad and your brand. Finally, *conative* objectives relate to the expected action from consumers, such as instilling loyalty and persuading first-time consumers to buy.

In addition, managers must define their short-term and long-term goals. Examples of short-term goals include immediate sales growth or greater downloads or hits. Examples of long-term goals are building brand equity and improving consumer education. It is always useful to establish beforehand how the firm defines the success of the advertising campaign.

Which Media Do We Choose?

Even though advertising and promoting on the Internet is beneficial, companies should also advertise in other media, such as network television and radio, for several reasons.

First, each medium targets a different audience. Radio targets commuters, for instance. Television reaches virtually every American household and offers something for each person in the family. Maximizing the number of media increases the potential exposure. Second, offline media have a larger reach: the Superbowl is, for example, watched by about 40% of all U.S. households. No online event can come close to this level of exposure. Third, some offline media target certain audiences coveted by online companies, such as National Public Radio (NPR), which boasts an audience that is affluent and highly educated. Finally, it may be easier to stand out in offline media, which is arguably less cluttered than the Internet. As a result, advertising in offline media can lead to a greater awareness.

Advertisements in offline media must work closely with the design of the web site and online ad efforts. This is the integrated marketing communication approach. Offline ads must reinforce the branding message being sent by online ads and on the web site. They can build traffic to the web site by prominently displaying the web site's URL. Offline ads can also be branding vehicles that direct interested consumers to the web site, where they are then exposed to information-based arguments.

Advertisers must look carefully at all media and choose those that meet their objectives. Table 6.5 summarizes the performance of the different online media options and the different strategic objectives. This can be used as a guide during the decision process.

Prescriptions for Advertisers

Managers must keep six guidelines in mind when thinking of the Internet as an advertising medium:

1. *Use multiple approaches.* The Internet is a versatile medium, with many avenues for advertising. Viral marketing can lead to a big boost if managed well. Banner ads and sponsorships are indirect approaches to advertising, and e-mail is a direct method. Many users locate information using search engines and optimizing search position should be taken seriously. Smart managers will realize that they have to use multiple approaches to successfully reach their audience. For example, a sponsorship at a leading portal lends the advertiser immediate credibility. However, banner ads may be necessary to shape the

Table 6.5

Choosing Between Online Communication Options

	Awareness	Knowledge Building	Targeting	Branding	Immediate Response
Viral Marketing	✓✓✓	✓✓	✓	✓	✓✓
Search Engine Optimization	✓✓	✓✓	✓✓✓	✓	✓✓✓
Banner Ads	✓✓	✓	✓✓	✓✓✓	✓✓
Sponsorships	✓✓✓	✓	✓	✓✓✓	✓
Spam	✓✓	✓	✓	Negative	✓
Permission-based E-mails	✓✓✓	✓✓	✓✓✓	✓	✓✓✓

identity of the brand and e-mail may be required to communicate new deals. Consumers who receive a promotional e-mail from a company whose logo they have seen at a major portal respond better than those who have not.

2. *Develop effective creatives.* Develop several banner creatives by varying colors, size, fonts, and execution styles. Similarly, develop different e-mail creatives by varying the number of links, the placement of the links, and the length of the text. Test these creatives out in real time and pick the ones that work the best. Rich media technology provides some ideas on improving banners. Rich banners can have a built-in order area, expandable order forms, and secure server technology to protect credit card transactions. They also cost more to produce and place, and they can slow down web-page loading times. But they are among the many options to explore, as are techniques new to the Internet that have been used effectively in other media. Using humor and celebrities, for example, will soon be common banner techniques.

3. *Measure, measure, measure.* As mentioned earlier, the click-through on a banner is an intermediate measure with no intrinsic meaning. Conduct marketing research to assess ad effectiveness using affective measures (e.g., awareness, recall, attitude) and cognitive measures (e.g., product knowledge). At the same time, correlate clicks to actual actions. When you approach a publisher, ensure that you understand exactly how they measure traffic to the site and the number of people who viewed the ad. Ask tough questions about the quality of the measurement. If you are tracking effectiveness over the long-run, ensure that you compare apples with apples (e.g., Net Ratings with Net Ratings).

4. *Build a customer database.* Develop a permission-based customer list (more information on permission marketing is available in Chapter 12). Obtain detailed profiles of who your customers are and what they want from you. Build customer trust.

5. *Don't put all your eggs in the Internet basket.* Advertising on the Internet should not mean abandoning other media. Instead, think of synchronizing your message across different media to come up with a well-designed advertising campaign.

6. *All industries are different.* When advertising in the B2B context, a factual and information-rich message may be most effective, while in the B2C context, brand building is most important.

Conclusion

In this chapter, we have used an IMC perspective to describe how to use online techniques to build customer traffic. The AIDA model guides us in this process by constantly reminding us that any successful promotional technique must eventually lead to an action.

Notes

(All URLs are current as of March 15, 2002.)

1. It is not possible to provide a comprehensive treatment of Integrated Marketing Communications here. Interested readers are referred to *The New Marketing Paradigm: Integrated Marketing*

Communications by Don E. Schultz, Stanley I. Tannenbaum, Robert F. Lauterborn, Stanley L. Tannenbaum.

2. Michael Pastore, "Internet Retailers Look Toward Profitability," August 30, 2000, <http://cyberatlas.internet.com/markets/retailing/article/0,,6061_449371,00.html>.

3. Danny Sullivan, "Search Engine Watch Page," <http://searchenginewatch.com>.

4. Richard Wiggins, "The Effect of September 11 on the Leading Search Engine," *First Monday,* 6(10), 2001, <http://www.firstmonday.org/issues/issue6_10/wiggins/index.html>.

5. Paul Bruemmer, "SEO and the Web Site Design Process," December 19, 2001, <http://www.clickz.com/search/opt/article.php/942651>.

6. The numbers presented by Advertising Age are different from those of the Internet Advertising Bureau. Using IAB figures doubles the share of Internet advertising. The dominance of large media is, however, unquestioned.

7. This study was conducted by Prof. Xavier Dreze of the University of Southern California.

8. Adapted from Jakob Nielsen, "Top Ten Mistakes in Web Design," May 1996, <http://www.useit.com/alertbox/9605.html>.

9. AssociatePrograms.com, "Home Page," <http://www.associateprograms.com/search/guide.shtml>.

REVIEW / CHAPTER 6

Discussion Questions

1. How would you define success for a viral marketing campaign?

2. Study Figure 6.1. How would you measure such social networks for an existing customer base?

3. When is it preferable to be listed in a search engine as opposed to a directory and vice versa?

4. Are some types of consumers more likely to use search engines to locate information?

5. Consider Figure 6.2. What do you think it would look like over the next ten years?

6. Can an advertisement be annoying and effective at the same time? Should Web ads be made more annoying to capture consumer attention?

7. Have you ever been motivated to buy something after visiting a company's web site? How would you define an effective web site?

8. What are the disadvantages of using free giveaways frequently?

9. How do you set the commission rate in an affiliate program?

E-Tasks

1. For the twenty last names in the following table, answer these questions:

   a. How many people do you know with each of the *last names* in the table? Include only people you know personally (e.g., friend, colleague, relative, neighbor). Enter the number of people next to each last name in column 1.

   b. For each row, indicate the number of people you are willing to contact by e-mail. Enter this in column 2.

   c. Finally, in column 3, enter the number of people from column 2 who are most likely to respond to your message. Base this on your previous experiences with them.

   d. Total columns 1, 2, and 3.

   Compare your totals in columns 1, 2, and 3 with those of your classmates. Were you among the top five in the class in terms of any of these totals? Did you know the person who came out as the most influential? Would you have picked him or her if you were launching a viral marketing campaign? Why do you think there is attrition between columns 1 and 2?

REVIEW / CHAPTER 6

E-Tasks (continued)

	Number of people 1	Number of people in 1 who you are willing to contact 2	Number of people in 2 who are most likely to respond 3
1 Avery			
2 Bradley			
3 Gutierrez			
4 Johanssen			
5 Kim			
6 Kelley			
7 Lim			
8 Martinez			
9 Macmillan			
10 Miller			
11 Nguyen			
12 Nance			
13 Olson			
14 Patel			
15 Perry			
16 Peterson			
17 Rominsky			
18 Sheth			
19 Steinmetz			
20 Strand			
TOTAL			

REVIEW / CHAPTER 6

E-Tasks (continued)

2. Customer retention is as important as acquisition. Visit http://www.e-loyaltyresource.com/quiz/ to take a quiz on how well you understand building customer loyalty.

3. Obtain a list of the top web properties for the last month from Jupiter Media Metrix (http://jmm.com). Now, obtain a list of the top ten online advertisers for the last month from the same company. Compare the two lists to study the relationship between advertising and traffic. What does it mean if a site has a lot of traffic but is not advertising the most?

4. Visit http://www.netratings.com. Obtain a list of the top ten banner ads (in terms of impressions) from the previous week. Rank these ads from the most effective to the least effective. What do you find?

5. A new ad type called pop-under has become popular. To learn more about this, visit http://www.popunder.com. Compare this ad format with the pop-up. Which is more annoying? Which is more effective? Can an ad be annoying and effective at the same time?

APPENDIX I / CHAPTER 6

Sweepstake and Contest Sites

1. http://www.sweepstakes4u.com/. Directory that offers over sixty different sites. Offers the ability to win cash and other prizes by filling out surveys and contests. Gives the option of entering as a return user.

2. http://www.huronline.com/. Web site that offers different categories of sweepstakes and contests, such as mail-in contests, slot machines, and bingo. On the side, there are advertisements for other sweepstake or contest sites, such as Lucky surf.com and iwon.com.

3. http://www.onlinesweeps.com/. Web site that offers the ability to choose from several types of sweepstakes, such as online sweepstakes, slot machine games, daily entries, and eQuiz trivia game.

4. http://contests.miningco.com/shopping/contests/. Web page that offers updates about sweepstakes, such as daily sweepstakes news, site giveaways, and going out of business sweepstakes. On the side of the page, called its "Site Guide," it also has formatted the page to categorize sweepstake sites in alphabetical order, home/family-oriented, and entertainment-oriented.

5. http://misc.webstakes.com/play/StandAloneReg?reg_id=1901. A web site that requires membership and providing personal information and interests before entering the site. After entering, it offers different sweepstakes and contests sites that you can visit.

6. http://www.webcontests.com/bestsweeps.html. Web site that is a subsidiary of web magnet.com that merely has a list of seventeen recommended sweepstake sites to visit. It also has a category of top twenty Web sweeps and top twenty web contests.

7. http://www.fatcatcafe.com/freebies/Contests_n_Sweepstakes/. Site that lists twenty-two sites that you can visit to win freebies through sweepstakes and contests. The prizes include Palm Pilots, money, and vacations.

8. http://www.volition.com/cgi-bin/prize.pl. Web site that poses as a bulletin board for sweepstake and contest users. On this page, contest postings are available. This site allows anyone to generate their own contest or sweepstake.

9. http://www.thezone.pair.com/contests/. Web site that recommends a list of ten sites to visit for sweepstakes and contests.

10. http://www.sweepstakesonline.com/index.php. Web site that lists sweepstakes and contest sites by prizes.

I thank my students Joni Grepo and Jennifer Lao for their help compiling this list.

APPENDIX II / CHAPTER 6

Free Stuff Links

1. http://www.easyfreebies.com. This site offers an e-mail option to receive information. This site provides monthly offers, freebies forum, rebates, and many links. The site is well decorated and looks professional.

2. http://www.free-stuff-net.com/. This site connects you to great coupons and contests. It acts as a directory and has categories such as top sites and cool sites. They also categorize by products.

3. http://www.100hotfreestuff.com/. One Hundred Hot Free Stuff cuts through the masses, bringing you the latest and best information on free offers you need today! And there's no need to waste your time surfing.

4. http://www.totallyfreestuff.com/. This site provides many different categories of freebies (e.g., books, health and beauty), and also has the option to search for freebie products.

5. http://www.top20free.com. Provides a list of the top twenty sites that offer free clipart, graphics, fonts, and much more. Rankings are updated once every fifteen minutes and the in/out counts are reset to zero every twenty-four hours. You must send at least one visitor every twenty-four hours to be listed on top twenty.

6. http://www.freebies.net. Find the best free stuff on the Internet, with new freebies being added daily. This site is a directory, visually similar to Yahoo!, with categories such as magazines and samples.

7. http://www.nojunkfree.com/qpolicy.asp. The best free samples available on the Web. This site rates freebies and promises no junk. They show you best freebies, best samples, okay samples, etc. Within these categories are various products.

8. http://www.sampleville.com/. At Sampleville, we don't just find the greatest free offers, we actually order them for you! What does this mean? The fastest access to samples.

9. http://www.bonanzas.com/free-stuff/index.html. Offers free stuff and trial offers, sweepstakes, games and contests, samples, magazines, catalogs, trials. This site is a link to other sites offering freebies.

10. http://www.freetweak.com. They are building one of the largest free stuff site directories on the Internet. They update daily, so be sure to bookmark. It also has the option of searching for products.

APPENDIX III / CHAPTER 6

Coupons Links

1. http://www.1amazingdeal.com/. Emphasizes no banners, no flashing images–just coupons to various retailers such as Amazon.com, buy.com, rei.com, and more.

2. http://www.bigbigsavings.com/. Coupons and deals for DVDs, CDs, books, and other products from major retailers. They have a newsletter, forum, search by category, and much more.

3. http://www.thegeeknextdoor.com/. They scour the Net everyday to find the best coupons and product deals for favorite Internet merchants. They carry hundreds of merchants and tons of deals. The latest deals are listed in a Daily Edition. Use the category or merchant links to browse all of the deals in their system. If they don't have a coupon for a store you like, they give you the option of letting them know.

4. http://www.listofcoupons.com/. Offers coupon codes, bargains, freebies, sales, and more. They promote that they have no flashy banners or ads that make downloading time consuming. Instead, it's very plain, but they advertise their great coupons and offer to search by category or alphabetically by store.

5. http://www.specialoffers.com/. This site is a directory of coupons, offers, freebies, and more. They have numerous categories and you can search for products.

6. http://www.shoppingcoupon.com/. A great place to find coupons. They allow you to search for coupons by category or store.

7. http://www.insanecoupons.com/. They will put you in touch with the most popular stores and provide you with their online coupons and specials to help save you money. Purchase anything–maternity clothes, gift baskets, cigars, flowers, DVDs–all without leaving your computer. They let you search by store or category.

8. http://www.imegadeals.com/. Offering online coupons, coupon codes, and products listed by categories. They offer a mailing list. They promote that they update the site several times a day. They offer a customer service e-mail if people have problems using the coupon codes or the site.

9. http://www.hotcoupons.com/. They offer local coupons and promotions on products and services you use every day in your home, office, or even when you travel. You can search by putting in your Zip Code or city.

10. http://247malls.com/GO/mall/topcoupons.htm. Shop from over 1,000 of the Web's best stores at 247 malls and get free valuable online coupons and special deals.

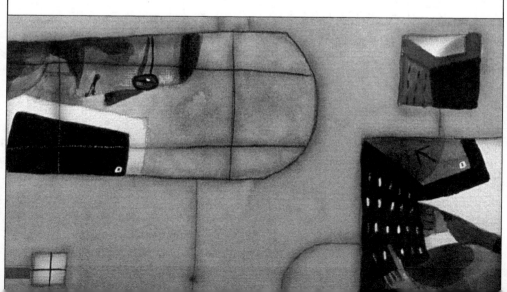

CHAPTER 7

Distribution and Logistics

Learning Objectives

▼ To understand the basics of supply chains.

▼ To understand how the Internet affects supply chains.

▼ To learn about the four stages of supply chain evolution.

▼ To understand the basics of distribution channels.

▼ To examine e-fulfillment issues for online retailers.

Executive Summary

A supply chain is a company's links to other corporations that help it deliver products to the individual consumer. A supply chain starts with the suppliers of raw materials (e.g., hops in the case of beer). The manufacturer then converts the raw materials into a finished product (e.g., Budweiser beer). Distributors help move the product to retailers. There are three flows within every supply chain—the physical flow of goods, the financial flow, and the information flow. The Internet can help reduce costs, serve markets better, and disseminate knowledge among the different companies in a supply chain. Supply chains evolve in four steps—traditional (no information sharing), integrated (information sharing within company), collaboration (information sharing with suppliers and customers), and synchronization (information sharing with partners). The portion of the supply chain from the manufacturer to the consumer is called the distribution channel. Companies use intermediaries to reduce the cost of distribution, shield themselves from market risk, target customers better, and provide better information to consumers. E-fulfillment is the process of executing a customer's order and ensuring that it reaches its destination on time. It is a costly and difficult process that can make the difference between profits and losses. This chapter discusses four e-fulfillment strategies—logistics postponement, resource exchange, leveraged shipments, and bricks-and-clicks; three typical e-fulfillment scenarios—direct to consumer (ship from retailer to consumer), consumer direct (ship from manufacturer to consumer), and sell-source-ship (ship from manufacturer to retailer); and e-fulfillment organization—centralized or decentralized—and in-house or outsourced.

Introduction

A supply chain consists of a company's links to other corporations that help it deliver products to the individual consumer. A supply chain starts with the suppliers of raw materials (e.g., hops in the case of beer). The manufacturer then converts the raw materials into a finished product (e.g., Budweiser beer). The portion of the supply chain from the manufacturer to the consumer is called the distribution channel. Manufacturers ship the product to wholesalers (usually state-level intermediaries) and then on to retailers (e.g., supermarkets, convenience stores) and finally, on to consumers. Other intermediaries, such as distribution and logistics providers and financial intermediaries, also facilitate the movement of goods.

Each supply chain is different, and not every one follows this neat sequence. Some distribution channels do not involve wholesalers. It has become increasingly common for manufacturers to sell directly to consumers while still working through the traditional physical distribution channel. Many retailers now have their own private-label brands (e.g., Safeway Select Soda) that compete with manufacturer brands (e.g., Coke, Pepsi).

Since customer demand drives supply chains, they must be customer-centric. Carefully observing the market helps reduce cost and improve efficiency. Some have even argued that the term "supply chain" should be replaced by "demand network" or "customer-driven Web."

Flows within a Supply Chain

There are three flows within any supply chain—physical goods, money, and information. The central movement is that of physical goods from manufacturers to consumers; financial flows and information flows facilitate this movement.

Financial flows are the movement of financial payments among the different companies that facilitate the forward movement of physical goods. Unless a downstream intermediary (e.g., wholesaler) has made the appropriate financial arrangement, an upstream company (e.g., manufacturer) will not ship the good. Companies may have complex financial arrangements with other agencies in the supply chain (e.g., credit, long-term contracts). Financial intermediaries also provide services such as insurance and escrow.

One of the most valuable resources within a supply chain is *information* about the marketplace (e.g., consumer tastes, demand patterns, inventory). The primary impact of the Internet and Web technology on supply chains has been to ensure that the right person has the right information at the right time. With better information about consumer demand, suppliers are better able to organize their production and manage their inventory. Information equals money in the supply chain. Every time a supplier can reduce inventory costs or produce the right type of product, it reduces costs and boosts profits. Information can also lead to conflict within the supply chain and battles to control information. Many companies are paranoid, for example, about the potential competitive implications of sharing information (e.g., a wholesaler may be in a position to share information with a competing manufacturer).

Despite these possible problems, effective sharing of marketplace information can help mitigate problems such as "the bullwhip effect." Even though customer demand may be relatively stable, one observes greater variability in orders as one moves up a supply chain. In other words, even a stable market demand could lead to a volatile order pattern for manufacturers. This phenomenon could be due to a variety of factors; one scenario would be retailers stocking up for future months when volume discounts are provided. Whatever the cause, the impact of the bullwhip effect on the supply chain can be huge: greater inventory may be held at different places in the chain, leading to greater costs; production facilities may not be used optimally; and so on. Better information flow between members of a supply chain can help avoid these problems. For instance, Wal-Mart is frequently praised for relaying point-of-sale information up the supply chain so that planning can be improved.

Benefits of Internet Technology

By facilitating better information flows in the supply chain, the Internet and Web technology can help supply chain management (SCM) in three important ways—sharing knowledge, increasing the speed of response, and reducing the costs of servicing a market.

First, using Internet and Web technology, it is now possible to share knowledge among participants in a supply chain. The large companies in a supply chain can easily provide intermediaries with information on market and industry trends. Specific information about the market collected by salespeople and retailers can reach manufacturers faster.

Second, using the Internet, companies can respond faster to changes in customer demand. Speedier sharing of information about changes in customer tastes or sudden inflections helps firms more quickly bring the appropriate product to the market and align product offerings with market demand.

The concept of a rolling warehouse illustrates the impact of this technology.[1] In turbulent markets with rapid fluctuations in customer demand, delivering a product over long distances (e.g., from Los Angeles to New York) can become problematic. Typically, trucks stop at multiple warehouses that service local markets. The problem is that the demand at each warehouse may be completely different at the time of delivery than it was when the truck started its journey. Some warehouses may want more units and others may want fewer. The rolling warehouse concept evolved to serve the needs of the market better. Instead of allocating the units ahead of time to a particular warehouse, the truck leaves without the information about what to drop off where; using recent demand forecasts, companies can provide the truck instructions along the way as to how much to drop off in different locations. Thus, the truck essentially becomes a rolling warehouse.

Finally, the Internet and the Web have helped companies reduce the costs of serving a market. Supply chains always have room for improvement. Causes of inefficiency abound and include rigid manufacturing systems, resistance to change, paper-based processes, and so forth. With a streamlined supply chain enabled by the Internet, the costs of each process drop, leading to a more cost-effective method of serving the marketplace.

A Note on Electronic Data Interchange (EDI)[2]

Starting in the 1970s, EDI (see the discussion in Chapter 4) has been the dominant technology used by large companies (e.g., Sears, Ford, Wal-Mart, and General Motors) to relay information among partners in a supply chain. EDI is a proprietary system that emerged as a way of getting departments within a large company to share information with one another. Over time, standards were developed that allowed multiple companies to use this system to talk to one another.

EDI systems are reliable: as one industry expert put it, "EDI is off the shelf, it's tried and true, it's an industrial strength workhorse." However, EDI systems are rigid and their potential for working with other applications is limited. In the words of another industry expert, "Where you have innovation, competition, rapidly changing business models, EDI is a drag." It's also expensive: the cost of transmitting information is $25 for every 1,000 characters.

Many companies that have EDI systems are deciding whether to scrap the entire system or gradually modify what they currently have. Most have taken the latter approach, and are trying to adapt EDI to the Internet, primarily to reduce transmission costs. All types of small business now have access to the Internet, which helps with some supply chains.

In addition to adapting EDI to the Internet, there is a movement to build extranets. *Extranets* are Web-based networks among invited partners. They are much more user-friendly than EDI systems because of the Web interface; however, successful extranets have to overcome the hurdles of security and integration with legacy systems.

Four Stages of SCM Evolution

Supply chains evolve in four stages—traditional, integrated, collaboration, and synchronization.

The *traditional supply chain* represents the lowest level in the evolution. At this stage, each company in the supply chain thinks of itself as an island that does not have to share any information with the others. Moreover, there is limited information sharing within the corporation, which results in inefficiency. Suppliers without demand information may produce too little or too much, and marketers without access to production schedules may distribute products inefficiently.

The next step in the evolution is an *integrated supply chain*. In this stage, there is information sharing within the business functions of a company; however, there is no information sharing with outside firms. As a result, several of the inefficiencies already discussed remain.

The next step in the evolution is a *collaborative supply chain*. In this stage, there is broader information sharing with suppliers and customers. As a result, transparency and collaboration lead to better responsiveness. As Hau Lee, an expert on SCM, puts it:[3]

The first problem companies face (in a supply chain) is a lack of visibility into your partners' demand forecasts. For example, 3M needs information about Procter & Gamble's production schedule of diapers so that it can plan for the components that go into the diapers. Meanwhile, P&G needs point-of-sale data from Wal-Mart to plan its diaper production. Having demand information from everyone in your supply chain lets you synchronize what you are doing with your customers and suppliers. It also helps you avoid some fatal mistakes, such as building too much manufacturing capacity—or too little.

Cisco is one of the firms that tried to achieve collaboration on a large scale:

Cisco's plan is to try to involve not just its first-tier suppliers but the second tiers and third tiers. What the company found is that sometimes when it has material shortage problems or delivery problems, it is because of the second-tier or third-tier supplier. For instance, the first-tier supplier to Cisco is Solectron. The supplier to Solectron might be Quantum. Then there are suppliers to Quantum. If the supplier to Quantum is late, that creates problems at Quantum, which would then stop production at Solectron. Cisco wants to have information transparencies at all these layers because if Cisco had gotten wind of these problems right away, it could have found an alternative supplier in time to avoid any delays.

Dell.com is another well-cited example: it has provided access to its data to 90% of its suppliers.

The tension involved in greater collaboration comes from two issues. First, companies are reluctant to share information with other corporations, because they fear that such sharing will lead to reduced power. They may also be concerned that their supply chain partners will share information with competitors.

As one CEO of a leading company said:[4]

As you know, it means we're all partners, right? I think it means everybody is trying to do the right thing—make decisions quickly and effectively so that everyone across the supply chain understands the ramifications. But every company has its own incentive systems in place. And the truth is, those incentive systems and those priorities and goals need to be in alignment across the supply chain. If they are not, it doesn't matter–you can call it collaborative supply chain until you're blue in the face, but it isn't.

An industry expert places companies into four categories when it comes to collaboration:[5] the not-nows, the nevers, the pretenders, and the real deals. The first set of companies feel that it is not the right time to push for this. The "nevers" feel threatened by collaboration and want to fight it until the bitter end. The pretenders have tried to incorporate collaborative initiatives, but have only made a token effort. On the other extreme, a small set of firms have actually implemented collaborative ideas into SCM practice. Heineken USA, Kmart, Bell Sports, and Hunter Douglas are some of the companies who fall into the last category.

The second negative aspect of increased collaboration is greater interdependence. As a result, if one firm faces a problem, it spreads quickly to the other parts of the system. For instance, if the company has forecasted demand incorrectly, its suppliers are likelier to plan incorrectly. Similarly, a supplier's labor or delivery problems have a more immediate impact on the company and its operations. Companies grapple with this problem by introducing greater redundancy in the system (e.g., adding more suppliers), but this leads to greater operational inefficiency and complexity. There is no easy way out of this.

A *synchronized supply chain*[6] represents the final step in the evolution. This type of supply chain distinguishes itself from the collaborative supply chain by even greater dependence. The goal is not just to share information, but also to synchronize operations. This type of supply chain uses systems that allow a company's operations to be visible to its suppliers and partners. As a result, operations can be synchronized so that there is a seamless transfer of information and products. In these supply chains, there is greater interactivity among the partners, and often some level of joint planning and shared decision making, rather than one company trying to dictate to everybody else. The boundaries between companies in the supply chain are blurred with greater sharing. Naturally, this type of a supply chain requires a radical transformation in the mind-set of the managers and the organization. Table 7.1 summarizes the potential benefits and challenges of synchronized supply chains.

Introduction to the Distribution Channel

The distribution channel is the portion of the supply chain that stretches from the manufacturer to the consumer. An organization needs intermediaries to distribute its products for the following reasons:[7]

1. Intermediaries reduce the cost of distribution. Consider a multiproduct company such as Procter & Gamble. If it were to attempt to distribute all of its products directly to consumers, the cost of contacting each consumer would be tremendous. It would not be feasible to run a store to sell Tide detergent. Working with intermediaries such as supermarkets, the company ensures that the supermarket bears the cost of making the product available to the consumer.

194

Table 7.1

Benefits and Challenges of Synchronized Supply Chains

Supply Chain Function	Synchronization Achieves	. . . and Requires the Ability to
Demand Generation	Richer understanding of customers' requirements More interdependent customer relationships	Translate customer data into valuable insights Communicate differently
Demand Planning	Reduced bullwhip effect	Align finance, sales, and operations forecasts Share information
Order Execution	Accurate demand plans Improved lead times and fill rates	Develop responsive and reliable fulfillment processes
Capacity Planning Materials Planning	Optimal capacity usage Supply/demand alignment	Maintain flexible manufacturing Utilize demand information for materials planning
Purchasing	Lowest total costs More interdependent supplier relationships	Rationalize supplier program Communicate differently

Source: David Anderson and Hau Lee, "Synchronized Supply Chains: The New Frontier," January 4, 1999, http://www.ascet.com/documents.asp?d_ID=198. Published by Montgomery Research.

2. Intermediaries shield manufacturers from risk. Consider the case of McDonald's, the global fast-food chain. The company has been able to expand its business rapidly by using a franchising strategy, in which the company provides the knowledge to run the restaurant and access to training and supplies, and a local businessperson puts up the capital required to open the restaurant. If a franchise flops because of low market demand, the risk to McDonald's is not great. The franchiser will survive, even if the local franchise does not.

3. Intermediaries help manufacturers target products. Go back to the example of Procter & Gamble. The company makes a large number of products, but not all of them are suitable for a supermarket. Although Pringles potato chips may be sold only in supermarkets, Pepto-Bismol and prescription drugs ought to be available in drugstores. Different retailers stock different types of products and, hence, appeal to different market segments. By matching a product to a target segment, the company can ensure that the right consumer gets the right product.

4. Intermediaries structure information essential to consumers. Individual buyers face search costs during their buying process: they must compare many products and choose the one that meets their need. Intermediaries provide an information framework that helps consumers shop. For example, supermarkets organize their products in aisles in a familiar pattern to help consumers locate products easily. Similarly, online retailers create a category structure and provide a search function to ensure that consumers can locate the product they want.

A distribution channel is most effective when each member is assigned the tasks it can do best and all the members' objectives are aligned to meet the specific goals of the channel. Of course, this does not always happen, and the result is conflict. Conflict can be horizontal or vertical, occurring between companies at the same level of the channel. An example of horizontal conflict is, two manufacturers distributing through the same wholesaler may fight over who gets preferential treatment. An example of vertical conflict is a retailer who may be unhappy with the treatment by the manufacturer. Managing this conflict effectively is necessary for success.

An In-Depth Look at E-Fulfillment— The Greatest Challenge to E-Tailers

Online retailers are not simply order-takers; they aim to provide the complete shopping experience, from the order to the product's delivery at the consumer's doorstep. A company must be able not just to take orders, but also to fulfill the orders successfully. Accomplishing this is no small task, and e-tailers have quickly realized that planning and managing their e-fulfillment operations efficiently directly affects their profits. (Even though this section is focused on e-tailers, much of it is relevant to B2B companies as well.)

E-fulfillment is not trivial. Consider this example: A consumer visits an online bookseller and orders six books produced by four different publishers. Once the order is received, the bookseller must figure out how to fill the order. One of the books is in the bookseller's warehouse because it is in great demand; the others require coordination with the publishers. Based on the relationships with the publishers, some can be shipped directly to the consumer, and others will come to the bookseller's warehouse and will then be forwarded to the consumer.

This is the level of complexity of *one order*. Imagine an online retailer at its peak with hundreds of orders coming in every minute from all over the world. Obviously, organizing e-fulfillment effectively is critical to the profitability of a company.

Online retailers that did not realize this learned a costly lesson during the 1999 holiday season when they were not able to meet shipping promises. In July 2000, the Federal Trade Commission (FTC) ruled that KBkids.com, Toysrus.com, CDnow, and Macy's.com did not tell their customers quickly enough about delays in the shipment of products. The last three companies on this list paid fines of about $1.5 million to the FTC. Major embarrassments to Toysrus.com forced the company to turn over fulfillment to Amazon.com.

A study conducted at Dartmouth College monitored the fulfillment of online orders worth $14,000 during November and December 2000. They found that:[8]

- It took an average of 9.5 days from order to delivery.
- 67% of the orders were delivered by the customer-desired date.
- 54% of the orders were delivered by the original e-tailer date.
- 88% of the orders were delivered by January 5, 2001.

- 3% of the orders were cancelled after customer discouragement.

- 70% of the orders received were preceded by an e-mail shipping notice.

- 32% of the orders used premium shipment (three days or less).

Online retailers are clearly struggling with their fulfillment operations.

Of course, many online retailers have learned from these fiascoes. A report on e-fulfillment released by Accenture, a leading consulting company, in December 2001 reported that 98% of all online merchants confirm orders using e-mail compared with 81% a year ago. The study also found that 72% of sites are now able to confirm that a product is in stock—up from 38% one year ago. However, the average number of days it takes for the product to arrive has remained steady at about seven days.

Fulfillment is expensive to every retailer. McKinsey conducted a survey of leading e-tailers (Webvan, Fogdog Sports, eToys, and Drugstore.com) in the fourth quarter of 1999.[11] In this study, fulfillment costs ranged from $10 to $14.29 for a typical order, or 12.3% to 60.8% of the revenue expected from the order. These figures do not include shipping costs, which can add from 1.2% to 22.1% of the revenue. Clearly, even if e-tailers brought prices down significantly, these costs would drive them into the red.

The role of fulfillment costs has become even more important considering the rise of free shipping as a permanent option among online retailers. In January 2002, Amazon.com announced that any order worth more than $99 would receive free shipping. It made this offer in response to a promotion run by bn.com since the middle of 2001 that made shipping free on all orders of two or more items.[9] This "free-shipping war" places more pressure on retailers' profit margins, and renders more urgent the need to reduce fulfillment costs.

Five E-Fulfillment Strategies

A company can adopt four e-fulfillment strategies—logistics postponement, resource exchange, leveraged shipments, and bricks-and-clicks.[10]

Some markets are turbulent. Customer demands change quickly, and competitors act swiftly. In such an environment, if a company is committed to shipping certain products to certain markets, it runs the risk of obsolescence. The product may arrive at the market too late or reach the wrong market, and the resulting product return and reshipping costs reduce company profits.

In such an environment, *logistics postponement* is a valuable strategy. Merge-in-transit is one approach to postponement. Instead of collecting all parts at a central location and assembling them there into the final product, merge-in-transit proposes using a logistics service provider located close to the consumer for assembly. This reduces shipping costs and ensures quicker final delivery.

Dell.com goes a step further. In its build-to-order system, the computer is built only when the customer order is received. Rather than acquiring the terminal and other computer parts, the company asks the terminal supplier to ship directly to the consumer. The rest of the computer goes from the Dell warehouse. This simple arrangement saves the company money and makes it more competitive in the marketplace.

The *resource exchange* strategy is important when distances are large. For example, Synchronet Marine provides an e-marketplace that lets shippers swap containers. Think of shipper A located in the United States who has to send some material from Hong Kong to San Francisco, but has no container in Hong Kong at the moment. Delay can prove costly. By participating on the e-marketplace of Synchronet Marine, shipper A can locate shipper B, who has a container sitting in Hong Kong, and make a deal to use B's container in exchange for cash or future swapping considerations.

The *leveraged shipments* fulfillment strategy is important when order size is small and consumers are distributed geographically. Streamline, a now defunct grocery delivery company, had an interesting fulfillment approach. The online grocery delivery business has proved to be very difficult, with many leaders failing because consumers are spread out and drivers can make only a limited number of stops in a day, leading to high delivery costs.

Streamline created an operating system that avoided this problem to some degree. First, the company put in place an efficient process for picking groceries off shelves, creating lower variable costs. Second, the company located its warehouse facility in a low-rent area far from the delivery areas, reasoning that a lower, fixed real estate cost could be traded against the slightly higher cost of driving longer distances to make deliveries. Customers got delivery on a day that the company specified: individuals who lived in one area all got their groceries delivered on the same day. Because Streamline pooled consumer orders, the average order size increased and that increased the efficiency of delivering.

Finally, the *bricks-and-clicks* approach essentially shifts the cost of delivering the product to the consumer. Consumers place the order online and collect the product at a nearby store or warehouse. Individuals benefit by not having to wait in line and being able to order online, while the company saves the cost of delivering the product to the individual's house.

This approach is also great for product returns. Every bricks-and-mortar store has an existing shipping arrangement with its suppliers and manufacturers to return items. Typically, items are consolidated over a period of time until there is enough to fill a truck. Instead of asking the consumer to ship the product back directly, asking him or her to return the product to the store allows the company to reduce return costs.

E-Fulfillment Delivery Models

There are at least three different types of e-fulfillment models:[12]

- Direct to consumer (ship from retailer to consumer)
- Consumer direct (ship from manufacturer to consumer)
- Sell-source-ship (ship from manufacturer to retailer)

In the *direct-to-consumer* approach, the consumer places an order with an online retailer, which has the product in stock and ships it directly to the consumer. If the retailer has a relationship with a bricks-and-mortar store (e.g., Rite Aid and Drugstore.com), the product can be shipped there for pick-up.

In the second e-fulfillment model, *consumer direct*, the consumer can order either from an online retailer or from the manufacturer's web site. The manufacturer ships the product directly to the customer.

In the third model, *sell-source-ship*, the order is placed at an online retailer, then passed on to the manufacturer, who ships to the retailer's distribution center. The product is then delivered to the customer.

Of course, there could be many more permutations of the fulfillment process. For instance, we have not discussed the role of wholesalers in this process. In some cases (e.g., books), wholesalers ship directly to the consumer. A product could also be assembled on its way to the consumer, in which case, an assembler must be factored into the fulfillment process.

Organizing for E-Fulfillment

When designing the organizational structure for an e-fulfillment operation, two interrelated decisions must be made.[13] The first decision relates to organizational structure and the second focuses on operation.

The first decision concerns the aspects of the operation that are centralized and those that are decentralized. The advantage of centralization is better economies of scale. The benefit from decentralization is that the fulfillment centers are closer to the market.

The second decision concerns which aspects of the operation are conducted internally and which are outsourced. This is the classic cost versus control debate. Conducting the operation internally leads to greater control, but higher costs. Outsourcing leads to less control, but lower costs.

Many online retailers have outsourced the fulfillment operations to an external party. Others have opened dedicated fulfillment centers to meet market demand (e.g., Amazon.com has bought warehouse space in the United Kingdom so that it can serve that market better).

Factors to Consider When Designing an E-Fulfillment System

Successful e-fulfillment systems take into account the following factors:

1. The true costs of online fulfillment must be measured, and a plan must be developed to lower all costs. Frequently, businesses do not fully consider such factors as manual rekeying of orders, call center costs, and warehouse labor costs. Adopting a total-cost perspective overcomes this.

2. Differentiation on the Web comes not only from web design, but also from back-end processes that the customer may not fully appreciate. Hence, it is possible to stand out as an e-tailer based on such factors as time to delivery and customer service.

3. Integration between the web site and the back-end processes is frequently underappreciated and put off until the last minute. Creating a plan to integrate avoids major headaches and creates a consistent user experience.

4. One must not assume that existing logistics operations are well suited for e-tailing. A process design exercise will ensure that the proper system is in place.

5. Similarly, one must not assume that existing suppliers can meet all needs. The capabilities of suppliers must be compared with required capabilities to assess their relative strength.

Conclusion

Supply chains are interrelated systems. Over time, greater information sharing and synchronization can lead to streamlining and better performance. The Internet can act as powerful enabling technology in this regard.

Notes

(All URLs are current as of March 15, 2002.)

1. Adapted from Hau Lee and Seungjin Whang, "Winning the Last Mile of E-Commerce," *Sloan Management Review, 42*(4), (2001):54–62.

2. This section was informed by two articles from CIO.com: Fred Hapgood, "Slow Train Coming," May 15, 2000, <http://www.cio.com/archive/051500/revisit.html> and Lynda Radosevech, "Electronic Data Interchange: The Once and Future EDI," January 1, 1997, <http://www.cio.com/archive/ec_future_edi.html>.

3. Sarah Scalet, "The Cost of Secrecy," July 15, 2001, <http://www.cio.com/archive/071501/guru.html>.

4. Sarah Scalet, "The World's Most Competitive Supply Chain," July 15, 2001, <http://www.cio.com/archive/071501/competitive.html>.

5. Gary Forger, "The Problem with Collaboration," November 2, 2001, <http://www.manufacturing.net/scm/index.asp?layout=articleWebzine&view=Detail&doc_id=54578>.

6. David Anderson and Hau Lee, "Synchronized Supply Chains: The New Frontier," January 4, 1999, <http://www.ascet.com/documents.asp?d_ID=198>.

7. Reason 4 is from Wroe Alderson, "Factors Governing the Development of Marketing Channels," in *Marketing Channels for Manufactured Products,* R. M. Clewett (ed.) (Homewood, Ill.: Richard D. Irwin, Inc., 1954).

8. Eric Johnson, "TuckShop 2000: An Efulfillment Study," 2000, <http://www.dartmouth.edu/tuck/news/features/TuckShop2000.pdf>.

9. Keith Regan, "Amazon's Free-Shipping Gamble: Will Rivals Ante Up?," January 24, 2002, <http://www.ecommercetimes.com/perl/story/15966.html>.

10. This is based on Hau Lee and Seungjin Whang, "Winning the Last Mile of E-Commerce."

11. Joanna Barsh, Blair Crawford, and Chris Grosso, "How E-Tailing Can Rise From the Ashes," *McKinsey Quarterly,* Number 3, 2000, <http://www.mckinseyquarterly.com/article_page.asp?tk=292854:879:24&ar=879&L2=24&L3=46>.

12. Pamela Rosario, "Direct to Consumer Fulfillment: Paving the Last Mile," October 3, 2000, <http://www.retailcouncil.org/events/tech2000/fulfillment>.

13. Fred Ricker and Ravi Kalakota, "Order Fulfillment: The Hidden Key to E-Commerce Success" Fall (1999), <http://www.ebstrategy.com/papers/SCM9911ecomm.pdf>.

REVIEW / CHAPTER 7

Discussion Questions

1. You are in a meeting with managers who are worried about sharing information with suppliers, wholesalers, and retailers. How would you convince them that sharing information and synchronizing activities is good?

2. Several reasons were provided for using intermediaries in the distribution channel. With the advent of the Internet and Web technology, which of these reasons has been weakened? Have any reasons been strengthened? Why have very few companies succeeded in eliminating intermediaries?

3. Amazon.com has made several investments in warehouses to improve e-fulfillment. Can a pure play succeed without any investment in warehouses? Do such investments diminish or enhance Amazon.com's competitive advantage?

4. How would you organize an e-fulfillment strategy for products such as furniture and flowers? How is that e-fulfillment approach different from product categories such as books and CDs?

E-Tasks

1. Visit the web site for "The Beer Game" at http://www.sol-ne.org/pra/tool/beer.html. Play the game as described there. What are the major points you learned from this game?

2. Visit http://www.petrovantage.com. This is an exchange for trading in petroleum-based products. Will big companies join this exchange? What are its advantages and disadvantages?

CHAPTER 8

Personalization

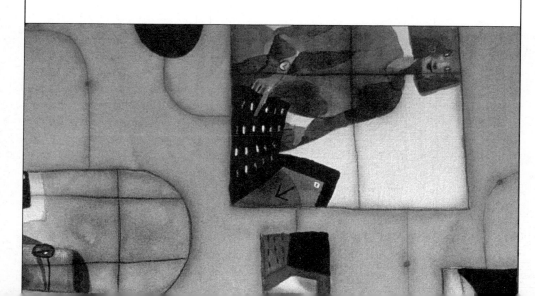

Learning Objectives

▸ To understand the basics of personalization.

▸ To learn how personalization differs from other targeting approaches.

▸ To understand when an organization should implement personalization.

▸ To understand the different technological approaches to personalization.

Executive Summary

Personalization is targeting taken to the extreme. It envisions creating a unique marketing mix for each individual. Personalization can lead to great customer loyalty. An organization should implement personalization when there is a great variety in customer lifetime value and needs, customers are sensitive to personalization, the process is amenable, the organization is looking for a competitive edge, and the organization is ready. Personalization may be either firm-controlled or consumer-controlled. The technology includes data collection and data analysis. Several personalization technologies are available: rule-based systems, simple filtering, collaborative filtering, and instant personalization or profiling.

Introduction

Personalization is targeting taken to the extreme. Customers respond better to targeted offers than to generic offers. In the past, corporations have targeted not *individuals*, but *groups* (e.g., eighteen- to twenty-five-year-old males living in the state of California).

Personalization proposes a consumer segment of size one. Rather than having one online storefront, one could have a million storefronts for a million visitors. This is no longer a dream—Amazon.com implemented this idea in September 2001. One of the tabs at Amazon.com has been named "your store" and contains information that is personalized to each returning customer. It has information based on past purchases, products the customer rated, and areas the customer described as favorites. Similarly, a site could offer a million newspapers to its million site visitors rather than one generic newspaper.

Rather than having one product or service for everybody, a company can customize its offerings based on the tastes of each individual. At a very general level, personalization is a system of providing a unique marketing mix (i.e., product and content, price, place, and promotion) for each customer. For example, the portal Yahoo! allows individuals to create My Yahoo! and control the content that they see each time. Dell.com is a pioneer in allowing consumers and corporations to personalize the hardware and software configurations of their computers. Marketers have sought to personalize promotions (e.g., Engage.com's multichannel promotional suite) and advertisements (e.g., Doubleclick personalizes banners). Priceline.com allows consumers to pick prices.

The following three scenarios using a fictitious e-tailer, Gizmos.com, illustrate the potential of personalization:[1]

Scenario #1. An individual arrives at Gizmos.com from an affiliate web page, Gadgets.com. Based on informational profiles, the marketing team at Gizmos.com has built for an individual coming from Gadgets.com, Gizmos automatically personalizes the site. Based on lifetime value information, an instant offer of "ten percent off your next purchase" pops up while the customer is browsing. After the customer has put a few items into his or her

204

Figure 8.1
How Personalization Works

shopping cart, the site makes specific cross-sell recommendations, based on information about individuals who have come to Gizmos.com from Gadgets.com, as well as what the customer has accumulated in the shopping cart. The Gizmos.com site can be tailored with banner ads, graphics, information, and articles more relevant to these individuals than the standard site.

Scenario #2. An anonymous visitor arrives at Gizmos.com. The marketing team at Gizmos.com needs ways to personalize the site based on the new individual's interests and must be willing to personalize in exchange for information. As a hook, the marketing team makes a "free shipping" instant offer in exchange for registration on the site, which includes just a few key questions about the visitor's interests. Then, as the shopper continues to browse, the real-time personalization application may recommend specific graphics, banner ads, and information. As the customer puts items into his or her shopping cart, cross-sell offers appear based on the product profile.

Scenario #3. A known customer visits Gizmos.com. The web site is already personalized with a welcome screen identifying the customer's name and, as this is a high-value customer, offers "free shipping on your next purchase over $100." As the customer places

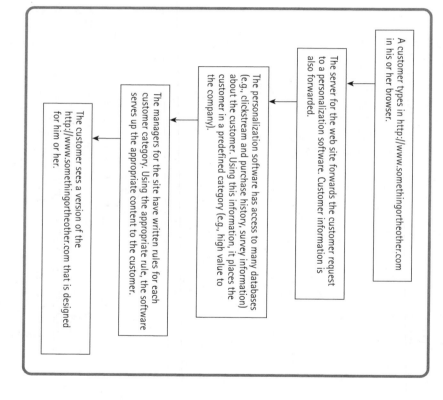

A customer types in http://www.somethingortheother.com in his or her browser.

The server for the web site forwards the customer request to a personalization software. Customer information is also forwarded.

The personalization software has access to many databases (e.g., clickstream and purchase history, survey information) about the customer. Using this information, it places the customer in a predefined category (e.g., high value to the company).

The managers for the site have written rules for each customer category. Using the appropriate rule, the software serves up the appropriate content to the customer.

The customer sees a version of the http://www.somethingortheother.com that is designed for him or her.

items in the cart, a live chat becomes activated and is displayed for this high-value customer to ensure that there are no barriers to purchasing. The high value associated with this customer has been generated from historical data, predictive analysis, and data from online and offline sources. Again, cross-sell items can be displayed based on a customer profile generated by sophisticated models.

Figure 8.1 shows an overview of the personalization process.

Terminology

Many popular terms appear to mean something similar to personalization. Therefore, before proceeding, you must understand the differences among these terms.

1:1 Marketing vs. Personalization. "1:1 marketing" is a term invented by Peppers and Rogers, the database marketing experts. It was a revolutionary term because it first focused the attention of marketers on the idea of a "segment of size one." However, 1:1 marketing focuses only on the company-led approach, whereas personalization also considers the consumer-led approach. In addition, 1:1 marketing does not incorporate content management systems.

Customization vs. Personalization. Customization is also company-led and not consumer-led. Moreover, the term "mass customization" was developed in the context of manufacturing and its focus was on developing production systems to enable a company to provide a unique product to a customer.

In short, "personalization" is the term appropriate for e-commerce, broad enough to include both company-led and consumer-led approaches to targeting a segment of size one.

Why Personalize?

There are both firm-side and consumer-side arguments in favor of personalization. From the consumer's perspective, personalization reduces the transactional burden. Consumers do not have to search through many untargeted alternatives and can focus on the few that are suited to their taste. Consumers may also find it convenient to use personalization to track new products consistent with their tastes (e.g., new books by their favorite authors).

From the company's perspective, personalization builds loyalty. One portal site reports that users who have personalized site content return five times more often than those who have not.[2] Personalization makes possible the ultra-targeted message, which is much more likely to be effective than an untargeted or poorly targeted message. Personalization also creates switching costs, making it harder for customers to move to your competitors. When customers personalize a portal such as Yahoo!, they are likely to return to their personalized page and not switch to a competing service such as MSN. In addition, made-to-order systems, such as Dell.com, have proven to reduce inventory costs, leading to price competitiveness.

When Must an Organization Adopt Personalization?

1. Dispersion in customer lifetime value and needs. Personalization makes sense only if customers differ in their value to the organization and if they have dramatically different needs. If customers are similar to one another, a homogenous marketing mix will suffice.

2. **Customer sensitivity.** The first question companies must ask themselves is: Do our customers care whether we offer more personalization? If the answer is no, the personalization potential is limited. In some product categories, the level of customer involvement may be low, and therefore the value of personalization may also be low.

3. **Process amenability.** The first obvious question in this multifaceted area is: Does the process technology that exists in your area allow you to personalize your product or service to individual customers? If it does, the next question is how extensive and how expensive would be the overhaul required to incorporate this technology into your existing process?

Another part of process amenability is marketing. Because the goal of personalization is products or services tailored to individual customers, an important question for companies to ask is: Does the marketing department have access to the level of detail regarding customer needs and the capacity to analyze such information?

A third consideration is design. Is your company capable of translating custom needs into actual specifications? The last consideration under this factor is production and distribution. Depending on the form and nature of your product or service, your production system may or may not be flexible enough to handle personalization.

4. **Competitive environment.** Are there competitive forces that would enhance or detract from the advantage your company might gain from implementing personalization? In other words, will you be the first in your market with a personalized product? How long might it take for competitors to react? And how will your competitors' customers react?

5. **Organizational readiness.** The last decision factor requires an honest assessment of your company's culture and resources. Is your company able and ready to capitalize on the opportunity inherent in personalization? Organizational change requires enlightened leadership, open-minded management, and financial resources. Each personalization strategy is unique to the company developing and implementing it; a strategy that works for one company might not work for another.

Two Approaches to Personalization

There are two fundamentally different approaches to personalization as practiced on the Internet: firm-controlled and consumer-controlled.

With the *firm-controlled* approach, the company builds a detailed profile of the consumer. This can be done without the explicit knowledge of the individual by observing each user's clickstream. The company might also ask the consumer for specific pieces of information to fill the gaps in its profile and to ensure up-to-date information. The consumer typically is not able to view or modify his or her own profile, and often does not even know that some personalization is taking place. Examples of firms that do this include Doubleclick.com.

With the *consumer-controlled* approach, the company strives to empower its consumers. Each individual enters into a relationship with a company willingly and with full knowledge of the implications. Then, consumers enter information about themselves so that they can receive promotions targeted to them. Essentially, the company implements permission marketing. The firm realizes that by providing full access, it is going to receive high-quality information from consumers. My Yahoo! is an example of this approach.

In many ways, the difference between the two approaches comes down to how the company treats its customer profiles. In the consumer-led approach, the individual has complete profile control. In the firm-led approach, the corporation controls the profile—with the understanding that it will provide value in exchange. Of course, the firm-led approach leads to a huge privacy issue about whether the company can share the data with others.

There is mounting evidence that individuals like to be in control of the personalization process. A recent survey featured in the *Harvard Business Review* indicated that 30% to 50% of users would like to be able to customize a site themselves (the variation is because of the subject area), while only 5% to 7% of users preferred to have a site personalized for them.[4]

Four Types of Personalization[5]

1. *Collaborative customization* (new product, new product representation).

This approach follows three steps: conduct a dialogue with individual customers to help them articulate their needs, identify the precise offering that fulfills those needs, and make customized products for them. Collaborative customization is most appropriate for those businesses with customers who cannot easily articulate what they want and grow frustrated when forced to select from a plethora of options.

2. *Adaptive customization* (same product, same representation).

Adaptive customizers offer one standard, but customizable, product that is designed so that users can alter it themselves. This approach is appropriate for those businesses with customers who want the product to perform in different ways on different occasions, and available technology makes it possible for them to customize the product easily on their own.

3. *Cosmetic customization* (same product, different representation).

This approach is appropriate when customers use a product the same way and differ only in how they want it presented. In other words, the standard offering is specially packaged for each customer.

4. *Transparent customization* (different product, same representation).

This approach is appropriate when customers' needs are predictable or can easily be deduced, and especially when customers do not want to state their needs repeatedly. Offerings are customized within a standard package for individual customers.

Personalization Technology

Personalization systems typically have two parts:

1. Data collection focuses on collecting and maintaining consumer data.

2. Data analysis focuses on matching content with profiles.

Data Collection

The goal of the data collection process is to build a customer profile. This profile is based on three types of information:[6]

- *Explicit information.* This is also called declared information and refers to information that is explicitly provided by the consumer through registration forms, surveys, and so on.

- *Implicit information.* The company gathers this sort of information using cookies and clickstream analysis as the user browses. The user does not explicitly provide this information.

- *Legacy information.* This is also called offline information and is collected through an offline relationship with the consumer or from offline list sellers.

Profiles can be either anonymous or contain personal identifying information (e.g., name, address, phone number). Profiles can be either naïve or intelligent. Naïve profiles contain raw data that is not analyzed; intelligent profiles combine the data with analytical models to make predictions.[7]

Data Analysis

There are several approaches to analyzing profile data to serve content. A discussion of the most important approaches follows.

Rule-Based Systems[8]

With this system, the company has the ability to set rules that govern the personalization process. The company might say, for example, that certain content must be shown only to repeat male users with a household income greater than $100,000. In this case, the personalization is governed by a series of "if/then" statements. However, the success of such a system depends on the depth and accuracy of the company's knowledge about the customer. The company makes educated guesses about special offers, promotions, and information best suited to the consumer (e.g., Broadvision, IBM's WebSphere Commerce Suite).

A typical rules-based system has three components: content, profiles, and rules. On the content side, the company must view each page as a collage of subcomponents that are dynamically re-created, rather than as a static document. This new way of thinking calls for dividing and subdividing information into content databases.

A profile is everything a company knows about its customer, from declared information in surveys and registration forms to inferred information from clickstream analysis and cookies.

As David Raab, an expert in this area puts it, the rules themselves "determine which content is presented to which profile(s)." Rules can vary from a straightforward lookup of the customer's preferred language to simple if/then logic to rankings based on automatically generated statistical models. Most of today's Web personalization relies on manually defined rules, sometimes drawn with a slick graphical flow chart, but more often written in Java or another programming language. A few systems include data analysis capabilities that let them discover relationships and propose new rules on their own, although even in those cases it is (wisely) left to the managers to decide which new rules to implement. Most systems can nest rules within rules, allowing considerable complexity."[9]

Simple Filtering[10]

Simple filtering relies on predefined groups, or classes, of visitors to determine what content is displayed or what service is provided. For example, online brokerages often classify their accounts by asset value or age group. Their sites can use simple filtering to provide preferential treatment to customers based on whether they are in the silver, gold, or platinum account class or, depending on the age group, the site could recommend savings accounts for college tuition or retirement.

Content-Based Filtering[11]

Content-based filtering works by matching the content to the user profile. A video recommendation system might, for instance, classify videos based on an objective criteria for the level of violence (1 to 10) and the genre (e.g., action, drama, international).

Collaborative Filtering

This technique matches customers with others with similar tastes (e.g., Firefly, Net Perceptions, Macromedia). The example that follows illustrates how this works.[12]

Consider this simplified example of how an online bookstore recommends books to one customer, Jack.

As customers have purchased and read books, they rate their selections on a scale of 1 to 5, 1 being "Did not enjoy," and 5 being "Enjoyed immensely." Jack has asked the bookstore to determine how he would be likely to rank Book D. Collaborative filtering uses the opinions of others, along with their prior agreement with Jack, to predict how well Jack will like the book.

| | Book | | | |
	A	B	C	D
Jack	1	1	5	?
Phil	5	2	1	
Jean	5	2	1	
Ted	2	2	4	5
Bill	3	3	3	3
Pat	1	1	3	4

In this case, Jean is not considered because she has not rated book D. Of the rest, Bill does not help much because his ratings for books B and C have nothing to do with Jack's ratings for the same books. Ted and Pat have tastes most similar to Jack's, and their ratings are used to predict that Jack will probably like this book. The resulting prediction is between 4 and 5.

The same data can be used in many other ways: helping the bookstore identify and promote books of interest to an individual, directing individuals to book reviews from like-minded people, targeting appropriate web page advertisements and announcements for each customer, or customizing a shopping guide for a particular end-user.

The disadvantage of collaborative filtering is that it does not work well when only a small number of customers sign up. A critical mass of consumer responses is required to obtain a fair amount of recommendation accuracy.

Computer-Assisted Self-Explication (CASE)

The purpose of this system is to help consumers reduce a vast choice set to a smaller set that they can consider seriously. The system asks questions about what an individual likes and dislikes and uses individual responses to eliminate alternatives (e.g., personalogic).

Instant Personalization or Profiling

All three preceding personalization techniques require time to get it right. With collaborative filtering, for example, the system has to learn about the consumer for a while before making appropriate recommendations. In instant personalization, when a visitor comes to a web site, the site automatically recognizes who it is and personalizes information to suit him or her.[13]

An overview of how all of these techniques may work in tandem is shown in Figure 8.2.

Figure 8.2
Overview of Personalization Techniques

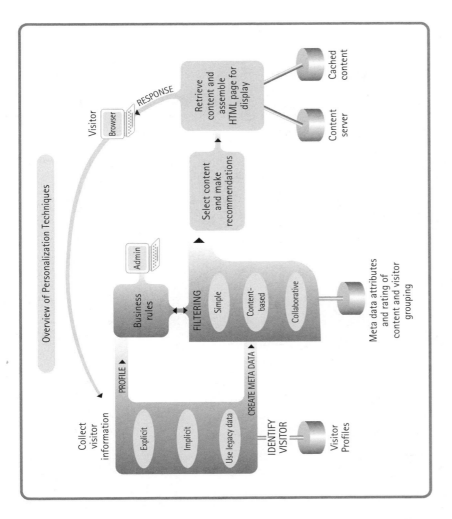

Overview of Personalization Techniques

Source: Web Site Personalization © IBM Corp. 2000. Reprinted by permission of IBM Corp.

Appropriate Level of Personalization

Maximum personalization should not always be a company's goal. Consider the situation where individuals have to provide information about themselves in order to receive a personalized service. MSNBC.com asks consumers to fill out only their Zip Code so that the news can be personalized for them. A site on the other extreme might ask consumers for detailed information about their lives in order to personalize content.

In the first situation, individuals have to provide very little personal information, but the level of personalization is low. In the second situation, detailed personal information is necessary, but, the individual is promised a very high level of personalization.

To understand why the second situation is not always better, one must realize only that *individuals hate to fill out forms about themselves.* Most do not mind providing one piece of information about themselves, but consider filling out long forms to be boring and irritating.

Two things happen as a result of this. First, the mental transaction costs rise at an increasing rate: for every additional piece of information obtained from the individual, the increase in cost is greater than the cost of providing that one piece of information. Second, the potential benefit from personalization increases at a steady linear rate with the amount of personal information provided. The net result is shown in Figure 8.3.

In Figure 8.3, the bold convex curve represents the rising mental transaction costs with the greater level of personal information required from the user. The dashed line represents the increasing benefits from personalization. *The threshold point is the maximum level of personal information one must obtain from an individual.* If more information is sought, the mental transaction costs from providing it outweigh the potential benefits from personalization.

Each customer differs as to both aspects of this curve. Some consumers may not care about providing information about themselves, in which case, the mental transaction cost may never cross the personalization benefit line. Likewise, some consumers may not see the benefits of personalization; to them, the cost of providing personal information is too high to do any business with the company.

Managers can improve the personalization process by trying to enhance the benefits of personalization or by reducing the hassles of providing personal information. The company might give consumers examples of the benefits of personalization and let them sample the site for some time so that they can see what they are missing.

There are two ways that companies have tried to reduce the hassle of providing personal information. The first approach is to use covert techniques to build profiles without the conscious knowledge of the customer. But in this case, mental transaction costs may be substituted by mental privacy costs—the costs incurred by the consumer who worries about his or her privacy. Companies must find a way to reduce concerns about privacy if they take this path.

The second approach is to collect personal information over a period of time. Consumers can be overwhelmed when a lot of information is asked of them in one session. Many

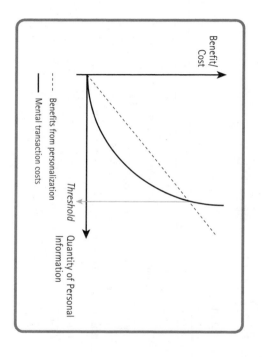

Figure 8.3
Optimal Level of Personalization

Benefit/Cost

Threshold

Quantity of Personal Information

---- Benefits from personalization
—— Mental transaction costs

companies divide questions into groups so that the individual does not have to answer more than two to three questions at any time. This approach risks a lack of standardization across profiles, and even a lack of important information in many profiles.

Personalization and Branding

Implementing personalization while ensuring that the brand remains strong may be a challenge for some companies. If the site redesigns itself for each user, it may become hard to define what the site stands for in the first place. As one industry expert put it,[14] "Don't focus too much on creating a great individual experience at the expense of a shared experience." In other words, maximizing the individual experience does not mean that the company can stop creating broader themes that define and inform its approach to personalization.

Put simply, a successful site clearly defines what it does while maximizing the individual's experience.

Tradeoffs in Personalization

Personalization appears to work best under the following circumstances:

- Relevance vs. information overload. No personalization algorithm is perfect. Personalization systems make mistakes because they don't fully understand the individual they are trying to serve. Consider a content management system, for example, that can learn about the reading habits of a user and present content that it thinks the user will like. The challenge in this case is not to leave out any relevant piece of information, but also not to provide too much information, leading to poor user experience. Balancing those needs is an important part of personalization systems.

- Profile accuracy vs. mental transaction costs. Most personalization systems work best when they have the most accurate and up-to-date profile about consumers. However, if consumers are constantly being asked to fill out surveys, they may get disgusted and end their affiliation with the company. Most personalization systems struggle with arriving at the right balance.

Arguments against Personalization

First, many personalization systems assume that people are no longer curious explorers. Even individuals bombarded with information and struggling to cope with clutter can still be curious. Personalization leads us to a minimalist trap where the system, in its zeal to provide consumers with the "right" information, limits their ability to explore.

Think of a personalized newspaper—"My XYZ Times." It may only show you news stories it thinks interest you. For example, if you have read stories in the international section in the past, it will feature those stories. But, this personalization is contrary to how most people read a newspaper. I, for one, don't always read stories in the same section: I choose stories that catch my eye. What I want, therefore, is the full newspaper!

Second, many personalization systems are bound to irritate because of their presumption of knowledge about you. When I go to Amazon.com, it greets me with an inane "Hi Sandeep!" Of course, the illusion that Amazon knows me is immediately destroyed by the link that says, "Click here if you are not Sandeep." This becomes a particular problem if there is no other tangible benefit from the personalization. Moreover, if the site does not clearly indicate what it is collecting from customers, customers might have exaggerated fears about the extent of the company's knowledge.

Third, many personalization systems seek to summarize a human being by a string of numbers. According to these systems, a human being can be defined by variables relating to past behavior and individual characteristics (e.g., demographics). I think this is a flawed approach, but my quarrel is not with the philosophy of the idea. Rather, I see this as a futile attempt to get at the core of a consumer. In fact, I would go so far as to say that "it is impossible to identify a set of behavioral or demographic variables that collectively describe the essence of a human being." Call it Sandeep's first law if you must. Individuals are not their past behavior; they are hedonic agents passing through life making idiosyncratic choices as they go. No single choice defines them nor does it satisfactorily predict their future behavior.

Fourth, many personalization systems lead to increased search costs. Think of Amazon.com's recommender engine. As soon as you choose a book, you are provided with information about other books that you must be interested in. A user now has to go through several titles to ascertain the fit between his or her tastes and the other books. But, didn't we start out by saying we wanted to reduce search costs? So, the assumption here is that the consumer prefers greater search costs provided it is on the marketer's terms.

Implementation Issues

Personalization software is expensive—it can cost from $50,000 to over $1,000,000. As a result, firms must be careful when purchasing and implementing such a system. Side-by-side comparisons are hard to find because personalization is frequently included as a feature of a larger software package (e.g., a content management system). One way of reducing the cost may be to outsource it to an application service provider (ASP). Also, integrating personalization systems with other systems already in place is typically a big issue.

Conclusion

Personalization is potentially a great idea; however, its value is directly proportional to what it adds to the user experience. Systems that require too much from the consumer, while providing too little, will have a tough time succeeding.

Notes

(All URLs are current as of March 15, 2002.)

1. Jennifer Sullivan, "The Challenges and Rewards of Personalizing Customer Interactions," *Customer Inter@Ction Solutions, 19*(10), (2001): 50–51.

2. Jesse Berst, "Why Personalization is the Internet's Next Big Thing," April 14, 1998, <http://www.zdnet.com/anchordesk/story/story_1977.html>.

3. Except for the first point, this is taken directly from C.H.L. Hart, "Mass Customization: Conceptual Underpinnings, Opportunities and Limits," *International Journal of Service Industry Management, 6*(2), (1995): 36–45.

4. William Hackos, "To Customize or to Personalize, That is the Question," May 2001, <http://www.infomanagementcenter.com/enewsletter/200105/customize_personalize.htm>.

5. This is based on the work of J.H. Gilmore and J. Pine, "The Four Faces of Mass Customization," *Harvard Business Review, 75*(1), (1997): 91–101.

6. IBM High-Volume Web Team, "Web Site Personalization," January 2000, <http://www7b.boulder.ibm.com/wsdd/library/techarticles/hvws/personalize.html#1>.

7. Robert Grossman, "Profiles, Personalization, Privacy, and all That: Some Questions and Answers," May 2000, <http://www.twocultures.net/epapers/ip-qa-v2.htm>.

8. More details about rule-based systems are available at <http://gobi.stanford.edu/personalization/frameset_rulesbased.asp>.

9. David Raab, "Personalized Web Sites," June 2000, <http://www.raabassociates.com/v9069.htm>.

10. Adapted from IBM High-Volume Web Team, "Web Site Personalization," January 2000, <http://www7b.boulder.ibm.com/wsdd/library/techarticles/hvws/personalize.html#1>.

11. Ibid.

12. This is taken from <http://gobi.stanford.edu/personalization/frameset_ffnote.asp>.

13. Personalization Consortium, "What is Personalization?," <http://www.personalization.org/faqs1.html#questiontwo>.

14. Annette Hamilton, "Personalization Panic: Beware the Three Deadly Pitfalls," August 12, 1998, <http://www.zdnet.com/anchordesk/story/story_2421.html>.

REVIEW / CHAPTER 8

Discussion Questions

1. Think of how Yahoo! will look in five years. Speculate on how the level of personalization will change on the site. Will there be more or less personalization? Will consumers be more or less satisfied with it?

2. What will it take for you to be comfortable with a firm-led, covert personalization approach?

3. Some managers argue that telling consumers about covert personalization simply makes them afraid of a relatively innocuous process. They argue that managers must downplay this. Do you agree with this argument? How would you communicate with your customers about the value of covert personalization?

4. I used the example of a newspaper as something that is hard to personalize. What is it about a newspaper that makes it hard to personalize? Can a magazine be personalized more easily? How about a work of fiction such as a book?

5. Is personalization an idea that is simply ahead of its time? Do consumer mind-sets need to change for it to work? If so, in what way?

E-Tasks

1. Visit Yahoo! and Lycos. Personalize these sites to your liking.

2. Visit Cnn.com and Msnbc. Personalize these sites to your liking.

3. Based on these experiences, answer the following questions:

   a. What are the differences in the personalization approaches offered by Yahoo! and Lycos and Cnn.com and Msnbc?

   b. Can news sites Cnn.com and Msnbc adopt the personalization strategy of portal sites (e.g., Yahoo!)? Why or why not?

   c. Are you more likely to revisit a site that you have personalized?

4. Find an example of a real site that you think will be hard to personalize. Explain why you chose this site.

5. Amazon.com has created a new feature called "Your Store." Go to the site to create your own online store. Did you find this experience satisfying? How can the company improve on this?

CHAPTER 9

Permission Marketing

Learning Objectives

To understand the basics of permission marketing.

To learn about the new insights it offers.

To study the differences between permission marketing and other forms of direct marketing.

To understand how to create, implement, and manage a permission marketing program.

Executive Summary

Permission marketing envisions every customer shaping the targeting behavior of marketers. Consumers empower a marketer to send them promotional messages in certain interest categories. The marketer then matches anticipated, personal, and relevant advertising messages with the interests of consumers. Permission marketing offers two new insights—cocreation and consumer control. There are many ways to obtain customer permission—opt-out, opt-in, and double opt-in are the best known. With opt-out programs, companies contact consumers on an unsolicited basis at first; consumers then have the right to leave. Opt-in programs contact only consumers who explicitly sign up. Double opt-in is even stricter: only consumers who opt-in *and* reply to a confirmation e-mail are permitted into the database. There are four business models associated with permission marketing: direct relationship maintenance, permission partnership, ad market, and permission pool. Every permission marketing program must include an explicit permission-seeking process, a verification process, a recognition of relationship, access to personal information, communication control, and a frictionless exit ability. The level of consumer interest in the program can be measured using metrics such as the opt-out rate and the virtual opt-out rate. In order to sustain consumer interest, the messages must be relevant and usable and the privacy of the consumer must be respected.

Introduction

Permission marketing[1] envisions every customer shaping the targeting behavior of marketers. Consumers grant marketers permission to send them promotional messages in certain interest categories. The marketer then matches advertising messages with the interests of consumers. In this way, consumers receive more advertisements relevant to their needs and interests, and marketers can locate the consumers most likely to respond to their ads. Many permission-marketing firms (e.g., Postmasterdirect.com, yesmail.com, CMGI) claim customer response rates that are dramatically better than those of banner ads.

Permission marketing did not begin with the Internet. For example, book-of-the-month clubs (see http://www.book-clubs.net/), which have existed for almost seventy-five years,[2] have permission to send customers a new book each month. Typically, individuals can sign up in book categories that interest them (e.g., science fiction, mystery), then, the club picks the books that go out to members. In some cases, noted celebrities (e.g., Oprah Winfrey) or newspapers (e.g., *Sacramento Bee*) may sponsor the club and may decline a book that does not interest him or her. The consumer promises to buy a predetermined number of books over a predetermined period of time. The publishers benefit from this arrangement because they do not have to worry about inventory costs. Consumers benefit from not having to travel to stores and not having to search for new books in their interest area. Consumers clearly expect to receive a book at periodic intervals. Other examples of permission marketing that predate the Internet include the Reader's Digest Sweepstakes, which used consumer preference information collected through surveys to better target individuals.

Even though permission marketing can work in any direct medium, the Internet gives it the potential for more widespread use. Two reasons for this are (1) on the Internet, the cost of marketer-to-consumer communication is low and (2) the Internet has enabled rapid feedback mechanisms due to quicker two-way communication. How do these two factors facilitate permission marketing? They allow for multiple exchanges between the company and the customer at a relatively low cost. A company can easily contact consumers for their permission, and consumers can easily contact the company to sign up or sign out of programs. As a result, it has become easier for a firm to solicit and maintain permission from consumers.

Insights Offered by Permission Marketing

Cocreation

Permission marketing envisions marketers and consumers as partners in creating a marketing mix. Individuals can control who sends them promotional e-mails by giving permission only to a select few firms.

Consumer Control

A key element of permission marketing is consumer control—the firm cannot send a message to a consumer who has not given it permission. This leads to greater commitment on the consumer's part, leading to better results from the advertising. Of course, the big managerial fear has to be that a significant number of consumers may refuse to give permission. Building permission takes time and a slow-growing database may be worthwhile if it generates an excellent response rate. Managers must not–in an attempt to boost permissions–resort to deceptive techniques such as burying the permission check-off box in a long legal agreement.

Permission versus Database Marketing

The essence of permission marketing is that it provides marketers a way to build a database of online customers. So how does permission marketing differ from traditional database marketing? Here are some key differences:

1. Traditional databases (e.g., from catalogs, department store transactions) rarely involve consumer consent. Consumers expect to receive promotions if they sign up for a catalog or purchase from one, but this does not mean that they have given the firms permission to send them a large number of promotional messages. Opt-out services for telemarketing and "junk mail" are available through the Direct Marketing Association, but they are cumbersome and restricted: only members of the DMA stop sending messages and consumers have to sign up for it every year.

2. Permission marketing programs using e-mail are much cheaper–the content creation and message delivering costs are both lower. Marketers can send multiple messages at a cost that is only incrementally higher; that is very expensive with traditional database marketing.

3. The most important difference may be speed and timing. As one industry expert said:[3]

In the traditional database marketing (DM) world, it may take two or three or more months for a campaign's final results to come in. And, depending on the mailer, the peak order time could be one, two, or three weeks out from the drop.

An e-mail campaign is typically finalized in three or four days, and the peak time is usually within the first 24 hours. The advertising web site (or customer service call center) needs to be prepared for the largest number of hits within that time frame. Conversely, a traditional DM advertiser needs to prepare his or her internal staff for the deluge at a completely different time.

E-Mail Is Synonymous with Permission Marketing

Many industry practitioners believe permission marketing may as well be called e-mail marketing, for many reasons.

E-mail introduces three capabilities: interactivity, rapidity, and reach. *Interactivity* means a two-way, rather than one-way, communication. E-mail is direct and personal, giving firms the sense that they are reaching the customer's living room. *Rapidity* means that a message can travel swiftly from marketer to consumer, allowing marketers to get quick feedback and fine-tune their offerings accordingly. In terms of *reach*, we live in the age of e-addressability—a large proportion of the population has an e-mail address.

The primary reason for the choice of e-mail as a promotional vehicle may be the effectiveness in terms of response rates. As shown in Figure 9.1, a survey of media buyers indicated that e-mail marketing is by far the most effective means of targeting customers.[4]

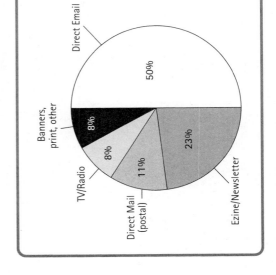

Figure 9.1
Media Buyers' Perception of Most Responsive Marketing Method

Table 9.1
Content Analysis of
Spam Messages

Categories	Number of Messages	Percent of Total
Pornography	29,884	30.2
Money Making/Get Rich/Work from Home	29,365	29.6
Other Direct Product or Service/Misc	23,326	23.5
Become a Spammer	4,200	4.2
Gambling/Sweepstakes	3,279	3.3
Health/Cures/Weight Loss (including Viagra)	9,804	9.9
Totals	**99,858**	**100.7**

Source: Study conducted by http://www.chooseyourmail.com, personal communication with CEO.

One of the problems with using e-mail as the main vehicle to execute permission marketing is that consumers still associate promotional e-mails with spam (unsolicited commercial e-mail). Consumers object to spam because of the high volume of messages; their irrelevance, deceptiveness, and offensiveness; and their targeting of vulnerable consumers (e.g., children). (Chapter 14 provides a full discussion of spam.) Obtaining e-mail addresses without the customer's permission is quite inexpensive—according to one spammer, 10 million addresses are available for $30. In addition, marketers incur similar costs whether they send out 1 or 10 million e-mails. As a result, the volume of spam messages tends to be high. In addition, spam messages frequently feature offensive topics. As shown in Table 9.1, a content analysis of about 100,000 spam messages conducted by Chooseyourmail.com revealed that the top two topics were pornography and get-rich-quick schemes.

Spam also creates a problem for legitimate advertisers. Individuals who are skeptical of unsolicited commercial e-mail tend also to be skeptical of other forms of e-mail promotion. Many consumers may simply stop opening any e-mail from commercial marketers.

Different Types of Permission

Opt–Out[5]

Opt-out refers to the situation where a marketer sends an unsolicited e-mail and then provides individuals an option of not receiving future messages. Each message includes a statement to the effect of "If you do not wish to receive such e-mails in the future, just click here." Typically, the consumer has provided personal information to a firm for some other purpose (e.g., purchasing a product, registering for a newsletter). Companies argue that this implies that the consumer has established a relationship with them and this opens up the possibility of sending out promotional messages. Buying from a company, the argument goes, is providing it implicit permission to send promotional messages. From the company's standpoint, this is less costly than acquiring customer permission, and it is a quick way for a company that already has a customer database to launch an e-mail marketing program.

Although companies may have the legal right to do this, leading anti-spam advocates (e.g., the Mail Abuse Prevention System or MAPS) have argued that opt-out programs place an undue burden on the consumers. They argue that although opt-out may work for offline arrangements (e.g., book-of-the-month clubs discussed earlier), on the Internet, this precedent could lead to consumers being deluged with e-mail. As a result, consumers may either start providing incorrect e-mail addresses to companies or create multiple e-mail accounts and provide the one they check least often to firms. Companies have argued that so long as they respect the privacy of the individual and act responsibly, this approach should be acceptable.

Opt-In

Unlike opt-out, opt-in requires the consumer to tell the corporation explicitly that it has permission to send messages. There are four business models that can be used to accomplish opt-in as shown in Figure 9.2.

Model 1 can best be characterized as *direct relationship maintenance*. Consider an example. At United.com, consumers can sign on for sales alerts from United Airlines, in

Figure 9.2
Current Practice of Permission Marketing—Four Business Models

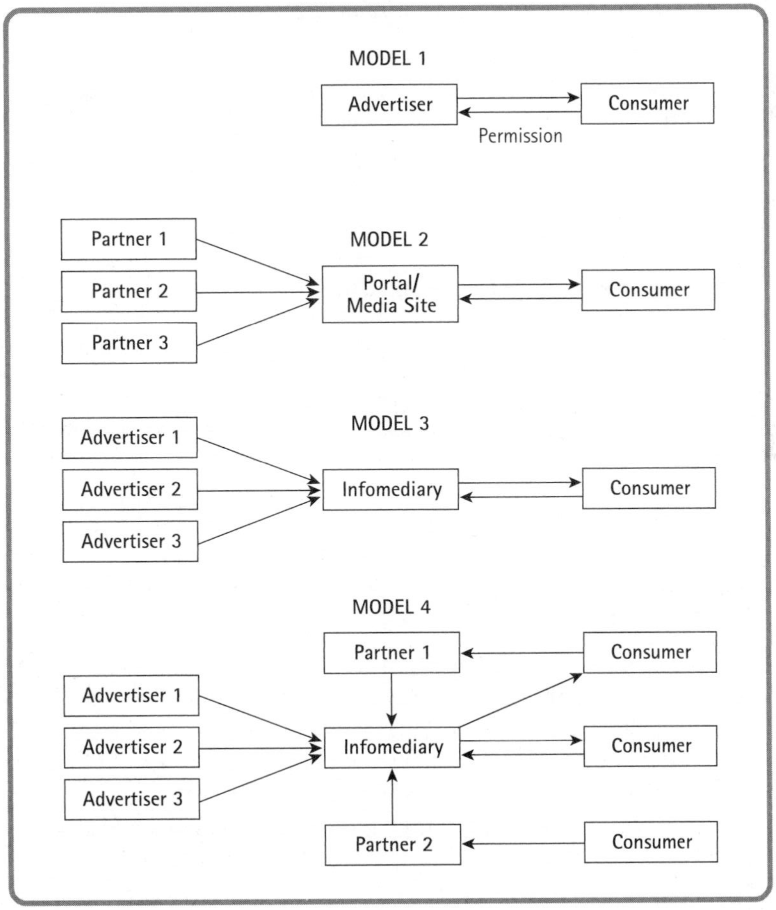

order to receive e-mail when prices drop on their desired routes or when a Web special is being conducted. Very little demographic or other personal information is requested. This is viewed as an additional service offered to customers to maintain a strong relationship.

Model 2 can be described as a *permission partnership*. Here, the consumer provides a portal or media site with permission to send him or her promotional offers. After receiving this permission, the intermediary alerts its partners that may be interested in sending out promotional offers. All consumers who have signed on receive all offers. Examples of this include nytimes.com and lycos.com. Permission partnership is commonly used to increase traffic to web sites.

Model 3 can be described as an *ad market*. A consumer provides detailed information about his or her preferences and interests to an infomediary, which then uses this information to identify advertisers. The ads supplied by these advertisers are then carefully matched with the consumer's tastes. Consumers win by reducing e-mail clutter and may get incentives to participate in the process. Advertisers find target customers for their promotions at a fairly low cost, and the infomediary makes a profit by facilitating this exchange. Examples include mypoints.com and chooseyourmail.com.

Model 4 can be described as a *permission pool*. Here, different consumers provide different firms with permission to send them promotional offers. These firms pool the information provided by the consumer, and promotional messages are sent out, targeting this larger pool. An example of this model is yesmail.com. In most cases, consumers have no idea that their personal information is being shared in this way, and that creates an ethical concern.

Many different types of intermediaries and infomediaries collect such information and use it to target consumers. Table 9.2 provides a partial list of such companies.

Double or Confirmed Opt-In

Opt-in misses one problem. Consumer A can sign up a friend (or enemy!) or associate, consumer B, for a service that B has no interest in. All of a sudden, B starts to receive e-mails for products that she does not care for.

In order to avoid this loophole, double opt-in calls for a stricter standard when building e-mail lists. It asks marketers to send a confirmation e-mail to all individuals who have opted in. When an individual confirms, the loop is complete and the organization can be doubly sure that it has the right person on its list. The Wireless Advertising Association announced in November 2000 that double opt-in will be the standard for ads sent to consumers through text messaging.[6]

There is a small premium in the marketplace for double opt-in e-mail lists. For example, PostMasterDirect.com, a leading e-mail list broker, charges about $0.15 per name for single opt-in lists and $0.35–0.40 for double opt-in names. The double opt-in lists are more effective (3–5% click-through rate versus 1.5–2.5% for single opt-in). However, the increased click-through rate may not be enough to justify the increased price. As a result, the gap may close, making it harder to maintain double opt-in lists.[7]

Table 9.2

Intermediaries and Infomediaries That Use Permission Marketing

Category	Description	Examples
Incentive Marketers	These web sites offer cash, discounts, or points in exchange for reading an advertisement or visiting a web site	Cybergold, MyPoints, Netcentives
Sweepstakes	Consumers register for sweepstakes in exchange for personal data	WebStakes, iWin, iWon
E-List Brokers	These web sites offer "tailored advertisements," particularly in markets with little information available (e.g., ballroom dancing or cold fusion development tools)	24/7 Mail, PostMasterDirect, Webconnect, YesMail, Email Exchange
List Managers	These sites (which offer e-mail list management services) are likely to move toward the e-list broker model	Topica
Community/ Lifestyle portals	While undeveloped, this category offers the most potential to introduce its members to relevant products and services related to its core content (i.e., profile data has depth, not breadth)	Women.com, iVillage, ETrade, SportsLine
Permission Managers	This category is an amalgamation of incentive marketers, sweepstakes, community portals, and e-list brokers. In one form or another, the web site develops a history of products and services in which the consumer has an interest	Yahoo!, AOL
E-Commerce portal	Based on buying history, the web site can introduce new products and services	Amazon, Yahoo!
Privacy Agents	Organize and protect a consumer's personal data; *Net Worth* by John Hagel describes this business model	PrivaSeek, Lumeria, PopularDemand
Personal Data Manager	Organize and facilitate the sharing of personal data (i.e., automated form fillers)	MS Passport, Novell's DigitalMe, Privacy Bank, Brodia, VerticalOne
"Wanted" Marketplaces	Receive consumer's permission and desire to seek out best deal for a wanted product or service	Imandi, Respond, iWant, eWanted
Comparison	These sites provide comparison shopping and reviews to help consumers find the best product	CNet, MySimon, DealTime, Epinions, Productopia
Gift Registries	Give list of desired products to intermediary; currently passed on to friends and family, but in the future could be passed on to advertisers (with consumer consent)	WishClick, Della, Wishconnect

Source: Jad Duwaik, Optink, http://www.optink.com/permarkt/index2.html, accessed August 2001.

The broader context in which one collects information—and not just the opt-in/opt-out policy—is important. As Jason Heller, chief executive officer of Mass Transit Interactive, said, "Double opt-in versus single opt-in versus opt-out means little if the user who signs up at jokeoftheday.com checks off that he/she is interested in computing and technology and then receives IT offers on a regular basis. We tend to pick lists for our clients that are contextually relevant to what we are offering. Over the years, we have found that the response rates are exponentially higher this way."[8]

Permission Marketing for Existing Customer Relationships

Permission marketing is applicable to existing customer relationships as well as new ones. The challenge is to use existing information about consumer behavior to infer whether the company has permission to send the consumer promotional messages. To do that, companies must take stock of their current relationship with the customer. Managers should seek answers to these questions:

- What is the customer's expectation from my company?
- What is the level of my relationship with the customer (e.g., level of purchase activity)?
- What did I tell the customer when I built the customer database?
- Does the customer feel that my company plays a role in his or her life?
- What level of permission has the customer given my company, if any?

The answers to these questions are not easy to find. Typically, companies may not have measurement systems in place to answer these questions in detail. Using the limited information a company has, the guide shown in Table 9.3 should help managers determine the level of permission they have from the consumer.

Table 9.3

Judging the Level of Permission with Existing Customers

Lowest level of permission	New customer
	Infrequent shopper
	Negative response to promotions
	Has complained about shopping experience
Medium level of permission	Steady purchase history
	Medium customer loyalty
	Responds to some promotions
	Contacts company for information
High level of permission	Loyal shopper
	High response to promotions
	Enthusiastic about brand
	Refers others to company
	Long purchase history

Depending on the characteristics described in Table 9.3, each company must place its customers in three or more categories with respect to permission. Then, the company must identify a plan to design an appropriate marketing mix for each segment based on permission. The company must also consider how to escalate the level of permission with customers in the low or medium categories.

Permission Marketing Best Practices

Ian Oxman, an expert in permission marketing, provides the following advice for building an e-mail list:[9]

1. Explain in simple English, and in plain view, the complete intended use of the e-mail address. Don't bury your intent in a privacy statement located on some other page. Yes, this will clunk-up the look and feel of your web page. Yes, your web designer will hate the idea. Just remember, e-mail marketing is about bottom-line profits, not web design awards.

2. Avoid using a "must-fill" field for the e-mail address. This sounds backward because the entire objective of opt-in marketing is to collect e-mail addresses. However, permission marketing works best when the user gives his or her e-mail address as opposed to your taking it. It may seem like a silly difference, but it produces a much more responsive e-mail list.

3. Always send a confirmation auto-reply immediately following registration. This confirmation e-mail fully reiterates the intent of the program and gives the registrant a last chance to opt-out. Some consumer advocates maintain that this confirmation should go even further and be opt-in rather than opt-out, for example, "In order to activate your registration, please click here." The registrant must click–opt-in–a second time to authorize his or her e-mail address to be added to the database.

4. Ask only critical targeting questions, minimizing the online collection of basic demographic data. Accurate demographic data, such as age, income, and marital status, improve list targeting, but approximately 50% of all self-reported online demographic data is spoofed.[10] Higher quality demographic data can be obtained by asking for a home address and then overlaying the demographics from a third-party provider. Focus your data collection on the specific information that directly predicts your customer's behavior.

Problems with Permission Marketing

Consumers are typically asked for their permission when they initially register, and then never asked to revisit their preferences. Obviously, as people change, the marketing messages become less and less targeted. Even if consumers are asked to revisit their profiles from time to time, they will do so only if they are provided with an incentive.

Another problem is that customers give their permission once, and are thereafter repeatedly targeted with marketing messages. Most consumers forget what they said they like to play, read, or drink and become passive recipients of messages, reducing permission-marketing systems to the level of direct mail. As marketers send more messages, the consumer becomes less engaged in the process and more irritated.

Consumers are frequently asked to opt-in to broad categories such as entertainment or consumer electronics. The problem with this is that they may be interested in only a small subcategory. They may receive ads for Sony television although all they care about are stereo systems, or although they buy only Magnavox televisions. Showing consumers ads for brands they do not care about raises the possibility of consumer irritation.

Finally, permission marketing places demands on consumers. Consumers have to work to get relevant ads—mainly by filling out surveys about themselves. Permission marketing may therefore fail to attract consumers with limited time.

Creating a Permission Marketing Program

The following elements must be included in every permission marketing campaign:

- Explicit permission seeking process

- Verification process

- Recognition of relationship

- Access to personal information

- Communication control

- Frictionless exit ability

The permission must be obtained explicitly rather than implicitly. This means that the firm must assume that it does not have the customer's permission to send out promotional e-mails. Then it must present the customer with a real choice of granting permission to the firm or not. The customer's right to be left alone must be honored. The permission-seeking process must be free from deceptive tactics.

The firm must verify the identity of each consumer in order to prevent consumers from signing on others without their knowledge. This is the "double opt-in" arrangement described earlier. Otherwise, consumers may sign up their friends and associates indiscriminately, placing an undue transactional burden on them.

The consumer must understand that he or she is entering an ongoing two-way relationship as a willing partner of equal stature who stands to benefit from this alliance. Indeed, the goal of permission marketing is to develop such win–win relationships. A well-designed permission marketing campaign creates well-defined expectations in the mind of the consumer about the nature and volume of messages. The consumer's and the firm's perceptions of the level of permission should be the same.

The consumer must know exactly what the firm knows about him or her, and be able to modify this information at any point. Such continuous access to one's personal information empowers and reassures the consumer; it also benefits the firm, since consumers who update their profiles more often are more likely to receive relevant messages and, hence, respond more often.

The consumer must be able to control the nature and volume of messages being sent to him or her, according to the true promise of permission marketing. They dictate the types of products and services they will see ads for by filling out forms on interests and product preferences. Many firms are doing this routinely today. Some firms (e.g., chooseyourmail.com) also allow consumers to control the volume of e-mail in any category.

The consumer must be able to exit effortlessly from a permission marketing relationship at any point. Not letting consumers exit at any point equates to assuming one has the permission to market to them when, in fact, one does not. Furthermore, frustrated consumers will no longer attend to the messages, leading to low response rates.

Measuring Consumer Interest in a Permission Marketing Program

Sustaining consumer interest in a permission marketing program is a challenge. Permission is a fragile concept that can be destroyed easily if the consumer loses trust in the company. A successful permission marketing program involves customers who are engaged in the process and who participate wholeheartedly. This definition allows us to create a set of metrics that can be used to identify programs in which consumers may have lost interest.

Let us discuss some of the key metrics:

1. Opt-out rate. This is the proportion of your database that has opted out of your program in any given time period (e.g., one month). One would like to retain members on the list, of course, but losing participants may not be as bad as it initially seems. It takes time to figure out that if a consumer decides the nature and style of the program are not for him or her, it is better that the person leaves. The company can then focus on those who are really interested.

2. Virtual opt-out rate. This is the proportion of your database that has not responded to any offer that you have sent out during a six-month period (to be more conservative, one could consider a one-year period). By not responding, this type of consumer may have *implicitly* withdrawn permission from you.

3. Zero communication rate. This is the proportion of your database that has not communicated with you in any way over the last six months (or one year). Naturally, this may be a sign of waning interest. Often the person has multiple e-mail accounts and uses the account that he/she has given you sparingly or not at all.

4. Profile updation rate. This is the proportion of the database that has updated its profile in the last six months (or one year). If this has not happened, once again, it may be a sign of waning interest in your program.

Measuring these rates and monitoring them over time allows the manager to gauge the level of consumer interest. Individuals who have withdrawn can be surveyed about why they did so. For instance, when an individual tries to opt-out, the organization may offer him or her an incentive as a last-ditch effort to persuade the person to stay. At a minimum, understanding the motivations of the individuals who have reduced their level of participation in the program helps managers make the program more effective.

Sustaining Consumer Interest in the Program[11]

Benefits increase an individual's level of interest in a permission marketing program; costs decrease it. There are two potential benefits: *message relevance and monetary benefit.*

The central reason why individuals join a permission marketing program is the promise of receiving relevant messages. Individuals value the relevance of promotional messages. At every point in his or her participation in the program, the consumer judges how relevant the advertising messages are to his or her needs. That consumer will lose interest if this judgment is negative, and gain interest if it is positive.

Permission marketing programs realize that it is burdensome for individuals to process messages. As a result, several offer consumers incentives to do so (e.g., airline frequent flyer miles to discounts for online purchases). Because individuals are interested in deriving some monetary benefit from direct marketing programs, these incentives are likely to lead to greater interest.

Most people are unlikely to join a permission marketing program simply to make some money. The main attraction is to receive promotional offers consistent with their needs. Therefore, if the promotional messages are highly relevant to an individual's needs, he or she might be willing to accept little or no monetary benefit in exchange for participation. Indeed, some large permission marketing firms believe that providing relevant messages is sufficient to maintain consumer interest (e.g., postmasterdirect.com, chooseyourmail. com).

At the same time, individuals face three potential mental transaction–related costs: *information entry/modification costs, message processing costs, and privacy costs.*

Many programs require that individuals provide detailed personal information, and then expect them to revisit and update their information. This is a huge transactional burden on the individuals. The more burdensome the data entry or modification process (e.g., longer forms, hard-to-understand questions), the lower an individual's interest in the program.

In addition, individuals face the cost of processing all of the promotional messages they receive. Individuals have to read the message before determining whether it is of any value. They must decide whether to "scan and discard" or "scan and read more," which places a cognitive burden on them.

If the design of the message is complicated and does not follow a logical sequence, even greater cognitive effort may be required of the individual. Although consumers desire message relevance, the transactional burden of processing the messages can affect their interest in the program.

Finally, individuals incur privacy costs. Privacy costs are defined as the mental burden of coping with the uncertainty of how the marketer uses one's personal information. When consumers on the Internet are concerned about their privacy, they are much more likely to take action such as providing incomplete information to web sites and notifying ISPs. Of course, individuals differ in terms of how they cope with privacy costs, and some place convenience ahead of privacy concerns. Most individuals have some privacy concerns, however, and if there are strong and credible assurances that lower these costs, they are likely to be more interested in the permission marketing program.

Thus, maximizing message relevance and monetary benefits and minimizing information entry or modification costs, message processing costs, and privacy-related costs lead to greater interest in any permission marketing program.

Conclusion

Permission marketing offers a new way of communicating with one's consumers. For it to be useful, marketers must truly respect the consumer as a partner in an exchange instead of trying to overpower him or her using deceptive techniques.

Notes

(All URLs are current as of March 18, 2002.)

1. Permission marketing is also called invitational marketing or participatory marketing.
2. This is mainly based on Robert J Posch Jr., "Enhanced Customer Choice is Never Negative," *Direct Marketing*, 62(9), (2000): 21–22.
3. Kim MacPherson, "DM and EM: A Comparison," December 18, 2000, <http://www.clickz.com/em_mkt/article.php/834191>.
4. Optinnews.com, "2001 E-Mail Marketing Study," May 4, 2001, <http://www.optinnews.com/news/showart.asp?DB=NewsTable&ID=360>.
5. Some have called opt-out the negative option and opt-in the positive option.
6. Christopher Saunders, "WAA Guidelines Affirm Double Opt-In for 'Push' Ads," November 8, 2000, <http://www.internetnews.com/IAR/article/0,,12_506341,00.html>.
7. Pamela Parker, "Beginning of the End for Double Opt-In," November 30, 2001, <http://www.clickz.com/feedback/buzz/article.php/931381>.
8. Pamela Parker, "Beginning of the End for Double Opt-In."
9. Ian Oxman, "How to Ask Permission," April 3, 2001, <http://www.digitrends.net/marketing/13640_15177.html>.
10. Graphic, Visualization and Usability Center, Georgia Tech, "GVU's Ninth WWW User Survey," 1998, <http://www.cc.gatech.edu/gvu/user_surveys/survey-1998-04/#highsum>.
11. This is based on Sandeep Krishnamurthy, "A Comprehensive Analysis of Permission Marketing," *Journal of Computer-Mediated Communication*, 6(2), (January 2001), <http://www.ascusc.org/jcmc/vol6/issue2/krishnamurthy.html>.

REVIEW / CHAPTER 9

Discussion Questions

1. Because opt-out has been used by direct marketers such as book-of-the-month clubs, should online marketers be allowed to use it? What makes e-mail marketing unique?

2. Should e-mail lists cost more than postal mail lists? What factors must be considered when pricing an e-mail list?

3. Which is more valuable: a database with a small number of consumers who have provided a high level of permission or one with a large number of consumers who have provided a low level of permission?

4. Is double opt-in out a more valuable strategy in some product categories than in others?

5. How can a company motivate consumers to modify their profiles more often?

6. Can you think of a way to implement permission marketing online without using e-mail? Can the Internet be used as a mechanism to implement a postal mail-based permission marketing strategy?

E-Tasks

1. Make a list of companies that you think you have a relationship with. You could, for example, list the names of department stores or supermarkets that you use. Now, try to think of the level of permission you have provided each of these organizations. What can they send you without giving you the feeling that they are overstepping their bounds? Do you think those companies know the level of permission you have given them?

2. Three levels of permission are noted in the text. Can you find examples in your own experience for each level? What do low-permission companies have to do to move you to higher levels?

3. A number of intermediaries who use permission marketing are listed in Table 9.3. Pick one company from three categories, visit their web sites, and sign up for services. How do these companies collect permission? Do they have the six elements every permission marketing program must have?

CHAPTER 10

Pricing and Distributing Digital Products

Learning Objectives

▼ To learn about the unique qualities of digital products.

▼ To understand the different pricing strategies for digital products and when it is appropriate to use them.

▼ To study the different ways in which digital products are distributed.

Executive Summary

Digital products are those that can be represented in digital form, including information of any sort, music, videos, and software. These products have unique properties: it is hard to judge their quality without experiencing them; they have a high fixed production cost for the first unit, but low marginal costs; they do not suffer from capacity constraints; and they are easier to retrieve, store, and share. Five pricing strategies are discussed: zero pricing, bundling, differential pricing, subscription, and site licensing. Companies offer zero-priced products for a variety of reasons: to generate trial and market acceptance, to convince users to upgrade to a better version, and to generate traffic to enhance advertising dollars. Bundling works well if the components are synergistic and the consumers' component preferences differ. Under some circumstances, differential pricing (also called price discrimination) generates greater profits, but because the Internet makes it easier for consumers to talk to one another, it is harder to use it online. Subscription pricing is primarily used by sellers because it reduces the uncertainty of the product's demand. Prior to beginning the distribution process, managers must first determine whether to classify it as a product (requiring a one-time upfront payment) or a service (requiring monthly billing). Versioning is another distribution approach that might be used. Because the illegal copying and distribution of digital products (i.e., piracy) is a major problem, strategies to limit its impact (e.g., lowering prices, offering customer support to legal users) are discussed.

Introduction

A digital product is anything that can be digitized (i.e., represented in digital form). Consider the classic *Huckleberry Finn*—it can be presented as plain text, a Microsoft Word document, or in Adobe Acrobat's pdf format. The following are examples of digital products:

1. Information-based services—research services

2. Literature—books, magazines, newspapers

3. Auditory information—music, lectures

4. Movies

5. Images—photographs, art, advertisements

6. Financial assets—stocks, bonds

7. Other information—recipes, directions, product manuals, maps

8. Communication—phone, fax

Digital Product Properties

All digital products share certain interesting properties that distinguish them from physical products and services.

Property 1: All Digital Products Are Experience or Credence Goods

In general, there are three types of products: search, experience, and credence. One can ascertain the quality of *search* products simply by gathering some objective information about them. For example, if one knows that a packet of salt has been iodized, it is likely a high-quality salt. Similarly, some industrial products can be completely described using certain technical specifications. As a result, obtaining information about the specifications is sufficient to determine the level of product quality.

Experience products require that the user actually consume or experience the product to determine whether its quality is good or bad. An excellent example is a book of popular fiction (see Appendix I on e-books). If one finds a book on a relevant topic and no other quality information is available, the only way to determine the book's value is to read it. Similarly, a song's quality cannot be judged without listening to it or reading its score.

Finally, a *credence* product may leave the user wondering about its quality even after it is consumed or used. This typically occurs when the consumer has little expertise and product knowledge (e.g., legal services, health care). On the Web, one frequently finds web sites containing controversial information that cannot be independently verified. Therefore, judging the quality of online information is difficult (see Appendix II).

Both experience and credence products require that consumers rely on impersonal and personal sources of information to give them a better understanding of the product's quality. Personal sources of information include early adopters of the product, opinion leaders, and reference or peer group members. Impersonal information sources include experts (e.g., movie critics such as Roger Ebert), objective third parties (e.g., *Consumer Reports*), and the popular press (e.g., editorial reviews). Amazon.com provides both types of information for all of its products through the use of editorial and customer reviews.

Property 2: Digital Products Have High Fixed Production Costs and Low Marginal Distribution/Selling Costs

Imagine a book's production process. It takes an author several months to locate the relevant information, organize it in the appropriate way, and write the book. After the author is done, editors and reviewers are involved in arriving at the final version. This entire process results in a high production cost for the first unit.

If, however, the book is digitized and presented on the Web as a downloadable file, the publisher does not incur a cost until someone downloads the book. Moreover, the incremental cost of additional downloads is typically low for the publisher. The publisher does not incur dramatically different costs whether 50 or 200 copies are downloaded in one day.[1]

Therefore, product pricing is tricky. Cost-plus pricing does not work because the marginal cost of the downloads is reduced. Although strategies such as break-even remain valid, new and innovative pricing strategies are necessary and are discussed later in this chapter.

Property 3: There Are Limited Capacity Constraints on the Production of Digital Products

For many physical products and services, there is a natural capacity constraint. For example, the number of planes that can be built in a month depends on the number of machines in a factory.

With digital products, however, capacity constraints do not arise very often. Consider a web site's downloading process. In general, if the capacity of a site's servers is sufficiently high, the site is able to meet most requests. For instance, consider the performance of the top fifty online retailers during December 2001. As shown in Table 10.1, even during peak hours, consumers were able to download the main page in about two seconds, and sites loaded properly 98.6% of the time—only one retailer on this list fell below 90%.

However, the capacity to download digital products is not infinite. During unusual periods of time (e.g., during the September 11, 2001, tragedy), sites faced with exceptional traffic had to shut down. According to Keynote Systems, major sites such as CNN.com, NYTimes.com, and ABCNews.com were completely unavailable between 9:00 and 10:00 A.M. EST on September 11. USAToday.com was down to an 18.2% availability (i.e., 18.2% of requests to download the site were successful), and MSNBC.com was reduced to a 22.0% availability. Although most sites started returning to normal access times during the next hour, many reduced the size of their home page drastically to ensure greater availability (e.g., CNN.com's homepage was reduced from 255 kilobytes to about 20).

Property 4: Digital Products Are Easier to Share, Store, and Retrieve than Paper Products

Compare a paper photograph with a digital photograph (e.g., .jpeg or .gif). If the paper photograph has to be shared with 100 people, it must be mailed 100 times. This is clearly a cumbersome and time-consuming activity. On the other hand, a digital photograph can be instantly e-mailed to 100 people; thus, making it easier to share. Similarly, using Napster, the file-sharing application, numerous users from around the world were able to share millions of files with each other on a daily basis.

Table 10.1
Performance of Top Fifty Online Retailers During December 2001

Keynote eShopping Holiday Performance Results Web Site Performance & Availability (Cumulative Results) Overall performance December 1–December 25

Sites	Perform-ance	Availability in %	Sites	Perform-ance	Availability in %
Buy.com	0.54	99.70	USPS	1.99	98.10
Victorias Secret	0.77	99.80	Smarterkids.com	2.08	97.50
Outpost	0.89	99.70	Nordstrom	2.1	99.60
REI	1	99.90	Bluelight.com	2.14	99.80
JCPenney	1.04	98.60	American Greetings	2.18	95.90
Land's End	1.13	99.70	Macy's	2.19	98.90
Neiman Marcus	1.17	99.30	Micro Warehouse	2.32	86.00
Dell	1.18	99.50	Airborne Express	2.33	99.80
Ashford	1.19	99.70	CompUSA	2.36	94.70
FedEx	1.19	98.30	Sam Goody	2.47	97.90
Half.com	1.24	99.30	Bluefly	2.66	99.00
Barnes & Noble	1.4	99.40	Wal-Mart	2.83	99.20
Eddie Bauer	1.44	99.70	eBay	2.85	99.20
Overstock.com	1.46	99.80	eGreetings	2.86	NM
Talbots	1.52	99.90	Sears	2.93	99.40
Best Buy	1.52	99.30	LL Bean	2.99	99.70
eToys	1.54	99.20	Pacific Sunwear	3.19	99.90
Target	1.55	99.40	Amazon.com	3.22	99.80
CDW	1.6	99.80	DHL	3.84	99.50
J. Crew	1.61	99.80	Hallmark	4.28	96.00
UPS	1.67	99.80	Best Prices	4.45	98.90
KBtoys.com	1.67	99.30	Saks Fifth Avenue	5.03	99.40
DELIA*s	1.78	99.80	Urban Outfitters	5.36	90.50
800.com	1.78	99.60	Gap	NM	NM
Orvis	1.91	96.70	Overall Performance of All sites	2.26	98.60
CDNow	1.98	99.80			

Keynote is measuring the performance and availability of top e-commerce web sites during the holidays, with results provided for the full week (5am–9pm PST). Measurements are taken by Keynote's Perspective service over T1/T3 connections from 25 metropolitan areas in the United States, a subset of Keynote's global network of measurement computers.

*Performance is the average time in seconds the URL took to completely download.

**Availability is the percentage of requests made that resulted in the main page being properly downloaded.

NM: Not Measured or Not Meaningful

Measurement data are not available for this site. This is not necessarily indicative of the performance of the web site. See below for more information.

Source: Keynote (Nasdaq:KEYN). Keynote, The Internet Performance Authority®, is the worldwide leader in e-commerce benchmarking and Web performance management services that improve the quality of e-business.

Pricing Strategies

Five pricing strategies are commonly used with digital products: zero pricing, bundling, differential pricing, subscription, and site licensing.

Zero Pricing

Digital products are commonly available at no charge. For example, users pay $4 for a paper copy of *Time* magazine in the United States, but can access its content for free on the *Time* web site: http://www.time.com. There are also many sites that specialize in connecting consumers with free offers (e.g., Volition.com, Freestuff.com). Similarly, beginning with Hotmail, consumers have had access to free e-mail accounts. Similarly, free software is available to consumers from sites such as http://www.cnet.com, http://www.jumbo.com, and ZDNET Downloads (http://downloads-zdnet.com.com/2001=20=0.html).

One of the issues that managers must understand is that there are many shades of "free." Even though a product is offered at no charge, the company may expect a consumer to provide something in return. It is common for companies to expect individuals to provide contact information through a registration process in exchange for a free product. In this case, even though the product is "free," the individual consumer incurs a mental transaction cost through filling out the forms.

Free software falls into three categories: freeware, shareware, and public domain. These terms are defined by webopedia.com as:

1. Freeware. Copyrighted software given away for free by the author. Although it is available for free, the author retains the copyright (you cannot do anything with it that is not expressly allowed by the author). Usually, the author allows people to use the software, but they cannot sell it.

2. Shareware. Software distributed on the basis of an honor system. Most shareware is delivered free of charge, but the author usually requests that you pay a small fee if you like the program and use it regularly. After sending the small fee, you can register with the producer and receive service assistance and updates. You can copy shareware and pass it along to friends and colleagues, but they are expected to pay the fee if they use the product.

3. Public domain. Any program that is not copyrighted. Public domain software is free and can be used without restriction.

The differences may seem subtle, but there are great variations as to what is expected from the user after the download.

Why Do Firms Provide Free Digital Products?

In many cases, the primary revenue stream in the company's business model is advertising. As a result, the company expects to make the greatest profit when it achieves the highest level of customer traffic or activity (e.g., web site visits, software downloads). The easiest way to accomplish this is by giving away free products. Consider Real Networks' Real Player, which is available as a free download from http://www.real.com. When playing a song with this player, one is shown advertising and sponsored content. The company, therefore, has an incentive to ensure that a number of users download the player and hopes to achieve this by providing the Real Player for free.

A digital product is frequently given away for no charge to encourage people to try it. Software, for example, is a complicated product with quality attributes (e.g., reliability, compatibility, performance, and stability) that cannot easily be determined without using the product. The challenge is to generate a trial, and the way to achieve that with minimal risk is to provide a form of the product for free. This is the method adopted by all shareware. Once a user is satisfied that the product performs satisfactorily, he or she pays to obtain the full version of the product on a permanent basis. Similarly, online retailers provide free sample book chapters and free sample songs to interested buyers in the hope that they will buy the complete book or CD.

Some digital products are provided at no charge in exchange for personal information. Personal information is a valuable commodity because it can be used to target advertisements. This generates higher advertising rates and higher revenues. Moreover, many sites sell market research reports developed from buyer information.

Many digital products are developed by individuals and small businesses without the budget or the influence to distribute using regular channels. Some of these programs are designed by hobbyists who have written the programs for their own personal growth and satisfaction. Others are written by small start up companies that want to establish their credibility in the marketplace. Distributing shareware is a great way for these people and firms to gain market acceptance.

Assessing the Demand for Free Digital Products

Seth Godin, a marketing expert, made his book *Unleashing the Idea Virus*, available for free on his web site using Adobe's pdf format. The book was also available in stores for a price. The download data is shown in Table 10.2. Over a period of twelve months, the book was downloaded 3,106 times by 4,389 unique visitors. The highest number of downloads occurred during the first month, and the first three months accounted for over 70% of all 3,106 downloads.

Table 10.2 indicates that making an online product available for free may draw the attention of the target audience for only a short period—there were 1,030 downloads the first month, but only 66 during the last month. Over time, the novelty fades, and it becomes harder to generate new users. Because a great deal of marketing accompanied the book's launch (e.g., articles in magazines such as *Fast Company*), demand surged during initial periods, then flattened out.

This is not, however, a typical download pattern. Some sites with free products languish because they are lost in the mix and nobody knows that they exist. Some sites become viable only after receiving support from an influential person or gaining prominence through a high rank by a search engine. In general, the launch of the free product must be integrated into the broader marketing and communication strategy of the corporation.

Table 10.2

Download Data for the Idea Virus Book

Month/Year	Number of Visitors	Downloads
July 01	156	66
June 01	136	61
May 01	187	85
April 01	143	65
March 01	192	96
February 01	241	120
January 01	322	148
December 00	237	112
November 00	263	141
October 00	506	496
September 00	487	686
August 00	1,519	1,030
Average	365.75	258.83
Total	4,389	3,106

Source: Seth Godin, "Unleashing the Idea Virus," 2000, http://www.ideavirus.com (accessed in July 2001).

Bundling

Bundling refers to offering a combination of products instead of selling the products individually. For example, Microsoft's Office Suite is a bundle of Word, Excel, Powerpoint, Outlook, Access, and other programs. Similarly, any web site can be thought of as a bundle of different content components. A newspaper is a bundle of stories. A music CD is a bundle of songs. Of course, bundling is not limited to digital products (e.g., cruise packages typically include hotel charges, airfare, and transportation to and from the airport).

Why is bundling an important pricing strategy for digital products? The classic explanation involves two individuals with diametrically opposed preferences.[2]

Suppose we were dealing with a proposal to start a newspaper that would have two sections, a business page and a sports page. Suppose also that there were just two potential readers, Alice and Bob. Suppose also that Alice needs to keep up with the financial world, and so is willing to pay $0.50 for the business page, but only $0.20 for the sports page, since she does not particularly care about sports, but might like to keep up with lunchtime conversations. Suppose that Bob's preferences are reversed, in that he is an eager sports fan, willing to pay $0.50 for the sports page, but only $0.20 for the business page, since all he cares about is occasionally checking on his retirement fund. Under those conditions, how should the proposed newspaper be priced? If each section is sold separately, then a price of $0.20 for each will induce both Alice and Bob to buy both sections, for total revenues of $0.80. If the price is set at $0.50 for each section, then Alice will buy only the business page, and Bob only the sports page, for total revenue of $1.00. On the other hand, if the two sections are bundled together, then a price for both of $0.70 will induce both Alice and Bob to purchase the newspaper, and will produce total revenues of $1.40. Thus the economically rational step is not to offer the two sections separately, but only bundled together.

A modern example of bundling, the Microsoft Office Suite, is illustrated in Table 10.3.

It is clear from Table 10.3 that the best buy is one of the bundles. Even if an individual only buys Word and Excel or Word and Powerpoint, the price ($678) is greater than the cheapest bundle ($479). The consumer is, therefore, given an incentive to buy the bundle instead of the components.

Table 10.3 also raises an important point. Microsoft offers the individual components, as well as the bundled product. This strategy is referred to as *mixed bundling*. *Pure bundling* occurs when only a bundle is offered on a take-it-or-leave-it basis. Recent research has indicated that if done prudently, mixed bundling leads to greater profits than pure bundling.[3]

When does bundling lead to improved profits? The following guidelines are useful:[4]

1. Bundling is more attractive if consumer preferences are diverse.

Table 10.3
Microsoft Office XP Pricing Scheme

Component Prices	Office XP Professional	Office XP Standard	Office XP Developer
$339	Microsoft Word 2002	Microsoft Word 2002	Microsoft Word 2002
339	Microsoft Excel 2002	Microsoft Excel 2002	Microsoft Excel 2002
109	Microsoft Outlook 2002	Microsoft Outlook 2002	Microsoft Outlook 2002
339	Microsoft PowerPoint 2002	Microsoft PowerPoint 2002	Microsoft PowerPoint 2002
339	Microsoft Access 2002		Microsoft Access 2002
169			Microsoft FrontPage 2002
Not Available			SharePoint Team Services from Microsoft
Not Available			Developer Tools
Not Available			Documentation
Bundled Price	$ 579	$ 479	$ 799
Component Sum	$1,465	$1,126	$1,634

Source: Compiled from data found at http://www.microsoft.com/office, accessed June 1, 2001.

2. Bundling is the preferred strategy if there is a synergy between the components (e.g., individuals can copy and paste documents between the Office programs).

3. Even if a large proportion of the population is indifferent about most of a bundle's components, it can be profitable if the total number of components is high.

4. Bundling is an appropriate strategy when there is a high degree of variability in the component prices. By presenting consumers with a bundle, the company can hide the price increases of some components by decreasing the prices of others.

5. When complementary bundles are provided, the company may be in a position to impose a surcharge for making the bundle available.[5]

Differential Pricing

The basis of this strategy is to charge different consumers different prices. In economic theory, this strategy is referred to as *price discrimination*. One of the most common differential pricing strategies for information products is to provide a discount based on purchase history. For example, loyal customers are provided a discount or the first-time buyer is provided an incentive to sign up.

An extreme form of price discrimination is to charge each individual a different price. This is called *identity-based or personalized pricing*. A company that is able to deduce how much each consumer is willing or able to pay for a product can set the price accordingly. For example, if a company can identify a consumer with a high disposable income and product interest, it can charge a higher price. Although the Internet allows a company to uniquely identify each individual based on his or her profile, it also allows individuals to talk to one another in public forums. When individuals find out that they are being charged much higher prices, they become resentful—and this leads to controversy and negative publicity.

This type of problem is illustrated by the DVD pricing case at Amazon.com. In September 2000, tests conducted by *Computer World* magazine indicated that some consumers could be charged as much as $10 more for the DVD *Planet of the Apes—The Evolution*. Similar variations in price were found when consumers purchased a DVD of the movie, *Men in Black*. Those consumers who had visited an online community called the DVD Talk Forum eventually discovered that this was happening. Prices varied according to which browser was used, whether a consumer was a repeat or first-time customer, and which ISP address a customer used.[6] The company denied tying the price variations to demographic information.[7] It refunded money to 6,896 online consumers and called the price test a mistake.

This embarrassing incident indicates how hard it is to implement identity-based pricing on the Internet. In another instance, large online retailers are providing loyal customers with coupon codes. When these customers enter this code during the shopping process, they are given a lower price. Unfortunately, there are now many sites that collect coupon codes and make them freely available to anyone. For example, consumers can locate codes at http://www.imegadeals.com/coupon_codes.htm. Similarly, using price comparison sites, such as MySimon.com, consumers can determine whether the price they are quoted at a web site is the lowest. This places pressure on those companies charging different consumers different prices.

Subscription

With subscription pricing, the buyer promises to buy access to content over time. For example, a buyer may pay a price to obtain multiple copies of a magazine during one year, to have access to a premier database such as ABI/Inform for six months, or to have Internet access for three years from a service such as AOL or MSN.

There are many different forms of subscription pricing used on the Internet:

- All content available to paid subscribers only (e.g., Consumerreports.com).

- Some content is free; premium content is available to subscribers only (e.g., Salon Premium, ESPN.com).

- All content is free upon registration (e.g., Nytimes.com).

- All content is free—no registration required (e.g., Cnn.com).

- Users are rewarded for browsing (e.g., cbs.sportsline.com).

There are a variety of reasons why subscription fees are an attractive way of pricing. First, it reduces the seller's demand uncertainty over time. If an individual buys a subscription for one year, the publisher is ensured of a demand for this period of time. Many publishers are willing to provide a price break in return for this reduced uncertainty.

Second, in some cases, it reduces the administrative costs of tracking transactions. Some experts argue that micropayments will abound on the Internet. Under this system, users pay a small fee for every transaction (e.g., reading a news story). The reality is that the administrative costs of charging by the minute or the byte are larger than the benefit. There is also some anecdotal evidence that consumers prefer simple pricing arrangements:[8]

In the 1970s, the Bell System experimented with charging for local calls. Typically, customers were given a choice of the traditional flat rate option, which might cost $7.50 per month, and allow unlimited local calling, and of a measured rate option, which might cost $5.00 per month, allow for 50 calls at no extra charge, and then cost $0.05 per call. Anyone making fewer than 100 local calls per month was better off with the measured rate option. However, they observed that typically around 50% of the customers who were making almost no local calls at all, and thus would have benefited from measured rate service, still stayed with the more expensive flat rate service.

Finally, subscription arrangements can increase consumer usage, leading to higher advertising and sponsorship rates. For example, when AOL moved from per-minute pricing to a flat fee in December 1996, the average time spent online increased from sixteen minutes to fifty-one minutes.[9] This was viewed as a bold and innovative move that defined the future of the company.

Site Licensing

This is a pricing practice used with institutional buyers. Typically, a large company or university pays a flat fee so that everyone in the institution, or some subset of individuals, can use a software program or gain access to an online database.

Licensing has several benefits for the software seller.[10,11] First, it places the burden of enforcing the license and checking for software piracy on the institution, not the software maker. Second, because it is a simple pricing model, it is easy to enforce. Third, it encourages new users to try a software package; thus, stimulating more usage. Over time, the organization may upgrade to a better package. Fourth, it reduces maintenance costs by standardizing the program's features.

The Distribution of Digital Products

Product or Service?

One of the properties of digital products is that they can be sold either as a product or as a service. Initially, this may seem odd. But, consider what Microsoft wants to do with its .Net initiative. Instead of selling its software as a CD that comes in a box with manuals, it wants to make all software downloadable from the Internet. Consumers pay a subscription fee. The company can then make incremental upgrades to the software instead of forcing consumers to buy one large upgrade. Those consumers with "always-on" connectivity (e.g., DSL or cable modem) will not notice the changes being made to the software—upgrades are made overnight, while they sleep.

The important distinction is that consumers do not pay for the product once—as they do for a product that comes on a CD. Instead, they pay a recurring service fee, similar to cable television or telephone fees. The company wants to build a billing relationship with each individual and create a new set of expectations.

The primary benefit to the consumer is *just-in-time functionality*. If a new feature is designed, the consumer has immediate access. Another benefit is the *seamless upgrade process*. Most consumers do not like upgrading their software because it is an onerous and technical process. Letting Microsoft upgrade the software from a remote location "while you sleep" may reduce the level of inconvenience associated with the process. Some consumers may also benefit by not having to pay a large amount to buy a product. By *spreading out the costs over time*, the service approach may improve the level of its access—those who cannot pay the total cost at once can still have access.

From the company's perspective, moving to a service distribution system is advantageous for many reasons: the costs associated with the upgrade process are reduced, if not eliminated; the company no longer pays to produce CDs and manuals; and by using bundling strategies, the company can create a more profitable pricing structure.

The challenge for the company is to change consumer mind-sets. Individuals used to buying a tangible product may balk at switching to a service. Similarly, consumers used to paying once for a product may be suspicious of paying monthly. Consumers may also have privacy concerns because the seamlessness of the upgrade process depends on the level of access the company has to the user's computer. The software's reliability may also become an issue with more frequent, smaller upgrades.

Versioning

Versioning involves creating a menu of products and charging different prices for each version. This is a very common strategy for selling digital products.

Consider *The New York Times* online (http://www.nytimes.com). Currently, it makes its content available for free on its web site. However, readers have long complained that this does not give them the same satisfaction as reading the newspaper. To meet this demand, the newspaper has created a new service. For sixty-five cents each, readers can now receive a digital copy of the paper formatted exactly like the paper version. The digital copy arrives in the form of a daily e-mail. Executives have said that they only require 5,000 readers for this venture to be a success—a figure they are expected to achieve.[12]

Similarly, an editor at Slate (http://www.slate.msn.com) wrote an article in July 2001 that related 101 ways to read the e-zine.[13] Readers can, of course, visit their web site. It is also possible to receive a daily e-mail with the latest stories. Slate stories are formatted for printing so they look like professional magazine stories. Readers can also play an audio version of a story or download it to a handheld device.

Digital products can be versioned in these ways:[14]

1. No banner ads. It is now increasingly clear that users absolutely hate banner ads. Most hate them so much that they are willing to pay so that they do not have to see the ads. Some publishers are, therefore, offering premium versions of their content with no banner ads (e.g., Salon.com). This demand may become greater as the ads become more annoying (e.g., pop-ups, audio/video, skyscraper).

2. Delay. This is designed for those information products with a value tied to timeliness. For example, most stock quotes are delayed by twenty minutes, but some web sites now offer real-time stock quotes to members for a price. Similarly, *WIRED* magazine uses an interesting strategy: The content of the print magazine appears online at http://www. wired.com/wired—thirty days after the print version is released. This is a strategy to motivate readers to pay for the magazine.

3. User interface. A fee is charged for sophisticated user interface.

4. Image resolution. A small, low-quality image is made available for free; however, a small fee is charged if the user wants better resolution.

5. Features. A stripped-down version is available for a low price, but, if the user wants to upgrade to the next level, he or she is charged a very high price.

6. Speed of access. This is a new dimension that is being used very successfully—consumers get a low access speed for free or a high access speed for a small fee. An example is the ISP Netzero. Their basic Internet service is free; however, if individuals pay a small monthly fee of $9.95 (as of June 2001), they receive Net Zero Platinum, which is Internet service with no banner ads and faster page loads.

Versioning does not work if two factors exist. First, if a higher-priced version can be easily changed into a lower-priced version, consumers become outraged, leading to a public relations problem. Microsoft faced this problem with its NT product—it was priced very low for individuals and very high for businesses.

The second factor is arbitrage—a user who has obtained the high-end product for a high price can easily make multiple copies and sell them to others. Alternatively, a low-end user can make the product available to high-end users who may not have access. These challenges must be considered when preparing a versioning strategy.

Content Provider

The Web is a very fragmented medium. A content-based site that simply focuses on its own site may not maximize its potential audience. In order to get wider exposure, many sites sell their content to other sites. This provides the sites with a steady stream of additional revenue with very little additional effort. Some examples include:

- Infospace.com offers standardized content—yellow pages, stock quotes, news, maps and directions, and a web search functionality to leading sites such as AOL, MSN, and Lycos.

- MSNBC.com has content partnerships with other leading news sites, such as Newsweek.com and WSJ.com.

- Some large news sites (e.g., ESPN.com) rely on wire services such as the Associated Press (http://www.apdigitalnews.com). It is not economical for every news site to have bureaus all over the world. Because the wire services have vast worldwide resources, the news sites can get high quality content at a low price. Unfortunately, this also means that the sites cannot distinguish themselves from one another.

In addition to supplying others with the content, content providers can make the information directly available to the consumer. For example, WSJ.com provides information on its web site and also shares it with MSNBC.com. Others primarily focus on supplying content (e.g., wire services).

If a large number of sites in a particular category are using content provider information, achieving differentiation becomes a challenge. Consider the sports category. Many sports web sites subscribe to wire services such as the Associated Press. Consumers who are interested in locating the game's score with a brief description can find the same information on many sites. This helps the small or local sites achieve the same level of credibility as the national sites and reduces the level of differentiation. It also puts pressure on the national sites (e.g., ESPN.com) to develop a more specialized content to attract consumers.

Software Piracy

Piracy is the illegal use (copying and distribution) of a software product. Software piracy is a major problem that costs businesses billions of dollars each year. As shown in Table 10.4, in certain countries, almost all of the software used is pirated. Moreover, as shown in Table 10.5, the losses due to piracy in the United States alone amount to over $3 billion dollars.

Table 10.4
Top Twenty–Five Countries by Piracy Rate

	1999	2000
Vietnam	98%	97%
China	91	94
Indonesia	85	89
Ukraine/Other CIS	90	89
Russia	89	88
Lebanon	88	83
Pakistan	83	83
Bolivia	85	81
Qatar	80	81
Bahrain	82	80
Kuwait	81	80
Thailand	81	79
El Salvador	83	79
Nicaragua	80	78
Oman	88	78
Bulgaria	80	78
Romania	81	77
Guatemala	80	77
Paraguay	83	76
Jordan	75	71
Honduras	75	68
Costa Rica	71	68
Dominican Republic	72	68
Kenya	67	67
Nigeria	68	67

Source: Business Software Alliance, http://www.bsa.org.

Table 10.5

Top Ten Countries in Terms of Total Retail Losses, Sorted in Descending Order in Terms of 2000 Losses (All figures in millions of U.S. dollars)

	1995	1996	1997	1998	1999	2000
US	$2,940,294	$2,360,934	$2,779,673	$2,875,185	$3,191,111	$2,632,438
Japan	1,648,493	1,190,323	752,598	596,910	975,396	1,666,331
China	443,933	703,839	1,449,454	1,193,386	645,480	1,124,395
Germany	775,898	497,950	508,884	479,367	652,379	635,264
UK	444,561	337,344	334,527	464,771	679,506	530,787
France	537,567	411,966	407,900	425,205	548,408	480,604
Italy	503,648	340,784	271,714	356,879	421,434	421,942
Brazil	441,592	356,370	394,994	366,688	392,031	325,617
Canada	347,085	357,316	294,593	320,636	440,101	304,999
Korea	675,281	515,547	582,320	197,516	197,269	302,938

Source: Business Software Alliance, http://www.bsa.org.

There are at least five ways in which software is pirated.[15]

1. The software can be *softlifted*. This involves copying a single piece of software on multiple machines in violation of the license agreement.

2. *Hard disk loading* is done by dealers who load unauthorized copies of the software on a machine that is then sold to the end-user.

3. *OEM unbundling* involves illegally providing a portion of a bundle to users without the authorization of the software company.

4. *Counterfeiting* involves selling fake CDs or manuals.

5. *Online piracy* is the fastest growing category. Illegal bulletin boards (also referred to as warez sites) provide users around the world with access to software.

What have software companies done to combat piracy? These companies have developed an *effective legal sales presence* in all areas of the world. Software has been made easier to purchase legally. Software producers also have filed lawsuits against corporations and work with world governments to develop strong laws against piracy.

One of the interesting approaches to stem software piracy is to offer *customer support only to legal users*. Because technical support is a valuable commodity, this is a strong incentive to buy legal software. This strategy, however, places software makers in a quandary—the better the product, the lower the need for technical service, the smaller the incentive to purchase legal software.

Whistle-blower programs run by software associations encourage employees to disclose the illegal use of software by their employers. In some cases, the program offers amnesty to the user provided the company signs the appropriate contracts and begins paying the correct amount.

One of the more controversial answers to piracy has been to *reduce software prices*. It is argued that individuals pirate software because of its high price. If the price is reduced, a large number of users may find it to their benefit to switch to legal software. Of course, firms are free to set prices in a competitive market, and this is not a strategy that is used widely.

Conclusion

Digital products have certain unique properties; yet, they are pervasive in today's e-business. Businesses must understand the unique properties of such products when determining pricing and distribution strategies.

Notes

(All URLs are current as of March 25, 2002.)

1. This assumes that the number of downloads is below the capacity of the publisher's servers. If there is a sudden surge in demand (as in the Stephen King example discussed in Appendix I), the publisher may have to incur additional server costs.

2. Andrew Odlyzko, "The Bumpy Road of Electronic Commerce," *WebNet 96—World Conf. Web Soc. Proc.*, H. Maurer, ed., AACE (1996): 378–389, <http://www.dtc.umn.edu/~odlyzko/doc/bumpy.road.txt>.

3. R. Venkatesh and Vijay Mahajan, "A Probabilistic Approach to Pricing a Bundle of Products," *Journal of Marketing Research*, 30(4), (1993): 494–509.

4. Odlyzko, "The Bumpy Road of Electronic Commerce."

5. A. Estelami, "Consumer Savings in Complementary Product Bundles," *Journal of Marketing Theory and Practice*, 7(3), (1999): 107–115.

6. Linda Rosencrance, "Testing Reveals Varied DVD Prices on Amazon," September 7, 2000, <http://asia.cnn.com/2000/TECH/computing/09/07/amazon.dvd.discrepancy.idg/hs~index.html>.

7. Reuters, "Amazon Apologizes for Random DVD Price Test," September 28, 2000, <http://asia.cnn.com/2000/TECH/computing/09/28/amazon.reut/>.

8. Odlyzko, "The Bumpy Road of Electronic Commerce."

9. Daniel Roth, "Well Connected," *Forbes*, 161(7), (1998): 44.

10. Odlyzko, "The Bumpy Road of Electronic Commerce."

11. Y. Bakos and E. Brynjolfsson, (In press), "Aggregation and Disaggregation of Information Goods: Implications for Bundling, Site Licensing and Micropayment Systems," in Proceedings of Internet Publishing and Beyond: The Economics of Digital Information and Intellectual Property, D. Hurley, B. Kahin, and H. Varian, eds.

12. Rebecca Fannin, "Paper Pushers," November 2001, <http://www.wired.com/wired/archive/9.11/mustread.html>.

13. Michael Kinsely, "101 Ways to Read Slate . . . and Counting," July 12, 2001, <http://slate.msn.com/?id=111843>.

14. Adapted from Carl Shapiro and Hal Varian, "Information Rules: A Strategic Guide to the Network Economy," 1998, <http://www.inforules.com>.

15. Eric Roberts, Web site for class on Computers, Ethics and Social Responsibility, "Types of Software Piracy," <http://cse.stanford.edu/classes/cs201/projects-99-00/software-piracy/types.html>.

16. AP, "Stephen King's E-Book Sets Record," March 16, 2000, <http://www.usatoday.com/life/cyber/tech/review/crg997.htm>.

17. AP, "Stephen King E-Book Earnings Lag," September 21, 2000, <http://www.usatoday.com/life/cyber/tech/review/crh539.htm>.

18. Netskills, "Your Internet Detective," <http://www.netskills.ac.uk/TonicNG/cgi/sesame?detective>.

REVIEW / CHAPTER 10

Discussion Questions

1. What digital product are you willing to pay for online? Why are you willing to pay for this product and not others? Are there market segments concerned with what people are willing to pay?

2. How would you assess the success of a product that is available at no charge?

3. Appendix I discusses the pricing strategies of two online Stephen King books. If you were advising him, how would you change the strategy for either book?

4. Consider a software program that is priced at $100. Now, assume that you have to charge for this program as a service. How would you approach the pricing decision? What cost information do you need to make your decision?

5. Develop a pricing strategy for an online course offered by a distance education program at a local university. How does it differ from the strategy used by a university such as Harvard, Stanford, or MIT?

6. Piracy is usually discussed in the context of software. However, the piracy of other digital products (e.g., music, video, e-books) is increasing. How does the issue of piracy vary in the different contexts?

7. How might e-books change libraries in the future? Universities and schools? The contents of students' backpacks?

E-Tasks

1. Jack Welch's new book, *Jack: Straight from the Gut* is now available through the leading online bookstores Amazon.com and bn.com. The book is available in multiple formats—hardcover, e-book, audio cassette (abridged), audio cassette (unabridged), audio CD (abridged) and audio download (Audible.com). Visit the relevant section for each format on the booksellers' web sites. How is the approach to pricing and presentation different in each case? Should more formats be created?

2. A distinction is drawn between pure and mixed bundling. Visit the web sites of three top software makers and study their product line. Do they offer pure or mixed bundles? Would you recommend a different approach?

APPENDIX I / CHAPTER 10

E–Books

Stephen King, the world-famous author of horror books, created a stir in March 2000 when he released a short novel (sixty-six pages) called *Riding the Bullet* online. The e-book was priced at $2.50 and was available at leading book-related sites. Bn.com and Amazon.com offered the book for free on their web sites as a promotion. The response to his offer was tremendous. Approximately 400,000 copies were downloaded during the first twenty-four hours.[16] The servers hit their maximum capacity quickly, so it was hard to access the book online for some time. This was a watershed event for e-books—many proponents believed that this proved its legitimacy.

Spurred by this success, King decided to experiment with another project. He offered a serial called *The Plant* on his web site. Instead of charging each customer, he created an honor system that encouraged consumers to make voluntary donations. He did not put the entire book online; rather, he made it available in installments and indicated that he would continue to write the book online if at least 75% of those who downloaded it paid $1. Unfortunately, only about 70% of the readers paid–172,004 people paid for part one and 74,373 people paid for part two. (Afraid that King might cancel the experiment, some readers actually paid more than $1 in order to compensate for the freeloaders.) Due to the drop in payments from part one to part two and "technical difficulties" (the serial was pirated by hackers), King has not finished the series as originally planned. This left the paying readers irate because they did not learn how the story ended. King has indicated that the first five parts are written. He has implied that he will charge for the first eight parts and then make it free. It appears that there will not be a voluntary payment system.[17]

Overall, King's online forays teach us many lessons. Few authors have the power to directly interact with consumers; however, King's two projects showed the world that it is possible to sell numerous copies of a book online. Nevertheless, pricing is tricky, and honor systems do not seem to work well. Security is also a problem. If the book is easily hacked, the ability to sell it online is significantly reduced.

So, what is an e-book? Although there is no definite answer to this question, there are at least three types:

1. Text files available on a web site for downloading to the user's PC. They are either free (e.g., Project Gutenberg, a long-standing project to make text files of old classics available) or paid.

2. Web-accessible files that can be read only by using a proprietary software such as Adobe Acrobat Book Reader. These "readers" present the information in a format that is much more pleasant to read on a computer screen. King's first novel fell into this category. It was written using Glassbook, now owned by Adobe.

APPENDIX I / CHAPTER 10

3. Web-accessible files that can be downloaded to a dedicated hardware device such as the e-bookman. If a user prefers "mobile" e-books, there are readers available for handheld devices. These devices offer additional features such as increased storage (ten to twenty books), portability, search capabilities, built-in dictionaries, highlighting capabilities, and audio and video capabilities.

E-books have several disadvantages. First, reading for long periods of time using the PC monitor or the LCD screen on handheld devices puts an excessive strain on the eyes. Second, users cannot print the books from the specialized readers; as a result, it is hard to share. Third, the readers display small amounts of information at one time; therefore, the pages are not easily compared.

Pricing e-books is an interesting topic. Because e-books have multiple components—the handheld device, the software, and the content—bundling is not a very viable option. It may be possible to sell the handheld device for a particular price (e.g., $250) and load it with ten books chosen by the purchaser. Users then pay for subsequent books.

Another approach is to focus on some of the most popular book titles and offer them as free e-books in order to get more people to use the book. A third approach uses a micro-payment system—users pay for each book based on the size of the book. It is not clear whether this is feasible because micropayment systems are not widely used, and not all books can be valued by their size—some very short books may be highly desired and can be priced higher.

Specialty categories, however, are expected to fare better. For example, loading textbooks onto e-book readers might be very successful—students have access to all of the textbooks necessary for their education at all times.

The bottom line is this: the future of e-books promises to be exciting!

APPENDIX II / CHAPTER 10

Judging the Quality of a Digital Product

When one finds a new web site, how can its quality be determined? One method of evaluating web content is provided by the Net Detective system.[18] Although they identify three sets of criteria for evaluating a web site, only two sets of criteria are presented here.

The first set of criteria pertains to the site's *content* and includes:

1. Validity—is the information well grounded, and is it appropriate?

2. Accuracy—is the information correct? Are there mistakes? Has the information been updated recently?

3. Authority—does the author know what he or she is talking about? Does the author have the appropriate credentials?

4. Uniqueness—is the information copied from elsewhere or is it original?

5. Comprehensive—are all of your questions answered?

The second set of criteria concerns how the information is organized or the *form* of the information. High-quality information is easy to navigate, is presented using appropriate technologies, and has strong user support.

Stanford Persuasive Technology Lab (http://www.credibility.org) has focused on the credibility of information obtained on the Web. They identify two dimensions that underly a web site's perceived credibility.

1. Perceived trustworthiness ("Are they good?")—whether the site is honest, unbiased, and truthful.

2. Perceived expertise ("Do they know what they are talking about?")—includes experience, intelligence, power, and knowledge.

They also have identified four types of credibility:

1. Presumed credibility derives from the general assumptions we have about the nature of the Web (e.g., sites with a .org domain name may be trusted more).

2. Reputed credibility arises when a site is referred by a trusted third party (e.g., doctor, American Medical Association). Similarly, if one sees a seal from a trusted third-party (e.g., TrustE's privacy seal), one may feel more comfortable with a particular site.

APPENDIX II / CHAPTER 10

3. Surface credibility involves the user's reaction to the aesthetics and design of a site. If a site is hard to navigate, has links that do not work properly, and has content errors, one is likely to find it less credible.

4. Experienced credibility relates to one's past experience with a site. For example, if a site crashed during a previous visit, one is likely to downgrade its credibility.

Strategies that firms can employ to communicate the quality of their digital products include:

1. Provide information from objective third-party sources to enhance credibility.

2. Improve the usability of the site by ensuring that there are no errors and that the navigation is smooth.

3. When there is a crisis, deal with customers in a prompt and professional manner.

CHAPTER 11

Online Community

Learning Objectives

▼ To understand the nature of a community.

▼ To identify the characteristics of successful communities.

▼ To learn how the Internet has enabled new types of communities.

▼ To understand how community members use the Internet.

▼ To learn how communities can help companies.

▼ To learn how to build a successful online community.

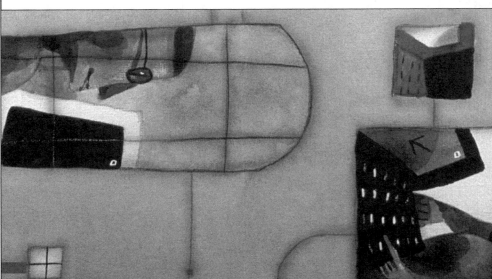

▼ To learn how to build a successful online community.

Executive Summary

In this chapter, an online community is defined as a gathering of individuals in a computer-mediated environment who are united by a common purpose and governed by self-determined policies. Every online community has five characteristics: purpose, boundary, mutuality, rules, and self-organization. Online communities are aspatial, anonymous, asynchronous, acorporal, and astigmatic. Individuals use online communities for a variety of purposes: some socialize, others network, and others have fun. Successful marketing to online communities conveys a positive message and helps new customers understand a product. The relationship between communities and companies progresses in three stages: denial, monitoring, and collaboration. Successful online communities create a strong sense of belonging among their participants. The nine-step process to build successful communities is discussed, as well as community building ethical issues.

Introduction

Online communities are everywhere. AOL users send 368 million e-mails and more than 1.3 billion instant messages are exchanged daily across the AOL network.[1] On Amazon.com, discussion boards, which provide consumers access to their peers and reviews by others, enhance the shopping experience. Trading communities, such as eBay, are very popular (see Case #3: eBay). On web-log sites, such as Metafilter and Slashdot, members contribute links to interesting news stories and information. Communities have successfully created new resources and products (see Case #5: LINUX).

Although the concept of "community" is very old, sociologists (and others) have long debated the proper way to define it. In this chapter, *an online community is defined as a gathering of individuals in a computer-mediated environment who are united by a common purpose and governed by self-determined policies.*

Managers must realize that although there are advantages to building online communities, it is not easy. Many Internet companies are now learning that simply providing the communication tools does not lead to community development. Consider what these three experts on online communities have said:[2]

Putting up message boards and chat rooms is a step towards community, but online community does not automatically happen just by throwing the tools at people. It requires thought. (Howard Rheingold)

Lots and lots of people at GeoCities (now part of Yahoo!) (don't care) about community. I interviewed hundreds of members, and most said, 'I don't know why you're contacting me. I just have a home page there because I want a Web space. (Amy Jo Kim)

There's a breakdown between what's being hyped and what's actually happening at these sites: Few of the members actually seem to be communicating with one another. Most people, it seems, just want a place to slap up a picture of their cat. (Janelle Brown)

Yet, when done correctly, online communities lead to unbelievable loyalty, great commitment, and a deep sense of kinship; for example:

More than 10,000 volunteers spend over 4 hours a week working for AOL. Their activities include monitoring chat rooms, hosting bulletin board discussions, helping kids with homework, offering technical advice. In return, the volunteers get a free America Online account and access to special community leader forums.[3]

The fact that this level of volunteerism is taking place in a for-profit company is commendable. By taking the right approach to building online communities, the company successfully reduced costs, while increasing a sense of involvement.

What Is a Community?

Every community has five features:[4] purpose, boundary, mutuality, rules, and self-organization.

1. Purpose. Every community has a mission that attracts its members. For example, surgicaleyes.com is a community that discusses problems with refractive eye surgery techniques such as Lasik. Flyfishing.com is a community of fly-fishers. It is important to clearly define the purpose of the community in order to attract the right audience.

2. Boundary. Every community must clearly define its boundary. Members must know what is relevant and what is irrelevant. Many communities may have an FAQ section that answers these types of questions for the novice user.

3. Mutuality. A community is comprised of members who have an interest in its purpose. Motivated members demonstrate high degrees of reciprocity toward one another. There is a strong sense of furthering the cause. A high level of shared interests leads to a win–win attitude instead of a competitive attitude, leading to cohesion and bonding.

4. Rules. Each community must define and communicate the rules of engagement to prospective and current members. For example, Metafilter does not permit new members to post content on the main page until they have developed a certain level of trust. The community also must determine how it will handle those who break the rules.

5. Self-organization. Communities evolve in the directions preferred by its members. Over time, a community must become self-sufficient, with key roles being played by volunteers. As shown in Figure 11.1, communities initially require more external management and control. Over time, the community becomes self-organizing.

Community and Internet Technology

The concept of community, of course, predates modern technology. For example, discussions at the village well, the local bar, or the water cooler are long-standing, powerful symbols of community. Even the idea of company-led communities is not new. Harley-Davidson developed the concept of Harley-owner-groups (HOGs) well before the Internet took root. The Internet and the Web simply helped companies, like Harley-Davidson, sign

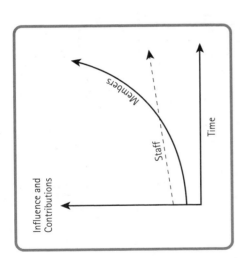

Figure 11.1
Evolution of Communities

Influence and Contributions

Members

Staff

Time

Source: Amy Jo Kim, "Three Underlying Principles," 2000, http://www.naima.com/community/intro/intro4.html.

up more people, provide better communication in members-only areas, and, in general, better communicate with their customers.

All online communities are characterized by the five "As".[5]

- *Aspatial.* Increasing the distance between participants does not affect the nature of their interactions. As a result, participants are spread out all over the world.

- *Asynchronous.* This is the opposite of being synchronous or real-time. Examples of asynchronous technologies are e-mail and discussion boards. Of course, not all communications are asynchronous—chat is an exception.

- *Acorporal.* In a virtual space, there are no bodies. Because individuals cannot see the other participants' body language, they do not observe grins, scowls, frowns, and so on. New technologies using avatar-based chats try to alleviate the problem by allowing consumers to create their own online persona.

- *Astigmatic.* In a virtual community, one cannot observe the trappings of power and status; therefore, individuals cannot observe the race, age, gender, office size, or fashion sense of other participants.

- *Anonymous.* Much of the communication in Internet communities is anonymous.

These characteristics lead to an interesting online communication dynamic. In many communities, members can only see an alias. As the famous *New Yorker* cartoon said, "On the Internet nobody knows that you are a dog." Generally, anonymous interaction allows frankness in conversations; however, it can also generate spiteful and mean behavior. In addition, because one does not know a person's reason for saying something, it is not possible to trust what they are saying. For example, a corporation's employees can praise a new product while masquerading as anonymous members of a community.

Online communities create a profusion of weak ties. The Internet makes it easy for individuals to develop casual relationships with numerous people: people report receiving e-mails from a casual college acquaintance and others belong to a mailing list but have not physically met any other member. Although some people have made major decisions (e.g., marrying) based solely on an online interaction, this medium typically leads to many casual relationships that never escalate further.

The five As also help to create an environment where there is more communication and more content. It is possible to start from scratch and rapidly learn about a topic. Successful online communities provide access to knowledge and content experts, as well as quick answers to obscure questions.

Why Do People Join Online Communities?

The activities people enjoy in online communities can be classified as follows:[6]

- *Socializing.* Communities created for meeting people, playing around, sharing jokes and stories, and just taking an interest in each other. Communities like this often center around bulletin boards and chat rooms (e.g., Electric Minds at http://www.minds.com).

- *Working (companies).* Distributed work groups within companies and between companies use online communities to build their team, keep in touch, and work on projects together. Very detailed descriptions of how online work groups function are located at http://www.awaken.com and http://www.bigbangworkshops.com.

- *Working (geographic community groups).* Freenets (http://www.freenetproject.org) offer local communities ways to communicate and work together. Some have even combined this with ISP service. Community groups, such as soccer teams and school groups, use online communities as forums for information and discussion, helping to bring the groups together.

- *Working (common interest).* Virtual communities are very important to people who share a common interest in issues and causes. People suffering with certain diseases, people interested in politics or the environment, or people studying together can form a nucleus for an online community.

- *Topical conversations.* Online salons and discussion forums, such as the Well (http://www.well.com), Salon's TableTalk (http://www.salon.com), and Cafe Utne (http://www.utne.com), have formed communities of people who enjoy conversations about particular topics and shared interests. ForumOne notes that the top eight topics of those forums registered on their site are: relationships (16%), "mega sites" (11%), business and finance (8%), health (5%), hobbies (4%), religion (3%), music (3%), and international (3%).

A survey conducted by the Pew Research Center identified the reasons why individuals make connections online[7] (see Tables 11.1 and 11.2). Most people join online communities to meet others who share the same interests. It is also common for individuals to join the online communities developed by those groups with which they are already affiliated.

Table 11.1
Why People Communicate with Online Groups

	Percent Who Thought It Was Important
Getting general membership news and information	76%
Getting involved with or learning about group activities	71
Discussing issues with others	68
Creating or maintaining relationships with others in group	49

Source: John Horrigan, Pew Internet & American Life Project, "Online Communities: Networks That Nurture Long-Distance Relationships and Local Ties," <http://www.pewinternet.org/reports/toc.asp?Report=47>.

Table 11.2
How the Internet Makes People Feel Connected

	All Surveyed
Find people or groups who share your interest	49%
Become more involved with organizations or groups that you are already affiliated with	40
Connect with people of different ages or generations	37
Find people or groups who share your belief	32
Connect with people of different economic backgrounds	29
Connect with people from different ethnic groups	27
Connect with groups based in your local community	26

Source: John Horrigan, Pew Internet & American Life Project, "Online Communities: Networks That Nurture Long-Distance Relationships and Local Ties," <http://www.pewinternet.org/reports/toc.asp?Report=47>.

Online Community Business Models

There are three major types of online community business models: community enablers, trading/sharing communities, and communities that are a feature of for-profit organizations:

1. *Community enablers.* These companies generate income by enabling the formation of communities. They do not have a specific interest in the topics of the communities they host—the topics can range from fly-fishing to ham radio. If the users stay at their site for long periods of time, the companies earn money showing them ads. Companies of this type include AOL, Yahoo! groups and clubs, and Talkcity.

2. *Trading/sharing communities.* These communities allow their members to trade or share products or services with one another. For example, eBay is a community where

users buy from one another in an auction format. Similarly, music-sharing sites (e.g., Napster and Gnutella) have users who come together for the primary purpose of sharing a product with one another.

3. *Community as a feature of a for-profit corporation.* The community is seen as a feature of a company's web site, and the company encourages interaction between its current and potential users. In exchange, its support and sales expenses are reduced. The topics in these communities are closely related to the business of the corporation. For example, Cisco Systems encourages its users to discuss issues related to its products.

Revenue Sources

Revenue sources for the community business models include:

- Subscription fees. AOL charges a monthly subscription fee for access to its Internet services, including community fees.

- Transaction fees. These are very common in trading communities. For example, eBay charges sellers to place an item and to sell one.

- Advertising. Many community sites still use advertising; however, in many cases, users leave the group when they see the advertising.

- Content fees. Users are charged a fee to access the material available at the site.

Community enablers that rely on advertising as their primary revenue source are struggling because advertisers are leery of placing their ads in discussion spaces where the tone can get unruly and risqué. Simply put, advertisers do not want to have their ads seen in a space where the content is unpredictable and organic. Although trading communities (e.g., eBay) have done very well, sharing communities (e.g., Napster) are struggling to find a way to make money because users are unwilling to pay prices high enough for the business to be viable, and other sources of revenue are proving to be unreliable.

Marketing to Online Communities

Consider this story.[8] When the movie *Lord of the Rings* was released in early 2002, it was the moment that many of the book's fans had long awaited. There are at least 400 fan sites devoted to this and other Tolkien books. Just before the movie was released, New Line Cinema decided to take a collaborative approach with these communities. Rather than antagonizing them, the company sought out the fan sites—a completely new approach in the film industry. When the movie's web site, http://www.lordoftherings.net, went up for the first time, the fan sites' webmasters played a major role in getting the message out. When a trailer was released in April 2000, it was downloaded by a record-breaking 1.7 million people.

This example clearly shows that working with online communities in a collaborative fashion can benefit a company's bottom line. In addition to tapping the communities' enthusiasm to get the message out, one of the greatest benefits is the reduced support and hand-holding costs. In many communities, problems that would normally require assistance from company employees are handled by the customer's peers. In other cases, peers help new customers familiarize themselves and learn the rules.

The relationship between companies and communities progresses through three stages: denial, monitoring, and collaboration. In the first stage, the company does not believe that communities have any merit. They either do not know that communities are talking about them or choose to ignore such conversations. In some cases, companies take an antagonistic approach and try to shut down the communities on legal grounds (e.g., copyright infringement).

The second stage is monitoring—company executives monitor what happens in communities that are related to their business. By being aware of how consumers view it, the company can take appropriate and timely actions. For example, executives might become members of large and influential mailing lists so that they can answer questions or address concerns in a timely fashion. If this is done, full disclosure must be the norm.

The final stage in the evolution is collaboration. As the *Lord of the Rings* example suggests, working in a collaborative fashion with communities can lead to win-win outcomes. Frequently, the company has to take the first step and approach the community—but it is usually reciprocated handsomely.

Benefits of Offering Communities on a Company Web Site

A study by McKinsey of seventeen major consumer-oriented web sites with community features revealed major advantages to hosting a community space.[9]

1. On transaction sites, community users represent about 35% of all users, but 64% of confirmed sales.

2. Contributors to community spaces are the most desirable consumers. They visit often—about four times more often than noncontributors and about ten times more often than nonmembers. They are also more loyal and purchase more.

Unfortunately, many corporations plunged into the arena of online communities with elevated expectations and are becoming somewhat disillusioned. This is more a function of overinflated expectations than the failure of community. Communities reflect consumer behavior, they do not change it.

Building a Successful Community

Price-Waterhouse-Cooper has developed a framework for building a successful brand community called the "community hexagon." The central construct in the framework is an individual's sense of belonging to the community.[10] In their framework, the company can enhance an individual's sense of belonging by providing the benefits of participation, precisely tailored content, greater brand identification, an opportunity to shape the development of the web site, an awareness of other like-minded users, and the ability to interact with others on the web site.

Amy Jo Kim is an online community expert who has consulted with a variety of companies and has extensive experience building communities. She has proposed the following steps to build an online community:[11]

- Define and articulate your PURPOSE

Communities come to life when they fulfill an ongoing need in people's lives. To create a successful community, you'll need to first understand why you're building it and who you're building it for—and then express your vision in the design, navigation, technology and policies of your community.

- Build flexible, extensible gathering PLACES

Wherever people gather together for a shared purpose, and start talking amongst themselves, a community can begin to take root. Once you've defined your purpose, you'll want to build a flexible, small-scale infrastructure of gathering places, which you'll co-evolve along with your members.

- Create meaningful and evolving member PROFILES

You can get to know your members—and help them get to know each other—by developing robust, evolving and up-to-date member profiles. If handled with integrity, these profiles can help you build trust, foster relationships, and deliver personalized services—while infusing your community with a sense of history and context.

- Design for a range of ROLES

Addressing the needs of newcomers without alienating the regulars is an ongoing balancing act. As your community grows, it will become increasingly important to provide guidance to newcomers—while offering leadership, ownership and commerce opportunities to more experienced members.

- Develop a strong LEADERSHIP program

Community leaders are the fuel in your engine: they greet visitors, encourage newbies, teach classes, answer questions, and deal with trouble-makers before they destroy the fun for everyone else. An effective leadership program requires careful planning and ongoing management, but the results can be well worth the investment.

- Encourage appropriate ETIQUETTE

Every community has its share of internal squabbling. If handled well, conflict can be invigorating—but disagreements often spin out of control, and tear a community apart. To avoid this, it's crucial to develop some ground rules for participation, and set up systems that allow you to enforce and evolve your community standards.

- Promote cyclic EVENTS

Communities come together around regular events: sitting down to dinner, going to church on Sunday, attending a monthly meeting or a yearly offsite. To develop a loyal following, and foster deeper relationships among your members, you'll want to establish regular online events, and help your members develop and run their own events.

- Integrate the RITUALS of community life

All communities use rituals to acknowledge their members, and celebrate important social transitions. By celebrating holiday marking seasonal changes, and integrating personal transitions and rites of passage, you'll be laying the foundation for a true online culture.

- Facilitate member-run SUBGROUPS

If your goal is to grow a large-scale community, you'll want to provide enabling technologies to help your members create and run subgroups. It's a substantial undertaking—but this powerful feature can drive lasting member loyalty, and help to distinguish you community from its competition

Online Community Ethics

When corporations benefit from online communities, several ethical issues typically arise. Consider these three cases:[12]

Case 1. Users must be warned before closing popular discussion boards. For example, AOL has closed large areas without giving a prior warning to its users. Another example is Netscape's Netcenter area, which was closed in April 1999. Such abrupt closures without prior notice cause frustration among the loyal users who feel betrayed.

Case 2. Some firms use a large number of volunteer workers to run major areas of the web site and this practice has been called exploitative. For example, at one time, AOL had 12,000 workers—10,000 were volunteers! Although AOL maintains that these volunteer workers participate of their own volition, the U.S. Department of Labor has scrutinized the practice. This completely new situation is not addressed by laws because volunteers rarely help for-profit corporations. AOL critics maintain that these volunteers must be paid because the company places strict guidelines on their work.

Case 3. On some community sites, individuals are encouraged to post links to commercial sites and are paid a commission on any resulting sales. This blend between community and commerce is criticized because the company benefits from using the good name of the community—it is similar to non-profit organizations collaborating with for-profit firms in cause-related marketing efforts.

Conclusion

Online communities represent a dynamic environment where individuals gather to talk to one another. Learning how to leverage these communities to meet organizational goals is an ever-increasing challenge.

Notes

(All URLs are current as of March 25, 2002.)

1. America Online, "Data Points," <http://corp.aol.com/whoweare/who_datapoints.html>.

2. Janelle Brown, "There Goes the Neighbourhood," January 19, 1999, <http://www.salon.com/21st/feature/1999/01/cov_19feature3.html>.

3. Janelle Brown, "Must AOL Pay Community Leaders?," April 16, 1999, <http://www.salon.com/tech/feature/1999/04/16/aol_community/index.html>.

4. Tony Clarke, "Communities and Business: A New Way of Organizing," paper presented at the Fourth International Conference on Virtual Communities (June 20–21, 2001), <http://www.infonortics.com/vc/vc01/slides/clarke_files/frame.htm>.

5. This is taken from Marc Smith, "Voices from the WELL: The Logic of the Virtual Commons," 1992, <http://research.microsoft.com/~masmith/Voices%20from%20the%20Well.doc>.

6. This has been taken directly from Sue Boetcher, Heather Duggan, and Nancy White, "What is a Virtual Community and Why Would You Ever Need One?," January 2002, <http://www.fullcirc.com/community/communitywhatwhy.htm>.

7. Pew Internet and American Life, "Online Communities: Networks That Nurture Long-Distance Relationships and Local Ties," October 31, 2001, <http://www.pewinternet.org/reports/toc.asp?Report=47>.

8. Marc Weingarten, "LOTR: Fellowship of the Web," January 2002, <http://www.business2.com/articles/mag/0,1640,35845,FF.html>.

9. Shona L. Brown, Andrew Tilton, and Dennis M. Woodside, "The Case for Online Communities," The McKinsey Quarterly, Number 1, 2002, Web exclusive.

10. James Old, "Revenue Models for Virtual Communities," "Communities and Business: A New Way of Organizing," papers presented at the Fourth International Conference on Virtual Communities (June 20–21, 2001), <http://www.infonortics.com/vc/vc01/slides/old_files/frame.htm>.

11. This has been taken directly from Amy Jo Kim, "Nine Timeless Design Strategies," 2000, <http://www.naima.com/community/intro/intro3.html>.

12. This is based on Chris Werry, "Imagined Electronic Community: Representations of Virtual Community in Contemporary Business Discourse," 1999, <http://www.firstmonday.org/issues/issue4_9/werry/index.html>.

REVIEW / CHAPTER 11

Discussion Questions

1. What is the difference between a company and a community? Are all gathering places communities?

2. When does one become a member of a community? Are lurkers (i.e., people who do not post or contribute) community members?

3. Three potential ethical problems were discussed in the chapter. Choose the least problematic (from an ethical standpoint for the company) and argue on the company's behalf.

4. What must a company do to build a successful relationship with a community?

5. When is marketing to a community unethical? How does one do it without incurring a back-lash?

E-Tasks

1. Join a Yahoo! club of your choice and participate for a week. How well designed is this community? How can Yahoo! improve its system?

2. Consider three communication technologies: instant messaging, discussion board, and chat. Join communities that offer one, two, and all three technologies. What is the individual value added by each technology?

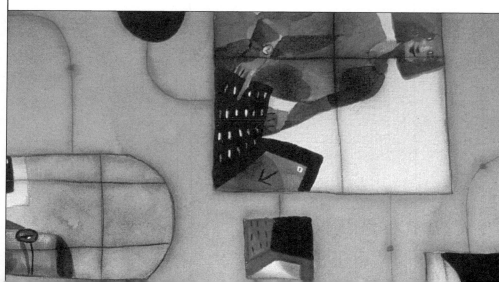

CHAPTER 12

Conducting
Online Research

Learning Objectives

▼ To understand how the Internet and the Web have affected the steps in the market research process.

▼ To learn about the different types of online market research: online focus groups, search log analysis, online environmental scanning, online surveys using e-mail or pop-ups, and clickstream analysis.

▼ To understand the challenges in conducting online market research.

Executive Summary

Companies conduct market research to better understand the conditions in the marketplace because a better informed corporation is more competitive. A well-designed market research system informs organizations of new opportunities, trends, and threats. There are four steps (all affected by the Internet) in the market research process: data collection, data storage and sharing, data analysis, and result reporting or action. The Internet allows the collection of information that was previously unknowable; facilitates efficient, low-cost, and rapid customer contact for surveys; allows companies to contact customers who were previously unreachable; and permits firms to view customer interactions. A digitized market research process eliminates the need to store paper surveys and reduces the human error potential during data entry or retrieval. Most of the field of statistics was developed for the days when information was scarce. With the Internet, we now have an abundance of information; hence, data mining has emerged as the new form of data analysis. This process involves an inductive analysis of the data to identify new relationships between variables. The last step in the market research process is result reporting or action. The Internet has reduced the gap between gathering information and action, leading to an adaptive style of management. Market research techniques can be classified on two dimensions: qualitative/quantitative versus customer contact/no contact. Online focus groups provide excellent insight into customer perceptions and attitudes. Search log analysis helps firms understand how individuals are searching for information. Online environmental scanning helps employees make sense of the vast amounts of information available on the Internet. Online surveys can be conducted using e-mail (for existing customers) or pop-ups (new customers). Clickstream analysis involves correlating the path a visitor takes at a web site with his or her actions. Finally, conducting online market research requires companies to meet several challenges (e.g., representativeness of the sample, spam).

Introduction[1]

Companies conduct market research to better understand the conditions in the marketplace.[2] A better informed corporation is more competitive, and a well-designed market research system informs organizations of new opportunities, trends, and threats.

Online market research has become increasingly important to all companies. For instance, it was reported in late-2000 that in 1998, General Mills conducted less than 1% of its research online. By 1999, this had increased to 20% and was anticipated to be about 60% of all research conducted during the year 2000.[3]

Impact of the Internet and Web on Market Research

It is important to note that market research was impacted by the advent of the PC—well before the Internet. For example, computer assisted telephone interviewing is used extensively to conduct telephone interviews using such techniques as random digit dialing to obtain representative samples. Similarly, virtual test markets (e.g., IShop from Indiana University) were developed for the stand-alone PC. These virtual test markets allow marketers to modify the types and number of products displayed and to monitor consumer behavior. Rather than focusing on these techniques, this chapter focuses on the value added by the Internet and the Web.

There are four steps in the market research process: data collection, data storage and sharing, data analysis, and result reporting or action. The Internet has affected all four steps significantly.

Data Collection

The Internet has affected data collection in five ways:

1. Collecting previously unknowable information. Traditional bricks-and-mortar retailers, for example, had access to purchase data, but only limited information on the buying process (i.e., what the customer goes through prior to purchase). A department store in a shopping mall cannot measure the time spent by an individual consumer at a given display or the amount of time the customer spent arriving at a decision or the path taken in the store. However, using the Internet, the marketer can measure all of these items in an online store. The marketer can virtually "observe" the consumer as he or she "travels" across the store. Although this example uses B2C commerce, the process is applicable to other online contexts: B2B commerce, communities, content, and so forth.

2. Efficient, rapid, and low-cost customer contact for surveys. All companies survey their customers from time to time to gather information about perceptions, attitudes, and so on. In general, this is a cumbersome and lengthy process: customers are sent surveys by mail or are contacted at their local mall by interviewers. The responses are then manually entered into a computer—this step takes the longest time and is prone to human error. In general, it is not uncommon for a company to wait three to six months to get the results of a survey. Using e-mail and pop-up ads, marketers can now survey customers quickly and obtain the data in electronic form. This approach also allows for a low cost per contact. One study found that a Web-based concept test involving 200 medical professionals cost $48,500 as compared to $59,500 using traditional methods.[4]

3. Large-scale information gathering. Because data collection is efficient, quick, and low-cost, it is now possible to gather information from consumers on an unprecedented scale. For example, every twenty-four hours AOL subscribers are invited to participate in a short survey. The company collected about two million responses from consumers over a period of eighteen months and used this data to evaluate its customer support.[5]

4. Contacting customer groups that were previously hard to access. Some customer groups are traditionally hard to access. For example, it is expensive to interview working professionals who are strapped for time and are reluctant to drive long distances to participate in a focus group. Similarly, customers in remote locations and those who are homebound are usually very hard to survey. Now, these groups can be contacted easily by using Web technology, leading to more representative samples.

5. Observing consumer interaction. Marketers know that word-of-mouth is a powerful marketing tool; however, they could observe only a small percentage of this communication. Now, marketers can visit discussion forums on topics closely related to their business and assess the concerns and knowledge gaps of the consumers. If a question continually arises, the company can quickly display the relevant information prominently on its web site.

Data Storage and Sharing

The Internet has enabled the complete digitization of the market research process. Instead of storing paper surveys, companies can store all research data digitally on computers. As a result, much more data can be effectively stored for a longer period of time.

Most organizations frequently reinvent the wheel—companies typically re-ask research questions that could be answered by data collected for some other purpose and stored within the organization. This is particularly a problem for large organizations—one department may be completely unaware of the type of information that another department is collecting. It is now possible to construct an intranet that enables all relevant employees to access the raw data and reports from previous market research efforts, allowing the organization to use its knowledge much more effectively.

Using the Internet for market research also changes the sheer scale of information collected. In large organizations, millions of records are generated each day and stored away; however, for various reasons (e.g., privacy concerns or a lack of an appropriate data model), most organizations have not formed a coherent research plan to use this information.

Data Analysis

Generally, data is subjected to a statistical analysis in order to make proper inferences. The data may be analyzed using statistical packages such as SAS and SPSS. Typically, the analysis begins with the descriptive statistics (e.g., mean, standard deviation), and moves to more advanced modeling techniques such as regression and clustering. The nature of data analysis changes substantially when the Internet is used to conduct market research. These changes include:

1. *Data mining*. Traditional statistical techniques were developed during the days when there was a *scarcity* of data. Now, there is an *abundance* of data. In many cases, it is no longer necessary to sample a subset of the population—a census can be conducted (i.e., data on the entire customer base of an organization can be made available). Large online companies generate millions of records per day; new variables are being measured for the first time. Data mining is the new label for a set of techniques that companies use to work on large datasets—it incorporates information from statistics, pattern recognition, machine learning, and database technology. Data mining can be defined as a process of inductive computer analysis of large datasets aimed at finding unsuspected relationships between variables. Because it is an inductive process, the researcher does not begin with a

set of hypotheses; rather, he or she starts with a large dataset and a set of objectives (e.g., to maximize sales). The relationships that emerge from the data mining process are exploited to fine-tune the marketing offering (e.g., web site design, price, promotions).

2. *Real-time data analysis.* Generally, there is a gap between data measurement and data availability. As a result, managers are looking at information about yesterday's marketplace—not today's market. With the Internet, managers can access information just-in-time. In many cases, the raw data is also processed to make the presentation more meaningful. For example, it is possible to produce a real-time chart of the number of orders placed at an online store. Of course, organizations must be careful about what metrics they use at this level of detail.

3. *Individual-level data.* All E-businesses have a customer database that includes such information as demographics, purchase history, attitudes, and response to promotions. The company now knows what each person is doing and can use that information to appropriately target each person.

Reporting or Action

The final step in the process is reporting or action. Using the Internet, reports can be generated and disseminated at periodic intervals. For example, the CEO can receive a daily e-mail with key market data, or department heads can receive the information broken down by product.

Using the Internet reduces the gap between information gathering and action. The Internet now permits real-time decision making using fresh market research. Consider Internet advertising. Systems now capture fresh customer response information in real-time. As a result, it is possible for a company to simultaneously release twenty banner ads with various creatives that target a subset of the market and the response to each ad is monitored in real-time. Based on the click-through and conversion rates, managers can quickly discard those ads that have poor results and focus resources on the ads that perform well.

This *quick-strike capability* is provided by the melding of fresh market information with quick marketing action. As a result, marketing objectives are met more effectively in a shorter time and with a lower cost. With the advent of the Internet, market research is not an activity that is conducted periodically with tenuous links to action; rather, its value lies in providing fresh market data to managers who can act quickly to maximize the ROI on marketing investments.

Classifying the Types of Online Market Research

Online market research provides us with new types of data and new techniques. As a result, it is necessary to redefine the categories of online market research. As shown in Figure 12.1, online techniques are classified on two dimensions: qualitative/quantitative and requiring/not requiring customer contact (for research purposes).

With the Internet, research can be done with or without customer contact. In either case, the information sought is about consumer behavior. Frequently, customers leave an imprint

Figure 12.1
Types of Online Market Research

	Customer contact	No customer contact
Qualitative	Cell I Online Focus Groups In-depth Interviews	Cell II Search log analysis
Quantitative	Cell III Surveys • E-mail • Pop-ups	Cell IV Clickstream analysis

that is recorded as they browse and shop over the Internet. These imprints are stored in logs that can be studied qualitatively or mined for the relationships between different actions, and the customer does not have to be contacted. Instead, the customer's behavior is used to draw inferences about how the customer thinks.

Qualitative research involves obtaining rich and textured customer information by asking the customers open-ended questions (e.g., What do you like about this product?; How can this service be improved?; Do you like this idea we are working on?). The focus is on obtaining deep insights into what the individual customer thinks—not applying a statistical generalization to a larger population. Instead of placing the customers into predetermined categories, the objective is to understand the categories customers use when thinking about a problem.

On the other hand, the focus of *quantitative* research is to quantify the magnitude of effects and to draw inferences about the statistical validity of the inferences. Survey research is quantitative. With survey research, it is not enough to determine that customers are more likely to buy when the price is set at $10 and the performance is set at 50 (on an index of 0–100) as opposed to a price set at $25 and a performance set at 90. Rather, the goal is to determine whether the difference is statistically significant to a sufficiently high level of confidence.

Cell I in Figure 12.1 represents research that is qualitative and requires direct customer contact. Examples of this type of research are online focus groups or in-depth interviews—the interviewer asks a single customer or a group of customers for their opinions about a product, service, or experience. The data collected is usually in the form of a transcript.

Cell II is research that is qualitative, but does not require contacting the customer directly. An example of this is search log analysis—whenever customers visit a web site and search for something, it is recorded in a search log. This log is studied to identify patterns of behavior.

Cell III is research that is quantitative and requires customer contact—a prime example is survey research. Individuals are contacted by e-mail or a pop-up ad and asked to participate in an online survey. The data is captured in a text file that is directly analyzed using a statistical package.

Cell IV is research that is quantitative and requires no customer contact (e.g., clickstream analysis and profiling). As the customer passes through the web site, data is recorded about his or her behavior and is analyzed using data mining models to identify relationships between variables (e.g., does greater time spent on a subpage increase the likelihood of a purchase?).

Online Market Research Categories

Online Focus Groups

Online focus groups can be conducted using either chat (see Figure 12.2) or bulletin boards. Using a chat forum is more common and generates better data. With bulletin boards, people don't return on a regular basis, so the data is not complete.

Online focus groups operate in a manner similar to regular focus groups: they are small (six to ten people); participants are directed to a public waiting area; they are screened; and those who qualify go to the focus group area where the moderator greets them. Generally, participants are paid from $40 to $250, and the group meets for sixty to ninety minutes.

There is also a subtle difference in the way questions are answered. In regular focus groups, one person speaks and has the undivided attention of the group. With online focus groups, multiple people can type in their responses at any time, generating more information.

A company's clients can participate in the process as well. They can log on to a special web site and watch the entire process unfold. Clients who want to ask a question are able to privately contact the moderator while the session is conducted.

Online focus groups have two primary advantages: cost and convenience. Participants do not have to drive to a location—they can log on from their homes or offices. This process allows those people who have trouble traveling (e.g., seniors, consumers in remote locations) an opportunity to participate. The software records a transcript of the entire conversation, and the speakers are clearly identified. As a result, the companies receive the reports quickly.

Online focus groups have a few disadvantages as well. Obviously, all nonverbal communication is lost when a focus group is conducted using a chat technology—one cannot see consumers roll their eyes or make faces. Also, it is not clear whether everybody is present all of the time—participants can leave to answer e-mail or the phone and nobody will know. As a result, the level of participant involvement may be less.

A recent study using undergraduate college students compared online, telephone, and face-to-face focus groups. It found that it was easier to recruit for and a greater rate of recruits participated in online and face-to-face groups than telephone groups. Interest-

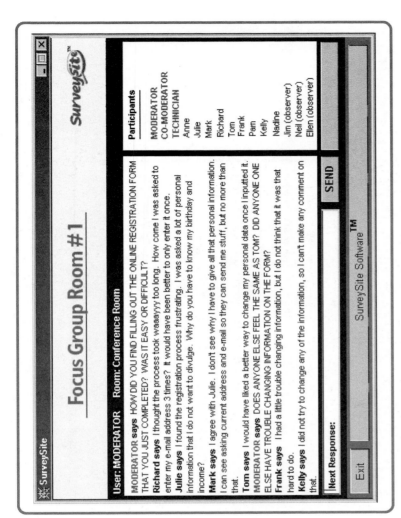

Figure 12.2
Screenshot of Online Focus Group

Focus Group Room #1

SurveySite™

User: MODERATOR   Room: Conference Room

MODERATOR says HOW DID YOU FIND FILLING OUT THE ONLINE REGISTRATION FORM THAT YOU JUST COMPLETED? WAS IT EASY OR DIFFICULT?

Richard says I thought the process took waaayyy too long. How come I was asked to enter my e-mail address 3 times? It would have been better to only enter it once.

Julie says I found the registration process frustrating. I was asked a lot of personal information that I do not want to divulge. Why do you have to know my birthday and income?

Mark says I agree with Julie. I don't see why I have to give all that personal information. I can see asking current address and e-mail so they can send me stuff, but no more than that.

Tom says I would have liked a better way to change my personal data once I inputted it. DOES ANYONE ELSE FEEL THE SAME AS TOM? DID ANYONE ONE

MODERATOR says DOES ANYONE ELSE HAVE TROUBLE CHANGING INFORMATION ON THE FORM?

Frank says I had a little trouble changing information, but I do not think that it was that hard to do.

Kelly says I did not try to change any of the information, so I can't make any comment on that.

Next Response:

[Exit]   [SEND]

SurveySite Software™

Participants

MODERATOR
CO-MODERATOR
TECHNICIAN
Anne
Julie
Mark
Richard
Tom
Frank
Pam
Kelly
Nadine
Jim (observer)
Neil (observer)
Ellen (observer)

Source: SurveySite, http://www.surveysite.com.

---

ingly, online focus groups took the longest time to complete and the telephone groups took the least amount of time.[6]

Search Log Analysis

It is common for a web site to permit a search of its contents. Most consumers use this search utility to locate the specific information that they desire. Every time a consumer types a search request, it is recorded in a search log (see Figure 12.3). An analysis of the log provides several useful insights into the marketing process (other types of logs are discussed in the section on clickstream analysis).

The log's analysis provides the marketer with raw consumer behavior. One learns what the consumer is thinking from the behavior instead of the responses to the company's questions on a survey. In a sense, search logs represent the ultimate truth and provide an unadulterated look into the mind of the consumer.

A search log can be mined to gain insight into the following areas:[7]

Figure 12.3
Extract from a Search Log

Keywords: albright; Options: All, Details; 11/26/97 12:47 PM
Keywords: cuba; Options: All, Details; 11/26/97 12:59 PM
Keywords: cuba; Options: All, Details; 11/26/97 1:00 PM
Keywords: International Boundary Commission; Options: All, Details; 11/26/97 3:35 PM
Keywords: russia; Options: All, Details; 11/26/97 3:35 PM
Keywords: mexico border; Options: All, Details; 11/26/97 3:35 PM
Keywords: International Boundary Commission; Options: All, Details, HTML Tags; 11/26/97 3:36 PM
Keywords: mexico border; Options: All, Details; 11/26/97 3:36 PM
Keywords: Embassy Beijing; Options: All, Details; 11/26/97 3:36 PM
Keywords: Manila; Options: All, Details; 11/26/97 3:36 PM
Keywords: mexico border; Options: All, Details; 11/26/97 3:36 PM
Keywords: mexico border; Options: All, Details; 11/26/97 3:36 PM
Keywords: Manila; Options: All, Details; 11/26/97 3:37 PM
Keywords: nationality visa; Options: All, Details; 11/26/97 3:37 PM
Keywords: paid internships; Options: All, Details; 11/26/97 3:37 PM
Keywords: Canada boundary; Options: All, Details, HTML Tags; 11/26/97 3:38 PM
Keywords: boundary commission; Options: All, Details, HTML Tags; 11/26/97 3:38 PM
Keywords: Eizenstat; Options: All, Details; 11/26/97 3:38 PM
Keywords: I 130; Options: All, Details; 11/26/97 3:39 PM
Keywords: 130; Options: All, Details; 11/26/97 3:39 PM
Keywords: jobs; Options: All, Details; 11/26/97 3:40 PM
Keywords: Form 130; Options: All, Details; 11/26/97 3:40 PM
Keywords: mexico; Options: All, Details; 11/26/97 3:41 PM
Keywords: Support 130; Options: All, Details; 11/26/97 3:41 PM
Keywords:; Options: Any; 11/26/97 3:44 PM
Keywords: inspector; Options: All, Details; 11/26/97 3:45 PM
Keywords: test; Options: All, Details; 11/26/97 3:55 PM
Keywords: authentication; Options: All, Details; 11/26/97 3:57 PM
Keywords: heath field internships; Options: All, Details; 11/26/97 4:03 PM
Keywords: heath field; Options: All, Details; 11/26/97 4:03 PM
Keywords: us consulate in canada; Options: All, Details; 11/26/97 4:05 PM
Keywords: canada; Options: All, Details; 11/26/97 4:05 PM
Keywords: Czech Republic; Options: All, Details; 11/26/97 4:05 PM
Keywords: charlotte; Options: All, Details; 11/26/97 4:06 PM
Keywords: travel; Options: All, Details; 11/26/97 4:06 PM
Keywords: north carolina; Options: All, Details; 11/26/97 4:06 PM
Keywords: UNIFIL; Options: All, Details; 11/26/97 4:08 PM
Keywords: Czech Republic Trade; Options: All, Details; 11/26/97 4:08 PM
Keywords: officers; Options: All, Details; 11/26/97 4:11 PM
Keywords: passport renewal; Options: All, Details; 11/26/97 4:12 PM
Keywords: Sub Sahara; Options: All, Details; 11/26/97 4:13 PM
Keywords: immigration law; Options: All, Details; 11/26/97 4:14 PM
Keywords: immigration law; Options: All, Details; 11/26/97 4:15 PM
Keywords: immigration law; Options: All, Details; 11/26/97 4:15 PM
Keywords: Arab Israeli conflict; Options: All, Details; 11/26/97 4:15 PM
Keywords: immigration; Options: All, Details; 11/26/97 4:15 PM
Keywords: germany; Options: All, Details; 11/26/97 4:15 PM
Keywords: immigration; Options: All, Details; 11/26/97 4:15 P

Source: http://tigger.uic.edu/~nrj/irb/searchlog.htm.

- *Unmet customer demand.* Typically, consumers type in a search request for what they want to find on a particular site. A study of search logs may show that consumers are searching for a product or service that is currently not featured on the site. As a result, the company can modify its product line to meet consumer demand.

- *Brand definition.* Search logs may indicate that consumers are searching for a product that is no longer offered, or that, in the minds of the consumers, the company stands for something that does not fit well with today's reality. A careful scrutiny of the search logs can help firms align their brands with customer perceptions.

- *Promotion validation.* Search logs can track how well advertising campaigns convey a company's message. If within the first days of a new product launch, consumers begin to search for the product featured in the promotion, it could be a sign of an effective campaign.

- *Consumer language.* Marketers might use the logs to communicate with customers through using the customer's own words. This helps companies steer clear of jargon and better connect with customers.

- *Web service and site feedback.* Search logs expose flaws in the web site's design. For example, if numerous individuals are searching for information contained on a sub-page, the organization may be better served by moving this information to a more prominent location. Similarly, users may be searching for information because they do not realize that they can access a pull-down menu if they scroll over a keyword–logs will reflect this action and indicate that a change is necessary.

- *Forecasting.* Search logs provide data that support forecasting–with a minimum of two years of history, a search log analysis can forecast the timing of seasonal changes in customer interests.

Online Environmental Scanning

The Internet is a huge information repository. Every company now has access to a large variety of news sources ranging from public news sites to private databases that require a subscription. Company employees can visit the competition's web sites to learn about their products and services. Public discussions about the company and its products also can be monitored.

Environmental scanning may appear to be an overwhelming task, but with some thought, the process is easily implemented. The first step is to design a plan that identifies the roles of the various employees. Although all employees must be vigilant, some employees should monitor the information collection on a full-time basis. Policies concerning how the information is disseminated within the organization are required. Some companies prefer that employees send out an e-mail to the entire organization, others prefer that they report to a particular office, which places the information in the appropriate context. Finally, the organization must decide which products to buy to meet its environmental scanning needs. Products can be classified as to their specificity (general vs. specific) and their impact on the company over time (short-term, medium-term, and long-term). An example of a long-term product is a technology assessment report.

There are four modes of environmental scanning:[8]

1. Undirected viewing—the individual is exposed to information with no specific informational need in mind. For example, a person may be at a news web site for some other purpose. The overall goal is to scan broadly in order to detect signals of change early. This is an exploratory process that skims many sources of information.

2. Conditioned (or directed) viewing—the individual focuses attention on information about selected topics or on certain types of information (e.g., a market research web site or the web site of a financial institution). The overall purpose is to evaluate the significance of the information encountered in order to assess the general nature of its impact on the company. The search is more focused than the undirected viewing.

3. Informal search—the individual actively looks for information to deepen the knowledge and understanding of a specific issue. It is informal because it involves a relatively limited and unstructured effort (e.g., using a search engine or directory or an online database). The overall purpose is to gather extensive information on an issue in order to determine whether there is a need for company action.

4. Formal search—the individual makes a deliberate, planned effort to obtain specific information or certain types of information about a particular issue. For example, it may involve an e-mail exchange with an expert or a search in a subscription online database (e.g., ABI/Inform). The search is very focused, and the overall goal is to systematically retrieve information relevant to an issue in order to provide a basis for developing a decision or course of action.

Online Surveys

Surveys are used to get consumer responses to specific company-generated questions. Surveys can be classified on the basis of the target audience: existing versus prospective customers.

Existing customers are typically surveyed to:

- Understand their level of customer satisfaction.
- Determine their perception of the web site's design.
- Learn about what they would like to see changed in the company's operations.
- Determine their intent to make future purchases.
- Gauge their interest in new product offerings.

Prospective customers are typically surveyed to:

- Understand why they have not done business with the corporation.
- Determine their perception of the web site's design.
- Learn about their perception of the company's marketing mix.
- Determine what will convince them to switch from one company to another.
- Gauge their interest in new product offerings.

The most important decision in the surveying process is identifying the sample. With existing customers, organizations usually have a list of e-mail addresses that can be used. In this case, the sample can be drawn randomly (e.g., one out of every ten customers) or in a targeted fashion (e.g., loyal customers who have shopped with the company for over two years). Using a random sample allows one to draw inferences over the entire customer population.

For prospective customers, there is no ready e-mail list, but there are some viable alternatives. There are market research companies that have a list of respondents who might be interested in participating. It is important, though, to question the agency about how the list is compiled and how it is maintained. For example, the average number of surveys completed by a participant should be known because "career respondents" (i.e., people who participate in every survey they can to earn money) are to be avoided–they may not be representative of your targeted population.

Another method is the use of pop-up ads. A company can use a market research firm that works with a suitable publisher. Alternatively, the company's web site can be used: Individuals are chosen randomly (e.g., one in every ten visits) to view a pop-up ad that invites him or her to participate in the survey. The individual then clicks on the link to go to the questionnaire. A company must be careful using pop-up ads–even though many market research firms report very high click-through rates, it is an inherently intrusive and annoying technique that may alter the results' validity.

The questions used in online surveys must be designed carefully. Of course, the usual considerations of survey design (e.g., choosing the appropriate words, sequencing delicate questions at the end) are important, but there are some considerations unique to online surveys:

- Length–if it is too long, consumers lose interest.

- Usability–can consumers clearly understand the survey's structure, and do they know how many more questions remain at any given point?

- Compatibility–will the survey load up in all browsers?

Finally, providing survey participants the right incentive is important. Does providing a greater incentive lead to a higher response rate? There is some research indicating that increasing the incentive does not increase the response rates for pop-up ads; however, with e-mail surveys, it appears that a greater incentive leads to more completed surveys. In many cases, companies merely provide a coupon for their store. Most offer straight financial incentives.

Clickstream Analysis

Clickstream data is the record of an individual's movement through time at a web site. This data is recorded in four types of logs:[9] access logs, agent logs, error logs, and referrer logs. Access logs contain most of the pertinent information about the user experience– they record information such as the user's IP address, the access date and time, and the nature of the user's request.

Agent logs provide data on the user's browser and operating system. *Error logs* provide information on specific requests that led to errors such as "Document Not Found." *Referrer logs* provide information on which sites directed the users.

The primary advantage to clickstream analysis is that the information about where a user goes on site and what he or she does there helps the analyst understand what type of person he or she is. Once a company learns more about the types of users, it can design its web site and product offerings to better match the users' interests.

Following are examples of what is being done with clickstream data:[10]

1. Path or navigation analysis. This analysis involves clustering consumers on the basis of the route taken to get to the site and the path used to navigate within the site. Typical research questions include: Where did they come from/go to? How many clicks did it take to find what they were looking for?

2. Advertising analysis (e-mail and web banners). Every organization wants to measure its advertising effectiveness. Clickstream data provides information about how the consumer got to the site. If he or she clicked on a banner or an e-mail, this is revealed in the clickstream. Examining what is contained in the clickstream helps measure the effectiveness rate of advertising vehicles.

3. Shopping cart analysis. One of the greatest problems with online retailing is that a large proportion of online shopping carts are abandoned after items are placed in them—some place this number as high as 75%. Using clickstream data helps to determine what interested your buyers, what turned them off, and when they left your site.

Currently, some research on visualizing a person's clickstream is being conducted and the results are being used to draw conclusions about what drives behavior.

Online Research Challenges

Using the Internet for online research has its own tricky issues. The most important are discussed in this section.

1. Population representation. Suppose you manage a bricks-and-clicks company. Will conducting an online survey help you draw inferences about the customers who visit your bricks-and-mortar store? In general, it does not. The online population tends to be more exclusive (e.g., more educated, higher income) than the mainstream. Therefore, in general, when conducting an online survey, do not draw inferences about the offline population.

2. Sample representation. Whether online samples are representative of the online population is a general problem. Consider pop-up ads. These are considered annoying by many consumers. At the same time, they remain one of the most popular ways of persuading a consumer to participate in a survey. Under these circumstances, it is valid to ask whether a segment of the population was systematically excluded because of the intrusive method used to ask people to participate. Ignoring consumers who do not use pop-ups

leads to a sample with systematic biases. To avoid this, use multiple approaches to contact customers.

Using annoying techniques (e.g., pop-ups) is only one way to lose sample representativeness; others include contacting only those users who have Internet access, contacting users who can read HTML e-mail and excluding those who cannot, and excluding non-English speaking and global users.

3. Spam. It is common to contact customers using e-mail, but should a company send a person an unsolicited commercial e-mail asking them to fill out a survey? In general, the answer is no. As a result, most e-businesses e-mail their current customers and use other techniques to identify prospective customers.

4. Participant recruitment. Many market research firms have panels of customers that they use for surveys and focus groups. Managers must determine how large the panel is and how it was put together. One must also ensure that the panel is sufficiently diverse (e.g., gender and age).

5. Privacy. Online research and the privacy of customer information go hand in hand. Companies that collect large amounts of customer information must be careful to use it only in ways that protect the privacy of the individual. Promises made at the time the data is collected must be kept. A more detailed discussion of privacy (including information about cookies) is available in the chapter on Internet and Public Policy.

Conclusion

The Internet has revolutionized the market research process. Although managers now have better capabilities and can conduct research more efficiently, they must understand all of the issues involved before using these techniques.

Notes

(All URLs are current as of March 25, 2002.)

1. The content in this chapter was influenced by Thomas W. Miller and Peter R. Dickson, "Online Market Research," *International Journal of Electronic Commerce*, 5(3), (2001).

2. In this chapter, the focus is on the external market. Of course, companies can use online techniques to poll employees or monitor their browsing patterns, but this is not covered here.

3. From D. Peterson and N. Hopkins, "Going Online with Consumer Research: The General Mills Experience," paper presented at the EXPLOR Forum, Chicago, IL, (2000).

4. R. Miller, "Interactive Data Electronically Acquired," paper presented at the EXPLOR Forum, Madison, WI, (1999).

5. M. Blackwood, "Taking Action on Satisfaction Measurement," paper presented at the EXPLOR Forum, Madison, WI, (1999).

6. N. I. Esipova, T. W. Miller, M. D. Zarnecki, J. Elzaurdia, and S. Ponnaiya, "Exploring the Possibilities of Online Focus Groups," paper presented at the American Association for Public Opinion Research Conference, Portland, OR, (May 20, 2000).

7. From Nick Maxwell, "Search Log Analysis: A Great Tool for Frank Customer Research," *Marketing News*, 35(24), (2001): 15–16.

8. This is based on the work of Chun Wei Choo at the University of Toronto <http://choo.fis. utoronto.ca>.

9. Mary Burton and Joseph Walther, "The Value of Web Log Data in Use-Based Design and Testing," *Journal of Computer-Mediated Communication*, 6(3), (April, 2001), <http://www.ascusc. org/jcmc/vol6/issue3/burton.html>.

10. Cognos.com, "Keeping Profits Flowing with Clickstream Analysis," <http://www.cognos.com/ au/cognews/pdf/profits.pdf>.

REVIEW / CHAPTER 12

Discussion Questions

1. As a manager of a leading consumer goods company, such as General Mills or Procter & Gamble, are you comfortable doing all of your market research online? Why or why not? Do you think your answer will change in a few years?

2. Are you as comfortable typing out your thoughts as speaking them? Will you be more or less vocal as a member of a virtual focus group or a traditional one? Now, as a manager, what does this tell you about using virtual focus groups?

3. What precautions might you take to ensure that an online survey is completed by the intended person (e.g., head of household as opposed to the daughter)? How do these precautions add to the cost of conducting online surveys?

4. How might you ensure that there are no spamming complaints from your consumers?

E-Tasks

1. Visit http://www.researchinfo.com/docs/software/index.cfm. Download a free online survey software. Create a small survey and administer it online. What were your impressions of this process?

2. Part I. Conduct a search on "Super Bowl advertising" using five search engines or directories: Google, Yahoo!, Alta Vista, Dogpile, and Metacrawler. How did the results vary across the search engines? What does this tell you about the quality of the information one receives from search engines?

   Part II. Now, conduct the same search on a paid information service such as ABI/Inform or Lexis/Nexis. What differences do you find? Find out how much your school is paying to access these services. Is this price justified?

3. Visit Yahoo! and use the chat facility to run an online focus group selected from your classmates on the topic "The Future of Shopping Online." What were its challenges and benefits? Do you think you could have obtained better results with a face-to-face focus group?

Slatanic—the Disastrous Move from Free to Paid Content: Case 4

Introduction

On February 12, 1999, *Slate* magazine announced that it had decided to make its entire web site, http://www.slate.msn.com, available for free once again. This was a dramatic and embarrassing step backward for the online magazine (also called e-zine), which had remained free from its launch in 1996 until March 1998. In April, the magazine switched to a subscription fee model—interested subscribers had to pay a fee of $19.95 per year to access its content. Yet, less than one year after starting to charge customers, the magazine had decided to reverse its decision and make its contents free—perhaps, forever.

The changes in *Slate's* pricing policy were closely monitored by the entire publishing industry. At its root was the fundamental question: "Can Internet users be charged a fee to view content on the web just as traditional print magazines charge readers a fee to purchase their magazine?" Hence, the decision to backtrack from the paid viewing position was seen as a landmark event in the publishing industry.

Slate was in a unique position because it was backed by an industry giant, Microsoft Corporation, and had a high-profile editor, Michael Kinsley. Industry observers were now asking if Kinsley and Microsoft could not develop an information product for which they could ask consumers to pay, could anyone else? This decision had the potential to shape the publishing world into a business driven exclusively by advertising.

Many questions remained. If subscription fees had not been a profitable strategy, why did *Slate* wait so long to announce the switch? Would *Slate* still charge a fee for some portions of its web site? What had led to the current decision? Was it wise?

Background

In June 1996, Microsoft launched *Slate* magazine with Michael Kinsley as editor. He was chosen because of his stature and credibility in journalistic circles. He was the editor of the *New Republic* and *Harper's* magazines and the contributing editor for *Time* magazine. His writing had appeared in such leading publications as *The Economist*, *The Wall Street Journal*, *The New Yorker*, and *Vanity Fair*. However, his most prominent job may have been as the liberal cohost of CNN's "Crossfire" from 1989 to 1995. Given these impressive credentials, he was considered a credible candidate to be the editor of an innovative online magazine such as *Slate*.

Microsoft, the world's largest software maker, is located in Redmond, Washington—just outside Seattle. Cofounded by Bill Gates and Paul Allen in 1975, Microsoft employed over 30,000 people worldwide and had an annual revenue of $19.75 billion and a net income of $7.79 billion in the fiscal year ending June 1999. Its products include the Microsoft Windows operating system, Office 2000, Internet Explorer, and Microsoft Network.

Slate was envisioned as a highbrow, high-end source of commentary on the news. The idea was to attract the most sophisticated and educated audience available on the Web. As the demographics of *Slate* users shown in Table C4.1 prove, the e-zine has been successful in attracting an educated, affluent, and sophisticated audience.

The Product

Slate's mission was to design a successful e-zine (also called Webzine or simply, zine)—a magazine available only on the Web. As Kinsley said, "The basic test was to show that serious magazine journalism can succeed on the Web. We tried to develop features that are both suited to the Web and useful to our readers."[1] *Slate* was going to be a serious magazine with a highbrow audience interested in analysis and commentary. A self-description of the magazine[2] reads: "Your quick, smart take on the news, politics and culture."

Slate does little original reporting. Instead, the e-zine strives for an incisive analysis of current news, events, and issues—fewer than ten full-time editors put it together. Kinsley explains this by saying that he does not think the world needs more scoops.

Slate's content can be divided into three categories: summaries, features, and dialogues. First, it provides a summary of current news and a commentary. Second, *Slate* developed a series of "meta-features"—intelligent and readable syntheses of news events and issues of the moment. Kinsley explained, "Our meta-features are intended to couple understanding with a little bit of wit. To save you the time and trouble of reading something you don't want to, and to direct you to what you do."[3] *Slate* has signed up prominent writers to act as columnists for these features (e.g., the distinguished economist, Paul Krugman, who writes a meta-feature called "The dismal science"). Third, *Slate* features an ongoing dialog between two writers on an issue. Also, readers can participate in discussions of articles or issues.

Given the background of the editor, it was natural to use the model of a magazine to design *Slate*. When the magazine started, it published long articles that could have appeared in popular print magazines. In its inaugural issue, June 24, 1996, *Slate* ran a 2,218-word article by Nicholas Lemann titled "Jews in second place: When Asian-Americans become the 'new Jews,'"

**Table C4.1
Demographics
of *Slate* Customers**

- Gender—67% are men and 33% are women
- Age—33% are 18–34, 71% are 25–54
- Average age is 41
- Affluent and well-educated—48% have a household income of $75K or higher
- 28% have a household income of $100K or higher
- Average household income is $83,126
- 63% have graduated college or higher
- 57% are professional/managerial/self-employed
- Seasoned online users—73% have been on the Web longer than three years
- 84% are on the Web five times a week or more
- Savvy online shoppers—94% have shopped online in the past six months
- 79% have transacted online in the past six months

Source: Slate.com, *Media Kit*, October 21, 2001, http://slate.msn.com//?id=95357. SLATE © United Features Syndicate. Reprinted by permission.

SLATANIC, THE DISASTROUS MOVE FROM FREE TO PAID CONTENT: CASE 4

"what happens to the Jews?" A profile of Bob Dole in the same issue had 1,648 words.[4]

Over time, the approach to writing articles for *Slate* evolved. The editor explicitly stated that the e-zine can no longer publish articles that could appear in *The New York Times* or *The New Yorker*. Instead, there is an explicit understanding that writing content for the Web is a somewhat different endeavor and writers must adapt to the new context.

Another major decision concerned how frequently the information on the web site was changed. *Slate* initially posted a set of articles that remained the same for a period of one week—it envisioned a static medium much like traditional magazines. It soon realized that this would never work for an e-zine—readers expected continual change. For example, users e-mailed *Slate* complaining that they had not posted something on their web site one and half hours after the 2000 World Cup soccer match was concluded. Users expected constant updates from news web sites such as cnn.com and the same was expected from sites that provided commentary!

The magazine also realized that posting new information on a frequent basis made sense from a production standpoint. All of the articles in any print magazine are not ready for printing at the same time. So, posting an article as soon as it was ready led to an efficient production process, while leading to a high level of consumer excitement.[5]

However, *Slate* has not moved completely to the dynamic model—it describes itself as a "weekly, evolving toward a daily." Some material is posted on a daily basis and other articles stay for over a week due to consumer interest. The magazine also provides an archive of older articles in "The Compost." This allows its writers to refer back to the older articles using links. This is obviously a feature that only publishers on the Internet can provide. Interested readers can also locate and read older articles. This was made a

paid feature when the rest of the e-zine was made free.

Slate also incorporated other new ideas. For example, the total word count for each *Slate* story was posted at the top. Kinsley explains the motivation for this: "A friend of mine made the point that, when you start to read a print magazine article, you flip through to the end to see how long it is. In this medium, there's really no reliable way to do that. We try to give readers some idea (by posting the word count)."[16]

Competition

Slate was by no means the first e-zine; however, it was perhaps the first that was launched by a major company with national, mainstream ambitions. Early e-zines include *Feed* and *Charged*. To these magazines and their readers, Kinsley was an East Coast elitist who did not understand the Web. Moreover, "Kinsley didn't help himself any by declaring, in the very first issue of *Slate*, that there was a deadening conformity in the hipness of cyberspace culture."[7]

Salon, out of San Francisco, California, has emerged as *Slate's* primary competitor. For the four-month span from October 1996 to February 1997, *U.S. News & World Report* named *Salon* "cool site of the year," *Ad Age* magazine named it "online magazine of the year," and *Time* magazine called it the "best Web site of the year." *Time* said *Salon* "does everything right. It looks fresh and dramatic . . . and it features first-rate writers." *Salon* was started using seed capital from Apple Computer. Its primary backers are major investors: the software company Adobe, the venture capital firm Hambrecht & Quist, the Japanese computer firm ASCII, and borders.com.

From a business model standpoint, *Salon* and *Slate* represent the two ends of the spectrum. *Salon* is a stand-alone content site (i.e., all they do is develop content for their online site); *Slate* is part of Microsoft's family of consumer-oriented sites under the Microsoft Network

(MSN) umbrella. This partnership with MSN provides *Slate* an advantage in terms of distributing the product. As Scott Moore from *Slate* said:[8]

There's no question that (our relationship with MSN.com) is a factor. The fact that Slate is distributed on the second-largest network on the Internet in the U.S. is a massive competitive advantage to us. I'm not going to dispute that and I certainly won't make any apologies for it. It's worth pointing out that most media companies tend to be large and that's because economies of scale really matter in the media business. One of the mistakes made a few years ago by Internet entrepreneurs was assuming that the Internet changes everything and that anybody with a good idea and a Webserver can throw up a Website, attract an audience, and sell advertising.

That's true, but if you look at standalone content sites, they have a much higher cost structure than a site like Slate, which is integrated into this large network and enjoys these economies of scale. We have 33 people dedicated to Slate, so if Microsoft decided tomorrow not to do Slate, they would save on a headcount of 33. They wouldn't save any more than that. Whereas Salon, even after all of the cuts they've made, is still in the neighbor-

hood of 100, and that's not to say they're being inefficient or profligate; it's simply that they don't enjoy the economies of sale, so it's much harder to make it work. That's really true in any medium you look at.

In general, the top news and commentary sites are not entirely online pure plays. As shown in Table C4.2, out of the top ten sites, only *Slate* and *Salon* are brands that have only an online presence. This illustrates the difficulty of building a strong brand online.

An article in the *Columbia Journalism Review*[9] distinguishes between the two magazines in this way:

For Michael Kinsley, the world has become a raging sea of content, its inhabitants floundering in an endless news cycle. What they need is a filter, and as the editor of the online magazine Slate, Kinsley is trying to provide one—a tool to help his readers navigate the political, technological, and cultural issues of the Information Age. For David Talbot, the editor and CEO of the competing online magazine Salon, the world is awash instead in commentary: opinion dispensed by wise men who comment passively from the shore. What readers need is more reporting. Wading into

Table C4.2

Top News and Commentary Sites, February 2001

		% Reach	Audience (in millions)
1	MSNBC.com	11.8	10,386
2	CNN.com	11.2	9,824
3	ABCNews.com	4.8	4,256
4	Nytimes.com	4.5	3,956
5	USAToday.com	3.6	3,160
6	Washingtonpost.com	3.5	3,084
7	Slate.com	2.2	1,966
8	Foxnews.com	2.2	1,930
9	Salon.com	2.1	1,844
10	Latimes.com	2.0	1,734

Source: Slate.com, "Who Our Readers Are," 2001, http://slate.msn.com/?id=95365.

SLATANIC, THE DISASTROUS MOVE FROM FREE TO PAID CONTENT: CASE 4

the currents, Salon relishes introducing new topics to the conversation, with the expectation that its readers will construct filters of their own.

Salon provides reviews of books, travel, music, and movies. It also provides commentary from well-known figures and interviews with famous writers. It has an interactive area on its web site called "Table Talk" where readers and others can comment on the contents of the site or the latest news. It has also initiated a project called Brainwave, which is "a joint online discussion with the staffs and readers of three other Web sites—Feed, Electric Minds and The Site—on a variety of issues."[10]

It never intended to charge its customers a subscription fee; rather, it was always managed as an advertising-driven business. *Salon* reported more than 400,000 visitors per month by early 1997. The extended coverage of issues related to Princess Diana's death were instrumental in this growth. *Salon* was next in the news to report a story about a five-year extramarital affair by House Judiciary Committee chairman Henry Hyde. This was a controversial story—other media outlets were aware of the story, but did not run it. This type of story increased its readership from 620,000 to more than one million visitors a month in September 1998. Three months later, *Salon* had retained half of those new viewers, and its readership was estimated to be about 850,000 visitors a month.[11]

Advertising versus Subscription

Since the beginning, the overall goal at *Slate* was very clear: The magazine had to be financially self-sustaining. Every magazine has two important revenue sources: advertising and subscription. If a sufficient number of consumers visit the web site, the magazine can sell banner ads to interested advertisers. In the advertising business, a general rule of thumb is that the greater the number of consumers, the higher the fee. The easiest way to generate the most users is to keep the content free. This should be *Slate's* path if it wants to pursue the advertising revenue stream aggressively.

Another source of revenue is the subscription fee from individuals. This is used by those traditional magazines that require both advertising revenue and subscription fee revenue to be profitable. Also, this is believed to be a sound way to manage a business because it generates revenue from firms, as well as individuals.

Slate was very clear that, in the long run, they wanted both sources of revenue. In fact, the magazine announced on Day One its intention to charge a subscription fee at some point. In November 1996, the company announced that it was interested in charging subscription fees—but could not do so for technical reasons.[12] In January 1997, the company stated that it was still interested in charging subscription fees but did not for business reasons. *Slate* first wanted to build a strong brand by keeping its content free and then leverage its brand strength by charging a subscription fee.[13] Finally, in March 1998, the company announced its subscription fee—and recanted it on February 12, 1999.

At its inception in June 1996, the magazine announced a goal of 100,000 paying subscribers. Soon after its launch, the magazine's estimate of unique customers was 25,000.[14] In January 1997, it received an average of 15,000–18,000 hits per day.[15]

In an attempt to increase customer traffic in January 1998, *Slate* stepped up its coverage of the Monica Lewinsky scandal. As a result, visits to the site were at an all-time high—270,000 separate consumers visited the site in January 1998. This was double the number of visitors from just the previous month. At the same time, two competitors, *Word* and *Charged*, folded up their business. This emboldened *Slate* to start charging its readers a subscription fee.[16]

Several pundits cautioned that this was a risky decision. Kinsley said, "There's no doubt that the day we slam the gate, the traffic will plummet," but expected readership to rise as *Slate*'s reputation and influence continues to grow." William Bass, an analyst at Forrester Research Inc., dubbed it the "Slatanic," and he predicted that it was headed for the "subscription iceberg" as readers simply abandoned *Slate* to read political commentary elsewhere.[17]

A few days after moving to the subscription fee model, the company announced that it had 17,000 subscribers.[18] By February 1999, this number had increased only to the "high 20,000s"–far short of the announced goal of 100,000 paying subscribers. *Slate*'s "Front Porch," the free section of its site, received almost 400,000 visitors.[19] The vast difference between the two numbers led the magazine to reconsider its subscription fee business plan. The managers had to acknowledge that, unlike its print counterparts, which used both advertising and subscription, advertising would primarily drive *Slate*.

As Kinsley said:

> In a nutshell, it now looks as if it's going to be easier to sell ads but harder to sell subscriptions than we thought a year ago. Ten to 15 people visit our free areas every month for each one paying subscriber. (That's counting a reader just once no matter how often he or she visits.) It's painful to think of turning away so many Slate readers from so much of our content–not to mention the potential readers who don't come in the first place.[20]

One other aspect of *Slate* pointed to an advertising-oriented business. The e-zine had done a good job drawing consumers with demographic characteristics attractive to advertisers. Sixty-three percent of its readers were college educated and the median household income was $83,126.[21] This was a good sign indicating that high rates might be charged to advertisers. The company, however, still was not profitable. *Business Week* reported that in 1997, *Slate* generated only about $1 million in advertising revenue, while its annual production cost was over $5 million.[22] The publisher, Moore, placed this in

context by saying, "I feel we are on the path to profitability and we do take a long-term view of success. We've only been at this for three years. Most magazines take about five or six years to become profitable."[23]

Analysis of the Decision

When analyzing the decision to switch back to a free web site, Kinsley noted that:[24]

> It may just have been that we were too early. There is too much free stuff out there, the process of paying and accessing what you paid for is too clumsy and unfamiliar, and so on. Some of this may change. But we also may have missed a couple of more fundamental truths about the Web. One concerns readers, and one concerns advertisers. Web readers surf. They go quickly from site to site. If they really like a particular site, they may visit it often, but they are unlikely to devote a continuous half-hour or more to any one site the way you might read a traditional paper magazine in one sitting. This appears to be in the nature of the Web and not something that is likely to change. And it makes paying for access to any particular site a bigger practical and psychological hurdle. Web advertisers, meanwhile, don't seem to place any special value on reaching paying subscribers. That was a bit surprising, since traditional magazine advertisers usually require paying subscribers.

In general, online publishers have had little success with a subscription-only strategy. According to a 1999 survey by Jupiter Communications, 46% of Internet users said they would not pay to view a web site's content. With such resistance, it is no wonder that sites similar to *Slate* have been unsuccessful.

Among subscription sites, there are two well-known success stories. *Consumer Reports Online*, which charges $24 for a one-year subscription or $3.95 a month, and *The Wall Street Journal Interactive*, which charges $59 a year. Each has generated more than 300,000 subscribers who enter a password at the site to gain access to

The Entry of Salon Premium

A little over two years after *Slate* made its decision to price content, Salon.com, announced a new product called Salon Premium. Rather than making all of its content free, it offered some content for free and some for an annual subscription fee. Paid subscribers got access to special content and did not have to watch banner ads. *Salon* hoped that this additional value would entice users to pay. *Salon's* publisher explained this to the customers in an e-mail attached as an Appendix. The magazine has cited many reasons for its timing. Many independent online content sites had folded up—notably Feed.com and Suck.com. From a competitive standpoint, this was probably a good time to launch.

Moreover, Table C4.3 indicates that the number of unique visitors to *Salon* had started to level off. In fact, there was a precipitous drop in stories or reports. Moreover, according to analysts, subscription schemes work well only for two major user segments: business and professionals.[25]

readership in December 2000. This sent a signal to the company that they may have hit the ceiling in terms of attracting new users. They could not take off to "the next level" relying only on their current model.

In addition, as shown in Table C4.4, Salon.com's financial situation was bleak. The company's losses had expanded and its cash level was running low. It wanted to attract additional investment money, but could not if it stayed with the advertising-based model.

Many felt that, in the long run, most content sites had to start charging a price. If that were true, then it made sense to be among the first to move to a fee-based model. As *Salon's* Patrick Hurley said:[26]

Consumers do have a finite budget. If there are 40 online subscription choices, they might be able to only select three. If they are passionate *Salon* readers we have a good chance of locking them in by offering a subscription option now as opposed to waiting until there are in fact a lot more sites seeking payment.

Table C4.3 Salon.com's Operational Data

	Unique Users	Page Views	Ad Impressions
June 1998	567,000	21,000,000	28,000,000
March 1999	1,150,000	40,000,000	99,000,000
June 1999	1,300,000	47,000,000	159,000,000
July 2000	1,430,000	N/A	N/A
August 2000	1,611,000	N/A	N/A
September 2000	1,543,000	N/A	N/A
October 2000	1,992,000	N/A	N/A
November 2000	2,163,000	N/A	N/A
December 2000	1,685,000	N/A	N/A
January 2001	2,178,000	N/A	N/A
February 2001	2,082,000	N/A	N/A

Sources: Marty Beard, "Give Us $30 for an Ad-Free Read," March 19, 2001, http://199.230.26.96/saln/Saln1015.pdf, http://www.medialifemagazine.com/news2001/mar01/mar19/3_wed/news5wednesday.html.

In Millions of U.S. Dollars (except for per share items)	12 Months Ending 03/31/01	12 Months Ending 03/31/00	12 Months Ending 03/31/99 Reclass. 3/31/00	12 Months Ending 03/31/98 Reclass. 3/31/00	12 Months Ending 03/31/97
Revenue	7.2	8.0	2.9	1.2	0.3
Total Revenue	7.2	8.0	2.9	1.2	0.3
Cost of Revenue	9.8	9.0	4.2	2.7	1.6
Gross Profit	(2.6)	(1.0)	(1.3)	(1.5)	(1.3)
Selling/General/Administrative Expenses	10.7	17.1	4.0	1.8	0.5
Research & Development	1.6	1.4	0.4	0.3	0.2
Depreciation/Amortization	1.2	3.4	0.6	0.3	–
Unusual Expense (Income)	3.5	0.0	0.0	–	–
Total Operating Expense	26.8	30.9	9.2	5.1	2.3
Operating Income	(19.6)	(22.9)	(6.3)	(3.9)	(2.0)
Interest/Investment Income, Non-Operating	0.6	1.1	0.0	0.1	–
Interest Income (Expense), Net Non-Operating	0.6	1.1	0.0	0.1	0.0
Other, Net	(0.1)	(0.1)	0.0	0.0	0.1
Income Before Tax	(19.2)	(21.9)	(6.2)	(3.8)	(1.9)
Income Tax	0.0	0.0	0.0	0.0	0.0
Income After Tax	(19.2)	(21.9)	(6.2)	(3.8)	(1.9)

Source: http://ir-web.finsys.com/results.asp?criteria=cik_code&CIK=0001084332.

Moreover, consumers online have strong expectations to receive numerous things for free. Patrick Hurley addressed this issue:

As for the idea of paying for content on the web, I think the whole zeitgeist is changing. Yes, you can only buy so many magazines or newspapers. And people have been conditioned to get things for free online. So now they're going to have to be conditioned that they're going to have to pay for some things. This is a difficult issue because the cost for content is much more significant than the general public ever grasps. We've got an 85-person staff to support. And we put up 15 to 20 new pieces of content a day. I think it's going to be an evolution, not a revolution. People are averse to change in anything. You can't just completely take something away from them that they've always had. But you can evolve in new services, new content and rationally charge them for it.

The company claimed that Salon Premium was profitable four hours after it was launched. The company has said that, in the long run, the vast

SLATANIC, THE DISASTROUS MOVE FROM FREE TO PAID CONTENT: CASE 4

majority of its content will be available only to subscribers.[27]

Skeptics, however, abound. Martin Nisenholtz, the CEO of New York Times Digital, made these comments about the Salon Premium decision:[28]

I've been modeling this stuff out since we started in 1995. I have to say, to date, the gated model (total subscription) simply isn't as compelling as the one that involves charging for specific premium products. I don't know what their goal is. I don't know whether to say that's a success because I don't know the yardstick.

Conclusion

The Slatanic case points out the difficulties of building a web site that features paid branded content. In February 2002, Kinsley stepped down as the editor of *Slate* (partly for health reasons). It is up to future editors to determine the business model. The jury is still out on the Salon.com approach—only time will tell if a sufficient number of customers are willing to pay an adequate amount for *Salon* to be successful. Future entrants will no doubt use the *Slate* and *Salon* experiences when they price their content.

Notes

(All URLs are current as of April 8, 2002.)

1. Nicholas Stein, "Slate vs. Salon: The Leading Online Magazines Struggle to Get the Net," *Columbia Journalism Review,* 37(5), (1999): 56–59.
2. Staff Writer, "Slate Backs Off on Web Charge," *The Atlanta Constitution,* February 14, 1999.
3. Stein, "Slate vs. Salon."
4. Stein, "Slate vs. Salon."
5. Michael Kinsley, "All the News that will Fit," *Forbes,* November 30, 1998, 222–223.
6. Martin J. Smith, "Michael Kinsley: From Page to PC," *Writer's Digest,* 77(1), (January 1997): 51–53.
7. David Shaw, *The Los Angeles Times,* June 18, 1997.
8. Jim Welte, "Five Questions with Scott Moore," June 15, 2001, <http://www.business2.com/articles/web/0,15757,FF,html>.
9. Stein, "Slate vs. Salon."
10. Stein, "Slate vs. Salon."
11. Stein, "Slate vs. Salon."
12. Michele Flores, "Slate Magazine's Plan to Charge Users Delayed," *Seattle Times,* October 18, 1996.
13. Russell Anne, "Slate to the Party," *Folio: The Magazine for Magazine Management,* 26(2) (February 1, 1997): 56–58.
14. Jonathan Miller, *Eastside Journal,* Bellevue, October 11, 1996.
15. Martin J. Smith, "Michael Kinsley: From Page to PC."
16. Richard Zoglin, "Is Slate Worth Paying For?," *Time* 151(11) (March 23, 1998): 66–67.
17. Steve Hamm, "Would You Pay to Read Slate?," *Business Week,* February 23, 1998.
18. Zoglin, "Is Slate Worth Paying For?"
19. Stein, "Slate vs. Salon," 56–59.
20. Michael Kinsley, *E-mail to readers,* February 1999.
21. Anonymous, "Media Insight: Slate Magazine," *PR News,* May 24, 1999.
22. Hamm, "Would You Pay to Read Slate?"
23. Staff Writer, "Slate Backs Off on Web Charge."
24. Michael Kinsley, *E-mail to readers,* February 1999.
25. Bob Tedeschi, "On-line Publishing Ventures are Still Looking for a Way Around Readers' Sales Resistance," *New York Times,* October 4, 1999.
26. Jeremy Schlosberg, "Web's Future Has Paid Written All Over It," May 21, 2001, <http://www.medialife magazine.com/news2001/may01/may21/1_mon/news3monday.html>.

27. Farhad Manjoo, "Salon: Last One Standing," June 15, 2001, <http://www.wired.com/news/exec/0,1370,44464-2,00.html>.
28. Ibid.

Discussion Questions

1. What is it about the Internet that is forcing magazines and newspapers to move to a free content model?

2. Why is it that *Slate* could not charge for its content?

3. *The Wall Street Journal*'s online web site (http://www.wsj.com) is one of the few sites that still charges its users. Why are they successful at charging their users?

4. How did *Slate* manage its announcement of a subscription fee?

5. Assume that you were managing *Slate* when it was founded. Devise a content pricing plan for the next one year, three years, and five years. What are the differences between your content pricing strategy and *Slate's*?

6. What makes some businesses suited to support by advertising and others by subscription fees?

Appendix

Announcing Salon Premium—A message from Salon editor David Talbot

Dear Salon reader,

For more than five years, Salon has operated as a fearlessly independent and iconoclastic Web newspaper, providing readers with a kind of political and cultural coverage that we feel cannot be found anywhere else in the media landscape. Publishing a daily "paper," even on the Web, is an expensive project. Staff and freelance workers must be paid, Web bandwidth must be purchased and servers maintained, reporting expenses must be taken care of—Salon's intensive coverage of the Florida election debacle alone cost the company tens of thousands of dollars in extra expenses.

Like many Web sites, we have tried to support our business primarily through advertising revenue. We have succeeded in signing hundreds of advertisers over the years. But this revenue has fallen short of covering our costs. And this year, Internet advertising dollars are in even shorter supply.

As many of you have read in the press, Salon has cut its budget repeatedly over the past year, laying off some staff and most recently asking our employees (managers included) to take a salary reduction. We feel we are now operating as cost-effective a daily media enterprise as possible. And we are doing this while working hard to maintain the quality of our product.

Now, we must ask our loyal readers to help keep Salon's unique voice booming.

Starting next month, for a $30 annual subscription, we will begin offering readers a special service, Salon Premium, that will include not only all the regular Salon fare but additional "bonus" features available only to subscribers. Premium subscribers will be able to view Salon without banner or "pop-up" ads. Over time we will add additional features, like an easy-printout download.

The new wave of Web ads that are now being adopted by many sites, including Salon, will be bigger and more prominent than current banner ads (you can see some of them on today's Arts and Entertainment pages). The revenue Salon derives from these advertisements is a crucial part of our support system, and we intend to

Source: http://www.salon.com/letters/editor/2001/03/20/premium/index.html.

293

SLATANIC, THE DISASTROUS MOVE FROM FREE TO PAID CONTENT: CASE 4

continue to explore innovative approaches to marketing online. The Internet has always been a medium built on personal choice, and Salon readers will have two options—continue to read a free, advertiser-supported site, or pay for Salon Premium and switch to an ad-free environment while also contributing to Salon's success.

Too much of our public life is banal and dull-witted; we are surrounded by a media universe that is a daily insult to our intelligence. This is why we hold dear such treasures as our local public radio stations—they help keep us from mentally decomposing.

We would like to think that Salon has also become an essential daily destination for many readers. Over the past several years we have brought readers unique coverage of the country's most urgent political dramas, from the Clinton impeachment to the drug war to the deeply disturbing coda of the 2000 presidential race. While the national press corps has been happily collecting nicknames from President Bush, Salon has been the Washington watchdog that the nation needs, barking loudly over the sale of government to the rich and powerful.

Salon has also published cutting-edge technology coverage, provocative entertainment writing and literary criticism, and resolutely uncuddly examinations of family life and parenting.

Salon has built a staff of remarkable journalists whose bylines have become household names to many of you. Their reporting and criticism is rounded out by columnists like Garrison Keillor, Camille Paglia, Joe Conason, David Horowitz and David Thomson.

If you want to help make sure that these unique stories and writers keep coming to you every day, please sign up for Salon Premium when it debuts next month (if you'd like to be alerted when the program launches, send an e-mail to premiumnews@salon.com). Or if you choose to remain a reader of Salon's free edition, click on the ads and do business with the companies that have been helping keep Salon in business.

As we all know by now, the Web didn't rewrite all the rules. A free press has its costs. By helping us defray these costs, you can assure that Salon's "presses" keep humming—and its voice keeps sounding.

—David Talbot, Editor

LINUX .com

LINUX and Open-Source:
Case 5

Introduction

LINUX is an operating system (the most important program on a PC—it provides a platform on which other application programs run[1]) that was developed by many volunteer programmers from around the world under the leadership of Linus Torvalds. LINUX is the leading star of the open-source movement, which calls for software makers to release the source code (i.e., program instructions in their original and fundamentally basic form[2]) for their products so that individuals can customize them to their liking and gain a better understanding of the software programs.

Economic theory dictates that such collective efforts are subject to social loafing and inconsistent effort. Therefore, conventional managerial wisdom dictates that the quality of the product is suspect. This has been the first reaction from many company managers. For example, Microsoft's Ed Muth has said,[3] "Complex future projects [will] require big teams and big capital. These are things that Robin Hood and his merry band in Sherwood Forest aren't well attuned to do."

Surprisingly, the reality is just the opposite: LINUX is commonly considered a superior product. In fact, internal reports at Microsoft reveal that LINUX did better than many Microsoft products on speed and reliability.[4] Microsoft has also explicitly labeled LINUX a threat to its long-term business (see letter in the Appendix). LINUX is being used in many companies to

handle mission-critical steps.[5] In 1997, Info-world magazine gave LINUX the "Best Operating System" award and also hailed its community for excellent technical support.[6] A partial list of companies[7] who have adopted LINUX includes names such as The United States Postal Service, Siemens, and Mercedes-Benz. In February 2002, Sun Microsystems announced that it will be adapting LINUX high strategic prominence by adapting those products that currently run on its Solaris operating system to run on LINUX and by offering a host of software and hardware products that could take advantage of the LINUX operating system.[8]

As a result, managers at leading firms are now taking open-source product development seriously for the first time. Other firms have announced that they will be making the source code to their products open-source; for example, Netscape's Mozilla project (now part of AOL-Time Warner).

Open-source is not limited to software products. Consider the MIT Open Courseware Initiative.[9] In April 2001, one of the world's leading universities, the Massachusetts Institute of Technology (MIT) announced that it is making the material from virtually all of its courses available for free. The goal is to have 500 courses online by the end of 2003. Students and teachers from around the world can access and benefit from this information. Universities world-wide are grappling with the implications of this move on higher education.

What Is Open-Source?

All open-source software packages are available for free; however, all free software programs do not necessarily fall under the open-source category. Many software packages are made available for free on a short-term basis and may have restrictions on their use. For example, WS_FTP is available for free to academic researchers, but its source code is not free.

All open-source programs are licensed. It is important that managers realize there is no one standard license; rather, there are a variety of licenses—each with its own unique twist. Perhaps the most well-known license is the general purpose license (GPL), which covers LINUX. The GPL has been criticized for its stringent requirement that users release the source code for any derived work (i.e., any work that uses the original source code).

Table C5.1 is a comparison of the leading licenses provided by Bruce Perens, the treasurer of the open-source initiative and an acknowledged expert in the field.[10]

There has been a general effort to develop a set of requirements for programs seeking to be classified as open-source. The requirements include:[11]

1. Free redistribution—anyone can pass on the entire program for free to his or her friends or peers.

2. Source code must be made available—any interested party has the right to see the source code for the entire package.

3. License applies to all derived works—if a person downloads an open-source program and adds a feature to it, the new product also falls under the open-source license.

4. Integrity of the author's source code must be maintained—the code must not be changed in a way so as to mutilate the author's identity.

5. No discrimination against people or groups.

6. No discrimination against fields of endeavor.

7. No additional license can be required.

8. License must not be specific to a product.

9. License must not contaminate other software.

Table C5.1
Comparison of Open-Source Licenses

License	Can be mixed with non-free software	Modifications can be taken *private* and not returned to you	Contains special privileges for the original copyright holder	Can be relicensed by anyone over your modifications
General Public License	no	no	no	no
GNU Library General Purpose License	yes	no	no	no
Berkeley System Distribution	yes	yes	no	no
Netscape Public License	yes	yes	no	yes
Mozilla Public License	yes	yes	no	no
Public Domain	yes	yes	yes	no

Source: Bruce Perens, "The Open Source Definition," http://www.perens.com/Articles/OSD.html.

Critics of the GPL license primarily object to the "derived works" requirement. As noted by Craig Mundie, Microsoft Senior Vice President,[12]

The General Purpose License (GPL) mandates that any software that incorporates source code already licensed under the GPL will itself become subject to the GPL. When the resulting software product is distributed, its creator must make the entire source code base freely available to everyone, at no additional charge. This viral aspect of the GPL poses a threat to the intellectual property of any organization making use of it. It also fundamentally undermines the independent commercial software sector because it effectively makes it impossible to distribute software on a basis where recipients pay for the product rather than just the cost of distribution.

Microsoft has proposed a slightly different idea called shared source (discussed later).

Open-Source by the Numbers

The most prominent open-source software products are listed in Table C5.2.[13]

Many of these programs are widely used. Consider Apache, located at http://httpd.apache.org/docs/misc/FAQ.html. A tracking survey conducted by Netcraft shows that Apache is the most widely used web server software—its market share is about 70%. A summary of their data is shown in Figure C5.1. Apache is heavily de-

ployed at hosting companies and ISPs that strive to run as many sites as possible on a single computer to save costs. Windows is most popular with end user and self-hosted sites where the host to computer ratio is much smaller.[14]

Even though Microsoft is still the market leader in operating systems, LINUX has grown impressively—primarily on the server side (i.e., the portion invisible to the user or client). For example, a survey conducted by the International Data Corporation revealed market share figures for 1998 and 1999[15] (see Table C5.3). A more detailed breakdown for the year 2000 is provided in Table C5.4.

There are many companies that distribute their own version of LINUX. At this point, as shown in Table C5.5, Red Hat appears to be the market leader in the United States.

Similarly, individuals can obtain LINUX in various ways: CD-ROM from a vendor or by using FTP from a site. Table C5.6 describes how people obtained a copy of LINUX.

Table C5.7 illustrates how various individuals actually use LINUX. There is a general misconception that LINUX is primarily used for back-end office applications such as servers. Although it is true that LINUX is used as the operating system for Web servers, firewalls, and

Table C5.2
Top Open-Source Software Programs

Name of Software	Type of Software
1 LINUX	Operating System
2 Darwin	Apple's operating system
3 Apache	Web Server
4 BIND	Provides Domain Name Server (DNS) for entire Internet
5 Sendmail	E-mail Transport Software

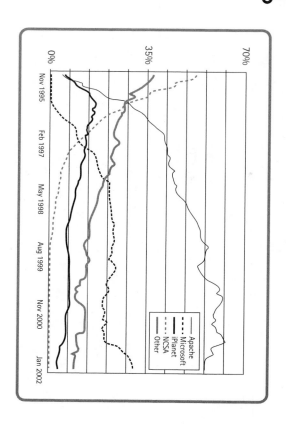

Source: "Netcraft Web Server Survey," http://www.netcraft.com/survey (accessed on February 12, 2002).

Table C5.3
Operating System
Market Share

	1998	1999
Windows NT	38	38
LINUX	16	25
Novell	23	19
UNIX	19	15
Other	4	3

Source: Adapted from Russ Mitchell, "New Numbers,
Historic Ramifications, February 10, 2000,
http://www.wideopen.com/story/499.html.

other servers, its highest use (61.27%) is as a
workstation, with programming ranking second.

Similarly, it is a misconception to think that
most people use LINUX at school or work. As
Table C5.8 shows, the vast majority uses LINUX
at home (89.04%), followed by about 44.5%
using it in their workplaces. LINUX is a global
phenomenon. As shown in Table C5.9, there are
LINUX user groups in at least seventy-four
countries around the world.

In many countries, the cost of software is very
high. As a result, open-source software is seen
as a way to reduce IT costs. For example,
Argentina is considering a law that would
require all government offices to use open-
source software.[16] This would make software
piracy moot and would expand access to software.

Table C5.4
Detailed IDC Survey for 2000

	2000
Client operating environments	
DOS and 16-bit Windows	7.5
Mac OS	4.8
Unix client	0.6
LINUX client	3.9
32-bit Windows, Windows NT and 2000	82.1
Other client	1.1
Total	**100.0**
Server operating environments	
Mainframe (all)	0.1
OS/400	1.5
Unix	15.1
LINUX	23.2
32-bit Windows, Windows NT and 2000	36.9
Other server	23.2
Total	**100.0**

Source: Adapted from IDC Research.

Table C5.5
Market Share Data
(As of February 12, 2002, 106,735 registrations entered 107,859 values)

Distribution	Count	Percent
Debian	22,262	20.86
Diy	1,415	1.33
Mandrake	17,810	16.69
Red Hat	29,246	27.40
S.U.S.E	10,645	9.97
Slackware	14,991	14.05
Others	11,490	10.76

Source: Harald Alvestrad, "The LINUX Counter Project," www.linuxcounter.org.

Table C5.6
How People Obtained a Copy of LINUX (As of February 12, 2002, 95,238 registrations entered 95,734 values)

Source	Count	Percent
CD	30,265	31.78
CD/InfoMagic	1,113	1.17
CD/Red Hat	3,063	3.22
CD/S.U.S.E	2,307	2.42
ftp	12,358	12.98
ftp/ftp.debian.org	953	1.00
ftp/ftp.redhat.com	1,216	1.28
Others	44,459	46.7

Source: Harald Alvestrad, "The LINUX Counter Project," http://www.linuxcounter.org.

Table C5.7
Uses for LINUX (As of February 12, 2002, 90,927 registrations entered 328,204 values)

Purpose	Number	Percent
Dns Server	15,760	17.33
File Server	21,471	23.61
Firewall	20,034	22.03
Ftp Server	23,062	25.36
Learning	35,571	39.12
Mail Server	20,848	22.93
Other Server	13,647	15.01
Programming	38,863	42.74
Router	15,774	17.35
Toy	24,799	27.27
Workstation	55,707	61.27
Www Server	29,872	32.85
Others	12,796	14.07

Source: Harald Alvestrad, "The LINUX Counter Project," http://www.linuxcounter.org.

Table C5.8

Where People Use LINUX (As of February 12, 2002, 90,927 registrations entered 328,204 values)

Place	Users	Percent
School	36,947	21.20
Home	155,207	89.04
Not used	21	0.01
work	77,593	44.51
somewhere	2,817	1.62
Total	272,585	100.00

Source: Harald Alvestrad, "The LINUX Counter Project," http://www.linuxcounter.org.

Table C5.9

LINUX's Global Picture: Number of User Groups Per Country (Accessed on February 12, 2002)

Country	Number of Groups	Country	Number of Groups
United States	150	Colombia	7
Germany	38	Denmark	7
Canada	27	Switzerland	7
India	24	Argentina	6
Russian Federation	23	Belgium	6
Italy	17	Netherlands	6
United Kingdom	14	Hungary	5
France	13	Sweden	5
Brazil	12	Ukraine	5
Australia	10	# with 4 user groups	4
Spain	10	# with 3 user groups	3
Mexico	8	# with 2 user groups	10
Norway	8	# with 1 user group	35

Source: Harald Alvestrad, "The LINUX Counter Project," http://www.linuxcounter.org.

How Can Enterprises Benefit from Open-Source Software?

The most important question for large corporations is deciding when they should make the code for their product open-source.[17] One paper provides the following suggestions:

- If by releasing the code in one segment of the market, profits will increase in a comple-mentary segment, the firm must make its code open-source.

- Releasing the code makes the most sense when one is very small or lagging behind the market leader significantly.

Open-source software development does not eliminate the need for large corporations to participate. In fact, large enterprises can play a variety of important roles:

LINUX AND OPEN-SOURCE: CASE 5

1. Version authentication. One of the drawbacks with many open-source software programs is that versions proliferate. As a result, it is hard for users to identify the current version! Enterprises such as Red Hat, Debian, and Mandrake play an important role by releasing their version of LINUX on CD-ROMs. Of course, each of these companies has a slightly different version of the software program.

2. Customer support. Many large companies do not trust a community of anonymous users to provide accurate customer support. As a result, many software vendors have a valuable supporting role to play in the installation, use, and maintenance of the software for large enterprises.

3. Facilitating new open-source movements. Remember that in open-source programs, software programmers are volunteers. They may be paid by their institution in some cases; however, in many cases, they are not. As a result, there is a dire need for companies that can support new open-source initiatives. For example, companies such as Red Hat provide grants for new efforts.

4. Adopting open-source ideas into new product development. Many large corporations are now incorporating open-source products into their existing product lines. For example, IBM has incorporated the Apache web server into its WebSphere suite. By doing so, companies tap into a vast global community of developers.

5. Source of information about open-source products. Many companies are vying to become the number one source of news and information about open-source products. For example, leading LINUX sites include CNET, NewsForge, and Screaming Penguin.

In addition, corporations can encourage the style of open-source communities within their organizations. For example, widespread code sharing within an organization is uncommon and is worth considering.

How Does an Open-Source Community Function?

A recent paper identified seven key principles that capture the activities of an open-source community:[18]

1. Open source developers work on projects that they consider important and significant additions to the software universe. They are not interested in products that lead to a dead end or make a small and marginal impact.

2. They focus on immediate and tangible problems. This is referred to as the "scratch the itch" strategy.

3. Because open-source developers are not paid, there is a constant search for efficiency and reusing what is already available.

4. A parallel process is used to solve problems. A number of people may generate multiple approaches to solve a problem. It is then possible to select the best solution to the problem.

5. Eric Raymond, a leading proponent of open-source, said, "Given enough eyeballs, all bugs are shallow." One of the roles of open-source is to leverage the sheer number of the community for debugging and testing.

6. There is a strong focus on documentation so that users can make sense of what is available.

7. Release early and release often.

There has been considerable debate as to why anybody would participate in an open-source project. Although some argue that it is altruistic behavior in search of a better world, others provide economic arguments. The main argument is that with open-source communities, users have an incentive to build a strong reputation that could be translated into a potential for future wealth.

A recent survey of participants in open-source projects conducted by the Boston Consulting Group and MIT provides more insight. The top five motivations of open-source participants were:[19]

1. To take part in an intellectually stimulating project.

2. To improve skills.

3. To take advantage of an opportunity to work with open-source code.

4. Non-work functionality.

5. Work-related functionality.

Interestingly, motives such as defeating proprietary software ranked low.

This study also classified participants into four categories: believers, fun-seekers, professionals, and skill-enhancers. Believers comprise 33% of all participants—they believe that code should be open-source. Fun-seekers form 25% of all participants—they do it to fulfill a non-work need and because it is intellectually stimulating. Professionals (21% of the group) participate for work-related reasons and to enhance their professional status. Finally, skill enhancers (21% of all participants) seek to improve their skills.

Advantages of Open-Source

Linus Torvalds, the creator of LINUX, identified several advantages to open-source products.

Large Developer and Tester Base

Traditionally, a company hires a finite number of developers to craft software. Next, testers work with the product to ensure that the number of bugs is small. At that point, it is launched to the market.

On the other hand, with the open-source method, numerous developers and testers can work on the product. Mr. Torvalds said:[20]

There are lots of advantages in a free system, the obvious one being that it allows more developers to work on it, and extend it. However, even more important than that is the fact that it in one fell swoop also gave me a lot of people who used it and thus both tested it for bugs and tested it for usability. The "usability" part comes from the fact that a single person (or even a group of persons sharing some technical goal) doesn't even think of all the uses a large user community would have for a general-purpose system.

So the large user-base has actually been a larger bonus than the developer base, although both are obviously needed to create the system that LINUX is today. I simply had no idea what features people would want to have, and if I had continued to do LINUX on my own it would have been a much less interesting and complete system.

Similarly, it has been argued that the open-source structure generates a rigorous review, leading to more reliable products:[21]

The central problem in software engineering has always been reliability. Our reliability, in general, is [terrible]. In other branches of engineering, what do you do to get high reliability? The answer is massive, independent peer review. You wouldn't trust a scientific journal paper that hadn't been peer reviewed, you wouldn't trust a major civil engineering design that hadn't been independently peer reviewed, and you can't trust software that hasn't been peer reviewed, either. But that can't happen unless the source code is open. The four most critical pieces of infrastructure that make the Internet work—Bind, Perl, sendmail and Apache—every one of these is open source, every one of these is super reliable. The Internet would not function if they weren't super reliable, and they're super reliable precisely because throughout their entire history people have been constantly banging on the code, looking at the source, seeing what breaks and fixing it.

In contrast, when an organization does not make its source code available to the public, it must employ several testers and developers at considerable cost, and the product quality may suffer.

Flexibility

One of the problems with regular software programs is that unless one works with all of the software from one company, one does not have the flexibility of "mixing and matching." According to Mr. Torvalds:[22]

In fact, one of the whole ideas with free software is not so much the price thing and not having to pay cash for it, but the fact that with free software you aren't tied to any one commercial vendor. You might use some commercial software on top of LINUX, but you aren't forced to do that or even to run the standard LINUX kernel at all if you don't want to. You can mix the different software you have to suit yourself.

Support from a Community

Traditionally, if a user has a problem, he or she has to contact the company's technical support division. In many instances, the level of support is poor. Moreover, after a time, users are asked to pay for this support.

With open-source software, one has an engaged community willing to answer questions. One could even talk to the actual person who wrote a software program in some instances!

Facilitating Factors for Success

A recent paper identified the factors that led to the success of LINUX.[23] Five factors are especially noteworthy:

1. The Internet. LINUX could not become a reality without the Internet. The sheer global scale of the endeavor and the complex coordination involved were not possible without the connectivity created by the Internet. Interestingly, most LINUX activities are conducted using older technologies such as e-mail, FTP, and USENET discussion groups. This led to an inclusive environment—people from around the world participated in the code's creation and maintenance.

2. Modular product. It can be argued that software, generally, is modular in nature. As a result, it is possible to delegate tasks to others easily,

Moreover, it is possible for individuals to contribute even when working alone. This low level of interdependency led to good quality control and a robust software product.

3. Strong leader with clear focus. Linus Torvalds is at the center of the worldwide LINUX community. His peers consider him a leader and a guru. His programming skills are considered to be among the best. As a result, he could set a clear agenda and generate participation from a large community. A leader must provide a vision, divide the project into small, well-defined tasks (modules), attract programmers, and manage the project. A leader with vision can assemble a critical mass of code to which the community can react and can offer a project with many exciting programming experiences.[24]

4. Parallel release structure. Most software companies adopt a sequential release structure—everyone is familiar with the 1.0, 2.0, 3.0 structure. Linus adopted a unique parallel release system with LINUX. According to Sproull and Moon:[25]

Perhaps, the most important management decision was establishing, in 1994, a parallel release structure for LINUX. Even-numbered releases were reserved for relatively stable systems and focused only on fixing bugs; odd-numbered releases were the development versions on which people could experiment with new features. Once an odd-numbered release series incorporated sufficient new features and became sufficiently stable through bug fixes and patches, it would be renamed and released as the next higher even-numbered release series and the process would begin again. The parallel release structure allowed Torvalds to simultaneously please two audiences who are often in conflict with one another. Users who rely upon a LINUX OS to support their production computing want a stable, reliable system in which new releases introduce only well-tested new functionality, no new bugs, and no backward compatibility problems. Developers, by contrast, want to try out new ideas and get feedback on them as rapidly as possible. The parallel structure offered both relative stability and certainty to users and rapid development and testing to programmers.

5. Consistent support from communities of practice. One of the most important aspects of software programs is the after-sale service that is expected from individuals and enterprises alike. LINUX is unique because individuals can pose technical questions to a group of experts who frequent a USENET group or an e-mail list and get answers rapidly. Of course, some of the larger companies, such as Red Hat, offer a similar service to their clients.

Open-Source Disadvantages

Even though open-source product development has several advantages, it also has its share of disadvantages:

1. Diminished role for commercial software makers. As indicated earlier, commercial software makers (e.g., Microsoft) have complained that the open-source license is unduly restrictive. The primary complaint involves the "derived works" requirement. For example, if Microsoft incorporates an open-source utility in its Windows 2000 operating system, it must make the entire source code available to the world. Because the company does not want to release its source code, it cannot benefit from any open-source software.

According to Craig Mundie from Microsoft:[26]

Shared Source is a balanced approach that allows us to share source code with customers and partners while maintaining the intellectual property needed to support a strong software business. Shared Source represents a framework of business value, technical innovation and licensing terms. It covers a spectrum of accessibility that is manifest in the variety of source licensing programs offered by Microsoft.

The principles of the Shared Source Philosophy are:

- Helping customers and partners to be successful through source access programs

- Building the development community and offering them the tools to produce great software

- Improving the feedback process in order to create better products for Microsoft's customers and partners

- Maintaining the integrity of our customers' environments

- Increasing educational access in order to get the technology into the hands of universities worldwide, and to seed the future of a strong technology industry

- Protecting software intellectual property based on the firm belief that software offers value as the basis of a successful business.

Microsoft views shared source as a tool that will help them work efficiently with their enterprise customers and distributors. For example, Microsoft has made its source code to Windows 2000 available to large companies, but with restrictive use terms.

2. Version proliferation. Consider the data in Table C5.10. There is a tendency for open-source software to have a proliferation of versions. This is certainly true for LINUX. As illustrated by the Table, there are at least twenty-three versions of the software running on user machines at this time. There is also a phenomenon called "forking the code," which refers to essentially creating two separate growth paths for the software. Forking can lead to even more versions.

3. Pace of innovation. Arguably, open-source product development may not be able to produce newer versions at the same pace as a for-profit corporation. Consider the lamentation of an open-source advocate: "It's nothing short of miraculous that Apache managed to retain its market share for about two years while

Table C5.10
Survey of LINUX Kernel Versions (Accessed on February 12, 2002)

Number	Kernel	Count	Percentage
1	2.0.32	3	0.10
2	2.0.33	3	0.10
3	2.0.34	5	0.20
4	2.0.34C52_SK	3	0.10
5	2.0.35	7	0.30
6	2.0.36	14	0.70
7	2.0.38	3	0.10
8	2.0.39	2	0.10
9	2.0.40	2	0.10
10	2.2.10	4	0.20
11	2.2.12	16	0.80
12	2.2.13	21	1.00
13	2.2.14	66	3.20
14	2.2.15	10	0.50
15	2.2.16	102	4.90
16	2.2.17	54	2.60
17	2.2.18	51	2.40
18	2.2.18pre11	2	0.10
19	2.2.18pre21	10	0.50
20	2.2.19	201	9.60
21	2.2.19ext3	2	0.10
22	2.2.19pre16	2	0.10
23	2.2.19pre17	12	0.60
24	2.2.20	71	3.40
25	2.2.21pre2	2	0.10
26	2.2.5	14	0.70
27	2.2.7	2	0.10
28	2.2.9	2	0.10
29	2.4.0	14	0.70
30	2.4.1	4	0.20
31	2.4.10	74	3.50
32	2.4.12	40	1.90
33	2.4.13	47	2.20
34	2.4.14	43	2.10

Table C5.10
(Continued)

Number	Kernel	Count	Percentage
35	2.4.15	5	0.20
36	2.4.16	192	9.20
37	2.4.17	376	18.00
38	2.4.18	27	1.30
39	2.4.18pre1	4	0.20
40	2.4.18pre2	3	0.10
41	2.4.2	67	3.20
42	2.4.3	40	1.90
43	2.4.4	46	2.20
44	2.4.5	26	1.20
45	2.4.6	9	0.40
46	2.4.7	85	4.10
47	2.4.8	76	3.60
48	2.4.9	178	8.50
49	2.4.9dual	2	0.10
50	2.5.0	3	0.10
51	2.5.1	5	0.20
52	2.5.2	3	0.10
53	2.5.3	5	0.20
54	Others	29	1.40
55	2	44	2.10
56	2.2	651	31.20
57	2.4	1,374	65.80
58	2.5	16	0.80
59	Others	4	0.20

Source: Harald Alvestrad, "The LINUX Counter Project," www.linuxcounter.org.

essentially treading water. Let's face it, in spite of a few point releases, Apache hasn't introduced any significant user features in two years."[27] It is not clear whether open-source can survive focused competition from such large companies as Microsoft and Sun Microsystems.

Conclusion

Open-source product development systems such as LINUX offer corporations much to consider. Organizations must, at a minimum, learn from the practices of these communities and incorporate them in order to be successful in the future.

Notes

(All URLS are current as of April 8, 2002.)

1. See Webopedia, "Operating System," <http://www.webopedia.com/TERM/o/operating_system.html> for more detailed information.

2. See Webopedia, "Source Code," <http://www.webopedia.com/TERM/s/source_code.html> for a more detailed description of the term.

3. OpenSource.org, "Halloween Document IV," <http://www.opensource.org/halloween/halloween4.html>.

4. OpenSource.org, "Halloween Document II," <http://www.opensource.org/halloween/halloween2.html>.

5. <http://www.bynari.com/BCG/cases/mclinux.html>, accessed September 2001.

6. OpenSource.org, "Case Studies and Press Coverage," <http://www.opensource.org/advocacy/case_studies.html>.

7. <http://www.bynari.com/BCG/cases/cos.html>, accessed September 2001.

8. Andy Patrizio, "LINUX Moving to Heart of Sun," February 8, 2002, <http://www.wired.com/news/business/0,1367,50311,00.html>.

9. "MIT Open Courseware Page," <http://web.mit.edu/ocw/>.

10. Bruce Perens, "The Open Source Definition," <http://perens.com/Articles/OSD.html>.

11. OpenSource.org, "The Open Source Definition," Version 1.9, <http://www.opensource.org/docs/definition.html>.

12. Craig Mundie, "The Commercial Software Model," May 3, 2001, <http://www.microsoft.com/presspass/exec/craig/05-03sharedsource.asp>.

13. A more comprehensive list is at OpenSource.org, "Products," <http://www.opensource.org/docs/products.html>.

14. "Netcraft Web Server Survey," <http://www.netcraft.com/survey>.

15. Russ Mitchell, "New Numbers, Historic Ramifications," February 10, 2000, <http://www.wideopen.com/story/499.html>.

16. Julia Scheeres, "Argentina Mulls Open Source Move," May 4, 2001, <http://www.wired.com/news/business/0,1367,43529,00.html>.

17. Tirole and Lerner, "The Simple Economics of Open-Source," December 29, 2000 <http://www.people.hbs.edu/jlerner/simple.pdf>.

18. Steven Weber, "The Political Economy of Open-Source Software," BRIE working paper 140, E-conomy Project Working Paper 15, June 2001.

19. Karim Lakhani, Bob Wolf, and Jeff Bates, "Hacker Survey," 2002, <http://osdn.com/bcg/bcg/bcghackersurvey.html>.

20. Rishabh Aiyer Ghosh, "What Motivates Free Software Developers: Interview with Linus Torvalds," 1998, <http://www.firstmonday.dk/issues/issue3_3/torvalds/index.html>.

21. Andrew Leonard, "Let My Software Go," April 14, 1998, <http://www.salon.com/21st/feature/1998/04/cov_14feature2.html>.

22. Ghosh, "What Motivates Free Software Developers."

23. Jae Yun Moon and Lee Sproull, "Essence of Distributed Work: The Case of the LINUX Kernel," 2000, <http://www.firstmonday.dk/issues/issue5_11/moon/index.html>.

24. Kasper Edwards, "When Beggars Become Choosers," 2000, <http://www.firstmonday.org/issues/issue5_10/edwards/index.html#p2>.

25. Moon and Sproull, "Essence of Distributed Work."

26. Mundie, "The Commercial Software Model."

27. Ganesh Prasad, "Will Open Source Lose the Battle for the Web?," August 14, 2001, <http://linuxtoday.com/news_story.php3?ltsn=2001-08-13-009-20-OP>.

28. Thomas Greene, "MS Promotes LINUX from Threat to "the Threat," December 11, 2001, <http://www.theregister.co.uk/content/4/2270.html>.

Discussion Questions

1. Is open-source thinking limited to software programs only? Can you think of other products where this may be a good idea?

2. In the Introduction section, MIT's Open Courseware project was discussed. If you were the president of a state university in the United States, would you be worried? How should your university respond? Will this put non-premier universities out of business?

3. With what type of software programs does open-source software work well?

4. Some have argued that open-source software will not thrive because the producers are not being compensated. What is your opinion?

5. Is a strong leader such as Linus Torvalds always necessary for an open-source program to be successful?

6. Will companies make more profit as a result of the open-source software movement?

Appendix[28]

Excerpt from Internal Microsoft E-Mail (Italics added for emphasis.)

From: Brian Valentine
Sent: Sat 11/10/2001 12:01 PM
To: WW Sales, Marketing & Services Group
Cc:
Subject: Hello again—long time no talk to . . .

LINUX Wins & Update

I'd like to share with you some great LINUX wins we've had recently. But before I do, I need to highlight a trend that we're seeing with many of our customers. They're fed up with expensive UNIX/RISC solutions from Sun, HP, and IBM. They're looking to move and they want to migrate to the Intel platform. Unfortunately, because LINUX is very similar to UNIX, and porting applications from UNIX to LINUX isn't that hard, we're starting to see customers move their UNIX applications to LINUX on Intel platforms. I need you to make sure that as many of these customers as possible continue to migrate off of UNIX, but on to Windows 2000 on Intel.

There are many other things that you need to watch out for with LINUX and the LINUX Compete Team has been busy creating some great collateral to help you win. *One thing you have to always keep in mind here—LINUX is the long term threat against our core business. Never forget that!* You should be smothering your accounts from every angle and if you see LINUX and/or IBM in there with it, then get all over it. Don't lose a single win to LINUX.

If you have not done it, you should inventory all of your accounts to know exactly where Unix (in any flavor, Sun, HP, IBM, etc) is and get engaged with them on how to convert them to the PC economics model and when doing that move to the best developer, application and OS platform in Windows. If you haven't done it at your customer sites—then do a walk-thru of their data centers and take inventory of where you see Sun machines, IBM, etc and ask them what they are running on those machines. Knock them out one machine, one application, one department at a time. I cannot stress how important this is!

PART THREE

Internet, Government, and Society

CHAPTER 13

E-Society

Learning Objectives

▼ To understand the unique nature of computer-mediated communication.

▼ To explore the appropriateness of the usage of Internet technologies in sacred and intimate human relationships.

▼ To learn about the potential for social isolation as a direct consequence of extended interaction on the Internet.

▼ To understand the issues involved with conducting elections online.

▼ To learn about the unique problems connected to gambling on the Internet.

▼ To understand the multifaceted nature of cybercrime and how it can be overcome.

▼ To learn about the digital divide locally and internationally and what can be done to reduce it.

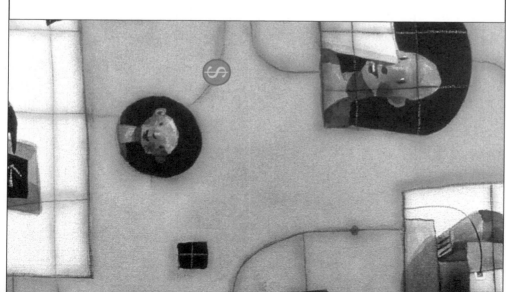

Executive Summary

The Internet has introduced computer-mediated communication (CMC) using such technologies as e-mail, discussion groups, chat, and instant messaging. CMC environments are unique because participants cannot view the full identity of all participants, participation is anonymous, and each individual is easily distracted. Using CMC in sacred and intimate relationships (e.g., virtual visitation, distance education, telemedicine) can create problems. Some studies showed that the extended use of the Internet leads to social isolation as individuals substitute casual, online relationships with substantial, real relationships. Today, it is possible to use the Internet to conduct large elections; however, this raises many issues such as security, the role of entrenched interests, and the impact of using a technology that is available to only a few. The Internet has made services such as gambling available to individuals in all corners of the globe. Gambling online can be problematic both on the consumer side (e.g., preventing children from gambling) and on the casino side (e.g., ensuring that the odds of winning are not unnaturally low). Cybercrime is on the rise and law enforcement worldwide is still grappling with the best ways to handle it. Finally, the Internet has created a digital divide in developed countries, as well as in the developing world. Trying to overcome this chasm by using innovative programs from the public sector, government, and independent agencies provides unique challenges.

Introduction

A society is defined as[1] "A group of humans broadly distinguished from other groups by mutual interests, participation in characteristic relationships, shared institutions, and a common culture." The Internet has impacted all aspects of society as described in this definition. It has changed the way individuals build and sustain relationships with one another and with institutions. It is now possible to develop a relationship with someone without ever meeting him or her. Controversial adult services are now available to minors, worrying parents and regulators. Others worry about those who do not have access to this technology—they will be left behind in a dramatic manner.

This chapter's focus is on the important ways in which the Internet has impacted society. One of the primary impacts of the Internet has been to facilitate CMC between individuals. Individuals can participate in electronic mailing lists, discussion groups, chats, instant messaging, and so forth. The vast majority of these forums rely on text-based communication between anonymous individuals mediated by a computer screen—a completely new way of interacting. The unique properties of this communication style are responsible for many of the challenges that the world faces today.

The topics discussed in this chapter are addressed from the CMC perspective. After a brief overview of CMC, the discussion turns to the impact of the Internet on sacred and intimate relationships. The questions addressed include: Can CMC be an effective tool in parent–child interaction? Or the interaction between a doctor and her patient? Between a professor and his student?

The second topic covers what CMC is doing to us as a society. Are we more connected to one another as a people or are we more isolated? Closely related to this is the issue of using the Internet for voting in elections. This use is viewed as a vehicle to reduce costs and increase participation. The question is whether it will ever be accepted as a suitable alternative.

The discussion next addresses the problems associated with Internet access to controversial services (e.g., online gambling, adult content, and hate literature). Related issues concern the distribution of products to an inappropriate consumer (e.g., liquor, drugs, and guns). The impact of the enhanced access to such services and products is discussed.

Finally, the concept of digital divide/dividends is covered. Throughout this text, we discuss the transformative power of the Internet. Some experts have started to ask whether the lack of access to this power will lead to an unprecedented separation between the "haves" and "have-nots."

A brief overview of cybercrime follows. Preventing criminals around the world from using the Internet to communicate and exchange money is a serious topic for law enforcement officials. Cybercrime is a phenomenon that affects both companies and consumers.

Face-to-Face versus Computer-Mediated Communication

Before plunging into the discussion of the specific topics, it is important to briefly discuss what CMC represents and its characteristics.

In CMC environments, *participants cannot see "the complete individual."* They cannot see the participant's body language (e.g., rolling eyes, raised eyebrows, strong handshake, blank stare). Several technology-based solutions attempt to overcome this problem. For example, some communication technologies encourage consumers to use *emoticons* (e.g., smiley face ☺) together with plain text to communicate their sentiments. In addition, consumers have created their own acronyms (e.g., LOL, which means "laughing out loud" or IMHO, which means "In my humble opinion"). Other technologies have created an entire persona (or avatar) for each individual based on their preferences. However, experts acknowledge that none of these approaches can replace human contact. Simply put, you cannot e-mail a hug or a handshake.

Many CMC environments promote *anonymous participation.* For example, most chat rooms require individuals to take on an assumed name before participating. Communicating with someone named "dannyboy" or "supergirl" is interesting, but not completely satisfying because of his or her concealed identity. This anonymity led to the famous line from *The New Yorker* cartoon: "Nobody knows you are a dog on the Internet." This quip focuses on a serious problem. Participants in CMC systems can project an incorrect image of themselves by accentuating the positives and hiding the negatives. They can pretend to be a different gender or age to reduce the barriers in others' minds. At the same time, this anonymity peels away layers of inhibition, leading to more open conversation. Many participants report that they are much more open about their feelings online. This is especially true in settings where the participants are all from one work group or organization.

Participants in CMC environments are *easily distracted*. Some participants may have other windows open and take time off to check e-mail or work on a memo. This is not always possible to detect. As a result, one may only have the partial attention of the participants. For example, it may be very hard for a teacher to regain control of an online class that is taken over by a few dominant participants.

CMC does not work well in environments that require *group decision making*. Consider telecommuting, for instance. In spite of its initial promise, most companies have made only limited commitments to it. In some cases, only the star computer programmer is given the opportunity to work remotely and even that is on a limited basis. The reason is that it is hard to manage problems that require a consultative decision-making process when a subset of the group is only virtually present. Many managers also expect to be able to drop into a colleague's office and chat about an issue. This ready availability is not always possible in a virtual organization.

Impact of the Internet on Sacred and Intimate Human Relationships

Consider the following scenarios:

1. (Kyron Henm-Lee is) a divorced mother in New Jersey who got a tech job offer in southern California. The new job required that she move her daughter, Katherine, a continent away from the nine-year-old's father. Mom's solution? Build a web site. Buy her ex-husband a web cam. And, click click, dad can communicate "directly with Katherine on a daily basis and review her school work and records. (He) would be afforded daily face-to-face communication with Katherine, albeit through an electronic medium."[2]

2. Coming soon to a hospital near you. The setting: An ordinary office conference room, barren except for a telephone, computer keyboard, television, and two remote controls. Suspiciously missing: stethoscopes, a sink, latex gloves, cotton swabs. Also absent: The patient. Dr. Pam Prescott hustles into the room and quickly consults her file. Jayne McVey is 44, diabetic, and, at this moment, sitting 100 miles away. The cameras begin to roll. It is the eighth time in a year and a half that the University of California–Davis Medical Center endocrinologist has seen this particular patient. But the two have never met. Instead, cameras film their every move and a secure, high-speed ISDN line transmits their images and sounds onto television screens—in real-time, of course—for the other to see and hear. Prescott reviews her patient's lab results and offers suggestions for keeping glucose levels stable. Twenty minutes later, their visit over, the two part amicably. A handshake, however, just isn't possible.[3]

3. In 1998, Washington State Governor Gary Locke remarked that universities can reduce costs and improve access by eliminating some professors and offering more online courses to bring education to the students' kitchen tables. Nine hundred professors at the University of Washington signed a petition opposing this move. One of the professors who signed the document said, "The thought of putting 19-year-olds and 20-year-olds into a program where they have no contact with teachers, no contact with fellow students, no contact with libraries, no contact with the atmosphere of a university–it's very disturbing."[4]

These are controversial examples involving Internet technology uses that have their share of opponents and proponents. Can virtual visitation be a substitute for actual interaction between a parent and a child? Is the quality of care adequate if the doctor is not able to physically examine the patient? Will the level of university education be the same if it is offered online?

In all of these situations, the primary question is: *"Can the Internet be effectively used to replace face-to-face communication in relationships that are held sacred or are intimate?"* The three relationships mentioned–parent–child, doctor–patient, and professor–student– are but a subset of the myriad relationships that are part of modern society.

The current conventional wisdom among experts is that the Internet cannot replace face-to-face interaction–especially in sacred or intimate relationships. It can, however, be used to supplement it. For example, many professors use the Internet to post their lecture notes so that students can read them before class and be better prepared. Also, systems such as Blackboard and WebCT, which allow instructors to manage communications with students in an integrated fashion, have successfully created a space that supplements the classroom. Similarly, having digital patient records and using complex decision-making tools allow doctors to make better decisions.

However, the allure of lowered costs is seductive. Frequently, policy makers under budgetary pressure promote the use of this technology in important areas such as university education. The availability of virtual visitation may tempt judges to reason that "virtual contact is better than no contact." Although this rationale may be true, the extent to which virtual visitation is a poor substitute must be emphasized and it must be adopted only in the rarest cases.

On the other hand, some scholars believe that anonymous interaction can be beneficial in some settings. For example, one study of an online course found that migrating online led to identifiable advantages:[5] students were more confident and participated more. There was also greater cross-cultural communication. Moreover, there was a higher level of informality and playfulness, leading to a greater degree of comfort among students. At the same time, online classes had disadvantages. There was greater aggression online and it was harder for the instructor to control the class. There was a degradation of trust when a female student's alias was misused and a negative message (flame) was posted using her name.

Does the Internet Lead to Greater Social Isolation?

A central aspect of every human society is the myriad relationships between individuals. We know others through our work, our neighborhood, or our extended family. Using the Internet, people can connect to others without ever meeting them, raising the larger question: "Does the greater connectivity provided by the Internet lead to better relationships between people?"

Although society may not yet have the answer to this larger question, a related question has become the focus of much debate: "Does the Internet lead to social isolation?" In other words, when people use the Internet for extended periods of time, does it lead to positive outcomes (e.g., greater happiness or satisfaction with life) or does it lead to negative outcomes (e.g., increased loneliness and sadness)?

A 1995 study conducted by researchers at the Carnegie Mellon University indicated that those who used the Internet frequently were much more likely to be less involved socially. Specifically, their longitudinal study of 169 individuals in the Pittsburgh area indicated that greater Internet usage led to "a drop-off in communication within a participant's families, the size of a person's social networks, and reports by participants of increases in loneliness and depression, psychological states associated with reduced social involvement."[6,7]

According to the study's authors, the primary reason for this reduction in social involvement was that many individuals were substituting casual friendships made online for vital and strong real-life relationships. The authors noted that:

You don't have to deal with unpleasantness (online), because if you don't like somebody's behavior, you can just log off. In real life, relationships aren't always easy. Yet dealing with some of those hard parts is good for us. It helps us keep connected with people.[8]

Follow-ups to this initial study have countered some of the more negative findings. Notably, a study by Larose, Eastin, and Gregg found that communicating on the Internet with people who are known can lead to lower depression—at least among some sections of the population. Interestingly, they also found that this may be driven by the level of a person's technology skill. Those who understood the technology enough to use it efficiently did not feel very isolated.[9] Another study found that the heaviest Internet users also tended to be more involved with nonprofit organizations, suggesting strong links with the community.[10]

Voting on the Internet

The Internet and the Web can be used to conduct elections online. Voters in the states of Alaska, Arizona, and Washington have already been allowed the opportunity to vote using the Internet.

There is considerable interest in this idea for two reasons: increased participation and cost. Over time, there has been a steady decline in the proportion of Americans who vote in presidential elections—less than 50% of eligible voters participated in the 1996 elections. Proponents hope that allowing people to vote using the Internet will encourage younger voters, voters in remote areas, and voters who are place-bound to participate in the electoral process.

The Internet voting mechanisms are less expensive than the traditional methods. Internet voting reduces the costs of counting and collating the ballots. Although security requirements may require the addition of new costs, the overall costs of an election are expected to be lower.

E-voting companies distinguish between two types of voting: e-voting and online voting. E-voting takes place at regional voting centers. Trained representatives identify voters and direct them to a voting terminal (i.e., computer) where they cast their ballots. The Internet simply acts as a "back-end" mechanism—it collects and transmits the information. Online voting occurs when voters actually cast their ballots using their home PC. Voters are mailed a PIN number after a signature process (to minimize fraud) verifies their identity.

Will Internet-based voting be adopted on a large scale? At this point, there are several barriers, primarily security and fraud—verifying the identity of the voter is paramount. Moreover, due to the digital divide (discussed later), there is concern that the proposed process is not democratic because large sections of the population do not have access to this technology. E-voting alleviates this concern somewhat, but not entirely. In the final analysis, entrenched interests and political considerations may well determine the ultimate outcome.

Access to Controversial Services Online

With the Internet's development has come increased access to controversial services by a larger portion of the world's population. Although there are a number of controversial or adult services offered (e.g., pornography, the sale of tobacco and alcohol), the issues raised are similar. Therefore, this section uses online gambling as its focus.

Overview

Gambling on the Internet is huge business. A search on Yahoo! on August 22, 2001, revealed that there are at least 1,417 Web-based gambling outlets. According to industry figures, "in May 1998, there were approximately 90 on-line casinos, 39 lotteries, 8 bingo games and 53 sports books. A year later, there were more than 250 on-line casinos, 64 lotteries, 20 bingo games and 139 sports books."[11] Initially, American casinos were prohibited from having online gambling. However, a new law, passed by Nevada, legitimized online gambling sponsored by American casinos.[12]

Online gambling is a very profitable business: "Whereas it might cost $300 million to build a new resort casino which employs thousands, ICI's virtual casino was developed for only $1.5 million and employs only 17 individuals. Warren B. Eugene, ICI's colorful founder, has said that his house cut averages about 24%, versus the typical U.S. casino house take, which ranges between 8% to 16% of each dollar wagered."[13]

Gambling on the Internet is also very easy. Individuals can choose from a selection of casinos located all over the world and can wager large amounts of money in a relatively short amount of time. Because of the easy access, Internet gambling has become a problem on college campuses across the country.[14] Consumer-related problems include:[15]

- Underage gambling—ensuring that adolescents do not access Internet gambling using a parent's credit card.

- Problem gamblers—preventing participation by compulsive or "addicted" gamblers.

- Gambling while intoxicated—ensuring that someone under the influence of alcohol or other drugs does not have access to Internet gambling.

- Internet gambling in the workplace—monitoring company employees to detect Internet gambling during work hours.

- Electronic cash—monitoring the amount of money spent on gambling. It is likely that the psychological value attached to electronic cash is less than "real" cash (similar to chips or tokens).

- Hours of operation—limiting the amount of time spent gambling. Because the Internet never closes, it is possible to gamble all day, every day.

There is also some concern that gambling service providers may be fraudulent:[16]

1. Gambling operators located overseas might misappropriate consumers' credit card numbers and they are not subject to prosecution under U.S. laws.

2. The games may be systematically biased in the favor of the gaming operator and the customer has no way to detect it. Because there is no requirement that a U.S. gaming body audit the gambling mechanisms, unscrupulous casinos can separate unsuspecting customers from their cash.

3. Online gambling is viewed as a way to launder money. Individuals can lose a small amount of their money gambling and cash out the remaining funds to an offshore account.

The U.S. Congress has proposed a law to prohibit Internet gambling within the United States.[17] Detractors argue that this is a misguided effort because "the architecture of the Internet makes prohibition easy to evade and impossible to enforce. As an international network, moreover, the Internet offers instant detours around domestic bans."[18] Interestingly, Australia's Northern Territory was the first to launch a government-licensed, fully regulated online casino open to bettors from around the world.[19] Such a supportive approach to gambling has been soundly criticized. Other world governments are still debating the best approach to regulating gambling.[20]

Implications

Several general themes arise from the discussion of Internet gambling, including:

- The Internet is a global medium. Many online casinos are located outside of the United States (e.g., Australia, Caribbean). Similarly, the Internet is viewed by many as creating global competition. For example, many American universities may use the Internet to deliver online courses to students in other countries. U.S. software manufacturers can increase profits by selling software that can be downloaded from the Internet by anyone in the world.

- Due to the lack of face-to-face communication, the Internet might become a haven for illegal activity. Businesses have no credible way of verifying whether a buyer meets certain requirements (e.g., adult-only content or products). As a result, children may be exposed to mature content (e.g., pornography) or products (e.g., alcohol, drugs). Massive fraud is another concern (e.g., gambling games with odds stacked against consumer).

- Regulation requires extensive coordination. It is impossible to regulate a global enterprise locally—it requires large-scale coordination using worldwide forums.

Cybercrime

The Internet is, unfortunately, also a place where criminals abound. Cybercrime reports on matters ranging from viruses to hacking to child pornography are everywhere. Total losses from cybercrimes in 1997–2000 are estimated to be greater than $650 million.[21]

Cybercrimes are generally categorized as follows:[22]

- Internal computer crimes—worms, viruses, trap doors

- Computer manipulation crimes—embezzlement, fraud, counterfeit, economic espionage, desktop forgery

- Telecommunication crimes—hacking, unauthorized access, telefraud, computer network trespassing

- Intellectual thefts—theft of trade secrets, computer hardware, software, components, and services

- Civil rights crimes via computer—extortion, bribery, slander, hate mail, threats, harassment

- Support of criminal enterprises—drug dealers, terrorists, money laundering

Leading experts believe that many factors have come together to facilitate the growth of cybercrime.[23] Because it is possible to hide one's identity and be anonymous on the Internet, criminality is hard to detect. In a digital world, criminals have adapted from a tangible world to one that is intangible. It is possible to arrange for large-scale fund transfers online, for instance. This is further enhanced by the use of cryptography and encryption. The technology has outpaced the legislation—many of the situations fall in murky legal categories with no precedents. With the Internet, determining jurisdiction is also challenging—especially in an international arena.

The general consensus is that several steps must be taken to stop cybercrime. First, the public must be made aware of the challenges of cybercrime. Second, law enforcement officers who are used to following criminals on the highway or in other traditional areas must be retrained to deal with cyber-criminals. Special cyber-units should be created using experts to assist the officers on duty. Third, laws must be updated—locally, nationally, and internationally. Clearly written cooperation agreements must be signed by all international bodies. Fourth, industry leaders must cooperate with the authorities to help them locate the criminals.

Digital Divide and Digital Dividends

The Internet and related technologies are powerful enablers of upward mobility and prosperity. Those individuals who have access to the Internet are able to access information faster and conduct various tasks in an efficient manner; however, access to these technologies is not uniform—the gap between the "haves" and the "have-nots" is continually expanding. For instance, not all web sites can be accessed by the disabled, so there is currently an initiative to expand the level of web site accessibility.[24]

A U.S. government study released in late 2000 found that:[25]

Persons with a disability are only half as likely to have access to the Internet as those without a disability: 21.6% compared to 42.1%.

56.8% of Asian Americans and Pacific Islanders have Internet access at home. In comparison, 23.5% of Blacks and 26.8% of Hispanics have access to the Internet at home.

86.3% of households earning $75,000 and above per year had Internet access compared to 12.7% of households earning less than $15,000 per year.

Nearly 65% of college graduates had home Internet access while only 11.7% of households headed by persons with less than a high school education had Internet access.

There is also a global digital divide. As shown in Table 13.1, the vast majority of Internet users live in Canada and the United States; only about 0.76% of world users live in Africa. Moreover, as shown in Figure 13.1, although the number of users in developed countries has increased at a fast clip, the number of users in developing countries has slowed down—less than 2% of the population in these countries has Internet access.

Barriers

A study by Ipsos Reid determined the following reasons why people do not use the Internet:[26]

- No need for it (40%)
- Don't have a computer (33%)

Table 13.1
Number of Internet Users

Region	Number of Users (millions)	Percent
Africa	4.15	0.76
Asia/Pacific	157.49	28.94
Canada & USA	181.23	33.30
Europe	171.35	31.49
Latin America	25.33	4.65
Middle East	4.65	0.85
World Total	544.20	

Source: Nua Surveys, "How Many Online?," February 2002, http://www.nua.com/surveys/how_many_online/index.html.

Figure 13.1
Internet Users in Developed and Developing Countries

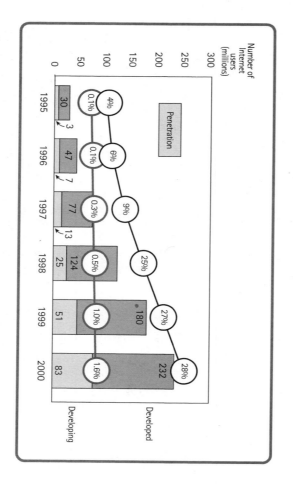

Source: Bridges.org, "Spanning the Digital Divide: Understanding and Tackling the Issues," http://www.bridges.org/spanning/chpt2.html.

Experts have also found that content-related barriers to Internet use exist in developed countries, including:[27]

- Not interested in it (25%)
- Don't know how to use it (16%)
- Cost (12%)

1. *Lack of local information.* There is very little information about local communities. While this is true for the large population, it disproportionately affects Internet users living on limited incomes, especially the nearly 21 million Americans over age eighteen whose annual income is less than $14,150 for a family of three (the level used by the federal government to define poverty). The challenge of developing content that will motivate these users to get online must be addressed.

2. *Literacy barriers.* Most of the information on the Net is written for an audience that reads at an average or advanced literacy level. Because 44 million American adults, roughly 22%, do not have the reading and writing skills necessary to function in everyday life, they cannot make use of the Internet.

3. *Language barriers.* Today, an estimated 87% of all documents on the Internet are written in English. Yet, for at least 32 million Americans, English is not their primary language, so they do not receive all of the benefits the Internet offers.

4. *Lack of cultural diversity.* The Internet can be a powerful tool to share and celebrate the uniqueness of the cultures in the United States and elsewhere. However, despite the tremendous surge in ethnic portals, there is a lack of Internet content generated by the ethnic communities themselves or organized around their unique cultural interests and practices. For many of the 26 million Americans who are foreign-born, the lack of cultural diversity in the available content serves as a real barrier.

In developing countries, the barriers are more basic—lack of electricity, large-scale illiteracy, the chokehold of traditional intermediaries, and poverty.

Digital Dividends

A new way of thinking asks whether a sustainable business can be built that focuses on the poorest section of a country. The idea is to stop focusing on the problem (digital divide) and move to solutions (digital dividends). Professor C. K. Pralhad stated that the real barriers concern how business managers think. He has identified five assumptions held by managers that act as key barriers to moving a business forward:[28]

Assumption #1: The poor are not our target customers; With current cost structures, we cannot compete for this market; "our cost structures are a given."

Assumption #2: The poor cannot afford and have no use for the products and services that are sold in the developed markets. Product is our focus, not functionality—"We worry about detergents not cleanliness."

Assumption #3: Only the developed markets appreciate and will pay for new technology. The poor can use the last generation of technology. "Innovations come from the top."

Assumption #4: The bottom of the pyramid is not important to the long-term viability of our business. We can focus on the top and leave the bottom tier to governments and non-profits.

Assumption #5: Intellectual excitement is in the developed markets. "Managers do not get excited with business challenges that have a humanitarian element to them."

He proposes that managers start thinking along new lines:

- Think of the poor as a market opportunity.
- Creatively bundle advanced technologies with local flavor.
- Selectively leapfrog technologies in the West.
- View achieving scale as critical.

Several new businesses have adopted Professor Pralhad's suggestions, including:

- Tarahaat.com—it is creating a commercial rural portal in India using kiosk technology.
- Grameen Bank's Grameenphone—it is empowering rural consumers with cell phones.
- The KnowNet—it is trying to disseminate relevant information to individuals all over the world. [29]

Conclusion

The Internet has created a brand new world. Individuals are relating to one another in new ways. Unfortunately, those who do not have access to the technology are being systematically excluded. Cybercrime has emerged as a legitimate area of concern. Online gambling has exploded. Overall, although the Internet has helped society in many ways, it has also raised new challenges. Coping with and overcoming these challenges requires new ways of thinking and cooperation on a global scale.

Notes

(All URLs are current as of April 8, 2002.)

1. Definition taken from <www.dictionary.com>.
2. Accessed in August 2001. http://www0.mercurycenter.com/columnists/armstrong/docs/005792.htm.
3. Julie Sevrens, "Telemedicine Alters Healthcare Delivery," October 29, 2000, <http://www.reporternews.com/2000/ads/health2/alter.html>.
4. Hiawatha Bray, "Long-Distance Learning Isn't Going to Put Harvard Out of Business. But Computer-Linked Classes are Spreading, for Better or Worse," April 11, 1999, <http://www.boston.com/education/college/col990411.shtml>.
5. Andrea Chester and Gillian Gwynne, "Online Teaching: Encouraging Collaboration through Anonymity," December 1998, <http://www.ascusc.org/jcmc/vol4/issue2/chester.html#LESSONS1>.
6. Carnegie Mellon University Press Release, "Carnegie Mellon Study Reveals Negative Potential of Heavy Internet Use on Emotional Well Being," <http://homenet.andrew.cmu.edu/progress/pressrel.html>.
7. Similar results were obtained in a somewhat-discredited study out of Stanford University.
8. Carnegie Mellon University Press Release, "Carnegie Mellon Study."
9. R. LaRose, M. S. Eastin, J. Gregg, "Reformulating the Internet Paradox: Social Cognitive Explanations of Internet Use and Depression," *Journal of Online Behavior*, 1 (2), 2001, <http://www.behavior.net/JOB/v1n2/paradox.html>.

10. Barry Wellman, A.Q. Haase, James Witte, and Keith Hampton, "Does the Internet Increase, Decrease or Supplement Social Capital?," April 11, 2001, <http://web.mit.edu/knh/www/downloads/netadd8b1-k.pdf>.

11. American Gaming Association Web Site, "AGA Fact Sheets," <http://www.americangaming.org/casino_entertainment/aga_facts/facts.cfm/ID/17>.

12. Accessed in August 2001, <http://www.hotel-online.com/Neo/News/2001_Jul_02/k.SJW.994101989.html>.

13. Cynthia Janower, "Gambling on the Internet," <http://www.ascusc.org/jcmc/vol2/issue2/janowerold.html>.

14. Ronald Reno, "NGISC Report: What Does it Say? What Does it Mean? Part 4," September 10, 1999, <http://www.family.org/cforum/research/papers/A0007727.html>.

15. Center for Addiction and Mental Health, "eGambling: The Online Journal of Gambling Issues," <http://www.camh.net/egambling>.

16. Reno, "NGISC Report."

17. Veronica Rose, "Federal Internet Gambling Prohibition Act," February 16, 2000, <http://www.cga.state.ct.us/2000/rpt/olr/htm/2000-r-0109.htm>.

18. Free-market.net Spotlight: Internet Gambling, "Smart Bet on the Net," February 24, 2000, <http://www.free-market.net/spotlight/gambling/>.

19. Mike Brunker, "Australia, US at odds on Internet Betting," July 9, 1999, <http://www.msnbc.com/news/287419.asp>.

20. Gaming Board of Great Britain, "Internet Gambling: Report to the Home Secretary," <http://www.gbgb.org.uk/intgambling.html>.

21. Wayne Williams, "Fighting Crime in Cyberspace," May 7, 2000, <http://www.nctp.org/docs/econcrime/index.html>.

22. Wayne Williams, "The Changing World of Cybercrime: What's on the Horizon," May 10, 1999, <http://www.nctp.org/docs/econcrime/tsld004.html>.

23. National Cybercrime Training Partnership, <http://www.nctp.org/docs/ECS_FINA.pdf>.

24. World Wide Web Consortium, "Web Accessibility Initiative," March 5, 2002, <http://www.w3.org/WAI/>.

25. Larry Irving, "Falling Through the Net: Defining the Digital Divide," November 1999, <http://www.ntia.doc.gov/ntiahome/digitaldivide/execsumfttn00.htm>.

26. Accessed in August 2001, http://www.ipsosreid.com/media/content/pdf/mr010613_1t.pdf.

27. Most of this is directly taken from Kevin Taglang, "Content and the Digital Divide: What Do People Want?," <http://www.digitaldividenetwork.org/content/stories/index.cfm?key=14>.

28. C. K. Pralhad, "The Poor As a Source of Innovations," <http://www.digitaldividend.org/ideas_informtn/ideas_informtn_03ss01.htm>.

29. The Public Voice, "The Public Voice and the Digital Divide: A Report to the DOT Force," March 2001, <http://www.thepublicvoice.org/dotforce/report_0301.html>.

REVIEW / CHAPTER 13

Discussion Questions

1. When is CMC superior to face-to-face communication?

2. Is telecommuting suited to certain types of jobs or industries? What are the conditions necessary to make such a program a success?

3. How long have you used the Internet? Do you feel a greater sense of belonging or do you feel lonelier? What do you think drives this?

4. Critically analyze the five managerial assumptions that act as barriers to targeting poor audiences. Are some unreasonable? Can the poor ever be a valid target market?

5. Using gambling as an example, discuss whether international laws can be developed to prevent inappropriate access to such a service.

E-Tasks

1. Visit one online casino that does not have a bricks-and-mortar outlet. Visit another that has a well-known bricks-and-mortar component (e.g., a Las Vegas casino). Which approach is more likely to be successful? How have these casinos differentiated themselves? Similarly, do you think consumers are more likely to visit a lottery run by a private company or by a state government?

2. Visit http://www.digitalpartners.org. Critically assess one of the projects featured there.

CHAPTER 14

The Internet and Public Policy

Learning Objectives

▼ To become aware of Intellectual Property issues and how they apply to e-business.

▼ To gain an understanding of Internet taxation issues.

▼ To learn about the implications of privacy on the operation of an online business.

▼ To understand why spam is a problem and how it can be limited.

Executive Summary

Intellectual property (IP) is any creation by the human mind that is unique and has value in the marketplace. IP is protected by using copyrights, patents, and trademarks. Many interesting legal issues arise in e-business in this arena. Some of the issues discussed include linking-related legal issues, business method patents, respect and integrity, domain names and trademarks, and the Digital Millennium Copyright Act of 1998. The taxation of e-commerce is a problematic issue. The two primary questions are: Who deserves to get the tax revenue (i.e., jurisdiction) and who collects this money? Currently, there is a moratorium on imposing new taxes on e-commerce in the United States. The European Union (EU) has developed three principles that will be useful to define the taxation landscape of the future. The privacy of consumer information is a theme that runs through many facets of e-business. Privacy is the right to be left alone. Because no e-business can exist without a customer database, prescribing rules and laws governing the responsible use of this information becomes vitally important. Most Americans are privacy pragmatists, but a small minority is very vocal about its privacy rights. Already, the FTC has identified five information principles: notice, choice, access, security, and redress. The EU and Europe's Organization for Economic Cooperation and Development (OECD) have also issued strict privacy regulations. Permission marketing may allow firms to successfully meet some of these new demands; however, there are also many technologies that customers can use to prevent a company from getting his or her information. Spam is unsolicited commercial e-mail. Because the marginal cost of sending e-mail is nearly zero, marketers have the incentive to send out large numbers of e-mail messages. There are various approaches that try to limit spam—technological (e.g., filtering at ISP and consumer levels), regulatory (e.g., anti-spam laws), and business-led (e.g., permission marketing).

Introduction

A corporation does not operate in a vacuum—the legal environment that surrounds it affects the nature of its business. Today, online businesses are facing cutting-edge legal issues. Current laws were developed in an older technological landscape and do not fully account for the nuances of the Internet and the Web. As a result, many controversies have emerged whose legal resolutions promise to change e-business in the future.

This chapter begins with a discussion of IP as it applies to online businesses. The Internet and the Web have spawned a host of unique issues related to protecting one's property rights online. The next section addresses the taxation of e-commerce. This is a fascinating area and the laws are still catching up with the technology. The Internet creates unique challenges to defining jurisdiction in terms of tax collection and payment.

A large section of this chapter is devoted to online privacy because privacy promises to be a complicated and thorny area that will have a dramatic impact on business. This topic is analyzed from both a business and a technological standpoint.

Finally, Appendix III at the end of the chapter discusses the issues involved with the use of spam, or unsolicited commercial e-mail.

Intellectual Property Issues

An IP is any product of human intellect that is unique or novel and has some value in the marketplace. In the context of e-business, IP examples include digital images, digital files, web sites, and online business models. IP laws protect the rights of the property owner (e.g., author, designer, photographer). A company can use three devices to protect its IP: patents, copyrights, and trademarks.

Patents provide the holder the exclusive right to prevent others from manufacturing, using, or selling the invention. A patent is granted for a period of twenty years. A *copyright* provides the author exclusive rights over his or her creation. Copyrights protect expressions, not the idea itself. In order to feature a copyrighted product on a web site, one must have the permission of the owner. If the owner detects unlawful usage, he or she can request that the product be taken off of the site. A trademark can be a logo, picture, image, musical phrase, and so forth (e.g., Microsoft logo). It must be registered with the U.S. Patents and Trademark Office to be enforced. A trademark is established through usage, not by invention or authorship.

The Internet and the Web raise many complex IP issues. The following discussion addresses several of the more interesting issues.

Issues Related to Linking

The Web uses HTML (i.e., hypertext). A link is a pathway to another site, and visitors go to a linked site by clicking on the link. Some linking practices are controversial from a legal perspective.

Consider the practice of *deep linking*—this occurs when site A has a link to site B, but the link is to a page other than site B's home page (e.g., linking to http://www.cnn.com/world, not http://www.cnn.com). This is viewed as a problem by site B because it may reduce the traffic to the home page, which may have banner ads. Moreover, deep linking disrupts the user's experience on site B—site B might want to control the user's experience by directing them to take a certain path.

Next, consider *meta-tags*—tags that help the "crawlers" from search engines locate sites and place them in different categories. The legal issue arises when site A places the name of site B in its meta-tag. If site A does that, everyone searching for site B is directed to site A. It is especially problematic when a competitor does that (e.g., Pepsi placing Coca Cola in its meta-tag).

Domain Names and Trademarks

Typically, a domain name is chosen because it is simple, intuitive, and suggestive of a brand name. Frequently, consumers search for a brand's web site by typing in "thenameofthebrand.

com." Therefore, a domain name is a valuable corporate asset. Consider a hypothetical brand, kawazoo, which has trademarked its brand name. If somebody other than this company owns the domain name kawazoo.com, there can be problems. Companies can sue such sites on the basis of trademark infringement, arguing that the practice creates customer confusion, dilutes the trademark, and constitutes unfair competition. ICANN, the international body in charge of domain names, has developed a uniform domain name dispute resolution policy that can be used to resolve these issues without going to court.

Business Methods Patents

Priceline.com operates a reverse auction—buyers make binding bids and sellers compete to sell to them. Even though the concept of a reverse auction is not new, Priceline.com obtained a patent on the process. This patent gives the company the right to exclude others from using this method to sell to customers. This and other business method patents in the e-business arena are viewed as controversial. On the one hand, some believe that businesses should have the right to protect their innovative business methods. On the other hand, critics argue that patenting methods that have existed for a long time can inhibit innovation.

Respect and Integrity

A number of Star Trek fans created web sites to talk about specific aspects of the show (e.g., certain characters). Paramount, the creator of Star Trek, sent out letters to the sites' webmasters in December 1996 demanding that they remove copyrighted materials within ten days or face legal action.[1] Although some members of the Star Trek community were unhappy with this action, the company explained that it was merely defending its copyright—the Internet allows end-users to copy other's work, pass it off as their own, or modify it.

Some argue that such activities do not threaten companies; however, others believe that companies have the right to protect their IP assets at all times. As with some of the other situations described later, the law in this area is complex and difficult to apply.

Digital Millennium Copyright Act of 1998

One of the most recent controversial cases in the copyright arena involved Napster. The music industry effectively used the Digital Millennium Copyright Act of 1998 to stifle Napster by forcing it to feature only music that is not copyrighted. The main points of this Act are as follows:[2]

- Makes it a crime to circumvent antipiracy measures built into most commercial software.
- Outlaws the manufacture, sale, or distribution of code-cracking devices used to illegally copy software.
- Permits the cracking of copyright protection devices to conduct encryption research, assess product interoperability, and test computer security systems.

- Provides exemptions from the anti-circumvention provisions for nonprofit libraries, archives, and educational institutions under certain circumstances.

- Limits the liability of ISPs for copyright infringement due to simply transmitting information over the Internet. ISPs, however, are expected to remove any material from users' web sites that appears to constitute a copyright infringement.

- Limits the liability of nonprofit institutions of higher education—when they serve as ISPs and under certain circumstances—for copyright infringement by faculty members or graduate students.

- Requires that "webcasters" pay licensing fees to record companies.

The Argument against Strong IP Protections

There is a growing school of thought (led by Lawrence Lessig) that excessively strong IP protections for firms are anticonsumer and anti-innovation. The copyright critics, for example, point out that software is generally provided copyright protection for ninety-five years and they argue that this was not the original intent. Moreover, studies now show that providing excessively strong IP protection does not always raise the level of innovation. As a result, there is a movement to modify the IP laws.

Internet Taxation[3]

Due to its vast scope and interconnected architecture, the Internet presents several taxation problems. Consider this scenario:

A company based in Portland, Oregon, has a web site on which it sells downloadable software. A consumer in London is interested in this software and downloads it, paying by credit card. The software is transferred to the consumer's PC in seconds.

This scenario raises three interesting questions:

- Is this a product-based or a service-based transaction?

- Who must collect the tax revenue?

- To whom does the tax revenue belong?

The first question involves the concept of *jurisdiction*. In the tax code, there is a clear designation of who deserves to receive the tax from any given transaction. In our scenario, the "who" is not clear. Who deserves to get the tax on this transaction—the authorities in the United Kingdom or the United States? Should the tax revenue be shared by the local, state, and federal levels?

Answering the second question is tricky. One way to resolve the problem is to ask the seller to collect all taxes and ensure that they are remitted to the appropriate authority. However, sellers argue that this process is terribly complicated and places a major financial burden on them. For example, there are approximately 6,000 taxing jurisdictions in the United States. If consumers are required to pay a tax, chances are they will not, and enforcement becomes a nightmare.

Currently, sellers are required to collect tax on the sale of some products, but not others. To understand why this happens, one must understand the concept of *nexus*. In a famous 1992 case, *Quill v. North Dakota*, 504 U.S. 298, the U.S. Supreme Court held that a remote seller (a catalog) could be required to collect sales tax only if the seller had the requisite nexus with the buyer's state; for example, the seller has a sales office or a sales agent in the buyer's state. If nexus is absent, the state cannot ask the seller to collect sales tax. For example, because Amazon.com is based in the state of Washington, only citizens in that state are charged sales tax.

Specific characteristics of the Internet and e-commerce created these problems:

1. The Internet allows for PC-to-PC transactions without a paper trail. Traditionally, taxing authorities have used a paper trail as the basis for determining taxes.

2. Electronic delivery of goods such as e-books and MP3 files.

3. Lack of information about buyers and sellers.

4. Global access to buyers and sellers.

In the United States, the Internet Tax Freedom Act was passed in 1998. The Act imposed a moratorium on placing new and discriminatory federal and state taxes on Internet-based transactions. The Act's provisions were recently extended to November 1, 2003. This moratorium does not prohibit the imposition of sales taxes on e-commerce transactions; rather, it prohibits new taxes.

The EU has adopted three regulations to govern Internet taxation:

1. No new or additional taxes will be considered for e-commerce; rather, existing taxes will be adapted so that they can be applied to e-commerce.

2. Electronic deliveries will not be considered goods; rather, they will be treated as services.

3. Only services consumed in Europe should be taxed in Europe (i.e., taxation should take place in the jurisdiction where consumption takes place).

In the future, Internet transactions will be taxed; however, a major international effort is necessary so that this is done in a fair, consistent, and efficient manner.

Privacy Online—An In-Depth Look

Privacy is the right to be left alone. It is the individual consumer's right to be in control of the personal information that describes every activity in his or her life.

In the digital space created by the Internet, customer information is arguably one of the most valuable commodities. Marketers covet it as a means to reach consumers in a more targeted manner. The following are some examples of how information is used by some e-businesses:

- Infomediaries collect customer information so that they can sell aggregate market research reports to interested firms.

- Permission marketing is based on better promotion targeting using customer interest data. Typically, consumers fill out a survey indicating their interests and preferences before entering into a relationship. This information is used to target promotions to the consumer.

- Personalization efforts involve building a customer profile based on previous shopping behavior, product preferences, and so forth.

- Banner advertising by companies such as DoubleClick and 24/7 Media involve keeping large databases that target consumers based on cookie information (discussed later).

In all of these situations, building a large customer database with individual profile information is an unavoidable step. There can be no e-business without a customer database. The issue then becomes how can a business manage customer information in an ethical and proper manner to ensure the success of their programs.

Controversies surrounding privacy are frequently reported in the press. Some of the more recent prominent examples include:[4]

- In July 2000, the FTC forced the bankrupt toy e-tailer, Toysmart.com, to abandon its plans to sell off its customer data to the highest bidder. The firm had promised site users that it would not divulge the information gleaned from tracking its users' activities on the site, but a court-appointed overseer believed the customer list was a valuable asset that should be sold to help pay the firm's creditors.

- In August 2000, Toysrus.com was accused of feeding shoppers' personal information to a data-analysis firm without revealing the relationship to consumers. In response to complaints, Toysrus.com added information to its privacy policy about how customer data is treated, but denies that the information is sold to outside vendors.

- In April 1999, IBM announced that it would not advertise on any site that does not have a privacy policy.[5]

- In November 1999, it was discovered that Real Networks (the streaming media company) was associating personal customer information with listening behavior using both the Real Player and Real Jukebox. The company changed this policy for future product releases.[6]

- In August 2001, a report by Cyveillance found that sites such as Yahoo! and AOL use covert monitoring technology known as Web bugs to track visitors to personal web pages without the knowledge of the page creator.[7]

- In August 2001, in response to criticism by privacy advocates, Microsoft announced that it was going to reduce the amount of information users have to provide as part of the Passport service—an integral part of Microsoft XP.[8]

How Do Managers Think of Privacy?

There is currently a broad spectrum of attitudes about privacy among business leaders. On one extreme are people like Scott McNealy, CEO of Sun Microsystems, who said, "You have zero privacy anyway. Get used to it."[9] Similarly, Bob Wientzen, president and CEO of the Direct Marketing Association said,[10] "(As consumers) we long ago quit worrying about safeguarding every piece of information about ourselves."

Others have said that some online firms are being lambasted needlessly. For example, an article in *The New York Times* stated that "the information collected by advertising networks is so fragmentary and so laden with errors that it is practically useless."[11] But, to privacy advocates, even the fact that they are trying to track consumers is objectionable.

There is a new wave of thinking among online firms that views privacy as a competitive advantage. Companies who take this approach are touting their superior privacy policy as an advantage to attract new customers. Consider this example:[12]

EarthLink, an Atlanta-based Internet service provider, has launched a $5 million-plus ad campaign aimed at positioning the company as a haven for those concerned about privacy. The company doesn't sell any customer data, and it provides privacy tools such as Spam filters on its site. In the third quarter of this year (2001), it will also be launching additional services, including ad blocking and IP address masking. "[Privacy] epitomizes our philosophy. We are there to serve our subscribers, not serve them up," says Claudia Caplan, EarthLink's vice president of brand marketing.

Overall, managers are quite diverse in their view of privacy.

Privacy and E-Commerce

The privacy of consumers is, of course, not an issue that is confined to the Internet or e-commerce—it is certainly a larger issue. Figure 14.1 is a map of all of the video cameras in the midtown Manhattan area put together by McCourt and Dahlman from the Department of Geography at the University of Kentucky. As is obvious from this figure, it is practically impossible to walk in this three-block area without surrendering one's privacy to an in-store camera.

So, how are privacy issues different in e-commerce? Following are three factors that make e-commerce different:[13]

- Exponentially increasing quantities of low-cost, digital information about individuals in corporate databases.

- Increased ability to easily share this information with others.

- Increased ability to combine disparate databases, and to mine those databases for information.

As one privacy consultant said,[14]

The ease and facility with which new technology allows data to be combined, collected, matched, transmitted, and otherwise manipulated in a nanosecond is a huge factor. What protected us, to

Figure 14.1
Uideo Camera Map of
Midtown Manhattan

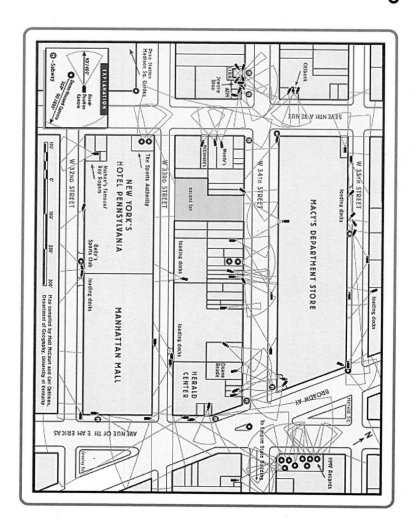

Source: Allan Reader, "To See and Be Seen," *The Atlantic Monthly,* July 1998, http://www.theatlantic.com/issues/98/jul/largemap.htm. Compiled by Matt McCourt and Carl Dahlman, Department of Geography, University of Kansas.

How Americans Think of Privacy

It is commonly understood that consumers typically fall into one of three categories when it comes to privacy.[15] The first set of people are called *privacy fundamentalists* (approximately 25% of the population). They are deeply concerned about privacy rights and potential invasions of privacy, and they reject any consumer benefits that require an oversight of their activity or the release of data about themselves.

At the other end of the spectrum are *the privacy unconcerned* (12% of the population)—people who don't care to think about privacy, don't have a problem with giving their

an extent, in the past was a wall of paper. Yes, the information was there, but it was scattered about and you had to really look to find it. Now electronic communication allows that wall to be penetrated very easily.

Moreover, with the Internet, greater amounts of consumer information are moving from the private realm to the public realm. For example, anyone can now look up the salary of a university employee at the University of Washington, and students can read the teaching evaluations of all of the university's professors.

information away, and don't worry at all about how that information might be used. (A quote that summarizes their attitude is: "If McDonald's offered a free Big Mac for a DNA sample, there would be lines around the block.")

Most people (63%) fall into an intermediate category called *privacy pragmatists*. Such people are always balancing the potential benefits from and threats involved with sharing information. They are particularly concerned about the secondary use (deliberate or inadvertent) of information that was originally divulged for one purpose only. Depending on what the privacy pragmatists receive in return for their information, they are willing to forsake different degrees of privacy protection.

Pew Internet Reports conducted a survey of over 2,117 Americans in July 2000.[16] The highlights of their report include:

- Individuals were in favor of permission marketing—about 86% of users favored opt-in as opposed to opt-out.

- The response for personalization was less positive—only 27% of users indicated that tracking is helpful because it allows the sites to provide information tailored to specific consumers.

- Users are unaware of privacy-related technologies—only 9% of Internet users had used encryption to scramble their e-mail, 5% of Internet users had used "anonymizing" software that hides their computer identity from the web sites they visit, and 56% of Internet users could not identify the primary online tracking tool (i.e., cookies).

- Concerns about privacy caused about 24% of individuals to provide fake personal information.

- 94% of Internet users wanted privacy violators to be disciplined with punishments up to a jail sentence.

- Privacy concerns typically did not stop individuals from using the Internet for a variety of activities.

Other surveys also have indicated strong sentiments about privacy, including:

- Georgia Tech's GVU lab's eighth survey consistently found that privacy is viewed as an important issue involving the Internet. The latest survey revealed that 72% of Internet users believe there should be new laws to protect privacy. The survey also found that 82% of users object to the sale of personal information.[17]

- A June 2001 Gallup poll found that 66% of users felt that the government must pass laws to protect the privacy of the citizens.

Consumers are understandably nervous about how their information is used by companies. As Jason Catlett from Junkbusters said,[18] "Consumers fear giving out information because they know they have almost no rights once it is out of their hands. If people had the right to force companies to delete information about them, they would more readily provide personal information."

This does not, however, stop individuals from giving out personal information if they think they will get something in return. In fact, "a Jupiter Research survey found that

65 percent of respondents would provide information online if they had a guarantee that the information would not be misused and 39 percent say they would do so to enter a sweepstakes. Other incentives to give up data include emails on products and services; access to more or better content; and the chance to gain affinity points, such as frequent-flyer miles."[19]

Approaches to Preserve Customer Privacy

There are at least three different approaches to preserve the privacy of customers. The *legislative approach* is based on the belief that most firms think like McNealy of Sun in that they don't really care about customer privacy. As a result, only passing laws either at the state or federal level can change behavior.

The industry has proposed a *self-regulation approach*. Their contention is that they can act responsibly when it comes to privacy. The main proposals in this area have been: privacy policies, independent third-party seal of approval programs and the Platform for Privacy Preferences (PPP) initiative.

Finally, the *technology-based approach* contends that neither the legislative nor the self-regulation approach empowers the customer. The legislative approach may protect the consumer—but only after the fact—e.g., through punitive damages. Similarly, some privacy advocates are skeptical of the self-regulation approach. The following discussion focuses on the self-regulation and technological approaches.

Self-Regulation

Privacy Principles

The starting point for self-regulation is the set of principles developed by the FTC. In a 1998 report, the FTC identified four fair information practices that firms must use online.[20] These principles are now widely accepted.

1. Notice. Data collectors must disclose their information practices before collecting personal information from consumers.

2. Choice. Consumers must be given options with respect to whether and how personal information collected from them may be used for purposes beyond those for which the information was collected.

3. Access. Consumers must be able to view and contest the accuracy and completeness of data collected about them.

4. Security. Data collectors must take reasonable steps to ensure that the information collected from consumers is accurate and secure from unauthorized use.

Notice is perhaps the most important of these four principles. Read, for example, the excerpt from the Direct Marketing Association's online privacy guidelines attached as Appendix I.

The Code of Fair Information Practices was primarily the contribution of the HEW (Health, Education, Welfare) Advisory Committee on Automated Data Systems.[21] The Advisory Committee released its report in July 1972. This code is based on five principles:

1. There must be no secret personal data record-keeping systems.

2. There must be a way for people to determine what information about them is in a record and how it is used.

3. There must be a way for people to prevent information about them that was obtained for one purpose from being used or made available for other purposes without their consent.

4. There must be a way for people to correct or amend a record of identifiable information about them.

5. Any organization creating, maintaining, using, or disseminating records of identifiable personal data must ensure the reliability of the data for its intended use and must take precautions to prevent misuses of the data.

Europe's OECD and the EU also have developed privacy guidelines. The primary guidelines include:[22]

- Limits on the collection of personal data.
- Personal data must be relevant and accurate.
- The purpose for which the data will be used must be stated clearly.
- Personal data can be used only for the purposes for which it is collected.
- Data should be safeguarded.
- An individual has the right to request his personal information.
- Major restrictions are placed on the transborder flow of personal information.

Privacy Policy

The FTC fair information principles influence the design of privacy policies by online firms—a good privacy policy addresses each principle.

A privacy policy can be as short as one sentence. For example, Seth Godin's site (http://www.permission.com) has this policy: "Note: we will never rent or sell your e-mail address to anyone." Others can be one or two paragraphs. For example, Carson's Publications' (http://www.carsonpub.com) privacy policy states:

This carsonspub.com privacy statement is very easy to follow because we are 100% dedicated to protecting your privacy, which is exactly why we do not collect any personal information on you in any way whatsoever. The only information we do collect is how many people visit the site, just numbers.

We do not really care who you are, where you come from or where you are going. We do not use cookies because we wouldn't even begin to know how. We do not share this information that we do not collect with anyone because there is not any collected information and we are here all alone, we don't have anyone to share it with. Thank you for looking into our privacy statement. Refreshing isn't it?

Most large companies have larger privacy policies (e.g., Amazon.com's policy is four pages long).

Are privacy policies sufficient to protect consumer privacy? The answer, generally, is no, because there are many problems with privacy policies. First, a privacy policy is not a contract. Second, a corporation typically reserves the right to modify its privacy policy at any point without prior notice to the consumer. For example, Amazon.com changed its privacy policy to indicate that it was free to transfer customer information if it bought a new company or sold itself.[23]

Also, most privacy policies are full of "legalese" and do not build trust with the consumer. Most consumers view the policy as a device to protect the firm from legal action instead of a forum for communicating the firm's intentions on how it handles privacy issues.

Finally, it is not clear whether privacy policies are impacting consumer behavior. For example, it is not known how many privacy policies are actually read by consumers. Many companies indicate that a very small percent of the traffic to the site is directed to the section on privacy.

Permission Marketing

As discussed in Chapter 12, permission marketing provides a new way of transacting with customers. Individuals indicate their interests and preferences and receive promotional messages targeted to them. In general, consumers can either opt-in (i.e., explicitly provide permission) or opt-out (i.e., have the freedom to stop transacting with the firm). Opt-in favors the customer, while opt-out favors the company.

Companies must be careful what they tell customers when they collect personal information. There must be a clear understanding of the level of permission provided. If the company wishes to change its policy at any time, consumers must be provided the freedom to opt-out.

Many implementation issues arise to ensure that the data gathered is consistent with the level of permission provided by consumers. First, a company has many channels of communication with the customer. If an individual opts out of one channel, does that automatically mean the customer should be removed from other lists? This is a major issue in the financial industry, for example, where a new law called the Gramm-Leach-Bliley Act requires banks to automatically opt-out a customer if the individual has so requested on one channel.[24]

Second, there is the issue of ensuring that the right person has provided permission. For example, person X may enroll persons Y and Z for a new service without their knowledge. When the company starts sending its e-mails to Y and Z, they may become irritated and call the company a spammer (see Appendix III for an in-depth discussion of spam). To avoid this problem, many companies now use a *double opt-in* system—individuals Y and Z receive a confirming e-mail and must take a specific action (e.g., replying, clicking on a link) to confirm their intentions.

Third, there is some ambiguity about when information can be shared with other parties. Most large e-businesses share some customer information with others and say so in their privacy policy. The question raised is: "Is permission transferable?" If I provide permission to firm 1, can it sell the information to firm 2, and does this automatically mean that firm 2 can send me messages? Some firms believe that this is true if firm 2 allows the individual to opt-out. However, a more stringent standard does not permit this type of information transfer. Indeed, the Gramm–Leach–Bliley Act mentioned earlier does not allow banks to do this.

Firms must carefully craft their permission marketing programs to ensure that the privacy of individuals is protected, while still providing the company a path to target customers. The Direct Marketing Association privacy guidelines in Appendix I may be used for this purpose.

Seal Programs

Because there are several problems with privacy policies, one approach to build the trust of consumers is the use of a third-party seal program—members agree to be audited on their privacy practices. Only those firms who meet the third party's requirements may display the seal on their web site. As a result, consumers who view the seal are immediately satisfied that the site has satisfied a set of requirements having to do with privacy.

The top two privacy seal programs are run by TrustE and Better Business Bureau (BBB) Online. TrustE is a nonprofit organization that allows licensees to display its seal on their web site if they meet certain requirements. Each licensee has to agree to an audit of its privacy practices and must agree to post a privacy policy. BBB Online's privacy seal program is part of the famous bureau's foray into the online arena.

Unfortunately, there are also problems with seal programs, including:

- The number of firms that have signed up for such programs is not very large. For example, TrustE reported that it had less than 2,000 members in June 2000. Compare this with the large number of firms online. Moreover, prominent firms such as Amazon.com have not signed up with TrustE.

- Although such seals may impact consumer perception, it is not clear whether the level of privacy being offered is indeed higher. This is compounded by TrustE's poor record of reprimanding members who have violated the privacy principles.

Platform for Privacy Preferences (PPP)

This initiative aims to automate the communication between a user and a web site as it relates to privacy. It works as follows:[25]

- A consumer's personal information is stored in his or her browser (e.g., Internet Explorer) in a standard format (name, address, credit card information).

- Web site privacy policies are translated into a standard format by answering a series of standard questions.

- The user sets their "preferences" in their browser. These preferences are based on the answers to the standard set of questions used by the web site (e.g., question to web site: Does web site release personal information to third parties? Possible answers: Yes, No, or Yes with specific permission from the user. User preference: If answer is "Yes" don't release information, if answer is "yes with specific permission" or "No" show a warning box).

- The privacy policy data is placed in a specific file at the web site and the user's browser automatically downloads the privacy policy when the site is accessed.

- The privacy policy is then compared to the user preferences and decisions are made automatically to transfer information, not to transfer information, or to show a warning before the transfer.

The proponents of PPP claim that it will ensure that an information transfer takes place only with sites that meet the privacy preferences of the individual. The critics of PPP have dubbed it *pretty poor privacy*. The concerns about PPP are summarized as follows:[26]

- It is designed not to protect data privacy but to facilitate the gathering of data by web sites. Were it designed to protect data privacy, it would make it harder, not easier, for users to pass their personal information to requesting sites.

- It oversimplifies and quite possibly misrepresents the trust interaction—always in favor of the web site that is asking for an individual's information.

- Many people do not understand that "privacy practices" are not the same as "privacy." PPP, therefore, allows sites to create an air of privacy while they gather personal data.

- It is a very one-sided information exchange: there are detailed data elements relating to the user (name, address, place of work, date of birth) and no data elements relating to the requestor.

- There is nothing about PPP that enforces or even aids in the enforcement of the "deals" that are struck through its algorithms. In this sense, PPP embraces the technical while ignoring the entire social context within which such a technical solution should exist.

Technology–Based Approach

The technology-based approach places the onus of privacy protection on the consumers. Several technologies have been developed to ensure the privacy of the individual during an online experience.

Secure E–Mail Services

In general, e-mail communication is not secure. All messages are sent through routers, and messages may be logged and backed up along the way. As a result, messages can be intercepted at intermediate storage points, compromising the privacy of the communication. To overcome this problem, several secure e-mail services are available. Some of the leading services are Hushmail.com, Ziplip.com, SafeMessage, Private Messenger, Mail2Web, and Ensuredmail. Mail2Web has now extended its service to cellular phones.

Anonymous Remailers

Remailers are designed to allow completely anonymous communication between two parties. Party A sends an e-mail to the remailer. The remailer strips away any form of identification and forwards it on to party B. A confirmation is sent to party A indicating that the e-mail has been sent to party B. When party B responds, the e-mail once again goes to the remailer. The remailer once again strips away all forms of identification before forwarding the e-mail to party A. More details about remailers are available at http://www.andrebacard.com/remail.html.

Anonymous Surfing Tools

Many software packages now allow users to browse anonymously. A great example of such a package is Zero Knowledge's Freedom.[27] This package allows users to create "nyms" or pseudonyms. These are identities the user creates for his or her online activities. The only difference is that the nym cannot be traced back to the user.

Cookie Cutters

Several programs now help consumers eliminate cookies (see Appendix II for an explanation of cookies). An example is Cookie Crusher available at http://www.thelimitsoft.com/cookie.html. Such programs allow consumers to accept or reject cookies before they are dropped. Eliminating all cookies is not in the consumer's best interest because they will not be able to shop in some stores and will have to remember their user name and password.

Disposable Credit Card Numbers

Because there is some concern among users that credit card numbers are not secure, leading credit card companies have adopted technologies that let users use credit cards in a secure way. American Express is a leader in this field—it provides its users disposable credit card numbers that are uniquely generated for each session. The credit card number expires after one online session.[28] Other cards, including Discovery, now offer similar services.

● Conclusion

We have discussed three important public policy issues related to the Internet: intellectual property, taxation, and privacy. All three play an important role in conducting business online. Managers must develop a solid understanding of these issues to be successful.

344

Notes

(All URLs are current as of April 8, 2002.)

1. Steve Silberman, "Paramount Locks Phasers on Trek Fan Sites," December 18, 1996, <http://www.wired.com/news/culture/0,1284,1076,00.html>.

2. The UCLA Online Institute for Cyberspace Law and Policy, "The Digital Millennium Copyright Act," <http://www.gseis.ucla.edu/iclp/dmca1.htm>.

3. I benefited from Global Internet Policy Institute, "Taxation of E-Commerce," 2000, <http://www.gipiproject.org/taxation/>, <http://www.ecommercetax.com/faq.htm> and Robert Sommers, "Taxation of E-Commerce," August 8, 2000, <http://www.taxprophet.com/pubs/outlines/Ecommerce.PDF> in writing this section.

4. Pew Internet and American Life, "Trust and Privacy Online: Why Americans Want to Rewrite the Rules," August 20, 2000, <http://www.pewinternet.org/reports/reports.asp?Report=19& Section=ReportLevel1&Field=Level1ID&ID=44>.

5. N. Wang, "IBM to Spurn Sites that Lack Privacy Policies," Internet World, 17 (April 12, 1999).

6. Chris Oakes and Jennifer Sullivan, "Real Damage Control—Again," November 6, 1999, <http://www.wired.com/news/technology/0,1282,32350,00.html>.

7. John Schwartz, "Web Bugs Are Tracking Use of Internet," Nytimes.com, August 14, 2001.

8. Accessed August 2001, http://www.msnbc.com/news/611917.asp?0si=-&cp1=1.

9. Polly Sprenger, "Sun on Privacy: Get Over it," January 26, 1999, <http://www.wired.com/news/politics/0,1283,17538,00.html>.

10. Jennifer Gilbert, "Privacy? Who Needs Privacy?," January 2001, <http://www.business2.com/articles/mag/0,1640,14437,FF,html>.

11. Rebecca Lynch, "What's All the Fuss About?," October 1, 2000, <http://www.cio.com/archive/100100_fuss,html>.

12. Dainty Duffy, "Get Ready for the Privacy Backlash," August 2001, <http://www.darwinmag.com/read/080101/backlash.html>.

13. Ian Graham, "Putting Privacy in Context: An Overview of the Concept of Privacy and of Current Technologies," June 28, 1999, <http://www.utoronto.ca/ian/privacy/privacy.html>.

14. Joann Greco, "Privacy: Whose Right Is It Anyhow?," The Journal of Business Strategy, 22(1) (2001): 32–35.

15. This is based on Toby Lester, "The Reinvention of Privacy," March 2001, <http://www.theatlantic.com/issues/2001/03/lester-p3.htm> and is based on the work of Alan Westin, the author of Privacy and Freedom.

16. Pew Internet and American Life, "Trust and Privacy Online."

17. Electronic Privacy Information Center, "Public Opinion on Privacy," <http://www.epic.org/privacy/survey>.

18. Gilbert, "Privacy? Who Needs Privacy?"

19. Ibid.

20. Federal Trade Commission, "Privacy Online: Fair Information Practices in the Electronic Marketplace," May 2000, <http://www.ftc.gov/reports/privacy2000/privacy2000.pdf>.

21. Taken from "1980: OECD Guidelines on the Protection of Privacy and Transborder Flows of Personal Data," <http://www.databasenation.com/cifp.htm#1980>.

22. Details are available at OECD, "Guidelines on the Protection of Privacy and Transborder Flows of Personal Data," <http://www.oecd.org/dsti/sti/it/secur/prod/PRIV-en.HTM>.

23. Matt Gallaway, "Amazon's Privacy Woes," December 12, 2000, <http://www.business2.com/articles/web/0,1653,8978,00.html>.

24. Mary Jo Parrino, "The Regulators Tackle Privacy," March 2000, <http://www.fmcenter.org/fmc_superpage.asp?ID=337>.

25. Privacy.net, "Platform for Privacy Preferences," <http://www.privacy.net/p3p>.

26. Karen Coyle, "P3P: Pretty Poor Privacy? A Social Analysis of the Platform for Privacy Preferences (P3P)," June 1999, <http://www.kcoyle.net/p3p.html>.

27. Accessed August 2001, http://www.freedom.net/faq/basic.html#3.

28. Maria Trombly, "American Express Offers Disposable Credit Card Numbers for Online Shopping," 2000, <http://www.computerworld.com/cwi/story/0,1199,NAV47_STO49788,00.html>.

29. This section is primarily based on Cookiecentral.com, "Cookies and Privacy FAQ," <http://www.cookiecentral.com>.

30. Scott Rosenberg, "Defending the Cookie Monster," May 7, 2001, <http://www.salon.com/tech/col/rose/2001/05/07/cookies/index1.html>.

31. Jupiter Media Metrix, "E-Mail Marketing to Soar to $7.3 Billion in 2005 Cannibalizing 13% of Direct Mail Revenues," May 8, 2000, <http://www.jmm.com/xp/jmm/press/2000/pr_050800.xml>.

32. Carolyn Duffy, "MsgTo.com Promises to Eradicate Spam," July 15, 1999, <http://www.cnn.com/tech/computing/9907/15/antispam.idg>.

33. Douglas Deckmyn, "Critics Say Self-Regulation Effort May 'Legitimize' Spam," Computerworld 33(35) (1999): 41.

34. Duffy, "MsgTo.com Promises to Eradicate Spam."

35. Accessed August 2001, http://www.spamsummit.com/presentations/leo/.

36. Randall Boe, "Testimony to Committee on Commerce, U.S. House of Representatives," September 28, 1998, <http://legal.web.aol.com/resources/legislation/housespam.html>.

REVIEW / CHAPTER 14

Discussion Questions

1. Can you think of a situation where company A might sue company B for having a link to A's site?

2. Are IP standards for digital products, such as software, too high? Do consumers deserve access to the source code of software before ninety-five years have passed?

3. Is the Internet very different from catalogs when it comes to taxation?

4. Do you think the EU and OECD principles on Internet taxation should be adopted in the United States?

5. The chapter discussed three privacy segments—the privacy unconcerned, the privacy fundamentalists, and the privacy pragmatists. Which segment would you place yourself in? Why? As a manager, should you pay attention to the loud complaints of the fundamentalists even when a large number of your customers are pragmatists or unconcerneds?

6. Has the privacy policy of an e-tailer ever influenced your behavior at its site? Have you ever looked at a privacy policy?

E-Tasks

1. Watch the movie "The Truman Show." Then, answer the following questions:
   a. Would you be willing to participate in a project such as "Truman"? Would you be willing to participate as an actor?
   b. Did the company actually benefit Truman by providing him a great life with a house, a job, and a wife? Were they doing him a favor?
   c. Should the company have told Truman at some point? Would that have made matters better?
   d. Why are individuals willing to provide a window into their life on reality television and web cams? What does that say about the consumer?

2. Visit http://www.privacy.net. Click on the link that says "Analyze your connection." Carefully read all of the information that is being passed on about you to web site owners. What pieces of information would you most like to block access to?

3. Visit http://www.spamcop.net. They allow users to send a public spam report to network administrators. Will this be effective in fighting spam?

APPENDIX I / CHAPTER 14

Extract from DMA's Online Privacy Guidelines

The notice should be easy to find, easy to read, and easy to understand.

A marketer should post its notice so as to readily enable the consumer to learn about the marketer's information practices in a manner that permits a consumer effective choice over the collection and disclosure of personal information.

For example, a marketer operating a World Wide Web site that collects personal information from individuals who visit it could post notice of its information practices on its home page or on the page where information is collected (e.g., survey questionnaire).

A marketer could provide an icon on its home page that, when clicked, will furnish the consumer with access to additional screens disclosing the marketer's information practices.

The notice should identify the marketer, disclose an e-mail and postal address at which it can be contacted, and state whether the marketer collects personal information online from individuals. If the marketer collects personal information online, the notice should contain disclosures about:

The nature of personal information collected with respect to individual consumers Depending on the circumstances, information collected about a consumer may include:

1. contact or locator information (such as name, postal and e-mail addresses),

2. billing information (such as financial accounts and credit card numbers),

3. transactional information (such as data on purchases a consumer makes),

4. navigational information (such as data revealing consumers' preferences or the choices they make among the range of products, services, or sites, and the times of day purchases are made), and

5. the content of correspondence or messages directed to a marketer.

For example, a marketer could include language such as: "We keep the information you provide in responding to our questionnaire."

Or, "We maintain your name, postal and e-mail addresses, telephone number, and payment and order processing information. We also may keep information on your communications with our customer service representatives." Or, "We collect information on the times and ways you use our web site."

Source: Direct Marketing Association, "Direct Marketing Association's Online Marketing Guidelines and Do the Right Thing," http://www.the-dma.org/library/guidelines/onlineguidelines.shtml.

APPENDIX I / CHAPTER 14

The Nature of Uses of Such Information

The information may be used, for example, to ensure that a consumer is properly billed, for marketing by e-mail, or for evaluating and understanding consumer reactions to content, services, or merchandise offered online. It also may include using the consumer's name and address for marketing by mail or other media.

For example, a marketer could include language such as:

> We will use your e-mail address only to contact you about merchandise or services you have indicated are of interest to you." Or, "We use information for billing purposes and to measure consumer interest in our various services or pages.

The Nature and Purpose of Disclosures of Such Information, and the Types of Persons to Which Disclosures May Be Made

This may include disclosure of names, postal and e-mail addresses to other merchants for marketing purposes, or to firms that conduct market research for the marketer, or disclosure of additional information for bill collection purposes.

The Mechanism by Which the Individual May Limit the Disclosure of Such Information

An opt-out will traditionally be the means offered to consumers to limit the disclosure of information collected about them.

APPENDIX II / CHAPTER 14

Understanding Cookies[29]

Technically speaking, cookies are a device to overcome the "statelessness" of the Internet. The way the Internet is designed, a web site can only see what you do in one session. As soon as that session ends (e.g., by logging off), the site knows nothing about you and has no way of learning when you return to the site. Therefore, simply put, cookies are a way by which a site tracks a user across different sessions.

A cookie is a small text file that is stored on a consumer's hard drive. They are a mechanism by which a web site can deliver simple data to a user's computer, request that the user's PC store the information, and, in certain circumstances, return the information to the web site when needed.

It is possible for any person to view his or her cookies and delete them. It is also possible for a user to change the browser settings so that cookies are rejected; however, most people do not do this because the browser cannot differentiate between "good" and "bad" cookies.

Some cookies can be useful. The following four scenarios illustrate the most common ways in which they enhance the browsing experience:

Alice is shopping at a particular web site that uses a shopping cart. She puts items into a shopping cart by clicking a link or an "Add to Shopping Cart" button. Cookies are used to store the contents of Alice's shopping cart so that she can continue to browse after adding an item to the cart. In this way, she can purchase a cart full of items rather than one item at a time.

Bob clicks around a web site that allows its users to view articles for a small charge. Cookies are used to store information about which articles he has viewed (i.e., a list of URLs) so that he can pay for them all at once (say, monthly) rather than each time he downloads an article.

Carl fills out a web site's form with his name, address, and other information. Cookies are used to store this information so that the next time Carl visits the site, the information is automatically uploaded and he doesn't have to provide it again. If the form contains sensitive information, such as a credit card number or a mailing address, the cookies can be delivered over the Secure Sockets Layer, which encrypts the information.

Don logs in to a web site that requires a user name and password. When Don's user name and password pair is successfully verified, the server passes down a cookie that functions as a "guest pass," allowing him access to certain areas of the web site. After a set time period, perhaps half an hour or a day, the guest pass expires and Don must log in again.

APPENDIX II / CHAPTER 14

Cookies cannot allow remote web sites to surreptitiously gather information from a consumer's hard drives. They also do not pass sensitive information such as an e-mail address unless the user has entered it and given permission to pass it on. Cookies issued by one site cannot be read by others.

Salon's Scott Rosenberg indicated that cookies are relatively benign for the following reasons:[30]

- Because cookies are simple text files, as opposed to executable code, they cannot propagate or create any sort of damage on the hard drive.

- The user remains in control and does not have to go through an opt-out procedure. He or she can simply delete the cookie.

APPENDIX III / CHAPTER 14

An In-Depth Analysis of Spam

Firms are increasingly using e-mail as a marketing tool to acquire customers, make them aware of new products, and build deep customer relationships. According to Jupiter Communications, the average number of commercial e-mail messages that U.S. online consumers receive annually will increase from 40 in 1999 to more than 1,600 in 2005.[31]

A significant portion of these commercial e-mails is likely to be unsolicited or spam. Most Internet users are affected by spam—over 90% of users receive spam at least once a week, almost 50% get spammed six or more times per week.[32] A majority of consumers perceive spam negatively. One of every three online consumers reported that they do not read e-mail from senders they don't know, and 16% said that they immediately delete messages that are not from friends, family, or colleagues.[33] Moreover, a survey showed that ISPs lose 7.2% of their new customers every year due to spam.[34]

Problems with Spam

Spam is a problem for consumers for four reasons—volume, irrelevance, offensiveness, and deceptiveness.

1. Volume. Most individuals generally feel that they receive a high level of promotional messages. Spam easily exacerbates this problem because the cost of obtaining a new e-mail address is minimal and the marginal cost of contacting an additional customer is nearly zero. Spammers easily obtain new e-mail addresses from web sites and Usenet groups by using software programs that "troll" the Internet and harvest addresses from such public sources as web pages and chat rooms. Because individuals provided their addresses at these places for other purposes, this "harvesting" violates their privacy rights. In addition, marketers incur nearly the same cost whether they send out 1 million or 10 million e-mails because of the automation of the e-mail transmission process. Therefore, high volumes of e-mail are disseminated continually.

2. Irrelevance. Most spam is irrelevant for most consumers. Marketers recognized the need to target a subset of customers early on because the cost of targeting the entire population is overwhelming and wasteful. Hence, the general approach to marketing can be best described as shown in Figure 14.2a. The outer ellipse represents the entire buying population, the shaded inner ellipse represents the targeted group, and the inner ellipse that is not shaded represents all users who find the message relevant.

As indicated earlier, the cost of obtaining an additional address and the cost of sending an additional e-mail is nearly zero. Therefore, even though a small proportion of the population is likely to be interested in a product, spammers are better off sending the message to everyone. With spam, the picture looks like Figure 14.2b. The outer ellipse is the entire population, which is targeted with the message. The inner ellipse that is unshaded represents those who find the message relevant.

Even though individuals care about receiving relevant promotional messages, they are likely to receive messages from spammers for pornography, offers to illegally sell them Viagra, get-rich-quick schemes, offers to sell e-mail addresses, and so on. Therefore, with spam, it is a certainty that a large portion of the population will not find a commercial message to be relevant.

3. Offensiveness. A significant portion of spam is offensive to many people. Some individuals view the Internet as a free and egalitarian space and are offended when they receive commercial messages for products they do not care about. Most people also con-

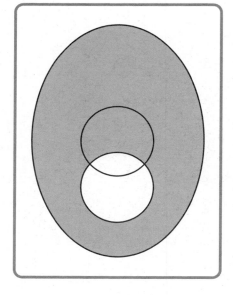

Figure 14.2a
Traditional Marketing
Message Targeting

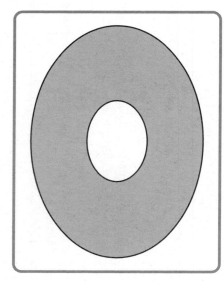

Figure 14.2b
Spam Targets
Indiscriminately

APPENDIX III / CHAPTER 14

sider spam to be offensive because the messages typically contain offensive material or use deceptive practices.

A survey[35] conducted by AT&T Worldnet asked consumers why they disliked spam. The top two reasons given were that it was time consuming to deal with and it obscured the legitimate e-mail that they received. Both of these reasons are driven by the high volume of messages.

Individuals are offended when they receive promotional messages for products that they consider inappropriate. For example, many individuals are offended when they receive ads for pornographic web sites at their workplace.

4. Deceptiveness. Deceptive practices are common with spam. For example, many spammers use forged e-mail headers (i.e., messages that mislead the recipient about the sender's identity). If a consumer tries to reply to the message, it bounces back or goes to a third party who is unaware of the spam. Such messages are, therefore, akin to direct mail packages without a return address. Another example of a deceptive practice is a misleading link. For example, consumers may receive a message that asks them to click on a link if they want to stop receiving such messages in the future. Clicking on the link either transports the consumer to, say, a pornographic site, or verifies for the spammer that the consumer's e-mail address is valid and the consumer receives even more spam.

In addition to consumers, spam also affects other stakeholders. Notable among them may be the ISPs that process the spam messages. AOL representatives testified in court that up to 30% of the messages it processes in a week may be spam.[36]

Responses to Spam

Many companies have recognized the harmful nature of spam, and their responses to spam fall into one of five categories. The first response category includes the laissez-faire attitude that spam is free commercial speech and, hence, nothing should be done to limit it. The second response type is technological. Companies such as Brightmail have proposed new methods to overhaul e-mail systems for the explicit purpose of limiting the extent of spam.

The third response category involves legislation. At least eighteen states have passed legislation limiting spam or are working on such legislation. In addition, there is an effort under way at the federal level—a law has just been approved by the House. The fourth response type has focused on consumer advocacy and education. Several nonprofit and industry groups have developed programs to spread the word about spam, blacklist spam advertisers, and provide consumers an opportunity to opt-out.

The last response category involves legitimate advertisers that wish to use e-mail as a marketing tool. They have proposed using a new technique of marketing to consumers called permission marketing (discussed in Chapter 12)—only marketers who have explicitly received permission to send an e-mail to a consumer may do so.

doubleclick.com

DoubleClick's Privacy Snafu: Case 6

Introduction

In February 2000, Internet marketing witnessed a major turning point. DoubleClick (http://www.doubleclick.com), the world's largest Internet advertising company, announced that it was shelving a major new plan to enhance its capability to target consumers with ads. The company had just paid $1 billion to acquire Abacus Direct Corporation, an aggregator of customer purchase history information from catalogs and department stores. Yet, just a few months after this acquisition, the company announced that it would not leverage the information made available to it through Abacus.

The company took this extraordinary step because of criticism that the new plan violates the privacy rights of consumers. The criticism came from such leading groups as the American Civil Liberties Union, the Center for Democracy and Technology, and the Electronic Privacy and Information Center.[1] For an example, read the open letter written by Jason Catlett, president of Junkbusters, in Appendix I. The harshest language perhaps came from the Michigan State attorney general, Jennifer Granholm, who accused the company of "cyber wire-tapping" in a formal announcement that it was suing the company.[2]

It had been a tumultuous month for the company. The stock price was at $120 in early February and had dropped to a low of $75 when the privacy criticism was at its peak. After the company announced its plans, the price went back up to $97.125.[3]

The general consensus is that Internet marketing has changed forever. Many questions swirled around: What exactly had happened? Why had DoubleClick taken this extraordinary step? What does it mean for Internet marketing in the future?

Background

DoubleClick was incorporated as a company in January 1996 and went public in February 1998. Figures C6.1, C6.2, and C6.3 show the phenomenal growth the company has had during its history.

As shown in Figure C6.1, the number of banner ads served up by the company has gone up from 5 billion in the first quarter of 1998 to a peak of 185 billion in the fourth quarter of 2000. During this time, the average growth rate between consecutive quarters was 29%.

Figure C6.2 shows the total number of customers in the DoubleClick advertising network. The total number of customers has risen from 1,400 in the first quarter of 1998 to a peak of 10,062 customers in the fourth quarter of 2000.

Figure C6.3 shows the trend in the gross revenue and the gross profit of the company. Once again, we see a phenomenal growth rate. The gross revenue has grown from $24.1 million in the first quarter of 1998 to a peak of $135.2 million in the third quarter of 2000. Similarly, the gross profit has risen from $12.2 million in the first quarter of 1998 to a peak of $77.9 million in the third quarter of 2000.

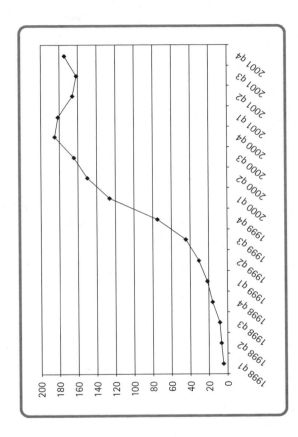

Figure C6.1
Number of Ads Served
(All figures in billions)

Source: Analyst Metrics available at DoubleClick's Investor Overview, http://media.corporate-ir.net/media_files/NSD/DCLK/reports/metricsq401.pdf. Reprinted by permission of DoubleClick Inc.

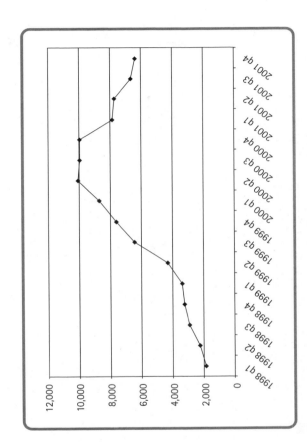

Figure C6.2
Total Number of Customers

Source: Analyst Metrics available at DoubleClick's Investor Overview, http://media.corporate-ir.net/media_files/NSD/DCLK/reports/metricsq401.pdf. Reprinted by permission of DoubleClick Inc.

Figure C6.3
Revenue and Profit
(All figures in millions)

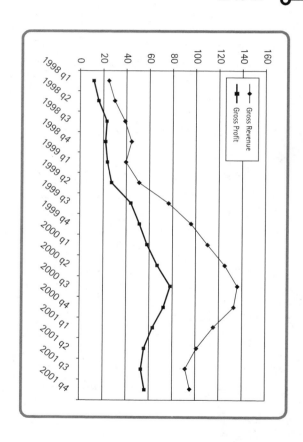

Source: Analyst Metrics available at DoubleClick's Investor Overview.
http://media.corporate-ir.net/media_files/NSD/DCLK/reports/metricsq401.pdf.

All indicators point to a profitable company with a sound growth rate. The more recent decline in the data on all three figures is from an overall weakness in the economy.

Targeting and the Internet

Targeting is the holy grail of marketing. Targeting provides a focus for the marketing effort, reduces the waste of marketing resources, and helps maximize profit by price discrimination. Most advertising media are not very good when it comes to the targeting ability they afford marketers. Consider a medium such as television—marketers can only "target on averages." If they want to target fifteen- to thirty-four-year-old females, they choose shows with an average customer profile that fits this description most closely. Of course, it is unlikely that *all* viewers of this show fall into the targeted category. As a result, some waste occurs (i.e., some ads are viewed by consumers who have no interest in them).

Direct marketing techniques, such as direct mail, promised to improve on the targeting.

However, these techniques have problems. For instance, they target consumers based on their past behavior and their demographics (e.g., gender, age, income). As a result, they do not generate high response rates (e.g., the average redemption rate for coupons is about 2%).

The Internet promised to usher in a new era of targeting technology. DoubleClick was one of the companies that recognized this early on and took a leadership role in delivering banner advertisements. Banners are small rectangles that appear on the top, bottom, and sides of a web site. When a user clicks on a banner, he or she is automatically taken to a web site selected by the advertiser.

The total expenditure on Internet advertising has skyrocketed over time. Table C6.1 indicates that spending in the first quarter of 1996 was approximately $30 million and spending at the peak in the fourth quarter of 2000 was $2.162 billion. Even though spending has decreased from this peak, the medium has established itself as a legitimate player. Moreover, according to the Internet Advertising Bureau, about

35% of the spending in the third quarter of 2001 was on banner advertisements, the strength of DoubleClick.

DoubleClick is an advertising network—it aggregates and matches demand from advertisers (for ads) with supply from publishers (i.e., ad space), benefitting both advertisers and publishers. Advertisers do not have to deal with a

wide variety of publishers to place their ads. Similarly, publishers have a reliable buyer for their advertising inventory. DoubleClick delivers millions of banner ads every day.

DoubleClick's DART system provides a state-of-the-art method to target consumers; however, all targeting done using banner advertising is covert—no customer input is solicited. When

Table C6.1
Total Spending on Internet Advertising

Year	Quarter	Amount (in millions)
1996	1	$ 30
1996	2	52
1996	3	76
1996	4	110
1997	1	130
1997	2	214
1997	3	227
1997	4	336
1998	1	351
1998	2	423
1998	3	491
1998	4	656
1999	1	693
1999	2	934
1999	3	1,217
1999	4	1,777
2000	1	1,953
2000	2	2,124
2000	3	1,986
2000	4	2,162
2001	1	1,893
2001	2	1,868
2001	3	1,792

Source: Compiled from press releases at Internet Advertising Bureau Home Page, http://www.iab.net.

you visit a web site, DoubleClick determines who you are and decides which ad is the best match for you. The company does this using cookies, unique identifiers, that are dropped onto your hard drive by all types of sites—including DoubleClick.

Cookies are small text files that uniquely identify each PC (see Appendix II in Chapter 14 for a discussion of cookies). These files are used by almost all e-commerce firms for a variety of applications (e.g., saving user name and password, filling a shopping cart with previous purchases). However, the cookie technology used by advertising networks such as DoubleClick is more powerful because it allows the advertisers to follow an individual as he or she browses on the Internet.

What DoubleClick Proposed

The cookie technology used by DoubleClick did not permit it to personally identify each user. They knew that a certain user logged on using a certain browser at a certain time and visited certain sites; however, they did not know if this person was Joe Blow or Jane Doe.

The acquisition of Abacus Direct Corporation changed all of that. Abacus is "the operator of a huge repository of consumer purchasing data, with a record of 2.9 billion transactions gleaned from everywhere from Williams-Sonoma Inc. stores to Federated Department Stores Inc.'s Bloomingdale's. If you've bought anything from a large department store or a catalog lately, Abacus probably has your name and address, what you bought and how much you spent."[4]

DoubleClick obtained from Abacus a detailed database of customer identity and purchase behavior information for 88 million U.S. households. The company intended to launch a targeting technology for banner ads that combined online information obtained from cookies with the offline information in the Abacus database.

Some sources suggest that DoubleClick has already amassed such detailed profiles on at least 150,000 individuals,[5] Privacy advocates suggested that this rich profile allowed DoubleClick to misuse sensitive financial and medical information.

FTC's Fair Information Practices

In a 1998 report, the FTC created four fair information practices that firms must use online.[6] These principles (see discussion in Chapter 14) are now widely cited and are likely to form the basis for future privacy legislation by the government. The principles are:

1. *Notice.* Data collectors must disclose their information practices before collecting personal information from consumers.

2. *Choice.* Consumers must be given options with respect to whether and how personal information collected from them may be used for purposes beyond which it was collected.

3. *Access.* Consumers must be able to view and contest the accuracy and completeness of the data collected about them.

4. *Security.* Data collectors must take reasonable steps to ensure that the information collected from consumers is accurate and secure from unauthorized use.

An analysis of the DoubleClick case on these principles allows us to identify possible infractions. Consumers were not provided with any notice that they were being tracked with cookies. Moreover, consumers did not give permission for the company to target them using personally identifiable information from the Abacus database.

After the criticisms of DoubleClick mounted, the company provided a site where individuals can opt-out of this tracking system. It is still available at http://optout.doubleclick.net/dclk/optout-success.html.

Privacy advocates have criticized this policy, saying that it does not provide an adequate choice to the consumer. They argue that instead of an opt-out policy, the company should choose an opt-in policy (discussed in Chapter 9). An opt-out policy's default setting places the burden on the consumers to exit the system. On the other hand, with an opt-in policy, only those consumers who are interested choose to enter the system. This is a contentious issue that has yet to be resolved.

Privacy advocates also pointed out that "opting out of the DoubleClick system puts an opt-out cookie on your hard drive. If you ever delete all of your cookies and then enter a DoubleClick network site, you'll start being tracked all over again."[7]

Currently, consumers cannot access their profiles and make any changes.

DoubleClick's Response to Privacy Concerns

It is important to remember that the company never expected their plan to evoke such high levels of criticism from the Internet community. Therefore, the firm initially did not take the possibility of a privacy backlash. In an interview, he plan seriously.

As described in a *Wall Street Journal* article,[8] "Just last November, Mr. Ryan, the company's president, had brashly dismissed even the possibility of a privacy backlash. In an interview, he predicted consumers would be just as comfortable giving out personal information online as they are handing their American Express card to a waiter in a restaurant. 'Some people forget that the No. 1 issue with credit cards 25 years ago was that someone is going to have a record of all my purchases,' Mr. Ryan said, in discussing privacy concerns. 'Now people are comfortable with that.'"

The February 2000 change in the company's stance is shown by a statement from DoubleClick's CEO Kevin O'Connor (see Appendix II). The company makes it clear that it had not

actually implemented the plan. In addition, the company pledged that "until there is agreement between government and industry on privacy standards, we will not link personally identifiable information to anonymous user activity across Web sites." The company wanted to end the brouhaha and appear as though it was decisively against using personally identifiable information.

Soon after this incident, the company hired a chief privacy officer, Jules Polenetsky (formerly the New York City consumer affairs commissioner), and has retained PricewaterhouseCoopers LLP to do regular privacy audits. The company felt that it had been unfairly singled out for this criticism. Kevin Ryan believed that all of the negative attention was a "penalty for success."[9]

In June 2000, the company announced that it had convened a panel of leaders to help advise it on privacy issues. This panel was headed by former New York attorney general Robert Abrams and included representatives from such well-respected organizations as the World Wide Web Consortium.[10]

Moreover, an audit conducted by the FTC in January 2001 was favorable. The FTC acknowledged that DoubleClick had never used personally identifiable information in a way that conflicted with its privacy policy.[11]

A group of online advertising networks, such as DoubleClick, has formed the Network Advertising Initiative (http://www.networkadvertising. org). This industry group developed a set of privacy principles in conjunction with the FTC. This collaborative effort should reduce the risk to DoubleClick from future legal actions.

These new developments are perhaps an indication that the company has turned the corner on this issue and has finally put it to rest. However, there are still rumors that the company may find ways of building profiles by merging the Abacus dataset with its customer database.

Notes

(All URLS are current as of April 8, 2002.)

1. Steven Cherry, "DoubleClick Recants on Privacy Issue," *IEEE Spectrum*, 37(4) (2000): 63–64.

2. Caroline Mayer, "DoubleClick Is Probed on Data Collection," *Washington Post*, February 17, 2000, E1.

3. Chris Oakes, "A Turning Point for E-Privacy," March 4, 2000, <http://www.wired.com/news/politics/0,1283,34734,00.html>.

4. Andrea Petersen and Jon G. Auerbach, "Online Ad Titans Bet Big in Race to Trace Consumers' Web Tracks," *Wall Street Journal*, November 8, 1999, B1.

5. Ronaleen Roha, "Prying Eyes," *Kiplinger's Personal Finance Magazine*, 54(8) (2000): 118–124.

6. Federal Trade Commission, "Privacy Online: Fair Information Practices in the Electronic Marketplace," May 2000, <http://www.ftc.gov/reports/privacy2000/privacy2000.pdf>.

7. Roha "Prying Eyes," 118–124.

8. Andrea Petersen, "A Privacy Firestorm at DoubleClick," *Wall Street Journal*, February 23, 2000.

9. Ibid.

10. Jennifer Owens, "DoubleClick Convenes Privacy Panel," *Mediaweek* 10(26) (June 26, 2000): 48.

11. Joel Winston, "Letter to DoubleClick Inc.," January 22, 2001, <http://www.ftc.gov/os/closings/staff/doubleclick.pdf>.

12. Taken from Jason Catlett, "Open Letter to DoubleClick," March 27, 2001, <http://www.junkbusters.com/doubleclick.html#four>.

Discussion Questions

1. Does DoubleClick have a right to target consumers with banner ads based on personally identifiable information?

2. If DoubleClick had informed consumers prior to announcing its plan, would it have made any difference?

3. Should the company be forced to get the permission of each and every consumer before targeting them?

4. Should targeting consumers by using cookies be held to a higher standard than e-mail advertising?

5. Are online advertising companies held to a different standard than direct marketing companies that send out junk mail?

6. Do you agree with the company's statement that it was unfairly targeted because it had grown?

Appendix I

Open Letter to Kevin Ryan, President, DoubleClick[12]

Dear Sir,

In a press release issued today (http://biz.yahoo.com/bw/010601/2316.html) your Chief Privacy Officer made the following statement: "DoubleClick is committed to executing its business in the most open manner possible." This claim is more suited to a Chief Propaganda Officer than a Chief Privacy Officer.

I have repeatedly asked DoubleClick to show the 88 million Americans what is kept in DoubleClick's Abacus Direct database about them, and I have met with repeated refusal. How could keeping billions of records in secret electronic dossiers constitute executing business in "the most open manner possible?" This flagrant boasting about what is manifestly untrue is simply one of the worst examples of public relations pabulum I have ever seen outside the tobacco industry.

The press release uses the phrase "fair information practices," but DoubleClick's own practices are nonconsensual, opaque and grossly unfair. If you examine the OECD's principles of fair information practice, available at http://www.junkbusters.com/fip.html you can see how remote DoubleClick's practices are from basic standards of fairness. You will note that openness is one of the principles, but it is one to which DoubleClick has failed to adhere.

Mr Polonetsky has not responded to my open letter of March 27, 2001, which is at http://www.junkbusters.com/doubleclick.html#four. In the name of openness, I call on you now to respond to that letter.

On March 26 DoubleClick declined to answer *The Wall Street Journal's* question of whether any data had been stolen by the hackers who repeatedly broke into its systems. In the name of openness, I call on you now to answer that question to the best of your ability.

On March 29 *The Wall Street Journal* reported that DoubleClick commissioned "PricewaterhouseCoopers LLC to conduct a security audit of its computer systems." In the name of openness, I call on you now to make that audit report public immediately.

The press release also solicits revisions to the policy. Here are a few of my suggestions, based on genuine fair information practices.

1. DoubleClick will only collect information about you or your browser if you explicitly consent to this collection.

2. DoubleClick will always show you the information it has associated with you or your browser.

3. DoubleClick always allows you to delete all information it has about you or your browser.

Please indicate whether you will adopt those revisions.

Sincerely,

Jason Catlett
President
Junkbusters Corp.

Appendix II

Statement From Kevin O'Connor, Chairman of DoubleClick

Available at http://www.doubleclick.net/company_info/press_kit/pr.00.03.02.htm.

NEW YORK, March 2, 2000—Over the past few weeks, DoubleClick (Nasdaq: DCLK) has been at the center of the Internet privacy controversy. During this time, we have met and listened to hundreds of consumers, privacy advocates, customers, government officials and industry leaders about these issues. The overwhelming point of contention has been under what circumstances names can be associated with anonymous user activity across Web sites.

It is clear from these discussions that I made a mistake by planning to merge names with anonymous user activity across Web sites in the absence of government and industry privacy standards.

Let me be clear: DoubleClick has not implemented this plan, and has never associated names, or any other personally identifiable information, with anonymous user activity across Web sites.

We commit today, that until there is agreement between government and industry on privacy standards, we will not link personally identifiable information to anonymous user activity across Web sites.

This action does not affect our core business activity. It means we are going to await clear industry standards before we decide the future direction of a number of new products. We will continue to expand our successful media, technology, e-mail and offline data businesses. We will also continue to abide by common industry practices in building anonymous profiles for ad targeting.

Since founding DoubleClick only 4 years ago, our company has grown to 1,800 employees with more than 7,000 customers worldwide. We are helping thousands of companies become successful in our new economy. I'm proud of DoubleClick's leadership as an innovator in improving the value of Internet advertising and

keeping the Internet free for consumers. Taking risks, inventing new products and services, and correcting mistakes are signs of responsible leadership.

Creating industry policies involving something so incredibly important to our global economy and individuals is not something to be taken lightly. We all agree on the goals: keep the Internet free while protecting consumer privacy. It is now time for industry, consumers and government to develop a clear set of guidelines that help create a healthy, free Internet while protecting the privacy of all consumers.

PART FOUR

Peering into the Future

Peer–to–Peer Systems

Learning Objectives

▼ To understand the nature of peer-to-peer (P2P) systems.

▼ To learn about the different applications of P2P systems.

▼ To study the two most well-known examples of P2P systems—Napster and SETI@Home.

▼ To understand the limitations of P2P systems.

▼ To explore the potential future business models for these systems.

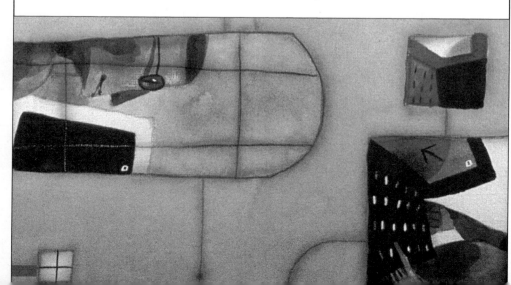

Executive Summary

If there is one thing you learn from this chapter, it should be that P2P does not equal Napster. P2P systems allow users to access the computers of other users like themselves (i.e., peers). Hence, instead of visiting the web site of a large company, a user has access to certain folders belonging to a user similar to himself or herself. Large companies such as Intel, McAfee, and Sun Microsystems have recently started to take P2P systems seriously because P2P technology is excellent for sharing resources. What is actually shared can be put into one of four categories—processor capacity (distributed computing applications such as SETI@Home), files (e.g., Napster, Gnutella), bandwidth, and content (e.g., Pointera, a P2P search engine). P2P systems play four roles in an enterprise—knowledge sharing, enabling commerce, groupware/collaboration, and reengineering the company's information technology (IT) infrastructure. P2P systems do have several limitations: security, free-riding, download failure, and scalability. Future P2P services will be based on subscription services, packet-based pricing, or will be positioned as enterprise-wide productivity tools.

Introduction

The Internet was intended to be a decentralized network that could withstand a nuclear attack; however, the Web has created a system of information dissemination that is centralized. Users interested in a particular piece of information visit a particular site and download it to their computer. If the main server that houses this information is destroyed, the information is not available.

P2P systems allow users to access the computers of other users like themselves (i.e., peers). Hence, instead of visiting the web site of a large company, a user has access to certain folders belonging to a user similar to himself or herself. The greater the number of users on the system, the greater the number of files each person can access. At Napster's peak, users downloaded 2.79 billion files from its system.[1]

P2P systems have received a lot of attention in recent times.[2] Intel's Chief Technology Officer (CTO), Patrick Gelsinger, said, "Peer-to-peer (P2P) computing could be as important to the Internet's future as the Web browser was to its past." In August 2001, IBM announced a commitment of $4 billion to a grid computing initiative that will use unused computer time to process information. Similarly, companies such as Sun Microsystems and Intel have made serious commitments to P2P technology. Sun Microsystems' chief scientist and cofounder, the well-respected Bill Joy, is now devoting all of his energy to build a software platform called JXTA (short for juxtapose) that will run P2P applications.[3]

Many applications are already in place. Instant messaging is a P2P technology. Similarly, McAfee, the leading provider of virus detection and killing software, has created a P2P application to quickly disseminate information about new product updates.[4]

McAfee ASaP is a service provided to large companies to let them distribute updates quickly throughout their organizations. Instead of making 10,000 individuals contact the McAfee

Web-site (a sure recipe for network overloads), a few initial systems contact the McAfee site, and they pass on the software to other systems in a chain. This is called rumor technology.

The primary reason why P2P is being taken seriously is that companies view it as a way of significantly reducing costs. As one proponent of P2P said:[5]

Companies can use P2P systems to effectively disseminate the right information to the right person at the right time at a dramatically reduced cost.

Applications of P2P Systems

- Collaboration. P2P computing allows users from around the world to interact with one another. Already, file-sharing systems such as Napster and Gnutella have empowered individuals to share music files with one another. Future P2P systems will unleash the potential for collaboration within large organizations.

  How much bandwidth does a simple peer-to-peer system like Napster save? Let's look at some rough estimates made by a company called CenterSpan, which makes a peer-to-peer content-sharing system called C-Star. They estimate that, if you put together Napster and the various Gnutella systems and all the knock-offs, you'd see about 3 billion songs traded every month. (Gnutella will be discussed in detail later.) Sounds like a high number, but it's been replicated elsewhere and could be pretty accurate. If you delivered all those songs from a central server, you'd need 25,000 T1 lines costing 25 million dollars a month. Peer-to-peer has to be more efficient.

- Edge services. P2P computing can be used to help a business deliver its services and capabilities more efficiently across a large network spread across the globe. Following is a tangible example:[6]

  A company with sites in multiple continents needs to provide the same standard training across multiple continents using the Web. Instead of streaming the database for the training session on one central server located at the main site, the company can store the video on local clients, which act essentially as local database servers. This speeds up the session because the streaming happens over the local area network (LAN) instead of the wide area network (WAN). It also utilizes existing storage space, thereby saving money by eliminating the need for local storage on servers.

- Distributed computing and resources. P2P computing can help businesses with intensive computing requirements. Instead of using one central supercomputer, P2P systems utilize idle computers from around the globe to efficiently process the information. The shining example of this is the SETI@Home project (discussed later).

- Intelligent agents. "Peer to peer computing also allows computing networks to dynamically work together using intelligent agents. Agents reside on peer computers and communicate various kinds of information back and forth. Agents may also initiate tasks on behalf of other peer systems. For instance, Intelligent agents can be used to prioritize tasks on a network, change traffic flow, search for files locally or determine anomalous behavior and stop it before it effects the network, such as a virus."[7]

An Overview of the Technology

P2P technology is basically used to share resources. What is actually shared can be put into one of four categories—processor capacity, files, bandwidth, and content.

Distributed Computing (Sharing Processor Capacity)

Distributed computing is based on using resources that would otherwise go to waste. It involves conducting computing operations using spare CPU cycles on idling machines. The process is eloquently described by this passage:[8]

Now, computers spend most of their time displaying zooming multicolored windowpanes or simulating an aquarium. These "screen saver" programs, which compute nothing, whose only purpose is to stir up pixels on the display screen, probably consume more of the world's computational capacity than any other kind of software. Go into almost any office and you'll find machines busily saving their screens all night and all weekend.

Even when a computer is ostensibly in use, it is mostly idle. Typing furiously, you might produce 10 keystrokes per second; that's not much of a distraction for a processor that can execute 100 million instructions in a second. Under these conditions the processor spends most of its time going around in a tight little loop, asking over and over, like a fidgety toddler, "What can I do now?"

Distributed computing predates the Internet; however, the availability of the Internet has led to access to a large number of computers. A number of scientific projects have been successfully conducted using distributed computing on the Internet (e.g., finding the largest prime number).

Even though distributed computing has its roots in the scientific and academic world, an ever-increasing number of for-profit companies are now using this technology. Biotech and financial services companies can benefit from this enhanced computing power. Here are some examples:

- Parabon Computing asks individuals to donate computing time. In exchange, users are paid or get the satisfaction of helping a cause (e.g., cancer).

- Avaki (previously Applied Metacomputing) provides software solutions to large corporations.

- United Devices helps organizations get more from existing computers by using a distributed computing approach.

- Intel's Cancer Research Project encourages users to donate their computing cycles to help cancer research.

- Intel has been using P2P in their chip design process.[9]

File Sharing Technologies

The Internet has provided us with several file-sharing mechanisms. At the most basic level, an individual can send a file as an attachment by e-mail or use services such as

Ofoto to share files with others. Programs such as FTP have long enabled users to move files from point A to point B. However, the most attention in recent times was devoted to P2P mechanisms, such as Napster and Gnutella, that facilitate the large-scale sharing of files such as music.

There are two types of P2P file-sharing technologies. The centralized P2P file-sharing technology is typified by Napster (see Figure 15.1) and the decentralized system's best exemplar is Gnutella (see Figure 15.2).

In the centralized system, users connect to one another. A central directory keeps records of all of the users and the contents of their PCs and helps users locate one another. More precisely:[10]

Figure 15.1
How Napster Works

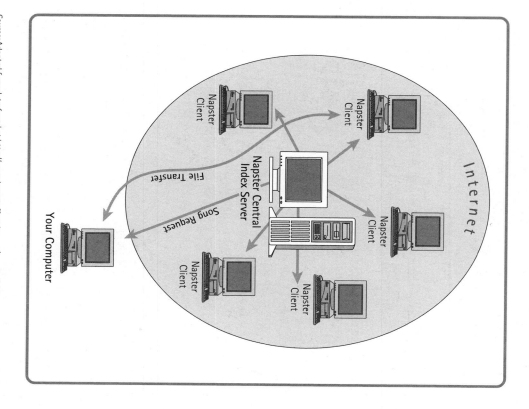

Your Computer

File Transfer

Song Request

Napster Central
Index Server

Napster
Client

Napster
Client

Napster
Client

Napster
Client

Internet

Figure 15.2
How Gnutella Works

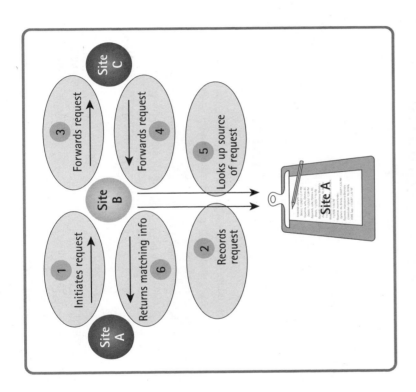

Source: Andy Oram, "Gnutella and Freenet Represent True Technological Innovation," May 12, 2000, http://www.oreillynet.com/lpt/a/208. Figure copyright O'Reilly & Associates, 2001.

Each time a user of a centralized P2P file sharing system submits a request or search for a particular file, the central server creates a list of files matching the search request, by cross-checking the request with the server's database of files belonging to users who are currently connected to the network. The central server then displays that list to the requesting user. The requesting user can then select the desired file from the list and open a direct HTTP link with the individual computer, which currently possesses that file. The download of the actual file takes place directly, from one user to the other. The actual file is never stored on the central server or on any intermediate point on the network.

On the other hand, "true" (i.e., decentralized) P2P technologies such as Gnutella and Freenet do not use a central directory. Rather, when user A gets on the network, he announces that he is alive to computer B. Computer B passes this message on to others, who pass it on to others, and so on. As a result, users are able to sense the presence of others without the need for a centralized directory.

Once "A" has announced that it is "alive" to the various members of the peer network, it can then search the contents of the shared directories of the peer network members. The search request will send the request to all members of the network, starting with, B, then to C, D, E, F, who will in turn send the request to the computers to which they are connected, and so forth. If one of the

CHAPTER 15 / PEER-TO-PEER SYSTEMS

computers in the peer network, say for example, computer D, has a file which that matches the request, it transmits the file information (name, size, etc) back through all the computers in the pathway towards A, where a list of files matching the search request will then appear on computer A's Gnutella display. A will then be able to open a direct connection with computer D and will be able to download that file directly from computer D.[11]

Bandwidth Sharing[12]

It is problematic to distribute large files (e.g., movie trailers) from a single site. P2P systems provide a solution. Rather than using a web site, the file is sent to participating individuals who can quickly share the file with their peers. The bandwidth load is distributed between many individuals instead of being borne entirely by a company. Companies offering such technologies include vTrails, Kalepa Networks, and Nextpage.

Content Sharing and Publishing

Consider a service such as Pointera. Most search engines cannot search more than 16% of the web and do not search for certain types of files. By using Pointera, the searcher has access to 500 million PCs and all of the files therein. Rather than searching on the Internet, the user has access to files created or downloaded by his or her peers. It is also possible to create private spaces using this service, limiting the access to a few trusted individuals.

Two Well-Known P2P Examples

SETI@Home (Distributed Computing)

The SETI (Search for Extra-Terrestrial Intelligence) project at the University of California at Berkeley is set up to search for life and civilizations on other planets and stars. The project uses a telescope located at the Arecibo observatory in Puerto Rico. The SETI systems collect about twenty gigabytes of information every day. The goal of the project is to detect patterns indicative of life; however, detecting weak signals requires more of computing power than is available even when using the large supercomputers available to the project team. The team, therefore, adopted a distributed computing approach to resolve the problem:[13]

People around the world will be able to get a copy of the SETI@Home screensaver and download a .25-megabyte chunk of data from the SETI@Home server. During the computer's down time, an educational screensaver will run in the foreground while in the background the data is searched for alien frequencies. When finished, the screensaver will log back in to SETI@Home, upload the processed data and download a new chunk.

This approach has been very successful. At the time of writing, 3.2 million users from around the world had participated in this project. The total processing time was in excess of 730,000 years.[14]

Napster

Napster is likely the most well-known P2P application. Over a short period of time, the company amassed 80 million registered users and lost a contentious fight with the recording industry.

The colorful history of this company began in May 1999 when Shawn Fanning, a freshman at Northeastern University in Boston, developed the Napster system to help users share MP3 files. Napster was Fanning's nickname in high school.

In December 1999, multiple record labels filed a lawsuit against Napster under the auspices of the Recording Industry Association of America (RIAA). The industry felt that Napster encouraged piracy on an unprecedented scale and feared that Napster would reduce the demand for its CDs and DVDs. On July 26, 2000, a U.S. district court judge ordered Napster to shut down. On July 28, 2000, Napster's appeal of this decision allowed it to continue operations until the case was tried.

On October 2, 2000, the RIAA appealed the decision of the Ninth U.S. Circuit Court of Appeals, and the U.S. Supreme Court ordered the injunction reinstated. Napster is now blocking about 90% of the songs it has access to due to copyright reasons. On October 31, 2000, Bertelesmann AG announced an alliance with Napster and withdrew from the case. On January 29, 2001, Bertelesmann AG announced that it would eventually charge fees to use Napster.

So, what did Napster do that was so contentious? It created a system by which individuals could share music (or any other) files with one another. Napster never gained possession of the file; rather, it maintained a large database of contact information that helped users reach one another. Once contact was established, users were free to swap files. Napster took the position that it was not infringing on the copyright protections because individuals were doing the actual copying. However, this position was not accepted by the courts, and Napster was forced to set up a system that checked for the copyrights of the songs.

As a result, the number of songs available for sharing on Napster was dramatically reduced. This did not, however, stop those who wanted to share files—they simply went off to other sites (see Table 15.1). As described earlier, Napster uses a centralized system and this was the flaw that allowed the recording industry to succeed in court. Many of the systems shown in Table 15.1 are decentralized—they have no information about who is contacting whom. Because this is likely to make it very difficult to hold them legally accountable, some level of file sharing is expected to continue over time.

The Role of P2P in Enterprises[15]

Perhaps the most important role for P2P within an organization is to help *manage and share knowledge* within the firm. Large organizations tend to have islands of great information that other sections could benefit from. It may not be available to others because it is not made publicly available on a search engine. Even listing on a search engine may not solve the problem when there is a lot of information. Companies such as Badblue,

Table 15.1

Change in Unique Audience

Site	Unique Audience		Percent Change
	May 27	July 15	
Napster.com	4,073,000	2,628,000	–36
KaZaA	179,000*	433,000	142
BearShare	197,000	274,000	39
Audiogalaxy	534,000	707,000	32
iMesh	262,000	331,000	26

Source: Michael Pastore, "Napster Users Fan Out in Search of File-Swapping Apps," July 23, 2001, http://cyberatlas.internet.com/big_picture/applications/article/0,,1301_806531,00.html#table2. Copyright 2002 INT Media Group, Incorporated. All rights reserved.

Magi Express, and Mangsoft have solutions that can turn every PC within an organization into a server that is accessible by a search.

Another application of P2P within enterprises is *groupware/collaboration.* P2P networks hope to offer integrated communication solutions in the future. For instance, virtual teams can use P2P systems to share information and work together. The leader in this arena may be Groove Networks, which was launched by the founder of Lotus Notes.

The third set of applications focuses on *enabling commerce by reengineering the supply chain.* These applications allow for P2P interactions between agents in a supply chain. In a way, this is a reincarnation of the extranet and the B2B marketplace as a P2P network. Companies working in this arena include Biz2Peer and Verai.

Finally, P2P applications within a company can *reengineer the company's infrastructure.* Rather than having a conventional centralized IT department, these solutions allow for the decentralized management of information. Obviously, this might be a challenge in organizations used to a strong, centrally run IT department. Companies working in this arena include Cytaq and Proskim.

How Managers Must Think of P2P

A 2001 conference hosted by Oreilly (http://www.oreilly.com) developed ten conclusions about P2P and where it was headed:[16]

1. P2P is a mind-set, not a technology or an industry.

2. To fully grasp P2P, you must think in terms of "PIE": presence, identity, and edge. These factors can be leveraged to turn an application into a decentralized networking platform.

3. P2P architectures offer powerful approaches for solving the seemingly intractable problems of the Web, such as bandwidth cost, denial-of-service attacks, and the cost of maintaining robust 24/7 systems.

4. P2P is not a binary choice between centralization and decentralization, but presents an enormous opportunity for creating a more efficient and robust Internet.

5. The future of consumer file-sharing services lies with licensed, subscription-based services. Hanging in the wings, fully decentralized services have a better chance of surviving legal attacks than do centrally managed services like Napster.

6. P2P content delivery networks have a tough road ahead: They must deliver solutions that are lower in cost and comparable in service to classic content delivery networks like Akamai.

7. Due to early adoption in the life sciences and financial services industries, distributed computation has the greatest short-term revenue potential in the P2P space.

8. Developments in both P2P and IM (instant messaging) point to the emergence of PIE. In a PIE-enabled network, resources at the Center migrate to the Edge; anonymous users gain Identity; and transient connectivity yields to Presence.

9. P2P creates the most significant challenges to the traditionally centralized IT departments, and to the current "intranet plus firewall" networking model of enterprise security and control.

10. Only two or three large providers of P2P groupware will survive; many of the current entrants will be acquired by larger players or exit the space.

Pitfalls of P2P Systems

Security[17]

The security of P2P networks is an important topic. In the words of a Frost and Sullivan analyst:

An obstacle to an effective enterprise P2P network is convincing network administrators that a P2P network can be secured to prevent digital assets theft. This will require significant resources from market participants to devote to education on P2P security features as well as potential benefits that can be obtained by implementing an enterprise P2P network.

For instance, the primary issue is to ensure that visitors can only visit those folders to which they are given access. Using Napster as an example, some argue that P2P networks can propagate information very quickly. Although this is good in some instances, it also means that it may be very fast in propagating viruses and worms.

Moreover, in large companies there is a sense that the IT departments will not have control over the process by which information is propagated. This loss of control is troubling to the managers in these companies.[18]

Proponents argue that there is nothing intrinsic about P2P that makes it secure or insecure. In their way of thinking, what is needed is a new way of approaching security issues, not a complete abandonment of the technology.

Free-Riding

An interesting study conducted by Huberman and Adar[19] at the Xerox PARC center revealed that free-riding is a major problem with P2P networks such as Gnutella. The problem is simple: Most people are interested in downloading information from others instead of providing any information themselves.

This is very apparent from the data shown in Table 15.2: the top 1% of hosts (also called super-peers) contribute as much as 37% of all files, the top 5% contribute 70% of all files, and the top 25% contribute 99% of all files. In other words, the remaining 75% of the participants in the network contribute only 1% of all files! Because their study was comprised of 33,335 peers, this means that as few as 333 people provided as much as 37% of all content. Clearly, a large proportion of the users are simply freeloading off of the efforts of others.

The study indicated that such large-scale free-riding creates major problems:

- The network may collapse if most people simply free-ride without sharing any files themselves.

- If only a small number of people are active on such networks, they could be singled out for lawsuits, they could lose their privacy, or could be the targets of denial-of-service attacks. Thus, the network is most robust if a large number of people are active.

Spamming on P2P networks is also expected to be a problem. Rather than adding value to the network by providing relevant information, spammers detract from its value with useless messages and corrupted or annoying files.

Download Failure

It is not always possible to locate the information one is looking for on a P2P network. First, the quality of the network depends on the number of members at any given time and the quality of information they are willing to provide to the network.

Table 15.2
Free-Riding on Gnutella

The Top	Number of Files	Provided This Percent of Content
333 hosts (1%)	1,142,645	37
1,667 hosts (5%)	2,182,087	70
3,334 hosts (10%)	2,692,082	87
5,000 hosts (15%)	2,928,905	94
6,667 hosts (20%)	3,037,232	98
8,333 hosts (25%)	3,082,572	99

Source: Adapted from Eytan Adar and Bernardo Huberman, "Free Riding on Gnutella," September 27, 2000, http://www.firstmonday.org/issues/issue5_10/adar/index.html. Reprinted with the kind permission of the author and First Monday.

Second, in decentralized networks, if users have to search the entire network, the computing power required is too high. As a result, users are only allowed to search between five to seven computers. Due to this restriction, some requests time out and are unsuccessful. Decentralized networks are also a poor vehicle for downloading rare content.

Current estimates indicate that as of March 2001, only about 25% of requests on Gnutella led to successes. Even though this figure is up from about 10% one year prior, it is still a very low number and a cause for concern.[20] It is likely that P2P systems will provide consumers easy access to popular files. However, it may be difficult to find rare content.

Scalability (Gnutella Scalability and Rebuttal)

One of the founders of Napster[21] has argued that a system such as Gnutella will not scale easily. As the number of users on the system increases, the number of searches conducted will be so large that there will not be enough processing power to accommodate it. As a result, the network will collapse. However, this is not the consensus viewpoint. Some P2P system architects pointed out that systems such as Gnutella set natural limits on the number of PCs a user can search and this limits the extent of the problem.[22]

Conclusion

If there is one thing you learned from this chapter, let it be that P2P does not equal Napster; rather, P2P is a mind-set that allows for a range of business applications. P2P technology is here to stay. File-sharing applications such as Napster will eventually become subscription services—sharing systems will charge based on the size of the downloads. Finally, P2P will reengineer several corporations and promote knowledge sharing and collaboration.

Notes

(All URLS are current as of April 14, 2002.)

1. Accessed August 2001, http://thestandard.net/article/0,1902,24127,00.html.
2. This is based on Morris Edwards, "P2P: Next Computing Wave or More Vendor Hype?," *Communications News* 38(10) (2001): 70–71.
3. Eric Schonfeld, "Bill Joy's New Passion: Industrial-strength P2P," *Business 2.0*, 3(1) (2002): 34–35.
4. Andy Oram, "Peer-to-Peer for Academia," October 29, 2001, <http://www.openp2p.com/pub/a/p2p/2001/10/29/oram_speech.html?page=2#fmd>.
5. Ibid.
6. Peer-to-Peer Working Group, "What is Peer-to-Peer?," <http://www.peer-to-peerwg.org/whatis/index.html>.
7. Ibid.
8. Brian Hayes, "Collective Wisdom," March–April 1998, <http://www.amsci.org/amsci/issues/Comsci98/compsci1998-03.html>.
9. Emelie Rutheford, "The P2P Report," January 12, 2000, <http://www.cio.com/research/knowledge/edit/p2p.html>.

10. Limewire.com, "Modern Peer-to-Peer File-Sharing Over the Internet," 2002, <http://www.lime wire.com/index.jsp/p2p>.

11. Ibid.

12. Geneer/Piper Rudnick, "Peer-To-Peer Computing and Your Business," <http://www.geneer.com/report/gbrissue03.asp>.

13. Janelle Brown, "The Geeks and the Aliens," May 6, 1998, <http://www.salon.com/21st/feature/1998/05/cov_06feature2.html>.

14. SETI@Home Berkeley, "Current Total Statistics," <http://setiathome.ssl.berkeley.edu/totals.html>.

15. Loosely based on Anne Zieger, "What Can P2P Apps Do for Enterprise Apps?," <http://www.peertopeercentral.com/EnterpriseP2P.pdf>.

16. Taken from Oreilly, "2001 P2P Networking Overview: Ten Key Conclusions," September 10, 2001, <http://www.oreilly.com/news/p2pconclusions_0901.html>.

17. Michael Pastore, "P2P Turning to Legitimate Applications," August 1, 2001, <http://cyberatlas. internet.com/big_picture/applications/article/0,,1301_858221,00.html>.

18. Rutheford, "The P2P Report."

19. Eytan Adar and Bernardo Huberman, "Free Riding on Gnutella," September 27, 2000, <http://www.firstmonday.org/issues/issue5_10/adar/index.html>.

20. Limewire.com, "Limewire: Network Improvements," March 2, 2001, <http://www.limewire.com/index.jsp/net_improvements>.

21. Jordan Ritter, "Why Gnutella Can't Scale. No, Really," February 2001, <http://www.darkridge.com/~jpr5/doc/gnutella.html>.

22. Ibid.

REVIEW / CHAPTER 15

Discussion Questions

1. What are the implications of file-sharing sites on online music retailers such as Amazon.com? Will users continue to pay for CDs if it is available for free?

2. If you are the manager of IT for a large company, how would you respond to arguments that decentralized informational systems are better?

3. What is the essential difference between having a search engine on an intranet and a P2P system?

4. If you are the head of a Fortune 1000 company, will you allow your employees to make their PCs available for distributed computing applications such as SETI@Home? What factors would you consider when making that decision?

E-Tasks

1. Visit Gnutella and download the application (this is still legal at the time of this writing). Download a file of your choice from the system. How does this experience compare to visiting the web site of an online retailer? Did you find the type of music you were looking for?

2. Participate in a instant messaging session at Yahoo! or a similar site. How do you compare IM to e-mail and chat?

CHAPTER 16

Mobile Commerce

Learning Objectives

▼ To understand the nature of mobile commerce (m-commerce).

▼ To learn about the differences between m-commerce and e-commerce.

▼ To understand the key wireless technologies.

▼ To learn about the primary applications of m-commerce.

▼ To take an in-depth look at the telematics industry.

Executive Summary

M-commerce is envisioned as a new form of commerce transacted on a variety of devices such as cellular phones, personal digital assistants (PDAs), pagers, intelligent information appliances, and automobiles. A technical primer on wireless technology is provided in Appendix I at the end of the chapter. M-commerce has five important characteristics: ubiquity, localization, instant connectivity, personalization, and time sensitivity. Due to the unique constraints of the user interfaces in mobile devices, the user experience is different than on a PC. Users cannot browse large documents, conduct transactions involving several steps, or type in long web site URLs.

Several key mobile technologies are discussed, including: short messaging system (or text messaging), mobile e-mail, 802.11 (also known as Wi-Fi), and Bluetooth. M-commerce has the potential to alter how large companies conduct their business. Potential applications are in three areas: strengthening customer relationships, improving supply chain efficiency, and enhancing employee productivity. The key applications discussed in this chapter include mobile portals, mobile gaming, mobile trading, and digital radio. Telematics (access to Internet/Web and other services in the car) is discussed in great detail.

Introduction

M-Commerce is envisioned as a new form of commerce transacted on a variety of devices such as cellular phones, PDAs, pagers, intelligent information appliances, and automobiles. Many of these devices may lack the complexity of a PC; however, they are expected to become widely available. For instance, as shown in Figure 16.1, the number of cell-phone users worldwide has exploded to 722 million in 2000. Moreover, EMC Cellular Database is forecasting that the number of cell-phone users will exceed 1 billion in 2001.[1] Already, 80% of Sweden's and 70% of Finland's population have cell phones.

The widespread availability of these devices is expected to facilitate new types of communication and commerce. The following scenarios capture the power that mobile access to the Internet/Web can bring:

- A business executive arrives at the airport. Instead of fumbling for change at the parking lot, she pays using a mobile device (e.g., cell phone). She is billed monthly for these charges if the total exceeds $50.

- A salesperson is about to meet with a client. He receives a text message just before the meeting that the inventory for one of the company's products is very high. He enters the meeting and offers a special deal on the product, making a successful sale.

- A consumer enters her local shopping mall. Her favorite store recognizes her and sends her a text message telling her that her favorite cashmere sweater is on sale at 30% off. She rushes to the store, makes the purchase, and leaves happy.

Figure 16.1
Number of Cell-Phone Subscribers Worldwide

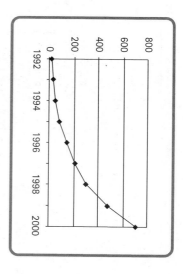

Source: GSMWorld, "Statistics Page."
http://www.gsmworld.com/membership/graph1.html.

Figure 16.2
Potential Wireless Commerce Scenarios

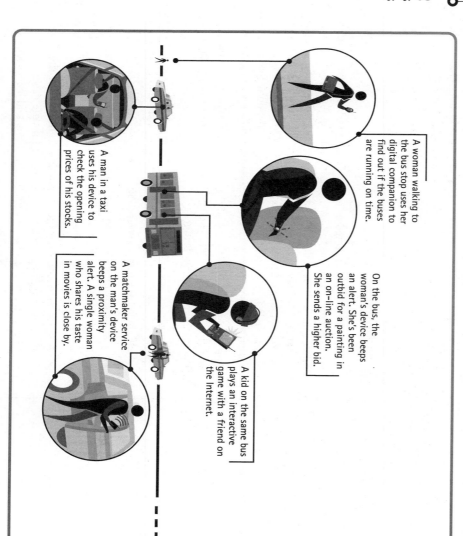

A woman walking to the bus stop uses her digital companion to find out if the buses are running on time.

A man in a taxi uses his device to check the opening prices of his stocks.

On the bus, the woman's device beeps an alert. She's been outbid for a painting in an on-line auction. She sends a higher bid.

A matchmaker service on the man's device beeps a proximity alert. A single woman who shares his taste in movies is close by.

A kid on the same bus plays an interactive game with a friend on the Internet.

Source: As seen in *Scientific American,* © 2002 XPLANATIONS™ by Xplane.com®.

- A family is on vacation. At the zoo, their ten-year-old son sees on his mobile device that his best buddy is also at the zoo. He sends him an instant message, setting up a rendezvous in thirty minutes.

- An investor receives an alert on her PDA that the stock she is interested in just dipped below the target price. She clicks a link and orders her electronic brokerage to purchase the stock.

- A consumer enters Starbucks. Using a monthly flat-fee wireless connection, his laptop is now connected to the Internet. He checks his work e-mail over a latte.

- A consumer enters a video store. He realizes that he wanted to check out a movie on the American Film Institute's top 100 movies. Within seconds, he pulls up their web site and locates the title that was eluding him. He makes the purchase and leaves the store.

Similar scenarios are shown in Figure 16.2. Some of these scenarios are already a reality (e.g., travelers on the King County bus system in Washington State can now check on the status of their bus at any time).

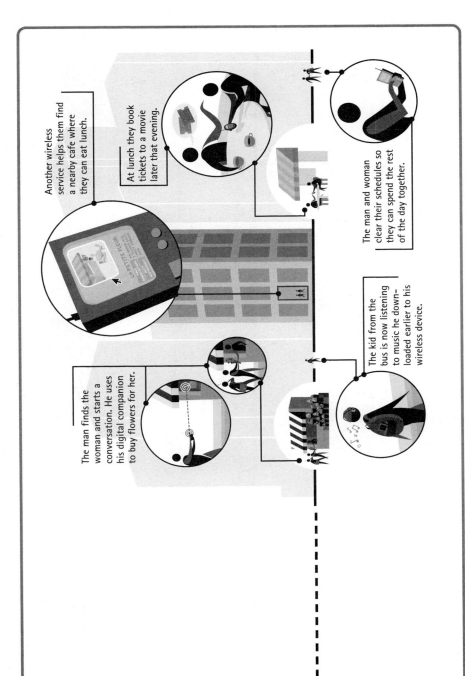

Another wireless service helps them find a nearby cafe where they can eat lunch.

At lunch they book tickets to a movie later that evening.

The man and woman clear their schedules so they can spend the rest of the day together.

The man finds the woman and starts a conversation. He uses his digital companion to buy flowers for her.

The kid from the bus is now listening to music he down-loaded earlier to his wireless device.

M-commerce is already here and its use is being considered very seriously by many companies. Consider these examples:[2]

- Ford Motor Co., the U.S. Army, and the U.S. Postal Service are deploying wireless radio frequency identification devices (RFID) to track assets such as equipment, vehicles, containers, and materials.

- Producers Lloyds and Progressive Insurance let agents with hand-held PCs access the account information of customers to file claims and authorize payments from remote locations.

- E-Trade and Fidelity Investments are providing mobile customers with two-way capabilities, enabling them to initiate transactions and receive information.

- Hertz and Thrifty Car Rental let their mobile customers make and confirm reservations using cellular telephones.

A summary of several typical key business applications for this technology in the B2B and B2C sectors are shown in Table 16.1. The conventional wisdom at this point is that

Table 16.1
Examples of
Wireless Applications

Class of Wireless Application	Sector	Examples
Mobile inventory management	B2B	Tracking the location of goods and services, such as boxes, packets, troops, or cattle
Product location	B2C	Locating certain items, such as TVs, VCRs, or cars in mall
Proactive service management	B2B	Transmitting information about aging components, such as automobile parts, to vendors
Wireless reengineering	B2B	Improving business services, such as claim adjustments or insurance
Mobile auction and reverse auction	B2B, B2C, C2C	Offering, selling, and bidding
Mobile entertainment services	B2C	Providing services such as video on demand
Mobile office	B2B	Providing services for businesspeople, such as traffic jam reports, airport and flight information, vacation reservations, and procurement of products and services
Mobile distance education	B2C	Offering classes using streaming audio and video
Wireless data center	B2B	Providing downloadable information from data warehouses
Mobile music and music on demand	B2C	Allowing downloading and storing of music from the Internet

Source: Adapted from Upkar Varshney, Ronald J. Vetter, Ravi Kalakota, "Mobile Commerce: A New Frontier," October 2000, http://www.computer.org/computer/articles/October/Varshney/Varshney.html. © 2000 IEEE.

the most lucrative opportunities will be in the B2B sector (enterprise applications). Wireless CRM systems, sales force management, and other related systems are expected to be most affected.

The Nature of M-Commerce

M-Commerce has five important characteristics:[3] ubiquity, localization, instant connectivity, personalization, and time sensitivity. (See also Appendix I for a technical primer on the wireless Internet.)

Ubiquity

With m-commerce, individuals no longer have to stay at their desks to access the Internet and the Web; rather, they can have access to important information anywhere at any time. A business executive can check his work e-mail from a mountain in Montana. An individual investor can track her investments while she shops or has lunch. This is the ultimate dream and the big promise of m-commerce.

Similarly, individuals can conduct commercial transactions from any location. For instance, while eating lunch, a consumer may receive a sale alert from Amazon.com. Simply by clicking on a button, she is able to finalize the sale and return to her lunch.

Localization

With m-commerce, the customer's profile includes his or her location in real-time. As a result, many new types of services can be offered. For instance, when a customer enters a mall, retailers can sense his presence and send appropriate ads or content. Already, "intelligent" taxicabs in Manhattan change their ads based on the physical characteristics of the streets they are on.

Location-based services will soon become more common in the United States because of a government mandate. The Federal Communications Commission (FCC) has indicated that, by October 2002, all cell-phone calls must be trackable for emergency purposes. This is likely to speed the broad distribution of location-aware cell phones and other devices will be sure to follow.

Time Sensitivity

Because most Internet access is currently through PCs, it is not always possible to target individuals at certain points in time. Thus, the time-sensitivity feature of communication and commerce is not as developed. However, with m-commerce, the user is no longer chained to the desktop and is "always on." As a result, it is possible to target him or her at the appropriate time.

For example, a consumer can receive coupons from competing restaurants a few minutes before lunch time. Similarly, it is possible for a user to receive an alert if a stock has dipped below a target price. Quick action can be taken, leading to a profitable decision.

Instant Connectivity

With the advent of third-generation phone systems and packet-switched networks, the user is "always on." The advantage of this is considerable and is comparable to the enhanced experience as a result of "always on" services for the PC such as DSL and cable modems. Users do not have to dial up each time they want to send an e-mail or browse the web.

Personalization

The basic concept of personalization was discussed in Chapter 8. M-commerce can enhance the level of personalization in several ways. First, the quality of the user data is enhanced—consumer profiles now include their location in addition to the previously measured variables such as purchasing and demographic characteristics. Second, because the consumer is "always on," the potential opportunities to target an individual rise. As a result, it is possible to personalize the user's entire daily experience.

The User Experience

Because the graphical user interface faced by consumers using m-commerce is constraining (e.g., cell phones, PDAs), the user experience is somewhat different—users cannot browse large documents, conduct transactions involving several steps, or type in long web site URLs.

These constraints create different search behaviors. First, individuals will do less browsing and more direct searching. They are much more likely to go to places that can be reached with one keystroke. As a result, individuals will visit fewer sites, but are likely to spend much more time at each of these sites.

As a result of these new search behaviors, it will be easier for one company to own the entire user experience. For example, today, Microsoft offers those users with Web-enabled phones or a PDA running CE or Palm to access Expedia.com Travel, MSNBC News, MSN MoneyCentral for Stocks information, and MSN Hotmail.

These behaviors also increase the emphasis on providing information to consumers. It is likely that such services as e-mail, stock quotes, weather, travel delays, traffic information and point-to-point directions will be the most popular. M-commerce will help consumers track their important activities anywhere. Therefore, communication alerts (e.g., stock price alerts, store sale alerts) will become much more frequent.

Currently, the evidence suggests that consumers are not very keen on adopting m-commerce to conduct transactions. For example, a May 2001 study conducted by A. T. Kearney, a Chicago research firm, surveyed 1,600 cell-phone users in the United States, Europe, and Asia.[4] Overall, 12% of users indicated an interest in purchasing using cell phones. Interestingly, only 3% of U.S. users showed any interest in purchasing using m-commerce. The study points to two barriers to the adoption of m-commerce. First, the slow connection speed (9.6K/sec in comparison to the standard 56K/sec or faster connection with the PC) has frustrated users who have to wait for long periods of time to download.

load web sites. Second, only a small percent of cellular phones have browsers or transaction capability—there is no critical mass.

Clearly, there must be an evolution in the quality of the handsets and the networks for m-commerce to be transacted on a large scale.

An Overview of Key Wireless Technologies

Short Message Service (SMS)

Currently, one of the top applications in the wireless arena is SMS (also known as text messaging). Consumers can send text messages to others from their PC or directly from their cellular phone. They can also sign up to receive messages about things they care about (e.g., weather, stock prices, horoscopes). The number of SMS messages sent out on global systems for mobile (GSM) networks (the leading network) reached twenty billion in May 2001 and, as shown in Table 16.2, has grown by leaps and bounds. It is also very profitable for the wireless carriers (e.g., it formed about 8% of Vodafone's year 2000 revenue[5]).

Table 16.2

Number of SMS Messages Sent Monthly on GSM Networks (All numbers in billions)

January 2000	4
February 2000	4
March 2000	5
April 2000	6
May 2000	7
June 2000	7
July 2000	8
August 2000	9
September 2000	10
October 2000	12
November 2000	13
December 2000	14
January 2001	16
February 2001	16
March 2001	18
April 2001	18
May 2001	20

Source: GSMWorld, "Statistics Page,"
http://www.gsmworld.com/membership/graph_sms.html.

There are three reasons for its success. First, it is easy to use—simply type out a message on a PC and it is relayed to almost any cell phone. It is possible to create messages on cell phones as well. Second, this is an incremental service offered by the phone company that already has a relationship with the customer. The charge for SMS shows up as a line item on the monthly cell-phone bill. Third, it is a service that has reached critical mass—it is on every GSM handset (see Appendix I for more details about GSM) and will soon be available on other systems.

The next step is enhanced message service (EMS). This extends SMS to allow the easy transfer of images and music. Recently, Ericsson, Alcatel, Siemens, and Motorola have announced plans to support EMS as a standard across their networks.

Mobile E-Mail[6]

Research In Motion's Blackberry is a breakthrough mobile appliance that allows users to log on to their existing e-mail accounts. It was the first device that worked with Microsoft Exchange and POP3 servers. All of a sudden, users realized that they did not have to use their heavy laptop to check e-mail; rather, they could check their e-mail on a small device.

Of course, the device has some disadvantages. First, the Blackberry device does not handle e-mail with attachments well—one has to buy an additional service for that. Second, the device does not work perfectly with e-mail in HTML and some other formats. Third, the device is expensive at $399. In the future, sending e-mail through handheld devices is expected to be common.

802.11 or Wi-Fi[7]

This is a wireless LAN technology that was developed by the reputable body, Institute for Electrical and Electronic Engineers (IEEE). It allows users to access the Internet with their laptops anywhere within a building without physically connecting to a phone line. The technology is capable of a connection speed of 11 megabytes per second (Mbps), which compares favorably to other Internet connections. Dell is already shipping computers equipped with this technology. Intel has promised to ship products using the 802.11a technology, which is about five times faster than the existing 802.11b technology.[8]

There are several applications for the 802.11 technology. For example, a university can allow its students to access the Internet all over campus. Because there is no need to rewire a building, there is minimum disruption. It is no wonder then that universities such as Stanford and MIT have implemented this technology, and venture capitalists are calling this "the next big thing."

Recently, Starbucks announced a partnership with Microsoft to implement 802.11 technology in its stores. It will be available in the Seattle, Dallas, and San Francisco stores first on a trial basis.[9] Consumers will be able to access it for a monthly fee.[10] Similarly, airports across the country are expected to be equipped with this technology in the coming months and years.

Bluetooth

Bluetooth is an alliance of companies, including 3Com, IBM, Microsoft, Motorola, and Nokia, that came together to design short-range wireless applications. The potential applications of Bluetooth are as follows:[11]

- Three-in-one phone. At home, your phone functions as a portable phone (fixed line charge). When you're on the move, it functions as a mobile phone (cellular charge). And when your phone comes within range of another mobile phone with built-in Bluetooth wireless technology, it functions as a walkie-talkie (no telephony charge).

- The Internet bridge. Use your mobile computer to surf the Internet wherever you are, regardless of whether you're cordlessly connected through a mobile phone (cellular) or through a wire-bound connection (e.g., ISDN, LAN, xDSL).

- Interactive conference. During meetings and conferences you can transfer selected documents instantly to selected participants, and exchange electronic business cards automatically, without any wired connections.

- The ultimate headset. Connect your wireless headset to your mobile phone, mobile computer, or any wired connection to keep your hands free for more important tasks when you're at the office or in your car.

- The automatic synchronizer. Automatically synchronize your desktop, mobile computer, notebook, and your mobile phone. For instance, as soon as you enter your office, the address list and calendar in your notebook is automatically updated to agree with the ones in your desktop, or vice versa.

It is fair to say that Bluetooth has not been a success thus far.[12] The technology's creators have been accused of hyping a technology that is not ready. The few products that have appeared on the market were very expensive and not received well. Moreover, the widespread success of 802.11 technology is viewed as reducing the potential of Bluetooth.

This is not surprising because 802.11 allows for faster connection (similar to a DSL connection) and provides for a greater range of usage than Bluetooth. The supporters of the technology say that there is room for both these technologies, but skeptics are dismissing the Bluetooth technology.

Key M-Commerce Applications

Enterprise Applications[13]

M-commerce has the potential to alter the way large companies conduct their business. Potential applications are in three areas: strengthening customer relationships, improving supply chain efficiency, and enhancing employee productivity.

Mobile applications can strengthen the relationship between companies and customers. By providing constant access to information and transactions, the mobile Internet can enhance the consumer's life by making it easier to conduct business with the company.

Introducing mobile access can also improve the efficiency of the supply chain. Mobile Internet technology enhances all of the flows within a supply chain: physical, informational, and financial. Physical flow is enhanced with applications such as mobile inventory auditing and mobile access to information for a sales force. The informational flow is enhanced by quicker feedback from agents in remote locations. For instance, an agent at a shipping warehouse can send an e-mail to the consumer as soon as an item is shipped, providing rapid feedback. Financial applications enhance the arrival and execution of orders and payments.

Finally, many large companies have made investments in huge business systems; however, given the mobility of their executives, access to these systems is lost as soon as the executive steps away from the desk. By providing employees with wireless access to company systems, a mobile workforce is created that can demonstrate excellent productivity.

Mobile Portals

Mobile portals provide users with a single entry point to the Wireless Web. Much like what AOL did for the Internet, mobile portals such as NTT DoCoMo (see Case 7), Vodaphone's vizzavi, and Halebop want to provide individuals access to Internet/Web services and content.

The successful portals are able to provide superior access to the service. Mobile portals, based on packet-switched networks that are "always on," have an advantage over those based on circuit-switched networks. Making the service available at a reasonable price is also important. Finally, mobile portals must decide whether they want to use an open or closed approach. Some (e.g., NTT DoCoMo) have taken a closed approach, using a small set of content providers; others (e.g., Europe's Halebop) offer open access to multiple content providers. Both paths can be successful.

Digital Radio

Most radio station signals cannot be heard thirty miles away from their source. Moreover, AM and FM radio stations rely on a limited spectrum. As a result, the number of alternatives available to consumers is limited. Audio quality on radio programs is spotty and static is a frequent problem, especially on AM. New technologies that can completely change the nature of radio are now on the horizon. They allow radio signals to be heard for thousands of miles from their source, provide digital quality sound, and access hundreds of channels.

There are three competing radio technologies: satellite radio (e.g., XM Radio, Sirius), Internet protocol (IP) radio (e.g., Airvana), and digital cellular (e.g., Almost live).

Satellite radio technology works by sending a signal from a ground source to a satellite. The signal is then beamed back to radio receivers located in a car. In the United States, two companies—XM and Sirius—paid about $80 million each for a chance to beam radio signals into cars. At this point, this is a subscription service. For $9.99 per month, subscribers to XM radio receive access to 100 channels of programming. Many (but not all) channels have no advertisements—those that have ads limit them to approximately seven minutes per hour. The list of content providers is impressive—USA Today, BBC, CNN/

Sports Illustrated, and The Weather Channel. It is important to note that satellite radio does not provide Internet or Web access to its consumers.[14]

The IP radio technology involves using the Web to deliver (potentially) millions of channels to the user. A typical monthly fee is expected to be $50/month with users paying approximately $400 for the device. The key advantage over satellite radio is that users receive live Internet access. This service is expected to be available only in large cities.

Finally, digital cellular technology offers the ability to listen to multiple channels from the Web as well. Users download content during the night and then listen to it during the day. The expected service fee is $20/month and users will pay $400 for the device.

Which of these services will triumph? It is hard to say. In the United States, cars are the most popular location to listen to the radio (41.6% of all listening takes place in vehicles). AM and FM broadcasters have dominated this market and have established brand names and relationships. At the same time, they are free and convenient—all a user has to do is switch it on! Therefore, competing with AM/FM services will be hard.

It is likely that each of these services will find a niche position. Users who care enough for a large selection of channels and can pay a monthly service charge will adopt the service. As for content and advertising, *typical radio is inherently a local medium*. The challenge for these services is to determine whether they want to change the character of radio or to provide local content to users.

Wireless Games

Gaming is expected to be a huge market in the wireless arena. The entire video game market in the United States was estimated at about $11 billion dollars.[15] Wireless gaming is expected to be the next frontier. Already, Sprint and Verizon have signed a deal with game maker Unplugged Games, and Motorola has an agreement with UIEvolution. Similarly, Microsoft has joined forces with Qualcomm to launch Wireless Knowledge. Wireless Knowledge has teamed up with Versaly Games to create gaming applications for the Web.

The key advantage of mobile gaming is that the user is no longer wedded to the PC or the game console. Because the game can go wherever the user goes, the intense involvement shown by gamers can be compounded several times. In addition to replicating features that are currently available on the PC-based Internet (e.g., global contests, live play with other opponents), mobile gaming is expected to create location-based games.

Creating games that can be played on a cell phone is a challenging task.[16] First, the elaborate graphics that players see on a PC are lost. Instead, participants are provided an overhead view of the game and this reduces the game's level of richness. Second, games that require frequent user input are not likely to make a smooth transition to the cell phone. Instead, those games that require more thought are likely to be more successful.

Most game creators do not view mobile gaming as an end unto itself; rather, it is viewed as an intermediate step in creating mobile services. For example, the technology of location-based games is easily transferred to other location-based services. Because gamers are usually early adopters, many view this as a design test bed where the technology can be perfected before being applied to other situations.

Mobile Trading[17]

Offering wireless services has become a necessity for electronic brokerages. For example, Mobile Etrade allows users to stay in touch with their portfolio using a cell phone or a handheld computer.

An IDC report forecasts that about 50% of all online users will be using mobile financial services by 2004. The report proposes the following ways of thinking about this statistic. First, the target customers are active investors—people who regularly monitor the markets and track portfolio performance—not necessarily the active traders. Second, the wireless Internet is more like a new channel than an extension of the existing wired Internet brokerage channel. Third, wireless investing services will not transform the industry like e-brokerage services did, nor will they generate significant new revenue; however, traders that do not offer these services will be at a disadvantage.

On the technology side, there are four barriers. The first barrier is its form limitation—the size of the screen is small and it is cumbersome to enter data into it. The second barrier is the underdeveloped device and network standards. The third barrier is data and transaction security, and consumer perceptions of this security. The fourth barrier is user technophobia.

On the business model side, pricing is viewed as a barrier because the industry does not plan to have a flat pricing scheme. Also, there is considerable conflict about who owns the customer relationship.

Telematics

A detailed analysis of this topic is contained in Appendix II.

Potential Winning M-Commerce Business Models

Currently, organizations are still experimenting with the technology to understand the best potential applications. New businesses plan to provide information (e.g., restaurants, stocks), communication (e.g., SMS) and entertainment (e.g., games) to consumers. Enterprise applications such as sales force productivity, remote inventory management, and remote location data access are expected to be much more widely used. Advertising on mobile media has already emerged as a legitimate area. The standards are in place—all ad messages are double opt-in (see Chapter 12 for a discussion of permission marketing).

Conclusion

Mobile technology applications promise access to the Internet and the Web at all times and in all places. It is fair to say that this is a technology that is still in the nascent stage, and companies are still studying the best way to use it. It is, however, clear that some form of the technology will impact our lives in the years to come.

Notes

(All URLS are current as of April 14, 2002.)

1. EMC, "EMC Forecasts Subscribers to Top 1 Billion by End 2001," July 16, 2001, <http://www.emc-database.com/website.nsf/index/pr010718#this-page>.

2. Taken from Ravi Kalakota and Marcia Robinson, "M-Business: The Race to Mobility," *EAI Journal*, 2001, <http://www.eaijournal.com/PDF/mBusinessKalakota.pdf>.

3. Adapted from Mobileinfo.com, "Separating Mobile Commerce from Electronic Commerce," <http://www.mobileinfo.com/Mcommerce/differences.htm>.

4. Bob Brewin, "Study: Mobile Commerce Loses Luster," May 11, 2001, <http://www.idg.net/ic_534414_5056_1-2889.html>.

5. Devin Pike, "Interview: The Future of SMS," June 19, 2001, <http://www.mbizcentral.com/story/news/MBZ20010619S0001>.

6. Michael Gartenberg, "BlackBerry Can Be Useful, But It Has Its Drawbacks," August 27, 2001, <http://www.computerworld.com/itresources/rcstory/0,4167,STO63296_KEY68,00.html>.

7. William Gurley, "The Next Big Thing: Try 802.11b," February 19, 2001, <http://news.cnet.com/news/0-1270-210-4848960-1.html?tag=bt_pr>.

8. Wylie Wong, "Intel to Ship Higher-Speed Wireless Tech," September 9, 2001, <http://news.cnet.com/news/0-1004-200-7093015.html?tag=pt.rss.feed.ne_7093015>.

9. Anthony Townsend, "Starbucks Charges for Wireless Access," June 19, 2001, <http://lists.nyc wireless.net/pipermail/nycwireless/2001q2/000146.html>.

10. Glenn Flieshman, "Tall, No-Foam Internet, with Plenty of Room," August 1, 2001, <http://www.80211-planet.com/columns/article/0,4000,1781_858101,00.html>.

11. Accessed August 2001, <http://www.bluetooth.com>.

12. Based on Chris Gaither, "Bluetooth Wireless Stumbles at the Starting Gate," August 20, 2001, <http://www.nytimes.com/2001/08/20/technology/ebusiness/20BLUE.html>.

13. Adapted from Ravi Kalakota and Marcia Robinson, "M-Business: The Race to Mobility."

14. Adapted in part from Kevin Bonsor, "How Satellite Radio Works, <http://www.howstuffworks.com/satellite-radio2.htm> and MIT Program on Internet and Telecoms Convergence, "In-Vehicle Alternatives: Can New Technologies Challenge AM and FM Radio by Offering Audio Programming to Vehicles?" <http://itc.mit.edu/itel/students/papers/invehradio_slides.pdf>.

15. Jay Wrolstad, "Report: Wireless Games Mean Big Bucks," May 18, 2001, <http://www.wireless newsfactor.com/perl/story/9805.html>.

16. David Coursey, "Games on Your Cell Phone? It's Only the Beginning," <http://msn.zdnet.com/zdfeeds/msncobrand/reviews/0,13828,2846322-hud00025hm3,00.html>.

17. Accessed August 2001, <http://www.idg.net/ic_467783_5056_1-2889.html>.

18. Most of the material is taken from Wow-com.com, "The WDF Wireless Data Primer," <http://www.wow-com.com/pdf/WDPrimer.rtf>.

19. CDG, "Third Generation Mobile Wireless: A Presentation on the Opportunities and Challenges of Delivering Advanced Mobile Communication Services," April 1, 2002, <http://www.cdg.org/3GPavilion/Detailed_Info/cdg_3g_presentation.pdf>.

20. EMC Press Release, "GSM Continues To Be the Leading Cellular Technology," 2001, <http://www.emc-database.com/website.nsf/index/pr010319#this-page>.

21. My thanks to my MBA students Jennifer Gregor and Randy Serroels for this mini-case.

22. Global Telematics, "The Meaning of Telematics," March 1, 2002, <http://www.globaltelematics.com/telematics.htm>.

23. Peter Dana, "Global Positioning System: Overview," 1999, <http://www.colorado.edu/geography/gcraft/notes/gps/gps_f.html>.

24. Jamie Anderson, "Telematics: Why CRM Strategy Will Be Crucial for Automakers," <http://auto forum.mckinsey.com/cont_2/cont_2_1_0.php3>.

25. Jay Wrolstad, "New Wireless Speakerphone Promises Noise-free Calls," April 6, 2001, <http://www.newsfactor.com/perl/story/8782.html>.

26. Telematics Update, "Chrysler Group Unveils Vehicle Communications System," October 26, 2001, <http://www.telematicsupdate.com>.

27. M. Scott Ulnick and William Haupricht, "The Current Market for Telematics: Great Products Searching for Demand," *Ducker Worldwide*, October 8, 2001.

28. Matthew Nelson and John Rendleman, "Reaching Too Far?," August 20, 2001, <http://www.informationweek.com/story/Iwk20010819950002>.

29. Federal Communications Commission, "FCC Acts on Wireless Carrier and Public Safety Requests Regarding Enhanced Wireless 911 Services," October 5, 2001, <http://www.fcc.gov/Bureaus/Wireless/News_Releases/2001/nrwl0127.html>.

30. Tellme.com, "Delight Callers While Reducing Costs and Complexity," <http://www.tellme.com/overview/>.

31. ITSA.org, "Chrysler's New Scalable Telematics Service Relies on Cell Phones, Bluetooth and Voice Recognition Software," October 25, 2001, <http://www.itsa.org/ITSNEWS.NSF/4e0650bef6193b3e85256235005a3a7/a5e31c96127dedc385256af0004ef370?OpenDocument>.

REVIEW / CHAPTER 16

Discussion Questions

1. Study the scenarios presented in Figure 16.2. Which of these do you see yourself doing three years from today? Which ones did you find unrealistic? Why?

2. Critically assess the potential success of wireless gaming. How popular will it be? Is it going to be a big part of the gaming industry?

3. Location-based advertising is viewed as a key application by some. Imagine driving on the highway and receiving alerts from a nearby McDonald's with coupons. Similarly, imagine receiving coupons from your favorite stores as soon as you enter a mall. If you were starting out in this business, what would you do to ensure that your wireless advertising is effective? Is it really different from e-mail and banner advertising? How?

4. What is the difference between a mobile portal and a portal for the PC-based Web? Does a portal designed for the PC-based Web (e.g., Yahoo) have an advantage in the mobile arena?

5. What are the challenges to making digital radio work? If you owned a local radio station, what would your strategy be?

E-Tasks

1. Order a book from Amazon.com using a PC and a Wireless Internet provider. What are the differences in the way the site appears and your experience? What are each more suited for?

2. Visit Yahoo! Mobile (mobile.yahoo.com/phone/tour). How is the service different from what PC users see? Is Yahoo! on the right track?

3. Visit the web site http://fulldemo.fonetastic.net/sms/v1/. Register to try a demo of SMS. What were your reactions? What are the advantages and disadvantages of this form of communication?

APPENDIX I / CHAPTER 16

A Primer on the Wireless Internet[18]

The first application of wireless technology was the telephone. The current thrust is to move from "voice" (i.e., phones) to "data" (i.e., mobile commerce and other Internet-based applications). The wireless data industry is defined by its four components: devices, network infrastructures, types of wireless access, and specialized content.

There are a variety of wireless devices available:

- Personal digital assistants (PDAs) (e.g., Palm Pilot, Newton)

- Smart phones (e.g., Mitsubishi, Ericsson, Samsung, Nokia Communicator, Sony)

- Handheld computers (e.g., Hewlett Packard)

- Two-way pagers (e.g., RIM, Skytel)

- Automobile applications (that is, telematics) (e.g., Highway Master)

- Wireless modems (e.g., Sierra Wireless, NovAtel, 3Com)

Each device has its own idiosyncratic edge that may suit one segment or another of the population.

Currently, there are three types of network infrastructure:

1. Global Systems for mobile (GSM) communications. GSM is a digital cellular or PCS standard used throughout the world and the *de facto* standard in Europe.

2. Cellular Digital Packet Data (CDPD). CDPD is a digital packet data protocol designed to work over AMPS (Advanced Mobile Phone Service, the original cellular network) or as a protocol for TDMA (time division multiple access—a digital air interface technology used in cellular and personal communications services). PCS (Personal Communication Service) is a two-way, 1900 MHz digital offering now being rolled out across the United States. CDPD was developed by such Wireless Data Forum (WDF) member companies as Bell Atlantic Mobile and AT&T Wireless.

3. CDMA (code division multiple access). This is a spread spectrum air interface technology used in some digital cellular, personal communication services, and other wireless networks. CDMA was developed by Qualcomm.

As per the CDG, CDMA accounted for 30% of the wireless market in the United States, whereas GSM accounted for only 7%.[19] Of course, GSM is stronger worldwide. Latest estimates put GSM at 442 million subscribers worldwide, with CDMA coming in second at 82 million.[20] China is the largest GSM market.

The types of wireless access fall into the following categories:

APPENDIX I / CHAPTER 16

- Full user mobility. Users can access data on the move (e.g., while driving a car). The CDPD technology described earlier allows for this; however, it takes place at slow speeds.

- Portable wireless data. These networks let users access the Internet while they are in the coverage area using a laptop or palmtop computer and a small wireless modem. These networks, however, don't offer full mobility during online sessions. If a user tries to access the Internet while in a moving car, the connection may drop. A prime example is the Ricochet service from Metricom, Inc. Speeds are generally higher than with fully mobile systems, but are still relatively slow when compared to today's dial-up modem technology.

- Fixed wireless data. This offers service to a location, such as an office or home, through larger customer-premises antennas than the mobile or portable setups. The fastest data throughputs—up to T-1 speed—are available over fixed wireless networks. Examples include Teligent and wireless T-1.

- In-building wireless. A key emerging area, data systems are of two types today: local-area network extensions and standalone, and "instant" networks. In the future, "personal area networks" and local communications will be used to combine in-building and wide area systems.

Using Microsoft's Windows CE and the Open Wave browser's new content and applications are expected to be possible in the specialized content area.

APPENDIX II / CHAPTER 16

Telematics—A Mini-Case[21]

Telematics is the integration of wireless, location, speech, and computing functionality to provide automobile drivers with a variety of mobile personalized voice, data, and Internet services based on where and what the drivers are doing.[22] Telematic solutions allow automobile drivers to access applications and services via a PDA, cellular phone, or an in-dash system. The only other requirements are a wireless service and a location-sensing technology like the global positioning system (GPS)[23] to determine the location of the telematic device. Once these connections are established, drivers can access applications and services optimized for the mobile environment. Most solutions combine these technologies with a call-center that can match a user's location with various informational databases (e.g., emergency response agencies, roadside assistance providers, hotels, restaurants).

Current telematic services include remote diagnostics, automatic maintenance scheduling, automotive safety systems, real-time traffic advisories, and audible/visible turn-by-turn navigation. The most popular telematic applications today are emergency calling, stolen vehicle tracking, automatic crash detection and response, route assistance, and concierge services. Figure 16.3 illustrates current telematic product offerings and their segmentation within the vehicle.

The Telematics Industry and Market Opportunity

The telematics industry is a new and growing market, and predictions of its future size vary greatly. A study by Forrester Research, McKinsey, and Deutsche Bank predicts that the worldwide telematics marketplace will grow from $5 billion in 2000 to nearly $25 billion in 2005.[24] There's no doubt that consumers have become comfortable using mobile devices, such as cellular phones, in the vehicle. Various studies have shown that a majority of wireless airtime is used in the automobile, with some estimates as high as 70% of all wireless calls occurring in the car.[25] The questions remaining are what telematic applications consumers will consider a significant value-add and how much they will be willing to pay for them.

OnStar helped jump-start the telematics industry when it launched in 1996 as a dealer-installed system in cars, offering subscribers emergency and security services through a call center. Today, OnStar is standard equipment in thirty-two of GM's fifty-four models. In February 2001, General Motors Corporation announced plans to add real-time trading and financial market data to its OnStar system. The voice-activated system, partnered with Fidelity Investments, allows users to ask the onboard computer for information; it checks the latest market quotes, then reads back the data. The telematic system also includes access to a twenty-four-hour-a-day service and assistance center, voice-accessible e-mail, and customized news services. BMW of North America announced in August 2001 that it would also offer wireless location, emergency, and information ser-

Figure 16.3
Telematic Market Segmentation

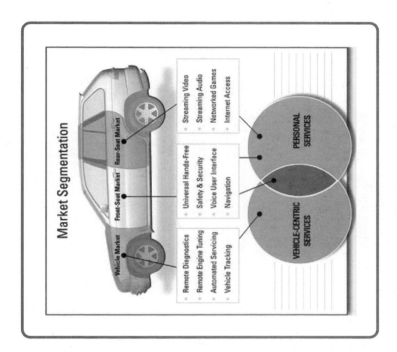

Market Segmentation

Rear-Seat Market
- Streaming Video
- Streaming Audio
- Networked Games
- Internet Access

Front-Seat Market
- Universal Hands-Free
- Safety & Security
- Voice User Interface
- Navigation

Vehicle Market
- Remote Diagnostics
- Remote Engine Tuning
- Automated Servicing
- Vehicle Tracking

PERSONAL SERVICES

VEHICLE-CENTRIC SERVICES

Source: Cellport.com, "Home Page," <http://www.cellport.com/>. Reprinted by permission from Cellport Systems, Boulder, Colorado.

vices that leverage the global positioning system (GPS)—as an option on all its 2003 model vehicles.

The companies positioned to benefit the most from the growth of telematics are those that provide services and connectivity. Because telematics provides the auto industry another way to differentiate their products and increase sales, that industry also has the potential to benefit significantly. Telematics can be used as an incredible CRM tool for the auto industry. Using telematics, automakers can have frequent contact with their customers, enhancing customer loyalty, enabling remote diagnostics, and easily communicating future service offerings.

The current telematics supply chain is shown in Figure 16.4.

Telematic service providers (TSP) integrate content from content aggregators, hardware and software, and the existing mobile wireless infrastructure to provide mobile services to

**Figure 16.4
Telematics Supply
Chain (Current)**

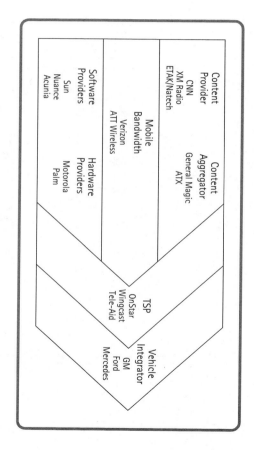

Content Provider	Content Aggregator	Mobile Bandwidth	Software Providers	Hardware Providers	TSP	Vehicle Integrator
CNN	General Magic	Verizon	Sun	Motorola	OnStar	GM
XM Radio	ATX	ATT Wireless	Nuance	Palm	Wingcast	Ford
ETAK/Natech			Acunia		Tele-Aid	Mercedes

Source: Reprinted by permission from Ulrick & Haupricht.

automobile drivers. The first wave of telematic products has focused on automobiles, and the supply chain model shows that the vehicle is the final delivery system for telematics. In the future, the auto will be only one of the vehicles for telematics—TSPs will expand their services to cellular phones as well and, eventually, the personal cellular phone will be the focal point for telematics. An individual telematics subscriber will be able to use telematic services in their car, at the mall, waiting for a bus, or at a sporting event. An example can be found in a recent announcement from DaimlerChrysler AG.[26] On October 26, 2001, Chrysler Group announced a new vehicle communication strategy utilizing Bluetooth technology and personal mobile phones. Chrysler's new system is operated through the user's cellular phone and works inside and outside the vehicle. The Bluetooth technology allows a customer's cellular phone to be integrated with their vehicle's telematic device so that only one device is in use at a time.

Future Trends

Currently the focus of most telematic services is on safety. As consumers become more comfortable with the technology and voice-recognition software improves, applications and services of convenience will start to become integrated components of our lives.

Ultimately, telematics will be a highly valued service that will enhance motorists' daily life. This technology will enable mobile society to download information to their car, such as maps, directions, a directory of restaurants in the vicinity of the moving vehicle, and so forth. It will also provide communication between a vehicle, office PC, home PC, a family member's cellular phone, or a business colleague's personal digital assistant device.

Risks

Will the telematics market grow at the rate predicted, and can TSPs be profitable? The telematics market faces a number of obstacles to the projected growth. A survey of telematic users conducted by Ducker Worldwide showed that a TSP could expect approximately 50% of current users to resubscribe.[27] OnStar acknowledges that an 80% resubscription rate is required for it to be profitable. A second risk to market growth is consumer acceptance of telematics. The Ducker survey found 60% of the people with telematics installed in their car had not used the system. The telematic market is in its infancy, and consumer acceptance is still low. A third issue is that of driver distraction. Governments around the world are enacting legislation to limit the use of handheld devices in cars. Although second and third generation telematics will have improved voice-recognition systems, drivers may still be distracted and the resulting accidents may cause additional legislative action. Given these risks, some researchers predict the consumer demand will remain low, and the market will grow at a much slower rate.

The path to safe, hands-free cellular phone usage in vehicles is strewn with stumbling blocks. Automakers and software vendors know they must first create voice-recognition systems capable of operating reliably in the face of wind, road noise, blaring radios, and little voices in the backseat. They must also figure out ways to connect cellular phones to radios and navigation systems, and then give the software the ability to understand voice commands.

There's also a potential for abuse. For some, the fact that a person's location can be tracked is in itself a breach of privacy. More worrisome is that someone with malicious intent could follow a person's every move. "When you start talking about having location-based services on every device, it's scary; it's Big Brother technology," says Amir Haramaty, chief operating officer of Nexus Telocation Systems Ltd., which plans to provide a service in Florida this year that will let people track vehicles, valuables, and even individuals. "This technology can help in emergency situations and improve efficiency, but we have to be careful."[28]

Yet another area of risk for telematic product providers is focusing product efforts more on "automotive telematics" and not on telematics in general. Although the use of telematics in a car is the first application of this technology, the mass market for telematics may be both inside and outside the vehicle. Today, telematics is driven by its use in the automobile; in the future, telematics will be a personal productivity and convenience product driven by personal cellular phones. Thanks in large part to a Federal Communications Commission mandate for Enhanced-911 that took effect October 1, 2001,[29] the

APPENDIX II / CHAPTER 16

next generation of cellular phones, due next year, is expected to include GPS chips to support location-based services. Wireless carriers are installing E-911 systems that, together with GPS, can identify (within fifty meters) the location of a cellular phone when it's turned on.

Conclusion

There is no doubt that the telematics industry will experience significant growth in the next five years. As Figure 16.5 shows, as the industry matures, the focus will move away from the vehicle integrator and toward wireless service providers. Wireless service providers are already beginning to offer voice-activated dialing and other services such as "Tell Me."[30] As consumers become accustomed to telematic applications in their vehicles, they will soon begin to expect them on their other mobile devices such as cellular phones and PDAs. Users will want to access their e-mail via a voice-activated system—and they won't want to pay two separate bills, one for the "auto" e-mail service and one for the "mobile" e-mail service. This will require an integration between auto manufacturers and wireless service providers similar to the alliance between Chrysler and AT&T Wireless utilizing Bluetooth technology.[31] Automobile manufacturers will move away from providing a full "telematic" system; rather, they will provide a system that allows a cellular phone to be plugged into the vehicle to use the phone's wireless connection.

In the short term, the most popular telematic services will remain those centered on safety and navigation. Telematic services that are quick and require minimal interaction between the system and the driver, such as making dinner reservations or checking movie

Figure 16.5
Telematics Value
Chain (Future)

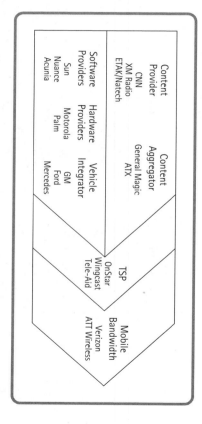

Content Provider	Content Aggregator	Vehicle Integrator	TSP	Mobile Bandwidth
CNN	General Magic	OnStar		Verizon
XM Radio	ATX	Wingcast		ATT Wireless
ETAK/Natech		Tele-Aid		
Software Providers	Hardware Providers			
Sun	Motorola	GM		
Nuance	Palm	Ford		
Acunia		Mercedes		

Source: Reprinted by permission from Ulnick & Haupricht.

APPENDIX II / CHAPTER 16

times, will also become popular. Services that require more interaction between the driver and the telematic device, such as receiving and responding to e-mail, will probably not be in high demand. These sorts of tasks require a high degree of multitasking and can distract drivers for extended periods of time. Although the use of telematic devices is on the rise, it will likely take several more years before a significant number of drivers are sufficiently comfortable interacting with telematic devices so that the industry can be profitable.

CHAPTER 17

Managing E-Commerce in the Future

Learning Objectives

▼ To understand the managerial challenges of the future.

▼ To learn about the consumer of the future.

▼ To study the business models of the future.

▼ To critically analyze ten cutting-edge technologies of the future.

Executive Summary

In the future, the Internet will fundamentally affect the strategic design of the company and its marketing activities. The search for competitive advantage will be constant and the Internet/Web can be a part of the solution. Consumers of the future will demand more convenience and privacy. Interactivity will be the norm rather than a one-way pushing of information. Future B2B marketplaces will offer the appropriate value-added services and will be industry-specific. Supply chains will be more nimble and companies in the chain will be more interdependent. The future of online media is in subscriptions. Online advertising is likely to get more intrusive and loud. Ten cutting-edge technologies in four categories are discussed: reinventing the computer (the wearable computer, home networking, pervasive computing, and natural language processing), security (biometrics), faster access to the Internet (broadband), and working from a distance (distributed instruction, tele-immersion, virtual labs, and digital libraries).

Introduction

This final chapter is about the future. The famous baseball player, Yogi Berra, once said, "It's tough to make predictions, especially about the future." This could not be truer in the context of e-commerce. In this rapidly evolving world, it is hard to make very specific predictions about the future. Despite knowing this, this chapter summarizes how the landscape for e-commerce will evolve.

E-commerce will evolve along the three dimensions identified in Chapter 1: business models, marketing, and technology. Improvements to one dimension will impact the other two. Technology will, certainly, change. The computers of the future will look different. The nature of the Internet and security will be more sophisticated. Business models will adapt to this, leading to new ways of earning a profit. The consumers of the future will also adapt to the technologies and will determine which ones will be successful. Marketing to these consumers will require a new imagination.

Think of digital rights management, the software that allows content providers to impose restrictions on users (e.g., preventing copying and pasting, limited "rental" duration, micropayments). In order to be successful, there must be clear synergies between the technology and the business model. The software developers must know how the business will use the software to charge customers and the business model designers must realize the constraints imposed by software design. It is not clear how consumers who are used to free content and ubiquitous access to copying-and-pasting will react to this. Setting appropriate expectations and managing the customer relationships will be challenging for the marketing function. Perhaps, a new pricing scheme may be required to gain customer acceptance. Customer feedback may lead to changes in the business model and software design. This illustrates the interconnectivity of the three dimensions and how they impact one another.

To focus the discussion, the rest of the chapter is broken down into the following sections: Managers of the Future, Consumers of the Future, Business Models of the Future, and Technologies of the Future.

Managers of the Future

A manager's thinking about e-commerce progresses in three phases:

1. Managers think of the Internet as a distribution and communication channel. They think of using it to gain access to new markets and communicate in new ways to existing customers. There is some interest in improving customer service.

2. Managers look inward. They realize that they can use Internet technology to reduce the cost of certain operations and improve the productivity of their employees. Companies in this phase launch intranets and e-training programs, for example.

3. The Internet begins to fundamentally alter the strategic outlook for the business. The technology may fundamentally alter the business model being employed. There is interest in creating a virtual organization and building online partnerships. The technology is taken seriously at the highest levels instead of being relegated to the Information Systems department. The thinking in this phase is that e-commerce is too important to be left to a few IT people sitting in a back office. Managers who get to the final phase faster than their competitors will do better. My vision is that all managers will end up in the third phase eventually.

The manager's search for competitive advantage is constant. Let me put it another way: there is no lasting competitive advantage. Managers must constantly innovate and rethink their business in order to be successful. The Internet and the Web can be part of this quest for competitive advantage in many ways. As discussed in Chapter 2, the Internet/Web can add value in six ways: enhancing the value proposition to customers, reducing operational inefficiencies within the organization, streamlining supply chains, increasing connectivity, making everything faster and eliminating distance.

Consumers of the Future

The Internet will lead to even greater convenience for the consumer in the future. Individuals will be able to place orders not only from their PCs, but also from mobile devices. The level of interactivity will rise. Consumers will expect to talk to firms and expect a conversation before a transaction. At the same time, getting the attention of the consumer will be exceedingly difficult due to increasing demands on their time and the explosion of clutter. Consumers will be very demanding about the privacy of their personal information and will want to set the limits of the usage of this information.

A question that currently remains unanswered is whether Internet technology can reduce the asymmetry of power between the company and the consumer. On the one hand, consumers could potentially be better informed about the prices of alternatives and the quality of the product. At one point, there was considerable fear that communities of consumers could exert influence on the activities of firms. For example, buying groups such as Mercata.com wanted to use greater cooperation and collaboration among consumers to force companies to reduce prices. These efforts have largely faded; however, some remain (e.g., Priceline's reverse auction allows consumers to name their price). It is not clear whether they actually provide more power to consumers. With Priceline, consumers have to agree to fly at an odd hour and may not pose restrictions on the number of stops.

Metcalfe's Law, discussed in Chapter 2, promotes the idea that increasing the size of the network leads to disproportionate returns. In the future, building this large network with a critical mass of consumers will be harder. Communities will splinter and it will be harder to locate large groups of consumers.

Business Models of the Future

B2B Sector

The B2B sector has seen two waves of firms. The first wave was comprised of independent marketplaces, such as eSteel, that hoped to make money by linking buyers and sellers. This set of firms has struggled because it is best suited in situations where there is fragmentation on the buyer and seller side. In many cases, large firms dominate and have no incentive to join a marketplace because that might require that they surrender their bargaining power. Even if they do participate, large firms use such marketplaces for only 1–2% of their overall expenditure.

The second wave of firms was formed by incumbents. A notable example is that of Covisint, which was formed by GM, Daimler-Chrysler, and Ford. Because these marketplaces did not have to build traffic on the buyer side, it led to a more efficient marketplace.

Writing in the *McKinsey Quarterly*, Berryman and Heck argue that:[1]

A third model—that of the "e-distributor"—lies between the two extremes of the stand-alone marketplace and the consortium. Like distributors in the off-line world, e-distributors take title to the goods they sell, aggregate those goods for the convenience of buyers, and (because they carry only certain products) in effect advise buyers which to choose. In addition, e-distributors perform a critical service for sellers by reaching hard-to-find buyers, such as small ones. The result, in many cases, is significant extra value for buyers and decent profits for sellers.

Future B2B marketplaces will offer three benefits. First, they will offer broadbased sharing of information among participants. This will not be an easy task because companies are scared of information sharing. Second, B2B marketplaces will be customized for industries or products. Different transaction models work in different contexts. Finally, the quest to find the appropriate value-added services will be constant. At this point, what matters to participants is basic financial services (e.g., settling transactions and conducting credit checks), not content or advertising. A great imagination will be necessary to find the right services.

Supply Chains

Many experts have said that, in the future, supply chains will be reconfigured as demand chains. What matters most in a supply chain is information about the marketplace. Getting that information to the right party at the right time is very important to ensure the success of the supply chain.

Future supply chains will be able to adapt easily to changes in market demands. The dependence upon firms will be greater and the entire ecosystem of interdependent firms will operate as one. Better measurability will lead to better understanding of the effectiveness of different processes. Agents who are ineffective and who do not pull their load will be weeded out.

Online Media

McKinsey conducted a study comparing online and offline media in 2001.[2] The main finding of this study showed that while the cost structure of online media is comparable to that of offline media, the revenue structure is not. Average revenue per user per month was much lower for online media—for online content services at $1.1 dollars per user per month in comparison to $10–15 for broadcast TV, $10–20 for cable TV, and $5–20 for print. Moreover, average cost was higher for online content services at $2.8 dollars per user per month in comparison to $10–13 for broadcast TV and $5–10 for cable and print. The authors of the study mainly attribute this to excessive reliance on banner advertising that has turned out to be ineffective. Advertising on the Internet is highly competitive both on the agency and the publisher sides.

The primary reason for this is the excessive reliance on advertising as a revenue stream. On average, about 78% of online media revenues come from advertising, compared to 56% for cable TV and about 66% on average for offline media. Moreover, because online advertising has not attained its potential, many large advertisers have stayed away, making it a weak revenue stream.

The future of online media is in subscriptions. *The journey is now from free to fee.* In February 2002, CNN International's president hinted that some form of subscription services may be necessary in the future.[3] If the three leaders of online news—CNN, MSNBC, and Nytimes—adopt some sort of subscription, it will have a rippling effect in the news business.

These points are worth remembering for the transition from free to fee. First, there will always be some free content. Second, restrictions will be placed on the users of free content (e.g., consumers who get free content may be exposed to more banner and pop-up ads). Third, additional value-added services will be provided to the users of paid content (e.g., they may be provided tickets to an event or provided first access to content before its release). Finally, once the billing relationship is established, other services will be sold to the consumer.

With the advent of digital rights management, publishers will have unprecedented access to new tools. For example, publishers can ensure that users do not copy and paste their content or that a music file is playable only for three days. These new digital rights management systems will enable creative pricing techniques, leading to a pay-per-view system. However, these technological advantages can prove to be illusory if they push a behavioral model that is unrealistic.

E-Tailing[4]

Multichannel retailing will be the norm. Pure-play online retailers such as Amazon.com will form partnerships with bricks-and-mortar retailers. The number of companies that will take the bricks-and-clicks approach will increase. Online shopping will be viewed as one channel for gathering information and shopping.

Online retailing will not succeed in certain product categories. Products that are hard to deliver in a cost-effective manner and those that require some sort of experience before purchase will be hard hit. Groceries may never be profitably delivered. Existing bricks-and-mortar stores with online operations may have the best chance of achieving a profit (e.g., Albertsons).

Online retailing will be a substantial part of the retailing business. In product categories such as toys and apparel, it could account for 10–12% of sales. In categories such as books, music, and software, it could be as high as 20–25% of all sales. The potential increases as consumers become more accustomed to ordering online.

The biggest detractor from purchasing online will be the shipping costs. Reducing the cost of fulfillment will be the highest priority. Fulfillment costs will decrease with better systems and greater coordination between the parties involved. There will be increased integration with offline ordering from retail, catalog, and other operations.

Customer service will be very important in building trust with consumers. Products must be delivered on time. Follow-up e-mails and calls must be made to ensure quality of service.

Brand strength will matter in this sector. Consumers shop at stores that they trust and like. Incumbents will have a strong advantage and will be hard to dislodge. The unique brand position of Amazon.com will be its biggest strength.

Online Advertising

Advertising on the Internet will be louder and more intrusive—it will look more like television ads. Consider the format some have discussed, the superstitial ad. When an unsuspecting user visits a web page, she is suddenly assailed by an ad that occupies the entire screen and plays the video of an ad. The experience is much like watching television—except that the user does not know when she is going to be hit with these ads. The users may be able to switch the ads off—sometimes.

The proportion of a web site that is content is going to shrink. Ads will occupy greater portions of screens. There will be greater confusion about where the content ends and the advertisement begins. Already, skyscrapers (large ads that occupy the entire length of the screen on one side) have expanded the advertising portion of a screen.

The greater intrusion of Internet ads will lead to more alienation of the customer. People will be simply turned off with these commercials and may actually pay to switch them off.

As the level of clutter rises, creative approaches to grab consumer attention will be the norm. Consider this "experiment" conducted by Yahoo! on a Friday in May 2001:[5]

Yahoo! effectively turned over its entire home page to an advertiser for the day. The result was the most memorable bit of advertising the industry has seen in a while.

Here's what visitors saw. The page loaded with a small banner picturing some birds below the Yahoo! logo. After a few seconds, the banner came alive; the birds flew down from the page onto a larger brownish banner (with "seeds") on the right. The birds then proceeded to peck away at that banner, gradually revealing a Ford Explorer logo.

Clicking on the ad brought a number of surprises. First, the whole browser window shook; then the entire directory of links—the heart of Yahoo!'s home page—disappeared. A truck appeared in the distance and drove right onto the page, and another logo appeared.

Measurement of ad effectiveness will improve. As a result, marketers will have access to individuals' attitudes about ads and will also be able to track offline sales. There will be a better understanding of the short-term and long-term effects of ads.

Wireless advertising will open new frontiers. These ads will be double opt-in, leading to greater relevance. They will most likely be less graphically intensive and more likely to engage the consumer. Their interactivity will require answering a few questions and receiving quick feedback.

Technologies of the Future

In this section, ten technologies that could transform the Internet are discussed. They can be placed in four categories:

1. Reinventing the computer: the wearable computer, home networking, pervasive computing, and natural language processing.

2. Security: biometrics (e.g., fingerprints, facial recognition, retinal scanning, hand geometry, and DNA profiling).

3. Faster access to the Internet: broadband.

4. Working from a distance: distributed instruction, tele-immersion, virtual labs, and digital libraries.

Reinventing the Computer

Wearable Computers

Even though m-commerce has much potential, the cell phone has many limitations as a communication device. Primarily, the screen size is small, limiting the potential applications that can be designed for it. Moreover, it uses the paradigm of the telephone, which requires an interruption of the consumer and can be intrusive.

The PC itself has become somewhat of a limitation. Users interact with it from their desktop. Laptops provide limited freedom, but bring fresh limitations.

A new technology may overcome these limitations. The wearable computer can project an image as big as a television screen to the eyes of those consumers wearing the proper equipment. As a result, users can easily browse the Web or perform other Internet-related tasks anywhere.

The MIT Media Lab has identified the following applications for this technology:[6]

1. Augmented memory: The Remembrance Agent. Wearable computers can alert the user about upcoming events. For example, when a user walks by a grocery store, the computer may alert the user to pick up some milk. Similarly, the user may be able to access detailed schedule information.

2. Augmented reality. The idea is to use wearable computers to create a blend of the real and virtual for an enhanced experience. For example, the MIT Media Lab has suggested visual filters that help the visually impaired by correcting blind spots and other weaknesses. Similarly, their Photobook face database system allows users to store up to 8,000 faces.

3. Desktop applications ported to wearables. Standard applications such as word processing, scheduling, and networking could be applied to these computers.

4. Wearable audio computing. The goal of this technology is to allow users to listen to any sound of their choice or to use sounds to enter commands.

5. Collective intelligence. Currently, this has been received as a niche technology:[7]

Using short-range wireless networks, aircraft mechanics and warehouse managers use them to maintain constant access to critical data. Doctors and nurses access patient records on their rounds. Work orders can be filed from the field. In the future, it's easy to see wearable computers finding their way into the hands of journalists, broadcasters, architects, paramedics or construction foremen.

At this time, the cost of a wearable computer is about $5,000—Internet services are extra. The manufacturers of these systems (e.g., Xybernaut) are targeting large businesses (e.g., manufacturing companies) rather than consumers.

Entering information on to wearable computers might be an issue. Users may have to strap on special keyboards. Voice-recognition systems are also now becoming available. Similarly, printing is not possible at this time. Due to these limitations, it is unclear whether this will become a mainstream consumer application.

Home Networking

About half of the U.S. population now owns a PC. The adoption rate of new PCs has slowed. As a result, there is considerable interest in home networking applications. The idea is to have a central network in the house powered by a PC that connects with all sorts of appliances within the house. This network can then make intelligent decisions, making life easier and better for the entire family.

Microsoft has identified four areas in which home networking can help.[8]

1. Security and wellness. The home network controls the curtains, coffeemaker, heat, lights, microwave, and other appliances. A user can set up a rule by which the heat turns on one hour before she comes home. It will be possible to turn the lights on in the evening when one is away so that the house is more secure.

2. Working at home. A home network can connect multiple PCs and peripherals such as printers. Using a high-speed Internet connection, users can work more effectively from home.

3. Friends, family, and community. The home network can be hooked to PC cameras that act as video-phones, allowing one to stay in touch with friends in other places. A new device called the automated family calendar can be placed on the refrigerator, automatically updating the whereabouts of everyone. Kids could find parents easily because the home network can track cell phones. An e-mail to the network is sufficient to obtain all sorts of relevant information.

4. Leisure: television, gaming, and music. Videogames downloaded from the Internet can be transferred to other points in the network. One can hook up to a live golfing lesson offered in a different location and talk to others in the class.

Pervasive or Ubiquitous Computing

The pervasive/ubiquitous computing movement has emerged as a real force. As shown in Figure 17.1, ubiquitous computing is the movement to move from the era of one-person-one-computer to one-person-several-computers. The idea is that many of these computers will be embedded in appliances that are used frequently and quietly add to the user experience.

There are three main applications of pervasive computing: human-information space interaction, task mobility, and nomadic data access.

1. Human-information space interaction refers to the user's interaction with a system of devices rather than with one device (e.g., PC or cell phone). Many of these devices will be invisible to the user and the interaction will be unobtrusive. Future devices will respond to changes in the words or gestures of the individual.

2. Task mobility computing frees the user from the desktop. Mobile workers will be able to access the Internet from remote locations. New input-output devices will lead to easier forms of communication.

3. Nomadic data access refers to the remote access of information. With pervasive computing, an individual will be able to access useful information instantly. To achieve this, persistent storage of information needs to be achieved.

Natural Language Processing[9]

Integrating natural language with computers so they can understand our language has been challenging for computer science and linguists. The benefits, however, of succeeding in the area of natural language processing (NLP) will far outweigh the efforts.

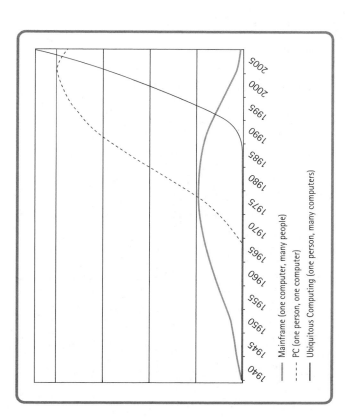

Figure 17.1
Major Trends in Computing

Mainframe (one computer, many people)
PC (one person, one computer)
Ubiquitous Computing (one person, many computers)

1940 1945 1950 1955 1960 1965 1970 1975 1980 1985 1990 1995 2000 2005

Source: Adapted from data found at http://nano.xerox.com/hypertext/weiser/ubihome.html.

Success in NLP comes in the form of an accurate interpretation of natural language via an application or computer component. In this sense, natural language represents speech or text processing. Although the actual design of such applications differs slightly, the goal of the core interpretative services takes either verbal or typed input and translates that input into an action. An example is speaking commands to a computer and, in turn, the computer running those commands.

In a business sense, the benefits of NLP can be felt in many ways. For example, enabling applications to respond to either verbal or typed commands improves usability. Thus, including NLP technology in products not only caters to a wider audience, but it also improves the ease-of-use and user productivity of NLP-enabled applications. Before going further, it might be helpful to learn about some of the goals and inner workings of NLP technology.

The following overview from Microsoft Research explains the nature of this technology:[10]

The goal of the Natural Language Processing (NLP) group (at Microsoft Research) is to design and build a computer system that will analyze, understand, and generate languages that humans use naturally, so that eventually you can address your computer as though you were addressing another person.

This goal is not easy to reach. "Understanding" language means, among other things, knowing what concepts a word or phrase stands for and knowing how to link those concepts together in a meaningful way. It's ironic that natural language, the symbol system that is easiest for humans to learn and use, is hardest for a computer to master. Long after machines have proven capable of inverting large matrices with speed and grace, they still fail to master the basics of our spoken and written languages.

The challenges we face stem from the highly ambiguous nature of natural language. As an English speaker you effortlessly understand a sentence like "Flying planes can be dangerous." Yet this sentence presents some difficulties to a software program that lacks both your knowledge of the world and your experience with linguistic structures. Is the more plausible interpretation that the pilot is at risk, or that the danger is to people on the ground? Should "can" be analyzed as a verb or as a noun? Which of the many possible meanings of "plane" is relevant? Depending on context, "plane" could refer to, among other things, an airplane, a geometric object, or a woodworking tool.

Our solution to this problem involves using our analysis system to learn that a "plane" is a vehicle that flies, that carries passengers, has wings, and so on. Our system learns by analyzing existing texts, including online dictionaries and encyclopedias, and automatically acquiring knowledge from this analysis. Such knowledge helps constrain the interpretation of the word "plane" in a sentence like "Flying planes can be dangerous."

Our group is developing NLP systems for seven languages: Chinese, English, French, German, Japanese, Korean, and Spanish.

Some of the applications that our system could be used for include text critiquing, information retrieval, and database query. The grammar checkers in Microsoft Office for English, French, German, and Spanish are early results of our research; Encarta uses our technology to retrieve answers to user questions; Intellishrink uses natural language to compress cellphone messages. As our system matures, it should greatly increase the accuracy of these products. In addition, other advanced products will become possible in any area where human users can benefit by communicating with their computers in a natural way.

Our work is distinctive because it: (a) acquires knowledge automatically; (b) is extremely broad-coverage; (c) applies to multiple languages and converges them at the semantic level; and (d) enables applications (and products) in many different areas.

As you can see from this overview, NLP is a complex area that combines many different areas of linguistics, such as syntax, morphology, and semantics, with the structured world of application development. However, there has been excellent strides made in this area, and the real-world business opportunities and value will continue to grow as NLP technology continues to evolve and mature.

Security

The issue of the security of computer systems has become extremely important after the events of September 11, 2001. At this point, Biometric technology, in one form or the other, holds the greatest promise to be the dominant security technology of the future.

Biometrics

The future of online security is in biometrics. This is the technology that identifies a user based on unique physiological characteristics (e.g., fingerprint, face recognition, retinal scanning). Biometrics improves on traditional systems that use passwords, because the person must be present and there is no fear of "forgetting" a password. As a result, unauthorized access to a web site will be reduced, if not eliminated.

Biometrics has been used extensively in forensics and to fight crime. Now it can be used to prevent unauthorized access to buildings, ATM machines, desktop PCs, laptop PCs, workstations, cellular telephones, wireless devices, computer files and databases, and both closed and open computer networks.

At this point, the technology is already available to the consumer. For example, Compaq provides a Biometrics PC Card. When installed on a PC, a small camera takes a photo of the individual's fingerprint. This is then used to identify him or her and simplify access to the PC. In general, biometrics is either integrated into the computer keyboard or is presented as a separate device.

There is a unique software solution known as biopassword. This program studies the rhythm and timing of an individual's typing to create a profile. This is then used to either permit or deny access. In the future, biometric technologies will be used in many contexts to prevent unauthorized access.

Faster Access to the Internet

Providing users faster access to the Internet is a constant struggle. Many solutions have been provided and others continue to be developed. For example, companies such as Cacheflow use the caching of frequently accessed content items to increase the speed of access. Others are working to create new routers, which will be more "intelligent." Similarly, there are efforts to create smarter packets, which will be tagged and directed in a certain way.

Broadband

One of the primary issues with the Internet is that most consumers do not have high-speed access at home. Although the vast majority of office workers have access to high-speed T1 connections, most home users still use a 56K modem. As shown in Table 17.1, by June 2001, only about 9 million users in the United States had access to a high-speed connection, with the vast majority of these users using cable modems.

If a large proportion of home users have high-speed access to the Internet, a number of applications become possible. For example, advertisements may include audio and video components, and users may be able to watch short films from home.

Table 17.1
The North America U.S. Residential Broadband Picture

	DSL	Cable	Total
Subscribers as of 6/1/01	2,913,636	6,450,916	9,364,552
Subscribers as of 3/31/01	2,543,938	5,800,103	8,344,041
Q1-01 Subscriber Additions	560,148	986,081	1,546,229
Q1-01 Average Adds/Week	43,088	75,852	118,941

A recent article indicated that four things must occur for broadband to be successful:[11]

1. The Internet's infrastructure must be reengineered so that it can support 1 Mbps (and higher) in millions of simultaneous streams.

2. New billing systems must be installed and adopted. Users will have to pay based on the size of the file they download, not a flat fee.

3. Content must be compressed for economic reasons and copy protected to reassure its owners. Compression reduces the burden of moving files and copy protection works with the new pricing systems to ensure steady revenue.

4. Large content providers (e.g., record companies and movie studios) must make their archives available online. This may be a challenge because these content providers will not be willing to participate unless they can be ensured profits.

There is considerable interest at this point in wireless broadband. The 802.11 or Wi-Fi technology described in Chapter 16 has now been modified for a much increased range. One service provider has hooked up the entire Big Island of Hawaii (300 sq. miles) with wireless broadband.[12] Future developments in this technology can lead to mobile Internet labs and unprecedented access to the Internet.

Working from a Distance

The Internet2 Project

One exciting source of future technologies is likely to be the Internet2 project (see www.internet2.org). This is a project launched by 185 universities across the United States, with the goal of developing a faster network that will enable new ways of learning, teaching, and conducting research. The faster network is expected to enable applications that were previously unfeasible.

The project members have identified four attributes that will be a part of future applications:[13]

The first is *interactive collaboration environments*, where you can truly interact with others without the barriers of distance. The second is to provide *common access to remote resources*, such as telescopes and microscopes. The third is using the network as a "backplane" to *build network-wide computation and data services*, such as those under development in the Grid (www.gridforum.org). The fourth attribute is *displaying information through virtual reality environments*—moving from static graphics and images to moving, three-dimensional animations.

Following are four application areas that embody these attributes.

Tele-Immersion

This technology enables users who are geographically spread out to collaborate with one another in real-time in a simulated environment.

In a tele-immersive environment computers recognize the presence and movements of individuals and both physical and virtual objects, track those individuals and objects, and project them in realistic, multiple, geographically distributed immersive environments on stereo-immersive surfaces. This requires sampling and resynthesis of the physical environment as well as the users' faces and bodies, which is a new challenge that will move the range of emerging technologies, such as scene depth extraction and warp rendering, to the next level.

Tele-immersive environments will therefore facilitate not only interaction between users themselves but also between users and computer-generated models and simulations. This will require expanding the boundaries of computer vision, tracking, display, and rendering technologies. As a result, all of this will enable users to achieve a compelling experience and it will lay the groundwork for a higher degree of their inclusion into the entire system.[14]

Figure 17.2 provides a picture of how this may work.

If successful, this technology is likely to change how teams work. For example, a manufacturing team that is spread out geographically could collaborate on a project. Similarly, in the health care arena, this technology can make some of the best medical services available to remote locations such as offshore oil rigs.

Virtual Laboratories

A virtual lab is a distributed problem-solving environment that allows scientists and researchers from around the world to work together. The lab includes large databases, scientific instruments, and software applications and tools. An example is the Grand Challenge Computational Cosmology Consortium, which is a group of theoretical astronomers and computer scientists engaged in collaborative research on the origin of the universe and the emergence of large-scale structures.

Digital Libraries

This set of applications is intended to establish a large-scale digital library that is accessible from anywhere. New technologies will enable users to retrieve information faster and read it more clearly.

Figure 17.2
Tele-immersion

Source: Reprinted by permission from National Tele-immersion Initiative/Advanced Network and Services, Armonk, NY.

Distributed Instruction

These applications create a networked learning environment. For example, an artist-in-residence at a university may be able to collaborate and "jam" with a high school jazz band on a high-speed connection. Instructors could access resources that were previously unavailable, creating a networked learning environment.

Conclusion

The manager of the future will face special challenges. New technologies will be available to companies and consumers. Consumers and their expectations and demands will change, and business models will have to respond. Above all, the future will be exciting for the adaptive manager who welcomes change.

Notes

(All URLS are current as of April 14, 2002.)

1. Ken Berryman and Stefan Heck, "Is the Third Time the Charm for B2B?," Number 2, 2001, <http://www.mckinseyquarterly.com/article_page.asp?tk=292854:1011:24&ar=1011&L2=24&L3=47>.

2. Jaques R. Bughin, Stephen J. Hasker, Elizabeth S. H. Segel, and Michael P. Zeisser, "What Went Wrong for Online Media?," *McKinsey Quarterly*, Number 4, 2001, Web Exclusive, <http://www.mckinseyquarterly.com/article_page.asp?ar=1121&ttk=292854:1121:17&L2=17&L3=65&page num=1> (registration required).

3. AP, "CNN Exec Predicts Fees for Online News," February 2002, <http://www.canoe.ca/CNEWS MediaNews0202/25_cnn-ap.html>.

4. Partly based on Ernst and Young's Online Retailing Report, cached version available at <http://216.239.51.100/search?q=cache:cHJ6WYlJaYEC:www.ey.com/GLOBAL/gcr.nsf/US/Online_Retailing_-_Thought_Center_-_Ernst_%26_Young_LLP+Ernst+Young+online+retailing+report&hl=en>.

5. Jeffrey Graham, "Online Advertising's Rich Future," May 9, 2001, <http://www.clickz.com/mkt/emkt_strat/article.php/84641>.

6. MIT Media Lab, "Wearable Computing," <http://lcs.www.media.mit.edu/projects/wearables/>.

7. Michael Martinez, "Merging With the Machine: Wearable Computers Offer Constant Access, for Better or Worse," August 20, 1999, <http://abcnews.go.com/sections/tech/DailyNews/wearables990820.html>.

8. Microsoft Home Networking, "Home Page," <http://www.microsoft.com/homenet>.

9. My thanks to Steve Fox of Microsoft for his help with this section.

10. Microsoft Research, "Natural Language Processing," <http://research.microsoft.com/nlp/>.

11. Charles Platt, "The Future Will Be Fast But Not Free," May 2001, <http://www.wired.com/wired/archive/9.05/broadband.html?pg=2&topic=&topic_set=>.

12. Erik Schonfeld, "The Island of the Wireless Guerrillas," April 2002, <http://www.business2.com/articles/mag/0,1640,38492,00.html>.

13. Ted Hanss, "Internet2 Applications Frequently Asked Questions," <http://apps.internet2.edu/html/faq.html>.

14. Internet2, "Tele-Immersion," January 19, 2001, <http://www.internet2.edu/html/tele-immersion.html>.

REVIEW / CHAPTER 17

Discussion Questions

1. Should the business model drive the technology or the other way around? Which should come first?

2. What is the core competence of Amazon.com? How will this change over time?

3. A unique online advertising effort that completely modified the content of Yahoo! for the benefit of Ford Motor Company is described in the text. What are the benefits from this to Yahoo!? What are the negative aspects? Will this approach be popular?

4. Devise a marketing plan for wearable computers. What are the hurdles that must be overcome in order to gain market acceptance? Who would be likely adopters of the technology?

5. Who is likely to use biometric technology? Will the B2C sector be affected by this? How about the B2B sector?

E-Tasks

The Future of E-Commerce

Let us use the last class to identify what we think the future (in 10 years) of e-commerce will look like. I have identified fifteen topics and they are listed below in no particular order.

1. Online retailing

2. Digital media

3. Micropayments

4. B2B marketplaces

5. Internet advertising

6. Consumer power

7. Virtual corporations

8. P2P computing

9. Desktop of the future

10. Distance education

E-Tasks (continued)

11. Digital rights management

12. The killer technology of the future

13. The e-commerce company to watch

14. A day in the life of a typical customer

15. A day in the life of a typical manager

Write one statement of no more than ten words for each topic. Keep your statements with you as a record of what you thought at this point—make sure your statements are thoughtful!

NTT DoCoMo.com

NTT DoCoMo's I-Mode Phone: A Case Study[1]: Case 7

Introduction

NTT DoCoMo[2] is a spin-off of Japan's telecommunication giant—Nippon Telegraph and Telephone (NTT). It is best known for its I-Mode phone, which has been a tremendous success in Japan. In February 2002, there were 40 million I-mode users in Japan, and the company had a market share of 62% at the end of December 2001.[3] In March 2000, an analyst counted an average of 40 million daily page views at NTT DoCoMo versus 70 million daily page views for Yahoo! Japan.[4] At one point, the company was so overwhelmed with demand that it had to temporarily shut down its services. The company is also immensely profitable—in the fiscal year that ended March 31, 2001, the company posted a record profit of $3 billion on revenues of $45 billion. This represented a 26% increase in revenues and a 45% increase in profit from the previous year.

This success has made DoCoMo the poster child for the proponents of the Wireless Web. While many other ventures providing access to the Internet and the Web have failed, DoCoMo seems to have found the "secret sauce" leading to success.

I-Mode phone users have access to the Internet and the Web. They can send e-mail and text messages to others. They can also visit web sites. There are two types of web sites on the I-Mode system: official and unofficial. Official sites are those that are approved by DoCoMo and they have a privileged position. They are easily accessible to users and any access charges appear on each individual's monthly NTT phone bill. Unofficial sites can only be accessed if an individual hears about it and then types in the entire URL. These unofficial sites do not have access to DoCoMo's billing system, so they must either establish direct billing relationships with users or earn money in other ways.

In addition to sending e-mail and text messages, I-Mode users can:

- Play videogames (e.g., the Hello Kitty game from Bandai)
- Reserve airline and concert tickets
- Find a restaurant
- Check their bank balance and transfer money
- Read news and weather reports
- Check train schedules and city maps
- Download wallpaper images, ringtone melodies, etc.
- Create photo albums that can be accessed from anywhere

As shown in Table C7.1, the most common applications of the I-Mode phone have to do with entertainment, news and tickets/living, with entertainment leading by far. As shown in Table C7.2, the most common activity of I-Mode users is to visit official sites, followed by e-mail. By one estimate, users spend 40% of their time on e-mail and 60% on Web functions. The average number of page views per day is about 10.5.[5] I-Mode has taken Japan by storm, and it is now a common sight to watch young people using

Table C7.1
Breakdown of I-Mode Accesses to Official Sites

Category	Percent
Entertainment	55
News	14
Tickets/Living	11
Financial	6
Town Info.	5
Business Tools	5
Travel	3
Restaurants/Recipes	1
	100

Source: Jeffrey Lee Funk, "The Mobile Internet Market: Lessons from Japan's I-Mode System," available at http://www.mobilemediajapan. com/resources. Reprinted by permission from Mobile Media Japan KK.

Table C7.2
Breakdown of I-Mode Traffic

Category	Percent
Official Sites	34
Mail	27
Automatic Messages	16
Unofficial Sites	14
Menu	9
	100

Source: Jeffrey Lee Funk, "The Mobile Internet Market: Lessons from Japan's I-Mode System," available at http://www.mobilemediajapan. com/resources. Reprinted by permission from Mobile Media Japan KK.

their portable phones on trains, in malls, and, in general, everywhere. Moreover, the success of DoCoMo has become a powerful symbol of Japanese success over its European and American rivals. As shown in Table C7.3, NTT DoCoMo is now among the top ten publicly traded Japanese companies in the United States with a market capitalization ahead of such companies as Toyota and Sony.

The Growth of NTT DoCoMo

NTT DoCoMo has grown at a tremendous clip. As shown in Figure C7.1, the number of customers has grown five-fold from April 2000 to August 2001. As of February 2002, the company had 40 million users. Moreover, new subscribers are still signing on at the rate of 43,000 a day, 1.3 million a month.[6]

Although the company still retains a lion's share of the wireless Internet market, it has strong competition within Japan. EZweb and J-Sky are the two other competitors. Table C7.4 provides a comparison between the three services—some of the differences may be accessible only to the technical reader. The EZweb and other services in Europe use the wireless application protocol (WAP—see the Appendix on WAP at the end of the chapter). This competing protocol has

Table C7.3
Top Ten Publicly Traded Japanese Companies

Rank	Company Name	Global 1000 Rank	Market Value U.S. $ Mil.	Sales U.S. $ Mil.	Profits U.S. $ Mil.	Assets U.S. $ Mil.	Return on Equity (%)
1	NTT DoCoMo	11	192,578	31,297	2,122	30,409	10.6
2	Toyota Motor	22	130,433	112,944	3,967	138,605	7.1
3	Nippon Telegraph & Telephone	33	99,942	96,063	3,906	178,540	NEG
4	Sony	49	70,745	61,522	141	57,290	0.7
5	Mitsubishi Tokyo Financial Group	78	54,129	NA	299	604,292	0.2
6	Sumitomo Mitsui Banking	91	47,746	NA	1,114	451,534	7.2
7	Mizuho Holdings	94	46,874	NA	1,780	375,700	3.4
8	Takeda Chemical Industries	101	45,279	8,109	1,236	12,346	14.6
9	Honda Motor	114	41,004	54,368	1,955	47,697	12.0
10	Nomura Securities	121	39,402	NA	1,529	158,407	12.8

Source: Adapted from data found at http://bwnt.businessweek.com/global_1000/index.asp?country=JAPAN.

Figure C7.1
Charting the Success of DoCoMo's I-Mode Phone

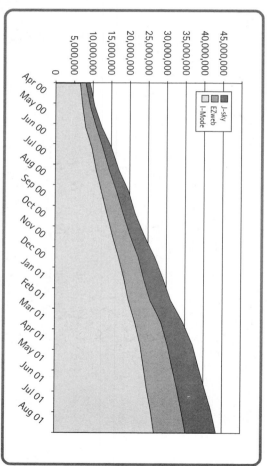

Source: Data from Jeffrey Lee Funk, "The Mobile Internet: How Japan Dialed Up and the West Disconnected," 2001: ISI Publications.

struggled to make any inroads on DoCoMo worldwide.

According to Takeshi Natsuno, executive director of I-Mode, the reason for their success comes from following the "Internet way of thinking" as opposed to the "telecom way of thinking." More specifically, he says that there are three components to the NTT DoCoMo way of thinking:[7]

First, *technology.* We selected Internet technology—HTML, MIDI for ring-tone downloads, Java. But telecom people only care about what's best for their infrastructure. So in Europe they invented a new technology (WAP) to fit the wireless space, but it was very difficult for Internet people.

Second, *business model.* US approach or European approach is to gain some mileage on content providers by sharing in their ecommerce revenue.

Table C7.4
Comparison of the Three Main Competitors in the Japanese Market

	NTT DoCoMo	KDDI/AU	J-Phone
Mobile Internet service	I-Mode	EZweb	J-Sky
Markup language	I-Mode compatible HTML	HDML (WAP)	MML
Microbrowser	Compact Netfront	EZbrowser	Proprietary
Numbers of official sites	576 (July 2000)	303 (August 2000)	287 (August 2000)
Mobile Internet fee	300 yen monthly basic fee + 0.3 yen per packet*	200 yen monthly basic fee + 0.27 yen per packet*	2 yen per request (no monthly basic fee)*
Image formats	GIF	BMP, PNG	PNG, JPEG
E-mail acquisition method	E-mail is sent to handset immediately	Notification of new e-mail is sent to the handset	Notification of new e-mail is sent to the handset
Sending e-mail	max. 250 double-byte characters (500 single-byte)	max. 255 double-byte characters (510 single-byte)	max. 3000 double-byte characters (6000 single-byte)
Receiving e-mail	max. 250 double-byte characters (500 single-byte)>	max. 2000 double-byte characters (4000 single-byte)	max. 3000 double-byte characters (6000 single-byte)
E-mail storage on server	50 messages for 30 days	200 messages for 7 days (inbox), 100 messages for 14 days (archive)	192 messages for 72 hours
E-mail attachments functionality	None**	Images and melodies	Images and melodies

[continued]

Table C7.4
(Continued)

	NTT DoCoMo	KDDI/AU	Tu-ka	J-Phone
Network	800 MHz Digital Packet switched PDC/P (TDMA)	Circuit switched PDC & 800 MHz Packet switched cdmaOne (CDMA)	1.5 GHz Circuit switched PDC (TDMA)	1.5 GHz Circuit switched PDC (TDMA)
Speed	9.6kbps (I-Mode), 28.8kbps (DoPa)	9.6kbps (PDC), 14.4~64kbps (cdmaOne)	9.6kbps	9.6kbps
Packet compatibility	I-Mode & DoPa	CdmaOne /PacketOne	Planned for summer 2001 (28.8kbps)	Not planned on PDC
Targeted users	Universal	Business people	Young women	Young women in their 20s & 30s
Color support	256 colors	256 colors	256 colors	256 colors
International roaming	Korea	Korea, Hong Kong, USA (Honolulu, San Francisco, New York City . . .), Australia (Melbourne, Sidney, Brisbane, Perth)	None	None
Phone usage basic fee plan (monthly)	Plan A: 4,500 Yen*	PDC: 4,400 Yen*, cdmaOne 4,600 Yen*	Business Plan: 4,500 Yen*	Standard Plan: 4,500 Yen*
Main mobile accessories	Pocket Board, Exire, Pacty, Camesse petit	Photo Palette, Web Palette, Mail Palette	Cara	Sky ePad, Sky Photo Pad
Affiliated Internet Service (ISP)	Mopera	Daredemo Internet	Internet Freeway	J-Phone Access Internet

*100 Yen = US$0.92

**Some I-Mode handsets can send ring tones as attachments via e-mail—but only to the same model handset.

Source: Mobile Media Japan, "Main Mobile Internet Services in Japan," November 2000, http://www.mobilemediajapan.com/stories/storyReaders$1432. Reprinted by permission from Mobile Media Japan KK.

But a normal fixed-line operator cannot take any portion of E-Commerce. We thought in the same way. By providing a better platform, transactions will increase—that is the biggest benefit to us. So we keep our traffic revenue, and they keep their transaction revenue—and if we can provide value-added services, like a billing system, of course we can share some revenue.

The third thing is *marketing*. In the telecom way of thinking, technology is very important. But AOL—they have never mentioned technology. Amazon.com—they just say, "We offer the best price." That is Internet way of thinking. So we never mention "Internet" or "protocol" or "wireless something," because content is everything.

Japan and the Internet[8]

PC-based Internet access in Japan is billed on a per-minute basis. As a result, consumers are not used to the unlimited usage that consumers in the United States enjoy.

Some key statistics about the online population in Japan are as follows:

- As of December 2000, 47.08 million Japanese consumers, or 37% of the population, were connected to the Internet, a 74% jump from the previous year.

- Of this total, 8.16 million users accessed the Internet solely through their mobile phone, while 15.48 million used both a mobile phone and PC, and 23.45 million used only their computer.

- 95.8% of companies with more than 300 employees had Internet access, compared to 88.6% a year ago.

- As of April 2001, there were 112,200 DSL subscribers and 784,400 cable Internet subscribers.

- Of those households with Internet access, 50.2% used 56K modems, 34% used 64K ISDN, 7.4% through persistent ISDN connections, and 4.6% through broadband.

Why Is I-Mode So Successful?

There are multiple reasons attributed to I-Mode's success. Perhaps the most important one is DoCoMo's strong connection with NTT. NTT owns an advanced packet-switched wireless network in Japan that was made available to DoCoMo. While its competitors continued to offer circuit-switching systems, DoCoMo was able to offer consumers an always-on connection, leading to a key competitive advantage. The connection with NTT also led to strong brand positioning within Japan, so there was no burden to create brand awareness. It also gave the company the necessary clout to form partnerships with handset suppliers. These suppliers worked closely with the company to design a world-class user interface.

The second major factor that contributed to I-Mode's success may have been the low PC penetration and high mobile phone penetration rate in Japan (as of December 2001, about 66 million Japanese users owned mobile phones[9]). Because PC-based Internet access is billed by the minute, it is an expensive proposition for most Japanese and was adopted by few. As a result, I-Mode was the first time many Japanese users were being exposed to the Internet and the Web, making it an exciting proposition.

Third, I-Mode instituted a system that benefits the official content providers immensely. The key attraction for the content providers is that they can piggyback on I-Mode's billing system. This reduces their costs and provides direct access to a consumer base. Of course, DoCoMo takes a commission for providing this service. Overall, this creates a strong win-win proposition. In many ways, this mirrors the business model of AOL for its Web business.

Fourth, I-Mode may not have become so popular so quickly without the easy-to-use handsets. I-Mode has been praised for the user-friendliness of its handsets. In contrast to its competitors (see Table C7.4), I-Mode was built for a packet-switched network using cHTML—

a stripped down version of HTML—while EZweb uses WAP. As a result, I-Mode's download speeds are much faster and the service is always on.

Fifth, I-Mode adopted an innovative billing system that charges users by the number of packets they send instead of a flat fee. Thus, users are not charged to compose e-mails—only to send them—and the charge is based on the size of their document. Similarly, individuals are charged for downloading web pages based on the size of the page. This innovative pricing system is really the first successful implementation of micropayments and was embraced by the market.

Finally, many cultural factors may have contributed to DoCoMo's success. The Japanese people have a strong love for gadgets. The first adopters of DoCoMo were teenagers and young people and they acted as catalysts in spreading the phone to the mainstream market.

Jeff Funk's Framework

Jeff Funk, author of a recent book,[10] argues that in order to understand DoCoMo and I-Mode, one must understand the positive feedback process connecting the different elements of the company's ecosystem. As shown in Figure C7.2, Funk asks us to think of the following six elements: users, content, phones and other devices, business models, search engines/portals, and services.

There are two positive feedback loops in this system. First, the six elements reinforce one

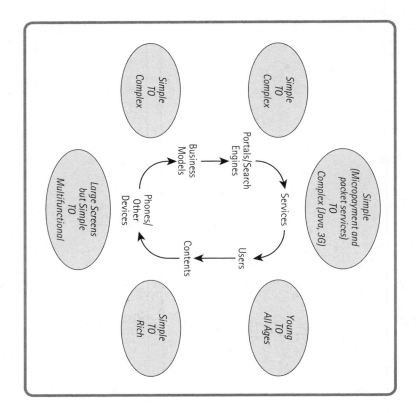

Figure C7.2
Feedback Loops Operating in DoCoMo

Source: Copyright © 2001 Jeffrey Lee Funk. All rights reserved. Reprinted by permission of the author and ISI Publications.

another to channel the company to desirable outcomes. For example, the company first marketed I-Mode to young users who were attracted to content such as e-mail and videogames. The company did not wait for the introduction of fancy 3G phones, initially reducing another potential barrier to adoption.

Second, *within each element* there is a positive feedback loop, leading to a natural progression in the company strategy. For example, although the company focused on young users initially, over time the average age rose. Similarly, although the initial phones were simplistic, the company has now launched phones that can operate on the 3G network. In many cases, the company started with a simple solution and progressed to a more complex and rich solution.

Further, he asks us to understand the concepts of richness and reach. "Richness" refers to the quality and quantity of information. Information that is sparse (e.g., traffic, directions, product location) is considered less rich. On the other hand, information such as a large web site is considered very rich.

"Reach" refers to the number of people who can participate in the sharing of the information. Mobile phones have smaller screens and keyboards and cannot access the level of rich information that can be accessed with a desktop computer; however, they have a higher reach than desktop computers and even PDAs. The larger reach of mobile phones comes from their greater diffusion, greater mobility, and faster power-up as compared to desktop computers. This is shown graphically in Figure C7.3.

A technology such as a wristwatch cannot handle very rich information; however, given its simplicity, it has ubiquitous reach. On the other hand, a PC is capable of complex computation and information manipulation; however, given its bulk and price, the portability is limited, leading to a limited reach. Technologies such as PDAs fall somewhere in between these two extremes.

In the wireless Internet space, the Japanese approach was to start with high reach and low richness and then steadily move to greater richness. On the other hand, the European and

Figure C7.3
Richness versus Reach

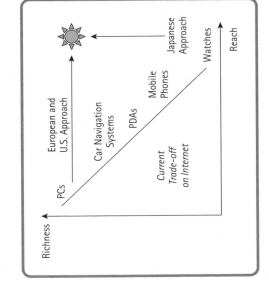

Source: Copyright © 2001 Jeffrey Lee Funk. All rights reserved. Reprinted by permission of the author and ISI Publications.

U.S. approach (i.e., WAP) was to start with rich applications targeted at corporate users. At this point, it seems that the Japanese approach was more appropriate—the I-Mode approach was driven by a "consumer electronics" mind-set rather than a "computing" mind-set.

Users

NTT DoCoMo initially selected young users as the primary target audience for the I-Mode phone. As Jeff Funk explains:

People under 25 generally spend a much larger amount of their time away from home and the office (if they have one), and make greater use of public transportation (buses and trains) and walk-ing, compared to older people.

As a result, these are ideal "first adopters" for a product such as I-Mode. Clearly, the company did not want to remain a company for young people only. Over time, the average cell-phone user also signed up for I-Mode, thus increasing the average age of the I-Mode user. Now, when a new user signs up for NTT's services, he or she also signs up for the I-Mode service.

Content

Content is very important to DoCoMo. Users are exposed to images of well-known and respected brands from around the world. Users can play a Disney game or get the latest headlines from CNN.

From a content perspective, I-Mode sites can be divided into two basic types: official I-Mode sites and unofficial or voluntary sites. Official I-Mode sites appear automatically on the I-menu of any I-Mode mobile phone because they have been officially checked, approved, and listed by NTT DoCoMo. Unofficial sites are not listed on the I-menu, but can be reached by typ-ing in the URL or sending a bookmark to the phone by e-mail. These sites have no official connection to NTT DoCoMo's I-Mode service. Some view I-Mode as a *walled garden* that is

carefully cultivated. Others argue that it is more of an ecosystem.

DoCoMo's approach to content is described by Mr. Natsuno:[11]

Our goal is very simple. We are providing links to the good-quality content. If you have three min-utes to kill, you don't have time to waste just on searching.

The company has twenty people monitoring the official sites and the content as the following excerpt explains:[12]

In fact, I-mode's success comes less from being walled than from being obsessively tended. Users are free to browse the thousands of unofficial sites and bookmark any they choose for instant access. But like the meticulously landscaped entrances to Tokyo office towers, I-mode is moni-tored by a small army of caretakers who, oblivious to the sprawling chaos around them, root out even the most infinitesimal weed in a campaign to ensure that here, at least, perfection reigns. "It's very carefully cultivated," says Kazutomo Robert Hori, CEO of Cybird, a company that creates I-mode sites. "Very carefully. Very, very carefully."

Because the service is billed by the minute, the goal of DoCoMo has been to carefully control the content available on their system. The goal of DoCoMo has been to create a branded expe-rience that is completely controlled by them.

Phones/Devices

In order to access the wireless Internet, users must have phones that are Internet-ready. Be-cause DoCoMo was able to control the design of phones, such phones were available early in Japan. As described by Jeff Funk:

Large displays are needed on mobile-Internet-compatible phones. The most popular Japanese mobile Internet phones have displays that are larger than two square inches. They first appeared in early 1999, and by late 2000 these display sizes and mobile Internet capabilities had become standard items on almost all Japanese mobile phones. These screens could display as many as 100 Japanese characters in spite of the fact that Japanese characters are far denser than Roman characters. And users could acquire many of these phones for less than $100 even if they were existing subscribers, as opposed to new subscribers.

Further, the positive feedback between phones, users, contents, business models, and portals/search engines has caused innovations to flourish in the Japanese mobile phone market. Phones with displays larger than two square inches keep getting lighter, while smaller and new functions keep being added because the basic electronic devices keep getting smaller. Polyphonic capabilities, a capability that is popular with young people, have evolved from four tones to 128 tones as of early 2001. Color displays had appeared by the end of 1999 and had become the standard for all phones by the end of 2000. Higher-resolution color displays that can display more than 65,000 colors had appeared by the end of 2000 and are expected to become the standard for all phones by the end of 2001.

Jeff Funk continued:[13]

The first keitai (cell phone), the so-called candy-bar models, had small black-and-white screens and were about half the size of Western cell phones. Now, with the advent of color and animation, the featherweight candy bars are giving way to slightly heavier, folding handsets with larger, high-resolution screens. They combine in one sleek device the functions of three separate gizmos in America: cell phone, handheld computer, and wireless email receiver.

Business Model

The basic business model of NTT DoCoMo shows that the company has two sources of revenue: individual consumers and official sites (corporate revenue was not expected to be very great). The company has a billing relationship with the individual consumer. As shown in Table C7.5, each consumer pays a flat monthly charge to sign up for the service. Then, the individual is charged on the basis of the number of packets transferred by him or her. Individuals can also sign up for specific content packages. The company takes a 9% commission from these service charges from the official sites. Not all official sites charge—one estimate is that about 50% of these sites charge. *The greatest money makers are downloadable ring tunes and wallpaper images for phone screens.*

Pricing by packets was a novel innovation. Many critics argue that consumers will never understand packets. The thinking in America is to encourage flat pricing with unlimited usage—the case of AOL switching to a flat fee is frequently discussed.

However, DoCoMo took the challenge because it felt that for the mobile user experience, this was the appropriate pricing model. Users who

Table C7.5
I-Mode Revenue per Subscriber per Month in Yen

	Revenue for DoCoMo	Revenue for Content Providers	Total Revenue
Monthly Charge	¥ 300	¥ 0	¥ 300
Packet charge	1,500–2,000	0	1,500–2,000
Paid Services	27	273	300
Total	1,827–2,327	273	2,100–2600

Source: Jeffrey Lee Funk, "The Mobile Internet Market: Lessons from Japan's I-Mode System," available at http://www.mobilemediajapan.com/resources. Reprinted by permission from Mobile Media Japan KK.

download large applications or chunks of data a pay more. This pricing system does not stop a user–it merely sets up incentives in the appropriate manner. For example, users are not charged for composing e-mail messages. The billing event is the act of sending the message.

Search Engines/Portals

Although DoCoMo provided a simple menu on the I-Mode phone with access to the official sites, traffic to the unofficial or voluntary sites exploded. As shown in Figure C7.4 and Table C7.6, the number of unofficial sites has grown at a tremendous rate.

As a result, users must use a search engine or a portal to locate the site they want. As described by Jeff Funk:[14]

By March 2001 there were more than 25 times the number of unofficial sites (more than 40,000) registered on the main search engine for these unofficial sites than there were official sites (1,480) on DoCoMo's set menu. Further, it was estimated that there were more than 20 times the

number of pages on unofficial sites than on official sites. *This dramatic rise in the number of unofficial sites and pages had caused traffic to these sites to exceed traffic to the official sites by the fall of 2000. The extraordinary growth in the unofficial sites has generated a large number of portals and search engines, which in turn are driving the number of unofficial contents and users.*

Services

In order to motivate a user, the company must offer an array of services. DoCoMo's packet-based pricing strategy allows users to try a variety of services.

Travails of Unofficial Sites[15]

The unofficial sites are in a tough spot. The fastest way to access them is to enter their Web addresses manually. This is a slow and cumbersome process on cell phones due to the small size of the device and its keypad.

Moreover, official sites get a cut of the monthly subscription fee charged by DoCoMo, but unof-

Figure C7.4
Number of Unofficial I–Mode Sites

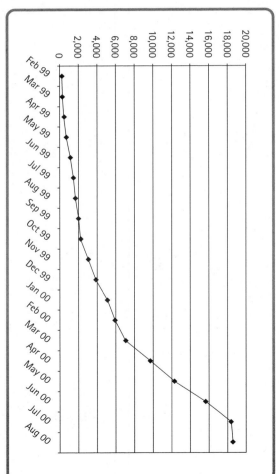

Source: Mobile Media Japan, "More Than 10 Million I-Mode Subscribers," August 6, 2000, http://www.mobilemediajapan.com/newsdesk/imode10million/. Reprinted by permission from Mobile Media Japan KK.

Table C7.6
Key Landmarks in I-Mode History

	Service launched
February 22, 1999	
June 28, 1999	Users Exceed 0.5 million
August 8, 1999	Users Exceed 1 million
March 15, 2000	Users Exceed 5 million
August 6, 2000	Users Exceed 10 million
November 22, 2000	Users Exceed 15 million
March 4, 2001	Users Exceed 20 million

Source: Compiled from press releases at http://www.nttdocomo.com.

ficial sites do not. Because they do not have a billing relationship with the customer, their options are limited. Many have contracted with credit card companies to charge directly.

Yoshihiro Shimizu, director of IT business for Mobilephone Telecommunications International (MTI), said that DoCoMo executives "have set themselves up according to their own group of exclusionary alliances centered on Old Economy companies." Even the government executive in charge of telecom policy said, "We have been inundated with complaints from companies that say they are unfairly shut out of DoCoMo sites." However, critics say that the government will not act because it owns a huge stake in the company. DoCoMo has promised to open its services to third-party ISPs when 3G services are established by 2003.

Global Expansion of NTT DoCoMo

NTT DoCoMo has no intention of being a regional player forever. It has made aggressive moves to become a global player. Following is a list of some of the company's key acquisitions:[16]

- Hutchison Whampoa–Hong Kong. In December 1999, DoCoMo acquired a 19% stake and in May 2000, Hong Kong became the second place in the world where I-Mode is available.

- Dutch KPN Mobile. In May 2000, NTT DoCoMo bought a 15% stake and they will be setting up Europe's first I-Mode service.

- Telecom Italia Mobile (TIM)–Italy. TIM has had a joint alliance with NTT DoCoMo since 1997 (with no exchange of equity) to exchange engineers.

- AT&T Wireless–United States. In November 2000, they bought a 20% stake for $9.8 billion and want to establish the first 3G I-Mode networks here in 2003–4.

- SK Telekom (South Korea's biggest mobile provider). In July 2000, DoCoMo purchased a 10% stake for $3 billion.

- KG Telecom–Taiwan. NTT DoCoMo has acquired a 20% stake in KG Telecom. The firms are to jointly provide wireless broadband services in Taiwan.

- Tele Sudeste Celular Participacoes. DoCoMo acquired a 7% stake in this Brazilian company.

In addition, DoCoMo owns 43.5% of AOL Japan and has established a strategic alliance with companies such as Palm.

Some observers are skeptical of the ability of NTT DoCoMo to go global. The primary argument from the skeptics is[17] that due to its association with NTT, DoCoMo has been sheltered in Japan. An example is DoCoMo's ability to set the specifications for handsets—not the manufacturers of the handsets! Moreover, DoCoMo did not have to bid for the wireless spectrum in Japan. It was simply given to them because of

NTT's stature. In addition, DoCoMo was able to dip into NTT's existing customer base.

DoCoMo will not be able to control the entire user experience in other countries. In Japan, the company controls all aspects of the user experience—design and sale of the handsets, types of phones, calling plans and rate structure, billing and service options, number and type of official content providers, and so on. This is not easy to replicate in countries outside Japan.

Naturally, the market characteristics may be different. Remember, in Japan, to many users the Internet/Web is synonymous with I-Mode because of low PC penetration. The major question is whether Americans (and users in other markets) will be as taken by this technology after being jaded with years of the PC-based Internet/Web. No company in the United States has tried to price based on the packet. Many have said that Americans are used to simple pricing schemes and this may not work. The usual issue of cultural differences is also raised.

Will American teenagers be excited by the same things as Japanese teenagers?

Finally, the technology may not be ready in American and European markets. The necessary infrastructure may not be in place for these phones. Building a packet-switched network may take time. The hardware may have to be modified to make it compatible with the new types of content.

These are certainly not easy challenges and the company's future depends on surmounting them effectively.

Conclusion

NTT DoCoMo's I-Mode phone has created a worldwide wireless industry. It has established that it is possible to successfully provide its users with access to the wireless Internet/Web. What remains to be seen is how much of their business model and approach can be transported to other markets.

Notes

(All URLs are current as of April 14, 2002.)

1. I am thankful to my MBA student, Tushar Mehta, for locating important information in connection with this case.
2. Docomo is a Japanese word that means "everywhere." The "I" in I-Mode stands for information. Also, "ai" is the Japanese word for love.
3. Mobile Media Japan, "Home Page," <http://www.mobilemediajapan.com>.
4. Techbuddha, "I-Mode: Lessons for Asia's Cellular Operators," August 2000, <http://www.techbuddha.com/nextlevel/wappt3imode.html>.
5. Charles Bickers, "The Way of the Mobile Warrior," Far Eastern Economic Review, 164(24) (June 21, 2001): 46–50.
6. Frank Rose, "Pocket Monster," September 2001, <http://www.wired.com/wired/archive/9.09/docomo.html>.
7. Ibid.
8. Japan Marketing News, "Japan's Technology Performance Index," <http://www.jmnews.net/v1i14_numbers.htm>.
9. Nikkei Communications, "Mobile Phone Subscription Rates Slow in Japan," December 11, 2001, <http://www.nikkeibp.asiabiztech.com/wcs/leaf?CID=onair/asabt/cover/159566>.
10. Jeff Lee Funk, "The Mobile Internet: Why Japan Dialed Up and the West Disconnected," 2001, ISI Publications.
11. Rose, "Pocket Monster."
12. Ibid.
13. Ibid.

14. Funk, "Mobile Phone."
15. Benjamin Fulford, "DoCoMo Call Home," May 14, 2001, <http://www.forbes.com/global/2001/0514/040.html>.
16. Palowireless, "Imode Resource Center," <http://www.palowireless.com/imode/background.asp>.
17. Daniel Scuka, "DoCoMo: Easy Cell," October 17, 2000, <http://japaninc.net/online/sc/ntt/oct00_sc_docomo.html>.
18. Accessed August 2001, <http://www.sciam.com/2000/1000issue/1000bannan.html>.
19. Eurotechnology.com, "The Unofficial Independent imode FAQ: Imode vs. WAP," <http://www.eurotechnology.com/imode/faq-wap.html>.
20. Jonathan Watss, "Japanese Craze that Could Wipe out Wap," June 15, 2000, <http://www.guardian.co.uk/online/story/0,3605,332060,00.html>
21. Jakob Nielsen, "Graceful Degradation of Scalable Internet Services," October 31, 1999, <http://www.useit.com/alertbox/991031.html>.
22. Rose, "Pocket Monster."

Discussion Questions

1. Analyze the case using the technology, business model, and marketing framework. What is DoCoMo's core competence?

2. What are the advantages and disadvantages of using a "walled garden" approach to content development and delivery? What makes this approach a success for cable TV and a failure for most Internet content firms?

3. What are the fundamental differences between starting with a low richness, high reach strategy and a high richness, low reach strategy? Which one is suited for which situation?

4. Can ISPs in the United States use packet-based charging? Why or why not?

5. Have other companies in the United States adopted the strategy of focusing on young users? When is this strategy appropriate? When is it not?

6. How important is the leverage of an existing billing relationship to the success of DoCoMo? Will AT&T Wireless be able to leverage its billing relationship with the customer base to create a similar success story in the United States?

7. What challenges will DoCoMo face in the American market? What will not be available to it here?

APPENDIX

WAP
An Introduction to WAP

The key competitor for DoCoMo is not a company; rather, it is an open standard, a protocol. WAP is a communications protocol and an application environment that works with various wireless networks. WAP was developed by The WAP Forum, an alliance of over 500 companies that includes such large giants as Ericsson and Nokia. It was started with technologies developed by phone.com.

The WAP protocol enables mobile systems, such as phones, pagers, smart phones, and handheld devices, to receive information and services from one another. Its focus is on maximizing the interoperability between different devices. Hence, it is not a specific application or a language.

One of the primary problems with cell phones is that they cannot handle HTML—the most commonly used language on the Web. As a result, WAP supports a special language called WML or wireless markup language.[18]

Because Web pages currently written in HTML cannot be read by WAP phones, web site owners who want their pages read by a cell phone have to create a different page in WML. This, obviously, creates a new layer of costs and only a few web sites have implemented WML pages.

DoCoMo *versus* WAP[19]

According to one study, I-Mode is the world's dominant wireless Internet system. As of November 2000, 60% of the world's wireless Internet users used I-Mode, 39% used WAP, and 1% used PALM. The various user types are distributed throughout different countries—Japan has about twenty million wireless Internet users (both I-Mode and WAP), Korea has two to three million users, and Europe has one to two million WAP users.

There are many differences between I-Mode and WAP. First, most WAP implementations in Europe are circuit switched, whereas the I-Mode phone uses packet switching. As a result, most WAP users must dial-up to connect, whereas I-Mode provides the more desirable "always on" capability. Interestingly, in Japan, the WAP implementations also use packet switching. The reason for this is that DoCoMo had access to NTT's packet-switching network, whereas other WAP operators had to build such a network from scratch.

I-Mode includes images, animated images, and color. On the other hand, WAP implementations in Europe currently use only text and no images. WAP in Europe is marketed to business, whereas I-Mode is primarily marketed to ordinary consumers. I-Mode handsets in Japan have large full-color (256 colors) displays and can display animated full-color gif images and ten lines of text or more, while European implementations of WAP today have handsets showing four lines of text in black/white without images.

The marketing of WAP-based services in Europe presently focuses on business applications (e.g., banking, stock portfolio, business news, flight booking), while the marketing of WAP-based services and I-Mode in Japan focuses on fun and everyday life (e.g., restaurant guides, games, images, ringing melodies).

WAP users are charged for the connection time. For example, if one user looks at a newspaper headline or a football result for ten minutes, he or she is charged for ten minutes of connection time. In Japan, I-Mode users are charged per packet of downloaded information. So, if an I-Mode user looks at a news item or at a football result for two seconds or three hours on his or her mobile handset, the charge is the same, as long as he or she does not download additional information. In addition to the information transfer charges, there is a basic charge and subscription charges for premium sites, and, in some cases, a transaction, download, or other charge.

WAP Usability

In December 2000,[20] the Nielsen Norman Group commissioned a WAP usability study in Europe. Users were given a WAP-enabled phone and were asked to use it for a week. They were asked to perform specific tasks, but they were also free to perform other tasks.

The study concluded that the usability of WAP phones was 70% negative. Specifically, checking the weather initially took the user 2.7 minutes. Even after using the phone for one week, the average user still took 1.9 minutes to check the weather. The study pointed out that with a newspaper this task takes ten seconds or less.

The study also pointed out that the user interface is impoverished for two reasons.[21] First, a tiny screen cannot show any context, nor can it show menus, or visualizations of alternatives. Second, telephone push buttons are poor controls for advanced functionality. As a result, the study dubbed WAP the "Wrong Approach to Portability." This study has been discredited by its detractors on the grounds that it was based on twenty users only.

Following is an example of a typical user story:[22]

(DoCoMo's) Kamada's microbrowser opened I-mode to anyone who can create a Web page. Satoshi Nakajima, a Japanese expat who heads a Seattle startup called UIEvolution, discovered what that means when he set out to construct a little wireless site that converts US measurements to the metric system. Because he knows HTML, he was able to create an I-mode site in one evening; a day later he discovered that several hundred people had already visited it. It took him two weeks to develop a WAP version for the American market. "It was a really painful experience," he says, "and at the end of it I got no hits."

Conclusion

At this point, it seems like DoCoMo's I-Mode service has trumped WAP. While WAP has languished, I-Mode has made its mark in Japan and now promises to replicate its success in the United States and Europe.

INDEX

double or confirmed opt-in option, 224–226
e-mail as vehicle to execute, 221–222
existing customer relationships, for, 226–227
Internet, advantages offered by, 220
metrics for judging consumer interest, 229
opt-in option, 223–224
opt-out option, 222–223
privacy issues, 334, 340–341
problems associated with, 227–228
relevancy of, 219
types of permission, 223–226
Personalization
adoption of, considerations for organization's, 206
advantages of, 205
approaches to, 206–207
arguments against, 213–214
branding, and, 213–214
computer-assisted self-explication (CASE), 210
consumer-controlled approach, 207
customization versus, 205
data collection and analysis, 208–210
filtering, 209–210
firm-controlled approach, 206–207
implementation issues, 214
instant personalization, 210
levels of, determining appropriate, 211–213
loyalty, customer, 205
marketing versus, 205
m-commerce, enhancement through use of, 384
potential of, 203–205
privacy issues, 334
rule-based systems, 208–209
technological aspects of, 208–210
tradeoffs in, 213
types of, 207
Pervasive/ubiquitous computing movement, 410
Physical companies
e-commerce by, implementation issues of, 61–62
marketing, 45
Piracy, software, 248–250
Place (distribution), value related to, 49
Platform for privacy preferences (PPP), 341–342
Portals, mobile, 388
Porter, Michael, 37

PPP. See Platform for privacy preferences (PPP)
Price, value related to, 49
Price discrimination, 243
Pricing strategies for digital products, 239–245
Privacy
anonymous remailers, 343
anonymous surfing tools, 343
attitudes of business leaders, 335
attitudes of general population, 336–338
business leaders, attitudes of, 335
competitive advantage, as, 335
controversial cases, 334
cookie cutters, 343
customer information, e-business use of, 334
customer privacy, approaches to preservation of, 338–343
disposable credit card numbers, 343
Doubleclick case study, 354–362
e-commerce, factors in, 335–336
FTC guidelines, 338–339
general population, attitudes of, 336–338
marketer, policy guidelines for, 347–348
online market research, considerations in, 281
permission marketing, 334, 340–341
platform for privacy preferences (PPP), 341–342
privacy fundamentalists, 336
privacy policies, 339–340
privacy pragmatists, 337
privacy unconcerned, 336–337
seal programs, 341
secure e-mail services, 342–343
self-regulation approach to, 338–342
technology-based approach to, 342–343
Private-value auctions, 100
Product
elements of, 49
service distinguished from, 245–246
Product portfolio analysis
distinguished from revenue stream management (RSM), 52–55
Products sold on Internet, categories of unsuccessful, 31
Profit or loss centers, 46–47
Profit path analysis, 57–58
Promotions
customer acquisition, 175–177

direct model of, 176–177
intermediary, through, 177
value, as method to deliver, 49
Pure-play businesses
Amazon.com. See Amazon.com
Business-to-Consumer (B2C) companies. See Business-to-Consumer (B2C) companies
Consumer-to-Consumer (B2C) companies. See Consumer-to-Consumer (C2C) companies
eBay. See eBay
examples of, 73

R

Radio, digital, 388–389
Reachability, 5, 9
Research, online. See Online market research
Resource exchange fulfillment strategy, 197
Retailers
e-fulfillment. See E-fulfillment
future of, predictions for, 407
online sales statistics, 6–7, 10
predictions for future of, 407
products sold, list of, 11
profit margins, 12
top twenty, 12, 13
Revenue equivalence theorem, 101
Revenue model, 14, 46
revenue stream management (RSM). See Revenue stream management (RSM)
Revenue stream management (RSM)
cost of obtaining revenue (COOR), 52
decisions, 56–57
dimensions of, 52
forecasting revenue streams, 58–59
free service to pay service, shifting from, 59–60
importance of, 52
interrelationship among revenue streams, 55–56
product portfolio analysis, distinguished from, 52–55
profit path analysis, 57–58
profits, methods of maximizing, 51–52
user experiences, decisions affect on, 60
Reverse auctions
benefits of, 91–93
examples of, 84